DEVELOPING KNOWLEDGE COMMUNITIES THROUGH PARTNERSHIPS FOR LITERACY

ADVANCES IN RESEARCH ON TEACHING

Series Editor: Volumes 1–11: *Jere Brophy*
　　　　　　　　Volumes 12–29: *Stefinee Pinnegar*

Recent Volumes:

Volume 19:	From Teacher Thinking to Teachers and Teaching: The Evolution of a Research Community
Volume 20:	Innovations in Science Teacher Education in the Asia Pacific
Volume 21:	Research on Preparing Preservice Teachers to Work Effectively with Emergent Bilinguals
Volume 22:	International Teacher Education: Promising Pedagogies (Part A)
Volume 22:	International Teacher Education: Promising Pedagogies (Part B)
Volume 23:	Narrative Conceptions of Knowledge: Towards Understanding Teacher Attrition
Volume 24:	Research on Preparing Inservice Teachers to Work Effectively with Emergent Bilinguals
Volume 25:	Exploring Pedagogies for Diverse Learners Online
Volume 26:	Knowing, Becoming, Doing as Teacher Educators: Identity, Intimate Scholarship, Inquiry
Volume 27:	Innovations in English Language Arts Teacher Education
Volume 28:	Crossroads of the Classroom: Narrative Intersections of Teacher Knowledge and Subject Matter
Volume 29:	Culturally Sustaining and Revitalizing Pedagogies
Volume 30:	Self-study of Language and Literacy Teacher Education Practices
Volume 31:	Decentering the Researcher in Intimate Scholarship: Critical Posthuman Methodological Perspectives in Education
Volume 32:	Essays on Teaching Education and the Inner Drama of Teaching: Where Biography and History Meet
Volume 33:	Landscapes, Edges, and Identity-Making
Volume 34:	Exploring Self Toward Expanding Teaching, Teacher Education and Practitioner Research
Volume 35:	Preparing Teachers to Teach the STEM Disciplines in America's Urban Schools
Volume 36:	Luminous Literacies: Localized Teaching and Teacher Education

ADVANCES IN RESEARCH ON TEACHING   VOLUME 37

DEVELOPING KNOWLEDGE COMMUNITIES THROUGH PARTNERSHIPS FOR LITERACY

EDITED BY

CHESTIN T. AUZENNE-CURL
Texas A&M University, USA

And

CHERYL J. CRAIG
Texas A&M University, USA

United Kingdom – North America – Japan
India – Malaysia – China

Emerald Publishing Limited
Howard House, Wagon Lane, Bingley BD16 1WA, UK

First edition 2021

Copyright © 2021 by Emerald Publishing Limited

Reprints and permissions service
Contact: permissions@emeraldinsight.com

No part of this book may be reproduced, stored in a retrieval system, transmitted in any form or by any means electronic, mechanical, photocopying, recording or otherwise without either the prior written permission of the publisher or a licence permitting restricted copying issued in the UK by The Copyright Licensing Agency and in the USA by The Copyright Clearance Center. Any opinions expressed in the chapters are those of the authors. Whilst Emerald makes every effort to ensure the quality and accuracy of its content, Emerald makes no representation implied or otherwise, as to the chapters' suitability and application and disclaims any warranties, express or implied, to their use.

British Library Cataloguing in Publication Data
A catalogue record for this book is available from the British Library

ISBN: 978-1-83982-267-4 (Print)
ISBN: 978-1-83982-266-7 (Online)
ISBN: 978-1-83982-268-1 (Epub)

ISSN: 1479-3687 (Series)

Printed and bound by CPI Group (UK) Ltd, Croydon, CR0 4YY

ISOQAR certified Management System, awarded to Emerald for adherence to Environmental standard ISO 14001:2004.

Certificate Number 1985
ISO 14001

INVESTOR IN PEOPLE

*We dedicate this book to
our parents through whom our stories exist,
our children through whom our stories grow richer,
and to the stories ahead, ready to be told.*

CONTENTS

List of Contributors *xi*

Acknowledgments *xiii*

Community, Identity, and Change: An Inquiry into Professional Development Partnerships for Literacy Education in Urban Context   *1*
Cheryl J. Craig and Chestin T. Auzenne-Curl

PART I
SEEING BIG: TENSIONS AND TRIUMPHS IN PARTNERSHIPS FOR PROFESSIONAL DEVELOPMENT

Innovation and Integrity: Working Through Disruption to Support Teachers in Their Roles as Literacy Educators   *21*
Tina Angelo and Maryann Gremillion

Reflections on Research and Professional Development Partnerships in Post-Harvey Houston: Writing the Rip Tide   *41*
Chestin T. Auzenne-Curl, Cheryl J. Craig and Gayle A. Curtis

Reflections on Principal Leadership and Writers in the Schools   *61*
Michael Curl and Cheryl J. Craig

Navigating the Role of Teacher Educators in the Field: The Case for Increased Community Support   *79*
Daphne Carr and Chestin T. Auzenne-Curl

PART II
SEEING SMALL: THE CALL FOR A CLOSER LOOK AT THE WRITERS IN THE SCHOOLS COLLABORATIVE

Reflections on WITS History and Challenges of Change 99
Robin Reagler

In Search of a Trellis: A Principal's Perspective on the Need for Cross-Institutional Literacy Partnerships 105
Terri Osborne

Tough Turf: Restoried Moments in the Dissipation of an Urban Knowledge Community 117
Abdulkader Mokhtari, Chestin T. Auzenne-Curl and KaLeah Hicks

The Beauty of Petals and Thorns: Negotiating Identity as Writer-Teacher 129
Sarah Jerasa

Reflective Conversation on the Value of Longevity as Collaborators in Education 153
P. Tim Martindell, Cheryl J. Craig and Chestin T. Auzenne-Curl

PART III
SEEING MORE: SOMETHING TO PURSUE

Gentrimigration: Two Tales, One City's Story of a Changed Community 171
Tenesha Gale

Poetry Is Not a Luxury: Engaging Learners in Multiple Literacies through Creative Poetics 193
Lobat Asadi

"After a Trip, the Suitcase Stays Full till I Need Something": Unpacking Narrative Truths from the Field 215
Chestin T. Auzenne-Curl

The Implications of Social Media Scholarship on Forming a Knowledge Community in Black Cyberculture: A Coconstructed Narrative *231*
Chestin T. Auzenne-Curl and Daphne Carr

"Research Across Four Pandemics: The End Is a Beginning" *245*
Chestin T. Auzenne-Curl and Cheryl J. Craig

About the Editors *253*

About the Contributors *255*

Index *265*

LIST OF CONTRIBUTORS

Tina Angelo	Writers in the Schools Houston, USA
Lobat Asadi	Texas A&M University, USA
Chestin T. Auzenne-Curl	Texas A&M University, USA
Daphne Carr	Humble Independent School District, USA
Cheryl J. Craig	Texas A&M University, USA
Michael Curl	St. Thomas University, USA
Gayle A. Curtis	University of Houston, USA
Tenesha Gale	Humble Independent School District, USA
Maryann Gremillion	Independent Consultant, USA
KaLeah Hicks	Goose Creek Consolidated Independent School District, USA
Sarah Jerasa	University of Houston, USA
P. Tim Martindell	University of Houston–Downtown, USA
Abdulkader Mokhtari	Goose Creek Consolidated Independent School District and Lee College, USA
Terri Osborne	Texas A&M University–Commerce, USA
Robin Reagler	Independent Consultant, USA

ACKNOWLEDGMENTS

Like many aspects of global life in 2020, this journey alongside the Writers in the Schools (WITS) Collaborative and our authors brought us challenges and triumphs. We formed a community, and it seemed that with every twist and turn, we grew closer to the project and one another. We would like to thank all of the contributing authors, the Emerald Publishing Group, and our family members for their patience, support, and diligence as we persevered in the face of a pandemic. A special thank you goes to Doctor Gloria Ladson-Billings for sharing space and insight that extended our lens on the intersection of content and culture, and to Dr Xiao Han, Dr Daphne Carr, and Ms Kaleah Hicks for their scholarly contributions and support in our editing phase.

Finally, we extend gratitude to the Writers in the Schools Houston Team for inviting us to be a part of their journey and to Robin Reagler and Jack McBride, former and current Executive Directors, for sharing our desire to bring the stories of the WITS Collaborative to a national and international reading audience.

COMMUNITY, IDENTITY, AND CHANGE: AN INQUIRY INTO PROFESSIONAL DEVELOPMENT PARTNERSHIPS FOR LITERACY EDUCATION IN URBAN CONTEXT

Cheryl J. Craig and Chestin T. Auzenne-Curl

ABSTRACT

Craig and Auzenne-Curl reflect on how their individual experiences and personal practical knowledge developed in context over time contribute to a collective review of the backdrop of the stories of experience shared in this volume. The chapter provides context for the study that inspired the collection and a preview of the chapters yet to come.

Keywords: Urban context; urban education; teacher identity; knowledge communities; education reform; literacy coaching

INTRODUCTION TO THE VOLUME

We hold John Dewey's assertion that articulation and communication are essential elements to a liberated democracy as a truth, and we acknowledge literacy education as vital to social interaction and cohesiveness, education, and life itself (Dewey, as quoted in Greene, 1982). The chapters in this volume are reflections of this truth. The work is seeded in a three-year study on collaborative professional development for K-12 writing instructors, but as the partnership evolved, we revisited the stories from the field, and in telling and retelling the lived experiences of knowledge-making (Ross, Chan, & Keyes, 2017), we were guided in inquiry by the following questions:

- How do knowledge communities support teacher growth and development?
- How do relationships influence the trajectory of professional development programs and teachers' growth in community?
- What do these narratives of experience tell us about the development of individual identity in relation to others?

We have challenged ourselves to engage in a layered conversation about conversation. We consider the impact of narrative authority (Olson, 1995; Olson & Craig, 2001) on the chapters presented here, and we reflect on the importance of literacy education and teacher development through serial interpretation of these accounts (Schwab, 1983). Above all, we hold true that partnerships for the improvement of literacy education are partnerships for the improvement of communication which bears impact on how we navigate both our work and lives. Literacy classrooms are a perfect setting for the study of language as an historic carrier of culture and a disruptor of the same. Hence, the words we speak and the words we write matter.

As editors, we asked ourselves two questions upon entering this work:

(1) *Through what unique lens did I approach the work preceding this volume?*
A response here requires some reflection on the personal practical knowledge (Clandinin, 1985) accumulated prior to engaging in our three-year cross-institutional research partnership. In many respects, it calls us to determine the hows and whys of our entry into the study and the "whats" of our pre- and post-study knowledge development, which we see as inseparable from the development of our "selves."
(2) *What shapes my understanding of the work reflected in the chapters collected here?*
This second question delves more deeply into the relational aspects of our work with one another and with our community of contributing authors. The questions within this question include considerations for not only the professional roles and standards associated with each of our titles but also the less frequently addressed considerations of age, race, gender, socioeconomic background, and intra- and international cultural history, which is both intentionally and unintentionally shaping our work.

In the following sections, we (Chestin T. Auzenne-Curl and Cheryl J. Craig as co-researchers and co-authors) respond to the aforementioned questions.

Cheryl's Story: Comprehensive School Reform in Greater Houston

I came to the work involving the WITS (Writers in the Schools) Collaborative with over 20 years of experience conducting research in Greater Houston's public schools. The largest initiative over that continuum of time was the Houston Annenberg Challenge reform movement, a $60 million change effort meant to improve Houston's urban campuses over a five-year period. I was invited to work with 5 of the 11 lead schools and served as the formal evaluator at a sixth lead campus. Later, I was invited to conduct research on four other campuses chosen for the second tier of funding by the Houston A+ reform movement. The previous experiences I brought with me to this WITS reform endeavor taught me a plethora of lessons about change. One was that the vast majority of campuses and educators are genuinely engaged in it but there are those who participate in name only. The main thing I learned – through hard-wrought experience – is that bureaucrats and philanthropies cannot make educators do anything; teachers and principals must commit to making changes themselves. The same goes for students. Despite grand claims to the contrary, change can only happen one person at a time.

When I first moved to Houston from Western Canada, I was shocked by the educational disparities that existed between different students and schools. While I knew that the segregation and desegregation of public schools had happened, I did not know how phenomena had played out over time. One might say I arrived in Houston with book knowledge only....

While working with the Houston Annenberg Challenge schools, their lived reality deepened my understanding of what had transpired. Two of the campuses with which I worked were still under an unresolved court order for their school district's failure to segregate properly. One of those campuses, Hardy Academy (Author Tim Martindell's school), had two reforms in it, both driven by private interest groups (philanthropy, business-led group). I was taken aback by these developments as well. In Canada, private interest groups would not have open access to public school systems. The Annenberg reform movement, on one hand, wanted to improve students' educational experiences and open up a full range of career possibilities to them. The business-directed change effort, on the other hand, wanted to prepare Hardy's mostly students of color to become workers in local oil and gas industries. This set up a "dueling banjos" scenario with the Hardy teachers being less willing to comply with the latter reform agenda. Resentment predictably built. The Hardy teachers rebelled against the heavy-handed business change proposition. The business reformers subsequently moved on to campuses more vulnerable than Hardy, schools with less-strong teacher defenses.

A second thing that stood out to me was the Annenberg reform designated funding for elementary schools, middle schools, and high schools. The initial Houston Annenberg awards did not take into account that one elementary school had 600+ students, one middle school had 1,500 students, and one high school had 125 students. That small high school, Destiny High School, received more funding than all the large elementary and middle schools and an equivalent amount to Eagle High School, which had 3,500 students. The fact that Destiny High School had the least number of students of color made the situation even more egregious. After the first year, the reform funding formula changed and became prorated by the number of students per campus. However, I always wondered why leadership believed the flawed funding formula would have been appropriate in the first place. Also, I discovered a backroom deal favoring the small high school as well. On the whole, I learned that private groups entering schools may have agendas flying beneath the radar that may not be in the interest of all public schools and all children.

Then, there were the stories that students told. At one elementary campus, a primary Latinx girl told her teacher about waking in the night to find "a rat on her tummy." When I spoke with the principal about what the child said, he shook his head woefully, saying that some neighborhood homes had dirt floors and tales like this were not out of the ordinary. Later on, during the Houston A+ Challenge, a Grade 3 boy was disciplined for being late first thing in the morning for practice testing for the state exams. When a trail of roaches was later found in the school – and that trail led to the young boy's backpack – it was discovered that he and another youth had been left alone for three weeks while their parents were away on a work trip. When the teachers heard this news, they wept. They said if they talked to students when they first arrived at school rather than testing them, they would have a better chance of troubleshooting difficult situations. And, at Eagle High School, a few blocks away, I conversed with a female student of color. After seeing me around the campus several times, she stopped me in the hallway, begging me to adopt her as her clothing had become too small and she needed right-size clothes. These student narratives, among many others, have stuck to me like glue since I first encountered them. Together, they have awakened me to experiences I never imagined possible. In many ways, they are the stories behind the statistics, the narratives that are able to bring about human change in ways that numbers – devoid of moral push and purpose (Bruner, 1986) – never could or never can.

Finally, I must say something about the reminder of the public schools located in Greater Houston. No extra funding was assigned to them, if they were not in the first rounds of awards. Many attending these remaining schools were also students living in challenging circumstances with food anxieties, among other urgent needs. These campuses also had exceedingly high turnover rates of teachers. In an article published after the Houston Annenberg Challenge reform movement ended, I reported that 80% of the teachers in the largest school district in Greater Houston had 5 years or less in experience and 50% of the administrators in the same school district had 5 years or less of experiences (Craig, 2014).

Consequently, when I entered the WITS work, I knew that both teacher experience and principal experience in the large school district were precariously thin. I also knew there were a very large number of children and young adults, mostly of color, who had extremely high needs. Therefore, it did not surprise me that WITS received dedicated funding from a local philanthropy to assist Greater Houston's most challenged schools with students' literacy development. Entering into a partnership agreement with WITS, I knew much more was needed than money poured into a project that other people would have to live. At the same time, I recognized that WITS could be part of a lifeline that was so desperately needed and so obviously missing.

Chestin's Story: How Educators Negotiate Identity in Education?

I approach this work, Black, female, cis-gendered, and from a middle-class Southern American upbringing – an author, an educator, and a mother. Born in the '80s and raised in the '90s, my experiences in school were impacted by factors including tracking, socioeconomic and racial resegregation through redistricting, and high accountability performance measures of standardized testing. I was identified and labeled gifted early on. This placed me in a social incubator of sorts. I had classes with the same classmates, under the direction of the most trusted teachers at each grade level for most of my educational career. I was also usually the only person of color in my classes.

To travel back a bit, I was a junior in high school when I was first introduced to the idea that being a writer and an educator was mutually exclusive. It came from my beloved English teacher from the year prior. I told her about how I would major in Literature. I thought it would make her proud, because she was truly a light in my life. Her classroom was a place in which I grieved the loss of my grandmother on page after college-rule page in my journal. I was safe in that class. It was in that classroom that I came to understand, as Joan Didion said, that "I write to know what I think, and in which I first pondered that others might do the same." Of course, we wrote some of the more prescriptive, extended analyses on the work of Steinbeck, Fitzgerald, and Shakespeare, but those I cannot remember. What I carry with me now is the sense of freedom I found in my journal. It held my voice, and when the teacher read excerpts from our journals, she always gave enough feedback to guide us in perfecting craft, but never a grade. She made it clear that these journals were *our* places, and we invited her in. She dared not overstep into a judgment. She made it seem that we honored her by allowing her to share in our worlds. So, you may imagine that hearing her say to me, "Please don't let them convince you to teach. You are a writer; not a teacher." quite shocked me. She said, "Remember that. It's your gift."

I stood, smiling in clinch-toothed confusion and replied "Of course" only to have her belabor, "A writer, Chestin." And so my wondering began. "How, exactly, could I prove her wrong, respectfully?" So much of this book aims to do so. In fact, I do not believe that it is possible to separate one's sense of self as an author from the reality that we want to be heard and thus hope to provoke thought. All writing is a lesson in something. Our teacher selves and our writer selves reflect a negotiation of "being and becoming" through the sameness of each role. Perhaps the teacher seeks most often to encourage this behavior outside of self, while the author searches most frequently within. Ruth Vinz in the literacy area underscored that preservice literacy teachers, like their students, are being and becoming as they learn alongside one another while engaged in reading and writing; this was true for me, and across my career I have noted the same truth for literacy leaders. It is their classroom teaching experience that shapes their interactions with their peers as they enter the role of teacher educator in the field. It was the same for me.

I began my teaching career in the very classroom that inspired me to teach. My teacher was moving to the Austin area and I was her replacement. I did remember her words. I was a writer. I majored in literature with an emphasis in writing and planned on teaching for three years in order to pay for law school, but when I stepped into the classroom which had been stripped bare of all resources, I knew I was called to teach. I covered the profanity on the cork board with borders and fabric and thought of the difference that I could make in that very special room.

I was not met with a warm welcome by my colleagues. They felt that my major in literature left me ill-equipped to manage a classroom and were shocked when that proved false. My first year teaching brought me recognition from the central office staff and most importantly from my students. I still wondered if my fellow teachers had a point, and so I began to reflect on what it meant to be a teacher. *Was it coursework? Was it conditioning? Was it on the job training?* By year two, I had spent minimal time concerned with the state writing assessment, but I had worked to make sure that I understood it enough to prepare my students. I was surprised to find out that by year three, my students, none of whom were advanced-placement or honors students, earned the highest passing rate in the district and the highest campus percentage for essays with distinguished state recognition. So I was called upon, by the campus Dean of Instruction, to become a mentor when I still needed one. She did not leave me without guidance. She attended many professional development sessions with me and we always debriefed. She asked me: *How did you feel about that training and why? What are some specific things that you heard the facilitator say about "insert topic"? If you were leading this session what would you want to do differently? What would you hope people would leave with?* I journaled about our meetings and dedicated time to applying the responses to my view as a mentor.

For me, this idea of professional being and becoming is heavily wrought in an examination of language and it led me to focus my broader research lens on qualitative methodology. Throughout my career, I questioned the stories that intersect in truth and how those intersections shape who we are. America's beloved female philosopher Maxine Greene (deceased) wrote that we are always in the making and never made. With this in mind, my evolving research body consistently centers the participant in context. It rarely excludes me from work as a participant observer in study. The questions which permeate my analyses of work on the education landscape are: *Who are we? How do the commonplaces in which we exist shape our journey? How are we shaped by the experiences of others with whom we share physical and abstract space? What can be gained by a sharing of self and personal journey when we enter into a community of reflective practice?*

THEORETICAL AND METHODOLOGICAL FOUNDATIONS

Every contributing author in this volume is a teacher. Though for some of us, our classroom walls have been made virtual, and for others, a classroom has become an auditorium, while others travel to conferences across the globe to share, our unifying identity is that of educator of different kinds. In beginning with our likeness, we address the following theoretical foundations of this volume.

Storied Experience

In her 2013 volume, *Engaging in Narrative Inquiry,* Jean Clandinin (2013a, p. 21) ushers readers into the process of inquiry with a quote from Nigerian poet and novelist Ben Okri. A portion of it deeply resonated with us:

> One way or another we are living the stories
>
> Planted in us early or along the way,
>
> Or we are also living the stories we planted—
>
> Knowingly or unknowingly—in ourselves
>
> We live stories that either give our lives meaning
>
> or negate it with meaninglessness.
>
> If we change the stories we live by,
>
> Quite possibly we change our lives.

This notion of living "by" and "in" stories calls us to be narrative inquirers. Cheryl, as a student of Jean, and Chestin, as a student of Cheryl, hold true that narrative is both a methodology by which to conduct research and a natural phenomenon to be studied in the field.

In entering a study, we "think narratively" (Clandinin, 2013b; Clandinin & Connelly, 2000) alongside our participants to gain insights into their lived experiences. Our interpretations and wonderings are influenced by serial interpretation (Schwab, 1978a, 1978b) of themes repeated and divergent in the stories with which we interact.

The field of educational research often reports data with an inclination toward measurement in solely quantitative methods, but we believe that in order to move from measurement to change, a deeper degree of exploration is necessary. The worlds of theory and practice align in research that highlights "the particulars" (Schwab, 1969). Those seemingly minute elements that influence the numbers lend themselves to fuller exploration. They are revealed in the voices of practitioners. Narrative discourse in education amplifies them, and we study them with a Deweyan lens of three-dimensional experience which explores each event as relevant to time (past-present-future), place (context), and interaction (relationships). A study of words and interactions, *through words and interactions*, made literacy education a perfect ground for these methods (Dewey, 1938).

Knowledge Communities and the Value of Personal Practical Knowledge

Highlighting the importance of reflective, experiential learning through the use of narrative inquiry, Cheryl has contributed a particularly relevant stem to the methodological narrative tree. Her work reflects the lives of teachers and the contextualized knowledge communities (Craig, 1995, 2007; Craig, Curtis, Kelley, Martindell, & Perez, 2020) in which they live and grow. Our work with the WITS organization shed light on professional development efforts for transforming literacy practices as "originating events" (Craig, 2007) for several intricately connected knowledge communities. As the chapters in this book reveal, the assigned groups were not always the center of the truest knowledge transfer, but they frequently seeded interactions that led to the development of organically formed communities where personal practical knowledge coupled with collegiality formed lasting relationships and professional support. In these knowledge communities, much discussion focused on navigating the dilemmas within the workspace, and pedagogical risk-taking influenced change inside and outside of the classroom. We were able to note these and other resonances through the study of stories shared with us.

THE INQUIRY IN CONTEXT

> We hear about declining literacy; it has become a fact of life – a drab presence, simply there. We look for scapegoats; teachers, of course; disintegrating families; shiftless children…. What do we mean by literacy? What is it for? –Maxine Greene

Though the quote above is nearly 40 years old upon the time of this publication, it resonates loudly with the present-day discourse surrounding literacy education. Our first with Tina and Maryann was an informal conversation on the same topics. They were administrators in the WITS Collaborative, and we were members of the Texas A&M University Research Team. The WITS Team was looking for a new approach to program evaluation. Their previous structure seemed maligned with their programmatic goals. So we ventured into a casual conversation with strong echoes of the views and questions that Greene expresses in *Literacy for What?* (1982).

Place

Texas is know2n for high accountability measures for standardized testing and also for poor performance in reading and writing by its own standards. During our partnership with WITS Houston, the state of Texas' average reading scores for third and eighth grade were at 40.5% and 48%. Writing scores, which is assessed in grades 4 and 7, were at 59.5% and 45.5% (Figs. 1 and 2).

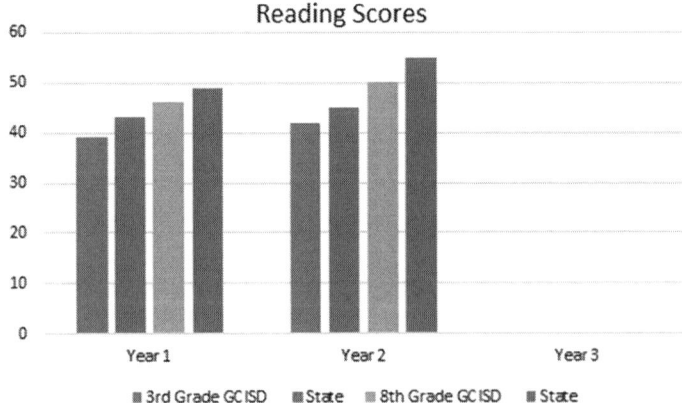

Fig. 1. Greater City ISD Reading Scores.

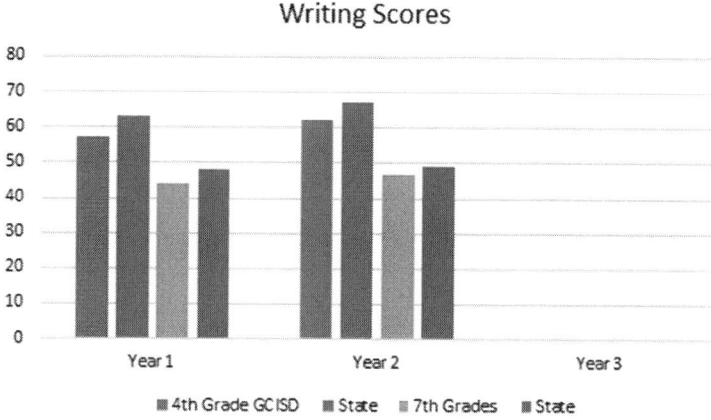

Fig. 2. Greater City ISD Writing Scores.

These scores become even more disparate when we view them according to socioeconomic status (Figs. 3 and 4):

Steven Klineberg's (2016, 2021) decades long study on Houston's demography revealed that the city's increasingly diverse population is a trend that the nation will certainly follow and that the trend centers the economically disadvantaged and historically marginalized population as the core for rapid population growth. These same groups struggle with conventional approaches to literacy instruction. It is little wonder that Cheryl noted significant student and school disparities when she entered the Greater Houston reform scene over two decades ago.

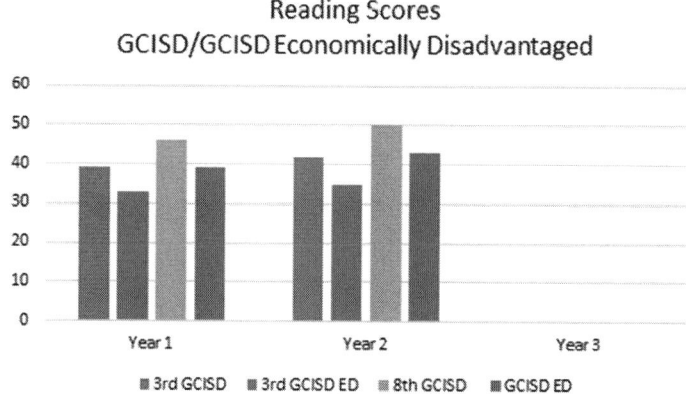

Fig. 3. Comparative Reading Scores (Economically Disadvantaged).

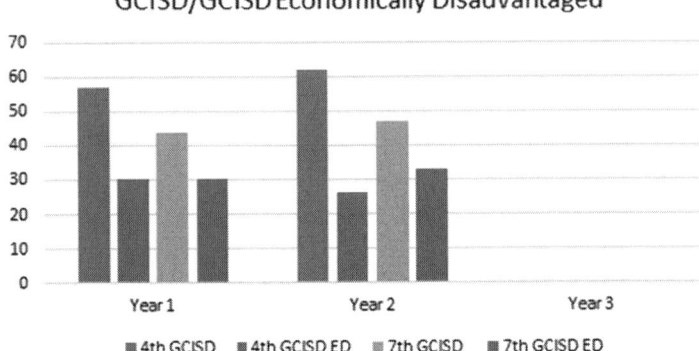

Fig. 4. Comparative Writing Scores (Economically Disadvantaged).

Time

The data reports representing our Y1-Y3 are complicated by the impact of Hurricane Harvey during our initial year, and in the final year, the COVID-19 shutdown. In Greater Houston, these three years were rampant with natural disasters, flooding, displacement, and illness that disrupted face-to-face education and "normal" curriculum, instruction, and assessment. The break from normalcy was a welcomed one for many marginalized populations. For these groups, "normal" had failed them for some time. The hurricane and the pandemic, along with troubling incidents of prejudice, police violence, and civil unrest, signaled that paradigmatic change of one sort or another may be on its way.

In an interview with Dr. Gloria Ladson-Billings (GLB), Chestin (C) asked her to reflect on the risks of returning to this "normal":

> C: What are the risks related to educators falling back into the comfort zone of a normal, and I feel restrictive, lens of writing as a performance-based accountability measure?
>
> GLB: The risks are obvious. We are likely to fall right back into the high rates of school failure among marginalized groups as well as a continued lack of engagement. The operative question for me is always, "What are we trying to produce?" If we have a vision of what we'd like to see at the end, perhaps it will give us some insight as to how to go about achieving it.
>
> I think you have a good infrastructure with WITS to encourage and support writing. I don't think the issue is getting really getting students to write but rather, getting teachers to teach and value students' writing.

When Chestin asked her about how writing instructors could create a portal to prevent us from falling back on the pedagogy of "normal" that proven to be ineffective with marginalized populations, she said

> ...There are so many outlets for innovative approaches to literacy and youth voice. I currently sit on the Advisory Board for Sacramento Area Youth Speaks (SAYS) and work with Urban Word NYC to select the National Youth Poet Laureate. I am also sharing a link for a long term and successful writing project we have here in Madison, The Simpson Street Free Press. These young people are amazing and start with upper elementary up through high school students.

These organizations centered student voices in an approach similar to WITS. WITS Writers worked with teachers to compile anthologies of the literature that students produced during the collaborative partnership, and WITS' poetry slams encouraged spoken word and young poets to integrate performance into their view of what writing can become outside of the classroom. Of equal importance to the venues for sharing work in multiple venues was the view and voice that adults in these organizations shed light upon. For teachers working in public education, especially in Texas in the twenty-first century, it was not that teachers disagreed with or lacked knowledge of the platforms. In fact, many of the teachers that we interviewed expressed a desire to move toward a voice-inspired curriculum, but without the assistance of partnering organizations, or institutions of higher learning, felt frustrated by a perceived lack of reinforcement for enacting such changes when they approached local administrators.

Tina, a founding member of the WITS Collaborative, recounted what she had heard from both WITS Writers and their partnering teachers in the field, "We are dealing with the stress of writing 26 lines on a page. Our state has given children this restriction of 26 lines to express themselves in." Chestin recounted her experience as a district level program coordinator,

> We had this discussion often in K-12, I know. The current assessment is not only a challenging exercise in the use of concise language and tight revision, it's unrealistic. I used to think that the 5-paragraph essay was a damaging restriction, but this is somehow worse. The literacy coaches with whom I planned the curriculum were never too shy to bring it up, they'd ask "How can we teach them that this is writing? It's not," and we gave pushback often. Sometimes we were successful, and other times, we were overridden by administrators who valued testing outcomes over learning outcomes. Still, in the end, we'd make the decision to do what we knew would benefit our students in the long run.

Tina added, "That is another thing that we hope WITS helps. We support the teachers in using authentic approaches to the writing process and to authentic products. What we know is that if we teach them what good writing is, the rest – the test – will take care of itself. So we make sure we share that with administrators."

Interaction

> If something that I teach a kid works only in the classroom, then it's not worth teaching, ... It has to work in the real world. –Cornelius Minor (in Formon, 2019)

The WITS Collaborative strives to make writing an authentic experience for all involved. "What we do is take a published author and bring them into our professional development circle, teach them the model for coaching, and then place them in a school with teachers so that kids get a natural and more engaging approach to writing instruction" said Tina. When we met, her primary role was to facilitate the preparation of the authors (WITS Writers) for field work. Maryann, who worked with Tina as a liaison with school leaders, added "We often meet leaders who want to put testing first. We strive to put communication first. Our goal is to show kids (through inspired teachers) that there are writers in the world, and that they can be writers, too." Both Tina and

Maryann spoke of the constraints under which many students and teachers were approaching writing. These whispers from the field brought Cheryl Craig back to her previous field observations in the Greater Houston schools.

Cheryl noted that there were historic literacy wars alive and well in the school districts in question. When one teacher at another Greater Houston campus had a literacy, reform forced down her throat, she wondered out loud whether her fellow teachers and her would ever graduate from the predigested curriculum they were expected to teach. Immediately, her principal authoritatively replied: "Never." This provoked the teacher to state that she was a "butterfly under a pin," an individual who used to be a curriculum-maker "in charge" of her teaching, but was now dictated to be a staff developer who policed every pedagogical move she made and forced her to live the teacher-as-curriculum-implementer image – and not of her personal making or choosing (Craig, 2012).

> Language is also a place of struggle. –bell hooks

The WITS Collaborative invited our research team into their community because they felt that previous evaluations were limited in their view of the Collaborative's work. As we listened to Tina and Maryann's discussion of these evaluations, the research team quickly understood that the past evaluations were not evaluations of the Collaborative. They were assessments of student performance. Texas has established a reputation for high accountability standardized testing and those measures had infiltrated the Collaborative's evaluation. We reflected on how the goal of the Collaborative did not seem to be restricted to student performance on tests. In fact, the Collaborative was largely functioning as a professional development structure for teachers. This would mean that the assessment of the program needed to be centered on the work of teachers.

Understanding how writing develops is essential to delivering effective writing instruction (Graham, MacArthur, & Fitzgerald, 2013; Graham & Perin, 2007; Kaplan, 2008). By growing in their understanding of composition theory and practice, teachers increase their ability to make informed decisions in the classroom that can make a positive difference in the growth of student writers. WITS is an inquiry-based program and thus a language based-program. In order to understand how it lived in schools, we would need to design a protocol for analyzing trends in Teacher Talk (TT) in order to drive decision-making (Phillip, 2018; Zepeda, Hlutkowsky, Partika, & Nokes-Malach, 2018) for continued professional development. Away from the previously presented high stakes testing methods that look to summative scores as primary indicators of success, this method draws attention to the process of teacher learning and student learning as it unfolds. Using narrative inquiry (Connelly & Clandinin, 1990) and reflective practices to bring to light narratives of struggle and success across the partnership, TT has been given increased attention in our study and across the body of educational research. Whether the research is centered on Teacher-to-Pupil Talk in language-based classrooms (Alkhazraji, 2018; Jing & Jing, 2018; Lee & Kim, 2016; VanDerHeide, 2017) where studies of how teachers and students communicate during the grammar and composition lessons are noted for relational and pedagogical analysis or on Critical Teacher Talk (Kim, 2016) that indicates introspection and craft, the research team moved forward in studying Critical Teacher Talk as relevant data in the area of teacher education and professional development in this project.

Application to the Study

As Cheryl and Chestin reflected on field recordings and transcriptions, trends revealed themselves. We discussed TT as it revealed the participating teachers' personal meaning-making experiences and Critical Teacher Talk as it indicated instructional strategies and technical approaches to writing. From these conversations, a new frame and rubric was developed to assist all members of the research partnership in active reflection on conversations regarding WITS-specific language of instruction. This language included but is not limited to the language of studies centered on workshop approaches to writing and the focus words of the School Reform Initiative protocols which Tim (Chapter 10) used in field preparation workshops for the WITS personnel partnering with classroom teachers. Words or phrases that are found on the state assessment rubric for student compositions and those unique to the coach or campus were also included, as we considered them influences on the cultural experience of the WITS professional development.

We broke down words and phrases into four categories: Praise, Critique, Workshop, and Inquiry. These categories are aligned to the WITS Collaborative Model's most promising practices in writing instruction (Graham et al., 2013, pp. 12–20) as follows:

- Most promising practice 1: Creating a supportive classroom environment where writing development can flourish
  Characterized by highly specific praise, critique, and inquiry. Workshop-rich practices permeate the culture by providing opportunity for gradual release
- Most promising practice 2: Teaching writing strategies
  Evidenced in the teachers' repetition and use of specific language of instruction.
- Most promising practice 3: Helping students acquire the knowledge needed to write effectively
  Heavily impacted by workshop practices such as modeling and paired practice.
- Most promising practice 4: Teaching foundational writing skills
  Influenced by inquiry and specific praise.

In observing TT, we listened for the frequency, depth of complexity, and specificity of language that was present during the discussion between WITS Writers and the classroom teachers with whom they were partnered. We found that this process yielded conversations that were centered on craft rather than scores, which often highlighted that language was, indeed, a place of struggle. Teachers often shared the complex lives of their students:

> I don't really think people understand how wrapped up in kids' lives we become when they ask us to have them open up and write a narrative. They share a lot. It gets heavy. (Middle School Teacher, Field notes, 2018)

> I hate talking about the test with kids. I try to tell them that it's just a test to tell them how far they have come with their writing, but in reality, it's not. The test doesn't measure whether or not [Dante] started really opening up to me, or if his ideas are more cohesive than they were in August. It just tells him how some phantom grader felt about what he did on one morning out of 187 school days – and it's part of whether he graduates or not. (High School Teacher, Field notes, 2018)

The echoings of frustration with accountability were compounded by a WITS program evaluation that returned to these isolated instances of performance. The Collaborative honored the process and the teachers' role in leading learning by example. One of the WITS Writers reflected on her observations of a teacher who had shifted his language and focus under the new TT protocols:

> I worked with Mr. Stanley last year and he was always frustrated. I could not get a kind word out of him and he was visibly disturbed when we would use the student data protocol. I am not sure if it was solely the protocol shift, but he definitely warmed up to discussion this year. He started talking about revision. That is huge. We tried to have teachers focus on revision before and it just felt like this act of terror. When would they have time to revise before the next assessment and the next data pull? You know.

> So when we started talking about the protocols, I think they – Mr. Stanley anyway – felt freed up to talk about the *process* of writing. We always valued that, but the new protocol highlighted it, I think. Process is more important than randomly collected products. That seems to be the message (interview with Mary, Spring 2018).

The protocols also demonstrated WITS Writers growing in their coaching role and in their identities as teachers of teachers. Chestin noted Mary's growth (Journals 2019):

> The WITS Writers are watching the teachers blossom into writers. They often share their observations about the teachers embracing their inner writer, but I'm watching the writers embrace their inner teacher! Watching Mary over the past year has been really interesting. She began as a writer, only. She told me that she was often hesitant to really assert a strategy because she was not a teacher, but now I'm listening to her use the language of instruction and the model lesson from the collaborative with confidence. She even said, "next week I'm going to teach…" and this is a huge mention. Last year she never said she taught, she "modeled," or she would say she "did" the lesson. Today she taught.

Having been a literacy coach, Chestin often reflected on the voices of other teacher educators in the field. Those for whom she said "cultivating in and empowering teachers to hold an image of self as autonomous creators" was a primary calling and daily struggle. "What we've seen in our study with WITS, and what we have experienced as researchers is an indicator of the power of language," She said. "Toni Morrison once said, 'We die. That may be the meaning of life. But we do language. That may be the measure of our lives.' In that, writing teachers, writing coaches, professional developers of writers, and of course – writers themselves – are always in the process of 'doing language' and therefore creating a standard of measure that I believe permeates this volume."

The collective body of authors here are from inside and outside the WITS Collaborative, and all provide us with introspective acts of meaning that are bound together by narrative threads of identity, communication, and the negotiation of which as they contribute to change.

IN THIS VOLUME

The chapters in this volume are presented in three parts: "Seeing Big (Part I), Seeing Small (Part II), and Seeing More (Part III)."

Part I: Seeing Big: Tension and Triumphs of Partnerships for Professional Development

In Part 1, "Seeing Big," four chapters that examine the larger landscape of twenty-first century professional development partnerships appear.

Chapter 2, authored by Tina Angelo and Maryann Gremillion, is titled *Innovation and Integrity: Working Through Disruption to Support Teachers in Their Roles as Literacy Educators.* In this body of work, Angelo and Gremillion tell how two disruptive forces – a hurricane and a pandemic – both drew to the surface inequities in education that the WITS Collaborative project sought to overcome.

In Chapter 3, Chestin T. Auzenne-Curl, Gayle Curtis, and Cheryl J. Craig address primary and secondary traumatic stressors in *Reflections on Research and Professional Development Partnerships in Post-Harvey Houston.* They discuss how stress from the hurricane trickled into the WITS Collaborative activities and influenced the initiative in both predictable and unpredictable ways.

Next up in the chapter lineup is Chapter 4 authored by Michael Curl and Cheryl J. Craig. The work chronicles what they know about principals' experiences of reform alongside Michael's sense of the WITS impact on the teachers and middle school students on his campus. The real-world example speaks to the power of a knowledge community of writers and teachers working productively to positively affect middle school students' life chances.

Chapter 5, authored by Daphne Carr and Chestin T. Auzenne-Curl, discusses their hard-wrought experiences in the field as teacher educators. *Navigating the Role of Teacher Educators in the Field: The Case for Increased Community Support* revolves around the need for additional support in the areas of *teacher* development, teacher educator retention, and the consistent engagement of campus and district level administrators. The chapter includes the importance of literacy coaches and the need for writing "interventions" such as WITS. The work also includes the preparation of preservice teachers and the critically important roles of teacher educators of different kinds. We then transition to Part II, Seeing Small: A Closer Look at the Writers in the Schools Collaborative.

*Part II: Seeing Small: The Case for a Closer Look at the
Writers in the Schools Collaborative*

Part II: "Seeing Small" is a section dedicated to the many layers of the WITS Collaborative. It begins with Chapter 6, *Reflection on WITS History and the Challenges of Change*, which is authored by Robin Reagler, former Executive Director of WITS. Robin openly reflects on the WITS approach to teacher professional development. She includes her perceived theory of how change happens within the WITS program.

We next move on to Chapter 7, *In Search of a Trellis: A Principal's Perspective on the Need for Cross-institutional Literacy Partnerships*. Authored by Terri Osborne, the work centers on the enactment of the WITS Collaborative on a secondary school campus. The campus's multitiered approach to school improvement and literacy intervention becomes instantiated through the principal's details about the partnership and tensions concerning its enactment. She additionally includes its implications for the field.

What follows is Chapter 8, *Tough Turf: Restored Moments in the Dissipation of an Urban Knowledge Community*. Authored by Abdulkader Mokhtari, Chestin T. Auzenne-Curl, and KaLeah Hicks, the work presents Mokhtari's reflections on his participation in the WITS Collaborative on two campuses in one more urban and one less urban community setting. In conversation with Chestin T. Auzenne-Curl and KaLeah Hicks, Mokhtari chronicles pivotal moments of success and struggle.

We then proceed to Sarah Jerasa's Chapter 9, *The Beauty of Petals and Thorns: Negotiating Identity as a Writer-Teacher*. In this chapter, Sara details the small step successes and systematic struggles she faced as an author as she modeled the writer's craft and enacted writer's workshop strategies with the teachers on her assigned campus. The chapter ends with a discussion of the important roles teachers navigate as they discover their best-loved-self teaching identity.

Chapter 10, *Reflective Conversation on the Value of Longevity as Collaborators in Education*, is authored by P. Tim Martindell, Cheryl J. Craig, and Chestin T. Auzenne-Curl. It revolves around a Zoom conversation that Tim and Cheryl had to, in which Chestin added field notes, visuals, and her and their reflections and analysis. The work is a life-like characterization of Critical Friends (CFG®) protocols in action. It furthermore features the fine points of Tim's facilitation of the WITS Writers alongside Tina Angelo and Maryann Gremillion. We now proceed to Part III, "Seeing More," which consists of our final four chapters and this book's conclusion.

Part III: Seeing More: Something to Pursue

Part III: "Seeing More" serves as a collection of divergent threads inspired by our work in the field. It first features Chapter 11, *Gentrimigration: Two Tales, One City's Story of a Changed Community*, which is authored by Tenesha Gale and written in parallel story form. The work unpacks two female teachers' perceptions of their peers' responses and attitudes toward students at various points during a defined period of demographic shift at the largest high school in Hope City District, Hope High School. As the community became more ethnically, socioeconomically, and linguistically diverse, the school climate changed, along with the teachers' attitudes. Chapter 11 raises long-standing questions about future stories to both live and leave by.

Poetry Is Not a Luxury: Engaging Learners in Multiple Literacies Through Creative Poetics is the title of Chapter 12, which is contributed by Lobat Asadi. The work examines the experiences of five high-school aged youth involved in WITS. Multiple Literacies Theory joins the tools of narrative inquiry as an interpretive device. All in all, Chapter 12 captures some of the benefits of art-based education and bildungsroman for marginalized learners. It also justifies the need for further research into art-based pedagogies and assessments, which may more fully capture and justify multiple literacies.

Auzenne-Curl recounts the process of meaning-making in *"After a Trip, the Suitcase Stays Full Till I Need Something": Unpacking Narrative Truths From the Field*, which is the title of Chapter 13. She restories two interviews, one with Poet Jasminne Mendez on community and the other with Gloria Ladson Billings on change. Each of these interviews added to her understanding of the role of writing instructors and her successful enactments of the role in the public education sector.

In Chapter 14, *The Implications of Social Media Scholarship on Knowledge Communities in Black Cyberculture: A Co-constructed Narrative*, Chestin Auzenne-Curl and Daphne Carr examine social media discourse among literacy teachers and coaches during the COVID-19 pandemic of 2020 and beyond. They argue that there is a close connection between the work of Black Womxn Scholars by virtue of their media presence and what is known about knowledge communities and their development, particularly as they apply at the present time.

Authored by Chestin T. Auzenne-Curl and Cheryl J. Craig, Chapter 15 discusses not one, but four pandemics that rocked the Greater Houston area – one after another, after another, after another – during the WITS Collaborative. *Research across four pandemics* summarizes the collective findings found in this book's chapters and interweaves what their respective authors and co-authors had to say about their effects and impacts. What this volume offers others nationally and internationally will also be spotlighted.

REFERENCES

Alkhazraji, A. M. (2018). Analyzing the impact of teacher talk on English grammar learning: With correlation to the procedures in classroom interaction. *Journal of Language Teaching and Research*, 9(5), 1109.

Bruner, J. (1986). *Actual minds, possible worlds*. Cambridge, MA: Harvard University Press.

Clandinin, D. J. (1985). Personal practical knowledge: A study of teachers' classroom images. *Curriculum Inquiry*, 15(4), 361–385.

Clandinin, D. (2013a). *Engaging in narrative inquiry*. Walnut Creek, CA: Left Coast Press.

Clandinin, D. (2013b). Personal practical knowledge: A study of teachers classroom images. In C. J. Craig, P. C. Meijer, & J. Broeckmans (Eds.), *From teacher thinking to teachers and teaching: The evolution of a research community. Advances in research on teaching* (Vol. 19, pp. 67–96). Bingley: Emerald Publishing Limited.

Clandinin, D., & Connelly, F. (2000). *Narrative inquiry: Experience and story in qualitative research*. San Francisco, CA: Jossey-Bass.

Connelly, F., & Clandinin, D. (1990). Stories of experience and narrative inquiry. *Educational Researcher*, 19(5), 2–14.

Craig, C. (1995). Knowledge communities: A way of making sense of how beginning teachers come to know in their professional knowledge contexts. *Curriculum Inquiry, 25*(2), 151–175.

Craig, C. (2007). Illuminating qualities of knowledge communities in a portfolio-making context. *Teachers and Teaching, 13*(6), 617–636.

Craig, C. (2012). "Butterfly under a pin": An emergent teacher image amid mandated curriculum reform. *The Journal of Educational Research, 105*(2), 90–101.

Craig, C. (2014). From stories of staying to stories of leaving: A US beginning teacher's experience. *Journal of Curriculum Studies, 46*(1), 81–115.

Craig, C. J., Curtis, G. A., Kelley, M., Martindell, P. T., & Pérez, M. M. (2020). *Knowledge communities in teacher education: Sustaining collaborative work*. Basingstoke: Palgrave Macmillan.

Dewey, J. (1938). My pedagogic creed. *School Journal, 54*, 77–80.

Formon, B. (2019, May 8). Five things we love about Cornelius Minor: Shining a spotlight on the ILA intensive keynote's dedication to equity in literacy. Retrieved from https://www.literacyworldwide.org/blog/literacy-now/2019/05/08/five-things-we-love-abou/t-cornelius-minor-shining-a-spotlight-on-the-ila-intensive-keynote-s-dedication-to-equity-in-literacy. Accessed on October 11, 2020.

Graham, S., MacArthur, C., & Fitzgerald, J. (2013). *Best practices in writing instruction*. New York, NY: Guilford Press.

Graham, S., & Perin, D. (2007). A meta-analysis of writing instruction for adolescent students. *Journal of Educational Psychology, 99*(3), 446–476.

Greene, M. (1982). Literacy for what. *Phi Delta Kappan, 63*(5), 326–329.

Jing, N., & Jing, J. (2018). Teacher talk in an EFL classroom: A pilot study. *Theory and Practice in Language Studies, 8*(3), 320.

Kaplan, J. (2008). The national writing project: Creating a professional learning community that supports the teaching of writing. *Theory Into Practice, 47*(1), 336–344.

Kim, N. (2016). Critical teacher talk: Successful English for academic purposes classroom practices in a global campus. *Journal of International Students, 6*(4), 96.

Klineberg, S. L. (2016, March 8). The changing face of Texas and America. *Fort Worth Business Press*, p. 10.

Klineberg, S. L. (2021). *Prophetic city: Houston on the cusp of a changing America*. New York: Avid Reader Press/Simon Schuster.

Lee, J., & Kim, K. (2016). Pre-service teachers' conceptions of effective teacher talk: Their critical reflections on a sample teacher-student dialogue. *Educational Studies in Mathematics, 93*(3), 363–381.

Olson, M. (1995). Conceptualizing narrative authority in (teacher) education. *Teaching and Teacher Education, 11*(2), 119–125.

Olson, M., & Craig, C. (2001). Opportunities and challenges in the development of teachers' knowledge: The development of narrative authority through knowledge communities. *Teaching and Teacher Education, 17*(6), 667–684.

Philip, G. (2018). How to evaluate the effectiveness of teacher talk. *International Online Journal of Education and Teaching (IOJET), 5*(3), 497–512.

Ross, V., Chan, E., & Keyes, D. (2017). *Crossroads of the classroom: Narrative intersections of teacher knowledge and subject matter*. Bingley: Emerald Publishing Limited.

Schwab, J. J. (1969). The practical: A language for curriculum. *The School Review, 78*(1), 1–23.

Schwab, J. (1978a). Eros and education: A discussion of one aspect of discussion. In I. Westbury & N. Wilkof (Eds.), *Science, curriculum and liberal education: Selected essays*. Chicago, IL: University of Chicago Press.

Schwab, J. (1978b). The 'impossible' role of the teacher in progressive education. In I. Westbury & N. Wilkof (Eds.), *Science, curriculum and liberal education: Selected essays*. Chicago, IL: University of Chicago Press.

Schwab, J. (1983). The practical 4: Something for curriculum professors to do. *Curriculum Inquiry, 13*(3), 239–265.

VanDerHeide, J. (2017). Classroom talk as writing instruction for learning to make writing moves in literary arguments. *Reading Research Quarterly, 53*(3), 323–344.

Zepeda, C. D., Hlutkowsky, C. O., Partika, A. C., & Nokes-Malach, T. J. (2018). Identifying teachers' supports of metacognition through classroom talk and its relation to growth in conceptual learning. *Journal of Educational Psychology, 111*(3), 522–541.

PART I

SEEING BIG: TENSIONS AND TRIUMPHS IN PARTNERSHIPS FOR PROFESSIONAL DEVELOPMENT

As foreshadowed by our opening discussion, the first four chapters of *Developing knowledge communities through partnerships for literacy* present a complex collection of stories of recognized tensions and triumphs across efforts to support teacher development in K-12 contexts.

The beginning two chapters, Chapter 2 and Chapter 3, address the impact of disruptive natural disasters on the enactment of teacher development programs when they are most needed. Tina Angelo and Maryann Gremillion, authors of Chapter 2, *Innovation and integrity: Working through disruption to support teachers in their roles as literacy educators*, discuss the hurricane, pandemic, and other influences on the structure of WITS' Collaborative and the on-the-spot planning and execution of modified protocols for professional development cycles. After that, Chestin T. Auzenne-Curl, Gayle Curtis, and Cheryl Craig take up the implications of the primary and secondary traumatic stressors as they surface on campuses as they describe in Chapter 3, *Reflections on Research and Professional Development Partnerships in Post-Harvey Houston*. Angelo and Gremillion's Chapter 2 is written from the position of WITS faculty, while Auzenne-Curl, Curtis, and Craig's positionality is that of researchers devoted to an insider perspective – albeit from a different purview.

Chapters 4 and 5 move us to a direct view of campus life in the view of campus and district level administrators and instructional specialists. As we enter Chapter 4, *Reflections on Principal Leadership and Writers in the Schools*, Michael Curl and Cheryl Craig present considerations for administrators who seek to reform practice and protect the essence of teacher's work in a knowledge community. This work is complimented by stories of Daphne Carr and Chestin T. Auzenne-Curl who close out Section I with Chapter 5, *Navigating the Role of Teacher Educators in the Field: The Case For Increased Community Support*. They home in on the nature and needs of literacy coaches and others who are in similar roles whether they are housed in or intermittently work on K-12 campuses.

INNOVATION AND INTEGRITY: WORKING THROUGH DISRUPTION TO SUPPORT TEACHERS IN THEIR ROLES AS LITERACY EDUCATORS

Tina Angelo and Maryann Gremillion

ABSTRACT

In this chapter, we describe our experiences creating and providing job-embedded professional development to teachers with an emphasis on creative writing. Our focus is on the intersectionality of communities. We share narratives and scenarios from each of the communities – the participating teachers/administrators and the writing coaches collaborating with them. The program's objective is to empower teachers to see themselves as writers to become more effective teachers of writing. We discovered the unique nature of each campus community of teachers/writers and also found the need to provide a space and intentional structures to enable writing coaches to support each other. To measure our impact on teachers, we describe a qualitative evaluation process. Using the lens of two disruptive forces – a hurricane and a pandemic – we explore the implications for the future of the work. Each disruption brought inequities in education to the forefront of our thinking.

Keywords: Job-embedded professional development; coaching; community; writing; collaboration; disruption; educational inequities

INTRODUCTION

This chapter explores our need to adapt in the midst of a regional natural disaster and an international pandemic while simultaneously nurturing the learning needs of teachers, students, and Writers in the Schools (WITS) Collaborative writers.

Taking a reflective turn back (Schön, 1991), we examine the structures of the WITS Collaborative and the program's response to the educational drought brought about by unanticipated disruption and the innovative changes made to maintain the integrity of the program.

WITS Collaborative as a Part of WITS Houston

As former Language Arts teachers, we recognize that setting is a key element in storytelling. We want our readers to get a sense of the city in which we live, the neighborhood where we do our work, and how the WITS Collaborative fits into the larger nonprofit organization known as WITS Houston. As we begin to tell our stories, we welcome you to envision us within this setting. We live in the fourth largest city in America, and one of the country's most racially diverse, but more than that, we live in a city that is composed of distinct communities. For example, residents of Houston identify themselves as living in the Third Ward, the Heights, Montrose, Oak Forest, Sunnyside, the Energy Corridor, and, of course, any number of suburbs. Houstonians depend on the support systems contained in these smaller communities within our huge city. We recognize that these community supports are not all equal, the needs of each community are not the same, and the education afforded to children in each community is not equitable. In fact, 19 independent school districts intersect the city limits of Houston. The city's largest district is responsible for educating over 200,000 children in 284 schools.

WITS Houston is a literary nonprofit that was founded in 1983 by Phillip Lopate and Marv Hoffman.[1] They saw an opportunity to bring talent from the University of Houston's Creative Writing program into Houston classrooms. WITS contracts with schools on a sliding fee scale based on the percentage of economically disadvantaged students enrolled. A resident writer visits a classroom for 24-hour-long visits over the course of the school year. Our mission is "to engage children in the joy and power of reading and writing" (Writers in the Schools, n.d.). Our vision is "to revolutionize the way reading and writing are taught, nurturing the growth of the imagination and awakening students to the adventure of language." In 2019, WITS impacted 65,000 students in over 400 Houston area classrooms. We have an office in a small red-brick cottage in the Montrose neighborhood one block away from the Menil Collection, an amazing art museum that was intentionally built to be part of this residential community. WITS is the educational outreach partner of the Menil Collection. For some of our students, the field trips that we sponsor to the museum are the only educational outing they will have for many years. WITS Houston writers not only work in school settings but also in hospitals alongside bedridden children, in community centers facilitating summer and after-school creative writing programs, and in public libraries offering free-to-the-public student writing workshops.

Our story focuses on WITS Collaborative, a job-embedded teacher professional development program. Unlike other WITS programs, this one is a result of suggestions made during community focus groups whose members wondered if the impact of WITS could be extended to teachers. The story of the WITS Collaborative begins here.

Chapter Organization

We have organized this chapter to reflect our lived experience in the educational communities we served, the structures we employed to support them, and the disruptions that impacted them. Our work with communities has enabled them to be flexible enough to respond to disruptions. We are not implying that any of this was easy or that our challenges both in the past and present are not ongoing. As we work within our sphere of influence in schools, we continue to educate ourselves, listen to members of our communities, and face challenges with brave conversations. Within each section of our Narrative Framework, we have infused our personal stories with scenarios, identified in a smaller font size, followed by an analysis of the disruptions and wonderings posed by Hurricane Harvey in August 2017, the COVID-19 pandemic of 2020, and social inequities in the educational system.

Our narrative begins with a brief history of the WITS Collaborative, a job-embedded professional development model for teachers founded on the research that teachers who see themselves as writers will be more effective as teachers of writing (Bifuh-Ambe, 2013; Wood & Leibermann, 2000). This work is also based on a series of interlocking professional communities that include the WITS writers, the school Language Arts teachers, and administrators on school campuses. Each group works together to create authentic communities of student writers. Our chapter explores the dynamics and challenges of each community including their responses to disruptions.

REFLECTIONS ON AUTHOR'S NARRATIVES

Looking back, we each pinpointed situations in our early teacher careers that brought about substantial changes in our practices as Language Arts teachers. Our author stories that follow illustrate how instructional challenges – when met with teacher reflection and integrity – can shift from disruption to innovation.

Tina's Story: A Paradigm Shift in Response to Disruption

My first lesson in disruption came in my fourth year of teaching, when I transferred to a larger district for better pay. Every eight years, school committees across Texas review the choices of textbooks to be adopted in their content area and vote on the one for their school to purchase. Unfortunately, my new district had made a "split adoption" of two language arts textbooks. I discovered this when I was last in line at the book room only to be informed that there were not enough textbooks of one kind for my 10th graders. I had to piece together enough textbooks for my students, but they would not each have the same one.

In the past, when all of my students had the same textbook, I could assign a story, everyone would read it, and then we would discuss it. But I was faced with a dilemma – all of my students could not read the same story. That was when I became a better teacher. To face my new situation, I adjusted my teaching and now had students read an assigned story in whichever textbook they had received with a guiding question around a writer's craft move. For example, rather than just reading "*The Lady or the Tiger*" and discussing the theme, now I would assign a story in various textbooks with the guiding question of "what techniques does the author use to describe the characters?" The resulting classroom discussions were richer, more engaging, and far more student-centered.

Maryann's Story: From Discomfort to Change: A New Way to Teach Writing

It was 1993, my first year teaching fourth graders at a neighborhood school north of downtown Houston. And the state writing test loomed. I was overwhelmed with teaching every subject, as is true for many teachers new to the profession.

But writing? I had no idea how to teach it. So I did what many nervous first year teachers do. I gave the kids test prompts from prior year state exams. The children passed the test, but they did not learn to write. That summer I read books about teaching writing and tried many approaches over the next four years. But something was still missing.

When I moved to another school in 1998, I watched a master teacher teach a writer's workshop lesson. I loved her focus on craft, how she talked about herself as a writer, and modeled from her notebook. The students wrote while she conferred one-to-one or in small groups. At the end, the children gathered to share and celebrate their work. After that, I attended summer institutes at Columbia University's Teachers College, kept a writer's notebook, bought children's books, and read Ralph Fletcher (1992, 2003), Katie Wood Ray (1999, 2000), and Lucy Calkins (1994, 2000). It completely changed the way I worked with students. I showed them that writers write from their own true lives, that writers read, that writers have choices about what they want to write about, and that we can all learn together to value our stories. I wish I had known how to do this in 1993. I have continued this work with WITS. We came together with writers and campus teachers to craft authentic ways for children to see themselves as writers.

CONCEPTUAL RESONANCES

We believe in the strength of educational communities as a support system for change. Specifically, the change we discuss through our stories is the concept that teachers who see themselves as writers become more effective as teachers of writing. In this autobiographical narrative study (Freeman, 2007) of educational communities with reflective narratives as our data source, we engaged in professional dialogue (Guilfoyle, Hamilton, Pinnegar, & Placier, 2004) to examine how external and internal forces impact the work of writing communities and the paradigm shift toward which WITS Collaborative is working. We recognize

- the organic and dynamic nature of communities and the impact it has on teacher practices. It is critical for teachers to be given the space and ongoing support in order for them to recognize the need for change in their teaching practices, specifically as it relates to creating a classroom community of writers composed of the teacher and students.

- the need for intentionality in choosing structures and protocols (McDonald, Mohr, Dichter, & McDonald, 2015) that serve specific groups and provide equity for all voices and ideas to be heard and considered. Part of this intentionality is listening to the concerns and needs of the group, thinking about objectives to be met, and choosing protocols to meet those objectives.
- that educational communities do not work in isolation, but are impacted by external forces such as hurricanes, global pandemics, and social unrest. This requires a certain amount of flexibility and unconventional thinking in order to respond effectively to severe disruption.

Our story begins with the creation of a professional development model for teachers that reflected these concepts.

NARRATIVE FRAMEWORK
How WITS Collaborative Started

What follows is Tina's story of coming to WITS, moving from the classroom to working for WITS, and developing the vision for the WITS Collaborative.

In 1983, when I was teaching sophomore English in a suburban school district south of Houston, one of my students was an immigrant student, a budding artist. He was one of those students who touch your heart and with whom you make an instant connection. As so often happens with teachers, I changed districts and lost touch with him. Fast forward to 1999 when my daughter was asked by her WITS resident writer to perform at the WITS Young Writers Reading. The Associate Director of WITS was the emcee and when I saw him, I could not believe my eyes. Here was my favorite student! As soon as the reading was over, I rushed down the auditorium steps to see him. When I asked what happened to his dream of being an artist, he told me that being in my sophomore English class had inspired him to pursue writing as a career. I experienced that rare moment as a teacher of seeing the impact I had made on a student. From that point on, I was involved with WITS.

Now instead of me influencing his life, my student was influencing mine. First, I applied for and received a Disney grant to bring a WITS writer into my classroom. I watched how Dr. Mal, our WITS writer, spoke with my students and led them step by step into their writing together. I wrote along with them. I had never thought of myself as a "writer" before, but here I was asking to sit in the author's chair so I could share my writing with my students. Just that one move changed the dynamics in my classroom. We became a community of writers taking risks with our writing and learning more about ourselves, each other, and the craft of writing. I listened as my WITS writer conferred with my students. I looked at their WITS folders to see the comments she wrote on their papers and saw a new way to help students enter into meaningful revision. I realized that basically I had been rewriting my students papers – not asking questions that would guide them into revision. I had used rubrics as a way of hiding from the real work of revision – the work that required me to feel confident as a writer. I was wearing myself out and the students were not learning.

This started me on the path to designing WITS Collaborative. In 2012, my former student asked me to join the staff and head up the new division of WITS – professional development for teachers. WITS had completed a 3-year strategic plan that included an expansion into professional development. Focus groups that included teachers had made the request. They recognized the impactful work that WITS had become known for and wanted the same impact to be extended to teachers. My first task was to envision how the WITS mission would include working with teachers. We had an opportunity to apply for a grant in the education division of a Houston-based foundation. I knew the relationship between a teacher and students in a classroom community is the key to learning. I kept going back to our organization's name, WITS. What did it mean to be a "writer in the schools?" When we used that phrase, to whom were we referring? At this point, the connotation was that the resident writer and the students were the "writers in the schools." The bigger vision needed to include a path so that teachers would also be seen as "writers in the schools."

In my search, I read national research articles and interviewed various WITS writers. I wanted to know what they were experiencing when they entered a classroom. What did the teachers do when the WITS writer was in front of the class? Was the teacher writing alongside the students or were they sitting behind their desk grading papers and entering grades into the computer? One of the writers I spoke with was Maryann. At that time, she was a seasoned WITS writer with a history of having been a classroom teacher in several Houston area elementary schools and a professional development consultant for an independent agency. She had brought all of this experience along with her own work as a visual artist and writer to her WITS classrooms. Together we lamented the fact that most teachers were not participating in the writing and talked at length about how that fact does not help build a sense of community in the classrooms. Our conversation centered around the question of "How do we get teacher commitment to the WITS writing experience?" Of all the writers I interviewed, Maryann was the only one who had focused on the teacher. I took copious notes and our conversation planted seeds in my mind for the WITS Collaborative.

The turning point in my search came when I focused on a writer who had been involved in a WITS pilot program, called the Whole Grade Immersion Model at a Houston high school. The English department chair had contacted WITS in response to the desire of his teachers to radically change the way they were teaching writing. The WITS writer described to me that she had met with the teachers several times in writing sessions, then taught in their classrooms, and finally met to debrief the classroom experience that the teachers had observed. As I talked with the writer and the department chair, we discussed ideas of how the program might look the following year. The pilot program mirrored the ideas that Maryann and I had discussed about how to involve teachers.

If we truly wanted teachers to feel that they were the "writers in the schools," we needed a program that would support them to feel confident as writers, knowing that only then would they become more effective as teachers of writing. In this era of standardized testing, teachers are forced to teach writing as a way to bring up a campus' test scores rather than to grow students into writers. To support a paradigm shift in teachers and impact a greater number of students, the focus of this professional development needed to be a collaboration between a group of teachers and a professional writer meeting during the school day. The purpose of the WITS Collaborative would not only be to write together but also to collaboratively take this same writing experience into the teachers' classrooms. The ultimate goal would be a community of writers in the classroom composed of both the teacher and the students exploring writing together.

My first attempt at growing the pilot program was not a success – but the lessons that I learned were invaluable. My first lesson was that we needed more structure to the program. Teachers and campus administrators as well as the WITS Collaborative writers needed a visual that would highlight the cycle and the key components of the Collaborative (Fig. 1).

Next, teachers and writers needed to see the commitments that each was making when joining into this work together. They also needed to see the commitments that their campus and the WITS administrators were making. Teacher commitments included attendance at Professional Learning Community (PLC) meetings with the writer, and campus administration commitments included naming a

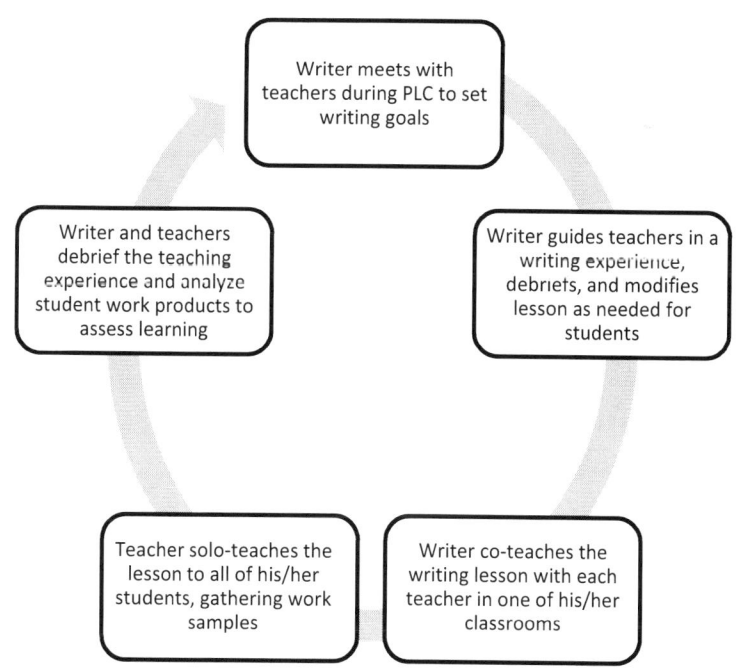

Fig. 1. WITS Collaborative Cycle.

mid-level administrator to act as a liaison with WITS and to ensure the time and space for the PLC meetings. WITS committed to scheduling mid-year meetings with the liaison to make any modifications as needed and to conduct a program evaluation.

But the most valuable lesson learned was the critical importance of the writer. I drew on my years as the Manager of Adolescent Literacy in my local school district where I managed all the literacy coaches. This work had taught me one big lesson – working with adults was very different from working with students. Pedagogy and andragogy are very different. The writers we chose to work in this program would need to either have some teaching experience or have a true respect for the work of teachers. Once these writers were chosen, they would need time to meet as a cohort to learn together, share their new campus experiences, and support each other in their new work. The professional development for the people who provide professional development for teachers is a critical but often neglected component. To structure these vital monthly meetings, I reached out to a consultant from the National School Reform Faculty to guide us in our work using Critical Friends Group Protocols.

The first WITS writer I invited into the cohort of Collaborative writers was Maryann. Over the years, Maryann moved from being an extremely successful Collaborative writer to being hired to join the WITS administrative staff as Program Director. Together we became partners in administering the Collaborative. The first project we worked on was a summer bridge program with rising ninth graders from three middle schools in a neighboring school district. We spent two weeks in the summer with teachers planning, teaching, and talking about writing strategies to boost student engagement and readiness for high school. Students wrote in response to lessons in the mornings, and in the afternoons, writers and teachers met to talk about student responses, what worked, and what we needed to consider for the next day. This model brought new understanding to teachers and a shift in the students and their attitudes toward writing. The following scenario is from Maryann's experience in one of these classrooms:

> Misha sat at her desk with arms folded. I knelt down to ask what was keeping her from writing. "Well, all my teachers say I'm angry and I guess I am since my mom died." I asked her to tell me the story. She shared a moment with her mom in the hospital, as she ran to get a nurse when her mom stopped breathing. I said to her, "That's the story you need to write." At the end of the two weeks, she read her story out loud. She told me, "I didn't know I could write like this, that it was okay to say what's inside of me." Later, the teacher told me no one had been able to reach Misha, and she understood much better the importance of students writing the stories they wanted and needed to tell. "I'm changing how I do things this school year and it's because of what I've seen these past two weeks."

We hoped to return the following year, but a change in administration and testing priorities did not match our writing philosophy. This is a typical example of one of the biggest disruptions we face every year: campus administrator turnover and the subsequent change in philosophies.

At the beginning of every school year, Maryann and I planned meetings together, made site visits, and counseled and advised writers. One of our first actions was to post a Request for Proposals in search of a new external evaluator. We chose a team from Texas A&M because they focused on qualitative evaluations based on narratives and had a background in urban education. We knew we had made the right choice when members of the evaluation team started by interviewing both the WITS Collaborative administrators and also our writers. They wanted to hear our stories from us. They wanted to understand us as a community in order to understand our goals, our questions, and our challenges. Members of the team joined us at all of our monthly meetings, taking notes, pictures, and recording our conversations around the table. Our biggest breakthrough was when our key evaluators, Chestin Auzenne-Curl, Cheryl Craig, and Gayle Curtis, met with us and asked, "Why have you been evaluating your program using student writing samples, when your focus is on creating a paradigm shift in teachers?" We were dumbfounded. But their question made us rethink and reexamine the approach to evaluating our program.

Together we discussed ways that we could use one of the Critical Friends Group[2] protocols, Looking for Trends in Student Work, as a basis for gathering more pertinent data. Our writers were very familiar with the protocol. We had practiced using it with samples of student work during our meetings, and the writers had long since taken the protocol into their PLC conversations with teachers. Our evaluators were proposing adding the element of taking notes about the conversations on student work that teachers were having at the beginning of the year (BOY), the middle of the year (MOY), and the end of the year (EOY). The comparison between the BOY, MOY, and EOY comments would yield the data to determine our program's effectiveness. Were teachers looking at student work in a more in-depth manner by the end of the year? Were they looking for evidence of what the students were doing right rather than focusing on their deficits? Were they asking different questions of themselves as teachers? The following observation from one of our writers demonstrates the findings of our new Teacher Talk evaluation tool.

> Ellie was working with a group of elementary teachers. She dutifully used the Looking for Patterns of Student Work at the beginning of the year with her teachers during PLC and noted some of their comments. At the end of the year, when the coaches met during our monthly meeting to compare their notes from the beginning and the end of the year, Ellie focused on one particular teacher who had made comments like, "He is not using capital letters properly. Look at his spelling. I know I taught them to use periods – where are they?" At the end of the year, Ellie's notes indicated that the same teacher was now saying, "I see what this student is attempting to do. I love how the student is bringing in his own experience to this prompt. Look at the sensory images that he is using." What a difference in point of view! The teacher was looking for strengths from which she could help the student grow rather than looking for deficits with which she could categorize the student as deficient. We had evidence of impact.

A Note about Disruptions

Even though we saw evidence of impact, we discovered that significant external forces challenge the work. These included Hurricane Harvey at the beginning of the 2017/2018 school year and the COVID-19 pandemic at the end of the 2019/2020 school year. The hurricane caused massive flooding and severe damage to many of the campuses we served within the 333 square miles of the Houston

Independent School District. In some cases, children from one campus had to share facilities with another campus. Because so many homes and apartments were now unlivable, schools lost track of their students and began the school year not really knowing who would be returning, who they lost, and what new students who had moved in with friends and family would now be attending. Our city was in chaos. One solution provided by the district was to refurbish old and unused facilities to house the students from school buildings that were damaged beyond repair. With the hurricane hitting in late August, the beginning of the school year was delayed. Although some undamaged schools were able to open as scheduled, most schools opened in a rolling start progression as the schools were repaired. This continued until November of that year. Administrators and teachers were so overwhelmed with adjusting in the face of this disaster, they were not even thinking about the support that WITS Collaborative could provide to their teachers and students. For us, this meant that we got a very late start in our work – sometimes only beginning in the spring semester.

The disruption of COVID was very different. With Harvey, we got a late start but were eventually able to return to our campuses and continue with the delivery of our Collaborative model and framework. With COVID, and with three months of the school year to go, all of the schools in the city were shut down overnight. After realizing that the schools were not going to reopen for the rest of the school year, WITS Collaborative writers and administrators quickly had to readjust to an online format delivery system. Our writers faced these challenges:

- Being on a steep technology learning curve (e.g., Zoom, Microsoft Teams, YouTube videos)
- Learning how to create video lessons
- Adjusting their lessons from 60 minutes to 10–15 minutes in length
- Dealing with the fact that they might be delivering lessons to up to three schools each using a different online platform

Both of these disruptions brought to the forefront the inequities between schools that had strong PTOs able to provide necessary support and supplies versus those who were so devastated and had such little support they expressed to us that what they really needed was notebook paper for their students. In the following sections, we explore more specific examples of the impact of these disruptions.

How WITS Collaborative Supports a Community of Writers

After the first year, we understood that building a sense of community is the foundation of our work. These communities include the writers in the Collaborative, the teacher cohorts on school campuses, and the students they teach. Each community required support for having a common goal, an ongoing process of exploration and reflection, and seeing where we needed to make changes. This system of support began with how the WITS Collaborative supported the writers.

Monthly Meetings
Every month from September to May, the writers gathered for two hours on alternating Tuesday evenings and Saturday mornings. The meetings always had an agenda with a specific focus and, of course, food, sometimes sandwiches and chips, sometimes pastries and coffee. We would gather around a group of tables pushed together in the WITS Meeting House, a small bungalow next door to the WITS office in a quiet city neighborhood. We talked with each other informally, sharing experiences from the past few weeks or telling stories about our families. Although each meeting had a different focus, we always wrote together. We wanted our writer meetings to reflect the fundamental principle that teachers who write make better teachers of writing. The writers needed time during our meetings to try out ideas and create lessons for the teachers. Through the use of Critical Friends Groups® protocols, writers shared a problem or a dilemma to the group for feedback, brought favorite texts to talk about, and shared their experiences and learned from each other.

Providing effective support meant the monthly meetings needed to be focused on what would best support the writers. The ideas and shape of our time together were about them and for them, not an idea we as WITS administrators thought they needed. At one meeting, Teresa said, "I need help. I can't seem to get through to my teachers how important it is for them to write." This led to several meetings about lesson design to engage the teachers. Since the WITS Collaborative community included both writers from graduate programs and teachers with classroom experience, it was important for writers to have an understanding and respect for teachers and the work they do each day. Everyone in the WITS Collaborative group is a veteran of WITS student-directed programs. The biggest challenge new writers faced was shifting their focus from students to teachers. The group meetings supported them to understand the difference.

Critical Friends Group® Protocols
Critical Friends Group® (CFG) protocols[3] were an essential tool in building a safe community with the WITS writers. We used these successfully to focus our thinking and give everyone an opportunity to speak. The protocols offered a variety of structures including looking at student work, problem solving, and lesson planning. The writers also used these with their teacher cohorts. The protocols became the foundation for every Collaborative writer meeting. Before each gathering, writers received a copy of the agenda to review and then received copies outlining the specific protocols to be explored. Using these allowed the monthly meetings to be writer-centered according to their specific needs. Writers came to the meetings to get ideas and support from each other, rather than being fed information from WITS administrators. Writers always reflected on the protocols we used to understand the process.

These are the protocols we used most often that brought our community of writers together:

Connections is a way to begin a meeting where participants have an opportunity to share what's on their minds in order to clear space for the work to come. The cardinal rule is not allowing any cross conversation. Participants do not have to speak if they prefer not to do so during the 5–10 minutes allotted. Because of this choice, there are many silences during the time period, which also serve to solidify the group in order to focus on the meeting's purpose. The fact that the group feels comfortable with these silences is a testimony to the sense of safety in the community.

Sharing/Receiving Feedback on Lesson Plans is a modification of the NYC District 79 protocol "Using a Tuning Protocol to Look at Lessons Plans." The objective is to examine the lesson of a colleague, acknowledge the good things found in that work, and modify the lesson to better achieve the stated objectives before sharing the lesson with the WITS writer's teacher cohort. The presenting WITS writer begins by providing the context of the lesson and posing a question to the group. After answering the group's clarifying questions, the presenting writer silently listens to the discussion and then reflects on the feedback. This process allows the individual WITS writer to tap into the collective knowledge of the group and also provides an avenue for sharing lessons with each other.

Consultancy protocol provides a structure for problem solving. The work of WITS writing coaches can feel very isolating because they work alone with a cohort of teachers on a campus. The writer describes a concrete dilemma, answers clarifying and probing questions from the small group, and then listens taking notes on their discussion. After the time for discussion ends, the presenting writer reflects on new insights gained and actions that they will take back to their campus work.

Looking for Patterns in Student Work is the basis for examining the program through Teacher Talk. More than any other protocol, this one has to be practiced in our monthly meetings before the writers take it back to their teachers. This is where the big change happens, the paradigm shift for teachers away from what the student cannot do to what he or she is actually doing. The writers examine several pieces of student work looking for patterns, themes, and inconsistencies in order to draw conclusions and generate implications for teaching next steps. When used with the teachers, this protocol allows for discussion of student work within a safe environment.

Microlab is a flexible protocol. The process is a sequence of questions asked in a structured and timed format. Based on the current environment or challenges faced by the entire group, we as administrators drafted the questions. After presenting a question, each participant writes in their journal and then take turns sharing with the group. We scribe answers and allow no discussion until the entire sequence of questions has been asked.

We found this protocol most helpful when the city of Houston issued a lockdown order in response to COVID-19. For example, to support each other in this disruption to our normal interactions as a group and with schools, we asked the following questions: "*What positive opportunities do you see in using Zoom to connect with your cohort?*" "*In what ways do you envision modifying* your lessons to fit the new online format?" and "*What challenges will we be facing in using this online format?*" The rich discussion after hearing each other's thoughts led us to develop new procedures and resulted in creating a structure to successfully complete the school year with our teacher cohorts.

Affinity Mapping is used at the beginning of the school year to set our group and individual goals for the year. Typically, we pose three sentence stems: *(1) What I would most appreciate from WITS Collaborative is... (2) Areas of growth this year for me are... (3) One goal I have for this year is....* Writers think about these questions individually, in triads, and in the larger group. As administrators, we take the responses from new and veteran writers and use this to help plan out monthly meetings for the coming year. It is important to listen to the group in order to give them what they actually need. Many writers use this to begin the school year with their teacher cohorts.

Text Rendering is a protocol used to construct meaning from a common reading and also clarifies and expands thinking about an article or a book. With no discussion and in a series of three rounds, writers share a sentence, a phrase, and a word that they felt were particularly significant. As administrators, we scribe their comments and facilitate a larger discussion as a group.

Chalk Talk is a silent way to reflect on a series of questions or statements that help generate ideas, share approaches, or solve problems. These questions/statements are posted in the center of large chart paper arranged around the room. Writers respond using colored markers to make comments and reply to each other's comments. Because it is done completely in silence and requires movement, this protocol gives a change of pace and a unique way to discuss and analyze. During discussion afterward, writers often express surprise at the similarities and new ideas generated on the paper.

Book Studies
Every year our group reads and discusses a book either in response to an area of need for both writers and their teacher cohorts or to study new ideas and thinking in education. We often use the text rendering protocol to facilitate our conversations.

In 2017–2018, the writers asked for help with showing teachers a way to confer with students. We read *How's It Going?* by Carl Anderson. Student conference during the writing time is a critical component to helping students individually. It is a conversation that allows teachers to find a teachable moment so students can try a craft move or make choices as a writer about what's next in their writing. Since this conversation has a clear purpose and a predictable structure, both the Collaborative writers and teachers found this helpful.

The following school year, after attending the NCTE conference in November, we read Christopher Emdin's book *For White Folk Who Teach in the Hood*. Emdin challenged our thinking around traditional school systems and offered other possibilities to serve youth in their communities whether urban or rural. This was our first response as a group to the national conversation on race. It was critical that we examine our assumptions and become sensitive to how we worked with teachers and model ways to teach students from diverse backgrounds.

In 2019–2020, the group looked deeply at Zaretta Hammond's *Culturally Responsive Teaching and the Brain.* A new member of the WITS staff brought this book to our attention. It includes step-by-step actions that teachers can take with their students. Writers translated the research in the book into conversations with teachers during PLCs and used this as an opportunity to explore what's happening currently in the larger world. The book also helped the writers look deeply at social disruption and the need for new approaches to address educational inequities. As an organization, WITS was also exploring equity, diversion, and inclusion. This book broadened our understanding about the realities facing so many students and teachers in education.

How WITS Administrators Support the Writer Cohort

The office is always open during business hours for writers who want to call or stop by after meeting teachers on their campuses. This helps us provide individual support. The following scenario illustrates a typical day at the WITS office.

"Tina, you have a call from Greta on the line." I knew exactly what she was getting ready to tell me. Her WITS Collaborative teachers were not coming to the PLC meetings with her. The situation had nothing to do with Greta's competency as a WITS Collaborative writing coach but had everything to do with the dysfunction of the school. We had the same problem the year before, but it had gotten worse. Because this was a small school, the teachers chosen for the cohort taught different grade levels and did not have the same common planning time. The campus administration was supposed to provide class coverage so the teachers could meet but were inconsistent with this support. Last year, at least we had a mid-level administrator working with us and had better attendance. But this year that woman had been promoted to a principalship at her own school and no one had taken her place. We were left dealing with an overworked and overwhelmed principal who did not really understand what we do in the Collaborative. Bottom line, Greta was frustrated. This had gone on long enough. I contacted the principal and made an appointment for Greta and me to meet with her. This had to be handled in person so we could come up with a mutual plan that we could all support. I needed the principal's buy-in, and I needed her to feel that our plan was her idea. We met and decided to focus only on third and fourth grades in January and K-2nd grades in February, thus needing fewer classes covered at one time. Before we left, the principal had us speak with the secretary who put these reminders into her calendar as we stood there. At the time of this November meeting, Greta had only been able to fulfill 30% of her contract. By the middle of March and with the plan fully implemented, 100% of the contract had been completed. Our WITS administrative support had opened the door for Greta to meet with teachers and model with students in order to complete 70% of her contract in just two months.

Activity Logs

Collaborative writers who work with both adults and students face very different challenges from the ones faced by writers who only work with students. We know that in addition to our monthly meetings and open-door support policy, we need to understand what each writer is facing in a specific and unique residency. We know that in addition to our monthly meetings and open-door policy, we need to understand what each writer is faciting in a specific residency. In order to gain more insight into individual cohorts, we have the writers complete an Activity Log to chronicle each of their campus visits.

- Did they meet with teachers?
- Which teachers are in attendance?
- What is the focus of the discussion?
- Did they model in classrooms?
- How many students are in attendance and whose classrooms are visited?
- What is the nature of the lesson taught?

These logs have many uses. We keep up with how many of the 50 program hours have been completed and talk with the writer if they appear to be having trouble completing their contract with the schools. By being able to review these logs, we are able to determine if a writer is meeting with all of the teachers who comprise the cohort and the percentage of PLC time and class modeling time. The logs allow us to get a sense of whether the writer is actually being used as a writing coach for teachers. These logs inform our mid-year administrator conversations with campus principals to ensure their support and fidelity to the WITS Collaborative program.

Site Visits

Although the main support for our community of writers is the monthly meeting, writers need more support than that. In addition to being at the planning meeting when the writer first meets the teachers, administrators make site visits to sit in on PLC meetings and debrief with the writer afterward. These observations allow us to get a sense of the group dynamics within the Collaborative community of teachers. It also gives us first-hand knowledge of the writers' frustrations or successes. That personal visit to a campus is vital not only for that specific writer but also for other writers. Through these observations we are able to share ideas with other writers. We are constantly saying, "You know the other day when I visited with Martha, I saw her do something that you might find useful or you might want to call and ask her about." These site visits allow us to become a conduit between WITS Collaborative writers – sharing the successes of one to help the challenges of another.

Disruptions

- During both Harvey and COVID, we had to make quick adjustments in order to serve our communities. As a group we discussed how to intentionally respond through the lessons that we brought to the teachers, the protocols that we employed, and the unique demands that these disruptions created for both the

teachers and students that we served. We recognized that we needed to keep what we were doing simple, direct, and relevant.
- We became true partners in a very human sense with both writers and teachers who had lost their homes to the Harvey flooding. The personal narrative writing that we brought to our writer cohort meetings helped each of us to process our emotions and tell our stories. The writers were then able to take these healing prompts back to their campuses for teachers and students.
- Although some writers struggled with the new technology demands of their job, they shared videos with us asking for feedback and during writer meetings they gave each other helpful tips.
- In COVID, our writers, like the teachers they served, were on a steep learning curve. They helped each other create engaging online lessons, posted on their own YouTube channels, and shared with the teachers. They quickly learned how to use and be comfortable in a Zoom or Microsoft Teams environment. This is the strength of the cohort.
- Our regular pattern had been to host the monthly WITS writer cohort meetings on either a weeknight or Saturday, both of which required our writers to leave their families and drive the distance across the city of Houston to our office. The surprise benefit of COVID was that we could now host our meetings on Zoom. As a result, our attendance increased, and we continued to use our protocols and have rich discussions. This was a positive lesson learned by the COVID disruption that we will take forward.

How the Collaborative Supports Campus Teachers/Administrators

The name WITS Collaborative intentionally reflects the primary relationship between the writers and administrators of WITS and campus administrators and teachers. WITS never comes into a school with the attitude of a know-it-all expert who is going to tell administrators and teachers what to do. Rather we view them as fellow professionals, and we truly believe in collaborating, in listening, and in planning together. Although we have a design that highlights the key components of our approach, and the teachers always know that they are going to be writing and sharing their work together, each of our campus cohorts is always unique. For that reason, we listen and ask questions during our program meeting with principals to discern which of our Collaborative writers would be the best fit for a specific campus. Is the cohort of teachers going to be composed of veteran or novice teachers? Does the campus need a Spanish-speaking writer? Have the teachers gone through other writing training together (e.g., Abydos[4] or Teachers College Reading & Writing Project[5])? Lessons learned over the years have also taught us to look for red flags. Is the district paying for our program or is the school dedicating some of its own budget? Is the principal talking about only bringing in teachers who need help or the whole grade level? Is the principal looking for a magic bullet to help the students pass the state test or looking for an approach to authentic writing? Is the principal willing to identify and have us meet with the mid-level administrator who will be our liaison or is the principal assuming that role? The following scenario illustrates the importance of clear communication:

Innovation and Integrity

The planning meeting sets the stage for the success or failure of a WITS Collaborative program on a campus. Many times, WITS will be contacted by a principal interested in bringing the Collaborative to the campus with a vision of either strengthening or in some cases, providing the teachers with a more authentic approach to the teaching of writing. The principal is all excited and the monies are earmarked in the budget. We make plans with the principal to schedule a planning meeting with the teachers, and the principal identifies the mid-level administrator who will be our liaison. Unfortunately, the principal does not always communicate any of this to the faculty. This happened at Bayou ES. The writer and I showed up for our scheduled planning meeting time with the 2nd and 3rd grade teachers. Our first red flag was that the principal was not on campus. A confused receptionist contacted the assistant principal, who quickly gathered the group in the library. And then – they just stared at us. They had absolutely no idea who we were, why we were there, or the goals of the Collaborative. Even the AP admitted in front of the group that the principal had not given her any details or directions. The writer and I quickly switched gears and explained the program. Needless to say, after this rocky start things just went downhill. We were 6 hours into a 50-hour program when the principal contacted us for a meeting. Her teachers were very disappointed in the program, they did not see a clear focus for each lesson, and they had no confidence in the writer. Maryann and I met with the principal to hear all the facts, then met with the lead 2nd grade and 3rd grade teachers to hear more about their goals. We went back to the office and identified a writer with a teaching background that would be a better fit for the school. The original writer was actually relieved not to return. She knew that we had gotten off to a bad start and that nothing she could do had worked to redeem it. With our lessons learned in hand, the writer, Maryann, and I had a new planning meeting. The principal and lead teachers were present and showed their excitement and support of the program's more articulated goals. The honest meetings we had with the principal resulted in a quick change of course and one of the best Collaborative programs of the year. In fact, they brought us back for the following year.

At the heart of the Collaborative is the community formed during the PLC meetings. Together the WITS writer and the teachers make decisions, plan lessons, and share their own writing. For this reason, no two Collaborative cohorts will operate in the same way. How could they? Each Collaborative cohort of teachers has its own needs, personalities, dynamics, and challenges. In order to focus on the work, the WITS writer hands each teacher the PLC agenda for the day complete with a focus, connection to previous learning, connection to student learning needs, debriefing, and next steps. Many times, writers will bring protocols to the group they have experienced during their monthly meetings, especially the Goal Setting Protocol at the beginning of the year. In this way, the work from one community (i.e., the writers) impacts the work of another community (i.e., the teachers). We have seen significant shifts in those schools that have partnered with WITS Collaborative over several years. Our first meeting with the teachers of one particular school had us shaking our heads when we left. They were teaching writing out of grammar books, their only request was that we help them build a set of grading rubrics, and they did not seem to communicate well together as a group. They were definitely not a "community." At our mid-year administrator's meeting during the second year, the school liaison reported that the teachers cherished the time to write together, had no more interest in creating a grading rubric, and were requesting that they be allowed to go off-campus to the Menil Collection with their writer in order to use the artwork as creative entry points into their personal writing. We were amazed at the transformation of a group of grumpy grammarians into a community of creative writers.

You never know the impact you are making. April had spent a frustrating fall semester at T. Morrison Middle School. Most frustrating was Mr. Pitts, an older man who had come into teaching after what he was more than willing to tell us was a "very successful career as a businessman." He had poor rapport with his students and was not a willing participant in the PLC meetings. I observed one of their meetings and saw him in action. He seemed to make an effort to be as ornery as possible. I dreaded my mid-year administrator's meeting with the principal. To my surprise the principal had glowing remarks about the impact Susan was making with this team of ELA teachers. He said that after a recent faculty meeting, he offered the teachers two choices: they could go back to their rooms to work independently or they could remain in the library and work together as a team. The Collaborative cohort teachers, including Mr. Pitts, was the only team that asked to remain in the library to plan together. The principal could not have been happier. This small step was all he needed to see a positive team-building impact of our program. The next year when I returned to the school, that same ornery teacher surprised all of us at the planning meeting when he talked about a turning point in his relationship with a student he had previously sent to detention. After reading his WITS writings, this teacher saw the student as a 3-dimensional person. He actually went up to the student at the start of the new school year and apologized to him for not understanding him better. You never know the impact you are making.

Disruptions

Although both Hurricane Harvey and COVID-19 presented the WITS Collaborative with challenges, they also helped us focus on which program elements we could modify, and what we needed to do to maintain the integrity of the program to ensure maximum effectiveness.

- Harvey presented a short-term disruption and resulted in a long-term lesson learned in the Collaborative evaluation process. Because schools opened on a rolling basis with some not opening until late October, we were not able to have three points during the school year to evaluate Teacher Talk. We were able to look at student work and Teacher Talk in January and again in May to discern paradigm shifts in the way teachers viewed their students' writing. We realized that going forward we simply needed an evaluation at the start of the program and at the end.
- When schools shut down due to COVID in March, connecting with campus administrators to complete the residencies was incredibly difficult. In some cases, we used backchannels like Facebook messenger if we knew the principals well enough. Writers were also encouraged to create an asynchronous video lesson to email their campus liaisons and teachers so they could visualize what we could offer during quarantine.
- During Harvey and COVID, both teachers and writers had their lives directly impacted. We recognized that writing as an act of healing was a way to acknowledge and process these emotions. Teachers needed to examine and work through their own stories about what they had lived through and were living through so they could take those same writing lessons into their classrooms. We experienced this during one of our site visits with the writer and her cohort of teachers. Both the writer and many of the teachers had lost their

homes or been severely impacted by the flood waters. The healing effect of the writing was evident in the tears of both those whose homes had flooded and those listening.

CONCLUSION

The WITS Collaborative model focuses on teachers as writers and the support of communities. Although it has survived in the face of disruptions, we are left with significant wonderings, challenges, and goals that inform our thinking about the future.

Wonderings and Challenges

Several of our wonderings focus on our dependency on school budgets. We recognize there are discrepancies between different campuses regarding the amount of money they have available for our programming. Some of our school programs are funded by very lucrative parent groups and other schools can barely afford us in their budgets. With decreasing budgets, will schools have the capacity to bring fine arts programs (theater, music, visual arts, and dance) to their schools? Can WITS Collaborative play a role in supporting teachers to integrate the fine arts as an entry point into writing in all content areas?

The age of COVID has highlighted the significant opportunity gaps between those students with access to technology and those who do not. With inequities around technology, we worry about the teachers and students that we are unable to reach because of the digital divide. As the school year begins with virtual learning, how does WITS Collaborative still play a viable role in the schools? In addition, our state suspended its standardized testing in the spring of 2020. What is the future of standardized testing in light of the gaps created during COVID quarantine? If the state continues to suspend standardized testing, could this be an opportunity for the WITS Collaborative to provide authentic writing experiences for teachers and their students?

Goals

Ironically, COVID has presented us with new opportunities to explore. For example, one of our writers created a series of online workshops for teachers to begin to see themselves as writers. The district included these in their summer professional development menu of online training options. Could this be a new avenue for supporting teachers? Another goal that our response to COVID has us considering is using a hybrid approach to our model. We found that the teacher and writer meetings being held online provided us with greater flexibility and attendance. In the future, our communities could meet online with classroom visits, modeling, and co-teaching continuing to be face-to-face. Our successful response to COVID has shown us the potential and possibilities for the future of WITS Collaborative. We no longer see ourselves confined to only our Houston community. We see a future taking this work to national and international levels and sharing the power of interconnected communities to a larger audience.

NOTES

1. Writers in the Schools (WITS) Houston website: https://witshouston.org/.
2. Critical Friends Group (CFG) is a professional development community whose members commit to improving their practice through collaborative learning and structured interactions or protocols with the ultimate purpose of improving student learning.
3. All protocols are available on the School Reform Initiative website https://www.schoolreforminitiative.org/protocols/.
4. Abydos is a research-based literacy project for educators in Texas.
5. A workshop approach to teaching writing as a process.

REFERENCES

Bifuh-Ambe, E. (2013). Developing successful writing teachers: Outcomes of professional development exploring teachers' perceptions of themselves as writers and writing teachers and their students' attitudes and abilities to write across the curriculum. *English Teaching: Practice and Critique*, *12*(3), 137–156.

Calkins, L. M. (1994). *The art of teaching writing*. Portsmouth, NH: Heinemann.

Calkins, L. M. (2000). *The art of teaching reading*. Englewood Cliffs, NJ: Prentice-Hall.

Fletcher, R. (1992). *What a writer needs*. Portsmouth, NH: Heinemann.

Fletcher, R. (2003). *A writer's notebook*. New York: HarperCollins.

Freeman, M. (2007). Autobiographical understanding and narrative inquiry. In D. J. Clandinin (Ed.), *Handbook of narrative inquiry: Mapping a methodology* (pp. 120–145). Thousand Oaks, CA: Sage.

Guilfoyle, K., Hamilton, M. L., Pinnegar, S., & Placier, P. (2004). The epistemological dimensions and dynamics of professional dialogue in self-study. In J. J. Loughran, M. L. Hamilton, V. K. LaBoskey, & T. Russell (Eds.), *International handbook of self-study of teaching and teacher education practices* (pp. 1109–1167). Dordrecht: Springer.

McDonald, J. P., Mohr, N., Dichter, A., & McDonald, E. C. (2015). *The power of protocols: An educator's guide to better practice*. New York, NY: Teachers College Press.

Ray, K. W. (1999). *Wondrous words*. Urbana, IL: National Council of Teachers of English.

Ray, K. W. (2000). *What you know by heart*. Portsmouth, NH: Heinemann.

Schön, D. A. (1991). *The reflective turn: Case studies in and on educational practice*. New York, NY: Teachers College Press.

Wood, D. R., & Liebermann, A. (2000). Teachers as authors: The national writing project's approach to professional development. *International Journal of Leadership in Education*, *3*(3), 255–273.

Writers in the Schools (WITS). (n.d.). About WITS. Retrieved from https://witshouston.org/about/our-story/

REFLECTIONS ON RESEARCH AND PROFESSIONAL DEVELOPMENT PARTNERSHIPS IN POST-HARVEY HOUSTON: WRITING THE RIP TIDE

Chestin T. Auzenne-Curl, Cheryl J. Craig and Gayle A. Curtis

ABSTRACT

As part of a larger study into the influence of a Writers in the Schools (WITS) professional development consultancy, this narrative inquiry began just as Hurricane Harvey, the second most costly hurricane to hit the United States, devastated the Texas Gulf Coast in August 2017 and drew to a close in late 2020 during the COVID-19 global pandemic. This chapter explores the 2017–2018 school-year interactions between WITS Collaborative writer, Mary Austin (pseudonym), and six writing teachers with whom she worked at McKay High School (pseudonym) in the aftermath of Hurricane Harvey. With record flooding and widespread damage causing school-opening delays, teachers, students, and WITS consultants navigated a rip tide of emotions as they strived to balance educational/professional needs and duties with personal loss and unexpected financial burdens. This inquiry examines how WITS teacher professional development was carried out in the midst of these trying circumstances.

Keywords: Narrative inquiry; professional development; teacher identity; knowledge community; disruption; literacy coaching

INTRODUCTION

As part of a larger study into the influence of a Writers in the Schools (WITS) writing consultancy on teacher and student growth, this narrative inquiry began just as Hurricane Harvey struck the Texas Gulf Coast in August 2017 and ended almost a year into the COVID-19 global pandemic in late 2020 with all online work. With two distressing events – a natural disaster and a health epidemic – bookending this chapter, WITS consultants and the teachers, students, and schools with whom they worked found themselves navigating new waters of unforeseen circumstances – not once, but twice, and for most, even more. This chapter explores the 2017–2018 school-year interactions between WITS Collaborative writer, Mary Austin (pseudonym), and six writing teachers with whom she worked at McKay High School (pseudonym) in the aftermath of Hurricane Harvey. With record flooding and widespread damage causing school-opening delays, teachers, students, and WITS consultants rode out a rip tide of emotions as they strived to balance educational/professional needs and duties with personal loss and unexpected financial burdens. This chapter examines how WITS teacher professional development was carried out in the midst of these struggling circumstances. We begin with a look back at the calamitous impact of Hurricane Harvey, the second most costly hurricane to strike the United States, an event that left the city of Houston on Texas' Gulf Coast still reeling and rebuilding after nearly two years.

Beginning August 17 and ending September 2, 2017, three days before the school year was to begin, an unfathomable 27 trillion gallons of rain fell over the state of Texas with record highs descending upon the Greater Houston area. The wind did not whip Houston; the water did. It fell slowly and steadily for a week, holding the city captive. It forced release from dams, and it caused the beloved bayous of the city to swell and overflow. In some areas, water stood 8 feet deep and rising, holding everyone – underserved, middle-income, and upper-class – captive and helpless. In other areas, it pushed through suburban streets and into homes – forcing evacuations with no time to pack belongings and nothing left unsaturated to which to return. Much like the water, stress and trauma took their turns wading in and out of people's lives. Families were physically and mentally displaced when school districts opened their doors weeks later. If there is one thing that became vividly clear in the wake of Hurricane Harvey's torrential rains, it was that the nation's most diverse city and its collective unique corners of the metroplex, regardless of their differences, were one in their frailties as human beings.

For most Houston area residents, particularly teachers, students, and the WITS writing consultancy that served them, the 2017–2018 school year was unlike any other they had ever experienced. Just as teachers in the Greater City Independent School District (GCISD) (pseudonym) were readying classrooms for students, Hurricane Harvey hit the Greater Houston area on August 25th, three days before the scheduled first day of school. A Category 4 hurricane, Harvey stalled for four days on the Texas coast "dropping historic amounts of rainfall of more than 60 inches over southeastern Texas" (Blake & Zelinsky, 2018, p. 1), causing catastrophic flooding across Houston – pummeling the city. With damages to the Gulf Coast region reported at 125 billion, Harvey is the second-most costliest hurricane on record. At its peak, Houston saw 203,000 homes damaged, 738,000 people registered for federal assistance (Amadeo, 2018), and an estimated

20,000 children homeless (Ballesteros, 2017). Of GCISD's 245 schools, 200 reported some form of standing water, 53 schools had major damage, and 22 had extensive damage (Fox News, 2017). In response to the countless school reparation needs, rolling start dates were put in place dependent on school conditions, with most students returning on September 11th and some students required to attend class at alternative campuses due to severe damages to their home schools. Although the start of school signaled some return to routine, Harvey took its toll on schools, students, and teachers alike as many individuals were confronted with recovery efforts at school and damaged or lost property at home, all the while coping with the human trauma associated with disasters. A ripple effect consequently occurred, impacting the work of WITS Collaborative writers, and these researchers as the WITS start-up dates were pushed much later in the school year than planned.

Post-Harvey Houston schools, like Post-Katrina New Orleans schools, became grounds of contagion with secondary traumatic stress (STS) for many educators (Hydon, Wong, Langley, Stein, & Kataoka, 2015). For some teachers, their personal loss was tucked away to make room for the comfort and consolation they offered their students, but the impact of this suppression, compounded with the chronic stress of working in already challenging urban school contexts, made the course of the school year (2017–2018) resemble a rip tide. It pulled them into an unknown sea of emotions and physical demands (e.g., basic needs, alternative housing, blue tarps, automobile replacement, home repairs, insurance claims, etc.) while they fought to stay on course with their lesson planning and to support students who were experiencing similar devastating home situations.

On the campus of Claude McKay HS (pseudonym) in Greater City ISD (pseudonym), our research team launched a three-year study on the professional development of its writing teachers. In the aftermath of Hurricane Harvey and its impact on personal and professional situations, we observed as WITS Collaborative program directors and writers adapted and adjusted to delayed school openings and repeatedly altered school schedules, all with the aim of improving student learning by supporting teachers. At McKay, we observed writing teachers form a community of knowing alongside published authors who worked in the WITS Collaborative program. The relationships established between Greater City ISD and WITS were strengthened. They proved to combat compassion fatigue and hinder the ability of the tide to draw anyone at any level into its tow and far-removed from the safety of a shoreline.

The inaugural year of the field study and its unique timing called the research team to launch a narrative inquiry into the professional development collaborative. The fluidity of the method and the embedded attention given to the temporality, sociality, and place of observed phenomena (Connelly & Clandinin, 2006) assisted us in narrowing our focus to Claude McKay HS (pseudonym) which is one of four campuses to which the research team was directed for observation. McKay was chosen for the ebb and flow of attention that the campus received even before Harvey. Since it had been identified by the state as a campus in need of improvement by virtue of its accumulated test scores, McKay was consistent in its enactment of WITS and the writer, Mary Austin (pseudonym), who led them through the program was identified by McKay's teachers as a

> ...reminder of the reason that [they] came to teach. In the middle of all the craziness and the confusion. [They] get to sit back and learn something, too. In the safe place with Mary. (Field notes, Spring 2018)

Since McKay was characterized by the state as persistently underperforming, post-Harvey WITS field sites like McKay also became safe places for the discussion of STS-induced factors and the psychosocial implications of working in a school on state watch for recognition as underperforming.

CONCEPTUAL UNDERPINNINGS

Teacher Professional Development

According to Schwab (1954/1978), in traditional professional development delivery scenarios teachers are kept in line over time through their "developed incapacity to understand" and "by the system of...programs and special texts by which [they are] given only as much of the new material as [their] continued usefulness may require" (p. 218). In response to this actualization, Meier (1992) stressed that professional development should take place in an intense and sustained way within the context of teachers' ongoing work in schools, in addition to outside of those schools. She declared that:

> at the very least, one must imagine schools in which teachers are in frequent conversation with each other about their work, have easy and necessary access to each other's classrooms, take it for granted that they should comment on each other's work, and have the time to develop common standards for students' work. (p. 602)

Meier's (1992) research was followed by a long line of research (Chan & Pang, 2006; Darling-Hammond, 2000; Darling-Hammond & Bransford, 2005; Richardson, 2003; Shulman & Shulman, 2004) supporting the assumption that effective teacher professional development is "anchored in teachers' reality, sustained over time, and aimed at creating peer collaboration" (Musanti & Pence, 2010, p. 73). When teachers come together to critically discuss their work and share stories of experience, teacher practices improve and student gains achieved. Furthermore, "students learn more and teachers experience greater satisfaction and commitment when they engage with their colleagues, improving instruction and strengthening schools" (Johnson, Berg, & Donaldson, 2005, p. 72).

Writers in the School Collaborative for Professional Development

The program for teachers of writing at McKay High School draws on Meier's (1992) perspective of professional development in which teachers collectively and collaboratively examine their work. WITS Collaborative writers, like Mary (the collaborative writer featured in this chapter), are "personal trainers" for campus teachers who share innovative lessons that are initiated with teaching teams, cotaught in writing classrooms, and next enacted by teachers who return to their teams to reflect on their role and the role of their students in the level of success of the lessons. This unique approach engages teachers and students in shared writing experiences while providing an embedded knowledge community (Craig, 1992, 1995; Curtis, Reid, Kelley, Martindell, & Craig, 2013) of safe space in which teachers story and restory their situated and contextualized experiences. In contrast to traditional professional development methods, Mary's (and WITS's) work employs an ongoing professional development model (see Fig. 1) which supports a creative and empirical base for teachers to retool (Cochran-Smith & Fries, 2001) and refine the tools that they bring to the collaborative.

WITS Model in Practice

Alongside their work in schools, WITS writers are coached in a collaborative lead by an outside consultant (P. Tim Martindell) who models the cycle with sample protocols. This portion of the WITS ensures that classroom teachers are presented with vetted, most-promising practices. Also, in this setting, the WITS writers form a knowledge community (Craig, 1992, 1995, 2007; Curtis et al., 2013) of their own in which to grow and advance their practice.

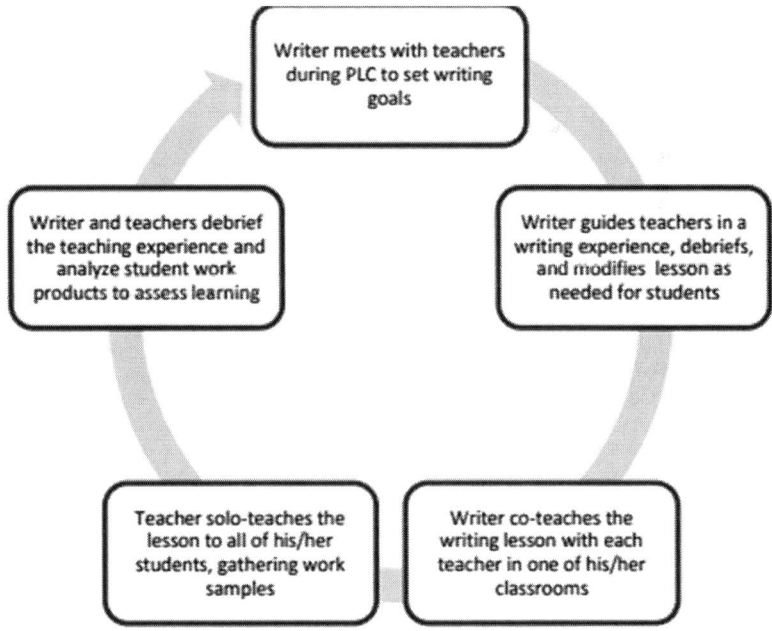

Fig. 1. Ongoing Professional Development Cycle Used by Writers in the Schools (WITS).

Story

Telling stories is a way that we humans make meaning of our experiences (Clandinin & Connelly, 1999). By storying the writing teachers' and Mary's experiences, the research team becomes a part of a relational act which creates connections "between teller and responder" (p. 16) and an educative act (Dewey, 1938) in that we each relive and reconsider experiences through retelling in effort to promote new understandings about WITS and the work of establishing and growing a knowledge community. Clandinin and Connelly (1999) assert that teachers engage in reflective practice (Schön, 1987, 1991) as they story and restory their lived experiences, constructing new meaning.

Narrative Inquiry

As a "study of experience as story" (Connelly & Clandinin, 2006, p. 477), narrative inquiry "is first and foremost a way of thinking about experience," with experience then being the phenomenon under study. Narrative inquiry is grounded in Dewey's (1938) notion of education as experience characterized by social interaction and continuity, or occurring over time. A three-dimensional research is formed at the intersection of personal and social interactions (sociality), experiences over time (temporality), and context (place). Consideration of the diverse elements within this space promote the uncovering of the "multiplicity of [participants'] lives and experiences" (Clandinin et al., 2006, p. 35), to aid in "understand[ing] the experiences in deeper and more complex ways."

Narrative Tools

The narrative tools of broadening and burrowing, and storying and restorying, employed through this inquiry were integral to identifying, examining, and constructing meaning from the narratives (Connelly & Clandinin, 1990; Keyes & Craig, 2012). The process of burrowing uncovered not only the foreground details of experiences of writer-consultant Mary Austin, McKay's teachers, and the research team, but also underlying motivations driving experiences and Hurricane Harvey–related preoccupations that moved in and out of situations like the tide. Broadening revealed many-layered narratives of school, district, community, and broader education landscape (Connelly & Clandinin, 1990) playing out in our participants' lived experiences. Storying and restorying are reflective engagements (Clandinin & Connelly, 2000; Connelly & Clandinin, 1990) by both participants and researchers. Ollerenshaw and Creswell (2002) explain restorying as

> ...the process of gathering stories, analyzing them for key elements of the story (e.g., time, place, plot, and scene), and then rewriting the story to place it within a chronological sequence...[providing] a causal link among ideas. (p. 332)

Highlighted participants in this inquiry included our Collaborative writer, Mary Austin (pseudonym), a white female, six McKay High School writing teachers (one Asian female, one Hispanic female, two African-American males, and two African-American females), and the authors as participant observers representing the research team.

Data Sources

Primary data sources included in the study are audio-recorded interviews with Mary Austin, the WITS Collaborative writer, audio/visual recordings of Mary's meetings with the team of six writing teachers, audio/visual recordings of WITS monthly Collaborative writers meetings, and four sets of researchers observation/ interview field notes per observation. Additional pertinent data were gathered from news agencies, state and federal websites, and school district publications. Data were analyzed and categorized according to emergent themes.

FINDINGS

The Claude McKay High School feeder pattern surfaced as an ideal setting for exploring the complexity of urban education in an age of accountability. This study is set in one of the largest urban districts in the most diverse city in the nation. Despite its recognizable title as "The Pulse of the City," Claude McKay HS and two of its feeder schools have struggled to achieve satisfactory performance designations for the decade preceding the study. During year one, the teachers at McKay were working under the leadership of a principal who was new to the campus. They saw the district's superintendent leave amid a budget crisis, and they found themselves on the frontline of resultant teacher position cuts. The campus was treading waters of state, local, and impending charter control. In the end, McKay was spared any kind of takeover for another year, and the victories were washed ashore.

With all the political battles and threats to autonomy from outside the building, McKay earned state recognition inside the building for the first time. The shifting tide was not only changing the way that teachers taught and thought, but it was also changing WITS. The following researcher field notes highlighted the situation.

> Mary indicated that WITS was experiencing "an identity crisis." With its original professional development model, it was about the writer and the students and the trust relationship that develops between them. WITS at McKay, in contrast, was not a direct relationship between the writer and students. (Field notes, Spring 2019)

Observer field notes further elaborated on the shifting tide teachers were navigating.

> "It is very indirect." Mary said. "It is about influencing students through developing the teachers as writers. It is about using teacher talk as the medium of exchange." She added, "We already know that trauma, floods, and hurricanes also shape students' lives and what they know." I could see and understand that in the moment, Mary had started to consider herself as a teacher of teachers. What those teachers understood about their students; Mary understood about the teachers with whom she worked.

Mary Austin began the year differently:

> I'm not a teacher, you know. My mom was. For years she taught around the corner from McKay. I know what she experienced and so I cannot call myself a teacher. I'm a writer and so

figuring out how to share that with teachers can be hard. I don't want them to think that I feel like I know more than they do about their classrooms.

Mary's trepidation regarding her dual identity as writer and teacher was all but gone by the end of the year, and her metaphorical classroom was deemed a success by the teachers that she served. We interviewed Rilissa Martinez (pseudonym), one of the teachers in the McKay cohort, before a session began:

Researcher:	How is WITS going?
Rilissa Martinez:	I really enjoy and learn so much from Mary. She has really good ideas that are practical ways to teach.
Researcher:	Anything in particular that you have most enjoyed?
Rilissa Martinez:	Definitely the work on helping students write better thesis statements for their paragraphs. I am sure I will use this approach for the remainder of my teaching career. I have already been creating information sheets and notes. The approach Mary took with them is really helping to "stage writing."

Hope Amid the Ebb: Teachers' Perspectives of WITS

As a group comprised veteran and novice teachers, the McKay writing teachers all considered their WITS sessions with Mary as valuable time in which they could share ideas.

Art (Teacher):	I love having Mary here. We all do. I brought my 13 writing samples and I'm ready to go.
Researcher:	So, is that an average class size for you? 13?
Art:	(Laughs) No. Not on the roster – in class yes. But I have 37 kids on the roster. About 13 show up on average and half are suspended and a lot are just not showing up. Some are displaced and some just don't like it here.
Researcher:	Can you tell me more about that?
Art:	There isn't much more to it. With the Hurricane we have lost kids and we have gained kids. School doesn't feel like it is the most important thing to them right now and to tell you the truth, some of the teachers feel the same way. This is one of the few times we can just relax and feel normalcy. Mary brings in great stuff.
Researcher:	What kind of things?
Art:	Protocols so that we are staying on topic when we are discussing student work, ideas for lessons and texts that take the kids minds off of all they are dealing with…and when we turn around and teach it, it's all ready. It takes that Collaborative time stress off, too.

The protocols introduced to the group by Mary presented new ways to look at how teachers work with and for students. Many were designed to increase meaningful discussions about different writing strategies and techniques, and how best to support their students' learning. During their time with Mary, the teachers self-reported growth in student achievement across several trait-based areas. These areas were identified by WITS protocols and model lessons; the teachers at McKay consistently voiced excitement and seemed enlightened and ready to extend the learning after each protocol.

"It was like a light bulb had gone off for me [when you finished modeling the lesson], and then I wanted to call you back," Phillip (a campus teacher) informed Mary. He seemed so genuinely impressed with WITS and himself. "I had to move on, but the next period! That's when I was on fire." (Field notes, Spring 2017)

The meeting conversations revealed how teachers came to rely on the consistent WITS structure and protocols for lesson design and review. The teachers began to ask Mary to target specific texts and populations in their discourse. They were celebrating the victories:

> Evelyn (Teacher): So, guess what, You Guys. Andrew wrote. It was about 6 lines, but one of them was all I needed, and I know that it had a lot to do with the model text that Mary gave us on homes. They all could relate to it. At first, I thought it was because they have homes and then Andrew wrote about not having one. It almost broke me, but it was so real. It was the only thing he has written all year.

Mary: Would you like to share it?
Evelyn: Not the whole thing, he is still working, and I would want to ask him because it's personal.
Mary: Okay, I understand.
Evelyn: But listen to the beginning! "I had a home, but Harvey snatch[ed] that and so much pain was locked inside it, I ain't really mad yet."

Evelyn went on to explain that she talked to Andrew about the content and structure of his poem and that he would be rewriting it. This sparked a conversation on how the engaging and socially relevant texts provided by Mary helped the students to work through things that were deep inside them as human beings in a recounting of what Horace Hill (2007) noted as poetry's power to engage students in acts of "agency that frees [them] from the constraints of social adversity" (p. 227). One of the teachers chimed in next (Fig. 2):

> You see all these posters that I have around the room? I worked on this lesson after the one you are talking about, Evelyn, and I realized that it was rough. I used the word Trauma with them and when you say that word, it is like you have to turn around and face your own. I really got emotional about a lot of things.

Nearing the end of the school year, the McKay writing teachers voiced their concerns that Mary's work with them was ending for the school year.

"We have no more sessions? What do you mean?", declared one teacher.

"This is our safe space!", another contended.

Mary explained, "The way it works is that [the schools] only pay for a set amount of sessions and tomorrow will be our last."

The writing teachers joked about pooling funds to purchase additional sessions, meeting discreetly for a happy hour, and other suggestions for continuing the collaborative work.

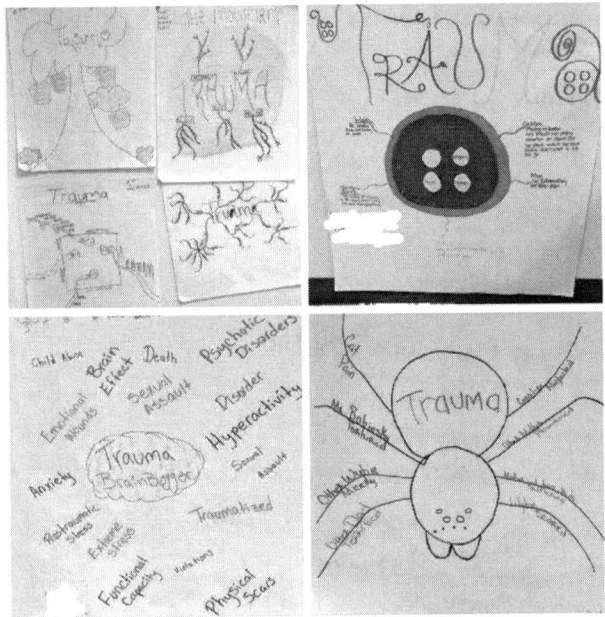

Fig. 2. Student Work on Trauma.

A Desire to Encourage Children to Learn and Create Freely

The school year was nearly over. It began in the fall with Hurricane Harvey and the spring hosted winter storm Ingrid, which led to an often unspoken of, but ever-present feeling of loss. There were lost instructional days, lost family members, lost homes, and a tendency for all parties to have lost focus.

Art:	I'm sorry you guys. I'm here but I'm not. It's just overwhelming. I was talking to one of my kids before class and she is dealing with a lot.
Mary:	No, that's fine. Do you want to talk about it?
Art:	She just...comes by for supplies and food and I know her mom isn't really at home a lot. I just try to encourage her to be a kid, but you can see her life hanging in her face. Today for the first time, though. She wouldn't write. I know she still isn't telling me everything, and she probably won't write tonight, but I gave her an extension.

Teachers often spoke about their students' needs, both personal and academic. Early in both semesters, the McKay team expressed to Mary that the days lost to the natural disasters were valuable time lost and that regardless of the time left, the desired to provide whatever was missing for their students. In a conversation on students' creativity and what could be done to promote it, teachers discussed how creative freedom advanced student performance.

"You know what worked? When I just gave it to them," one teacher said to Mary. "Really? I had to fight and add another mentor text. Just something silly," said another. Still another teacher shared his experience with creative writing in the classroom, "It felt like [the students] were so used to structure that they didn't know what to do without it. They didn't know how to just 'do them.'" In tone, it became apparent that the teachers themselves also needed to be affirmed and wished to be valued for what they could do. This is not an uncommon phenomenon among teachers in challenging urban context. The battle for autonomy and appreciation is often countered by "a deficit image of teachers needing to be told when, where and what to do" (Craig, 2012, p. 100).

Managing School-based Inconsistencies

As a consistently low-performing school, various professional development teams were brought into McKay, in addition to WITS. This often resulted in repeated schedule conflicts that, at times, prevented the writing teachers from participating in the full hour-long sessions with Mary. For example, in one professional development session that Mary facilitated, teachers were called out of the meeting to participate in a demonstration of a reading support program. The administration and the teachers agreed that there was a need for both trainings – the reading program demonstration and their writing work with Mary – but teachers voiced concern with the conflicting schedules and expectations.

> "I'm sorry guys, I am just popping in today and I need to take Evelyn and Art with me." The Department Head seemed quite in a hurry. He was dressed much more formally than usual. In the full suit and tie, he was unrecognizable.

Rilissa chimed in, "Why today? I wanted to see it, too, but I need to ask Mary about these essays." There was no answer, just a smile through tightly pursed lips and a shrug. He walked away, and she remained. She turned to the researchers and said, "A little over 40% of our 9th graders are reading on a third-grade level. I get it. So please don't think I am complaining. It's just that they don't let us focus on one thing at a time."

This issue of overscheduling was echoed in the subsequent meeting as they were called from their professional development with Mary to meet with the principal. Seven minutes later, they returned seeming somewhat disappointed that they were being mandated to forgo English instruction for the rest of the year in order to support the upcoming Biology and History Tests. Each of them entered the room with a very thick stack of bound papers. "Word searches!" one yelled. "See this? I looked through it, and its word searches," she continued on in frustration stating that she was not qualified to or interested in teaching Biology, but she knew that word searches were not an answer to students who may be struggling. Others erupted, but like a wave, the discussion tapered off and the conversation fell back into the protocol, as if it were an escape from reality. Mary reiterated the writing teachers' frustrations. She explained that due to demands on teacher time as a result of accountability expectations and the school's low-performing status, her WITS sessions were often canceled. "Sometimes I don't know when I will actually get to facilitate. After driving all the way here, I have to turn back home because of last minute meetings being called."

Mary explained that her work at McKay was "a different animal" from what she had been used to while working in WITS. The collaboration between writers and teachers was new to Mary, who previously worked in a different program called "Student Innovation." In the Student Innovation program, writers worked directly with students on writing models. WITS, in contrast, gave writers less time with students, and much more time as teacher coaches.

> WITS and the Student Innovation program are "enormously different." She said. They are, to use her turn of phrase, "different animals." WITS is indirect and often involves getting ready for the state test. It's very "practical," she says.

This aspect of state testing being ever-present when working with teachers was not a surprise to the research team, but we experienced it firsthand on several occasions. The following field text entry reflects just such an occasion.

> That day, I arrived first. I was met with kindness and enjoyed observing the interactions and staff in McKay's welcome area. One of the clerks even gave me a note to pass on to the teacher in whose classroom our meeting would be held. Then, the Dean of Curriculum spied me. "Who are you? Why are you here?" She's a curt African American woman – a no-nonsense person. "I say Texas A&M evaluators here to observe the WITS projects."
>
> No kind words, no apologies...

The field text entry continued:

> Well, she says "Today is a testing day...State requirements take priority... You will have to wait until another day." I am not put off. I state that there are others coming and I will sit in the classroom until they arrive.

Then, a little later:

> Ms. Martinez is back with the key and Mary has arrived as well, followed closely by the other research team members. The Dean of Curriculum comes by again and says the teachers will need to attend a training for state assessment. I say we will take the opportunity to interview Mary beforehand. (But soon Ms. Martinez returns...Today 5 teachers are absent and a 6th one is late The state priority cannot continue ...There is no quorum...) Our research at the school, though, can continue as planned.

Accountability Pressures and Budget Concerns

As the year progressed, Mary's group of writing teachers expressed to her their growing concern over the school's state accountability pressures. Performance status, anticipated leadership changes, and district budget cuts greatly impacted by Hurricane Harvey–related costs were looming over every conversation. Teachers were confronted with the possibility of the state restructuring the school, a charter school taking over direction of the school's professional knowledge landscape, and the district's eminent teacher position cuts. Who would be affected? One of McKay's teachers, Anya, shared her unexpected exit from the school.

> You don't have to worry about me. I've got the second-round interview across town. I'm not coming back to this, God willing. I want to stay for the kids, but I wonder how good am I for them? I feel like I have to sneak around to implement some of the things we work on in here. Why should I have to sneak around to do what I know is best?

These words came as somewhat of a shock to the team, as Anya, a strong voice, all year had never revealed any hint of leaving during our observations. As an immigrant from Asia who grew up in an all African-American area of Houston, she voiced feeling at home and also knowing what it was like to be "counted out because you're different" in school. Through Anya's voice, we heard triumph and motivation amid the pressures. Now, she had begun to story herself away in front of us. It was a floodgate. The other teachers were not surprised, and in the last WITS session of the year, the cohort discussed the next school year, revealing that many of them would not be returning. Many, like Anya, had already gone on other interviews, and some had accepted offers. The younger African-American male teacher spoke last, "I left my last job to come here – took a pay cut, no problem. I thought I could help here and make a difference he said to us on his way out of the door. I just guess I was wrong." The year ended solemnly and in a silent storm with a magnitude not unlike the physical one that delayed the unusual year's start.

Shifting the Tide: Writers' Perspectives of WITS

As Mary and other WITS writers continued to work with teachers, they observed noticeable shifts in teachers' perspectives as teachers recounted their students' progress in becoming writers. The following field note entries reflected such observations.

> Ms. Martinez said that the writing process has allowed her students to write that Leaders cause voices to be heard and that Followers cause revolutions. She said that it is as if a block has been opened up and there are no longer barriers in their brains. She can see that that they have the ideas in their brains – that they just need to get them onto paper. (Field notes, Spring 2019)

An earlier entry caught similar teacher thoughts on a student's growth as a writer.

> Yes. They have thesis sentences now, but they need to develop them into body paragraphs, which is the next step. Mr. Derek (teacher) was happy that most of them have introductions, general statements and hooks to develop readers' interests. He said all of this is important for the state test. (Field notes, Fall 2018)

Teacher comments also indicated their appreciation of Mary's collaborative WITS work with them, as well as the respect she showed them as teachers with agency.

> Art said, I will probably leave here, but not leave Mary. He laughed and looked around the room with deep narrowed eyes, as if he were recalling or searching, and he spoke again. The program is great. The way I see my kids trying and making steady increases in their writing, you know? But this was really for us. I don't know if it plays out that way everywhere, but we looked forward to Mary for the lessons and things, but really for the space and the respect. (Field notes, Spring 2018)

Teaching as a Writer

Mary's interviews were always insightful into the research team and always covered her work in the field and how it was coupled with the preparation she received in the WITS Collaborative program. As previously stated, Mary did not view herself as a teacher in the early stages of the program. She stated this several times in the community of peers (her community of knowing) in WITS Collaborative:

> I know a lot of you have taught before and I can't say that I have. You know, the time that I spend as an adjunct just doesn't count to me. My mother was a teacher for real and I can't say that I know all the education talk or anything and the pressures of the test, so these meetings are great for me. I love listening to what is going on in your lives and [about] your experiences as teachers, because I try to fold that into my understanding of the teachers that I work with. It can be nerve racking to go in as a writer and not have that.

Mary always exhibited a deep respect for her mother's profession but had stood firm in her belief that she was not a member of it. Perhaps it was the time spent on campus, or her welcomed presence as a member of the community, but she started to see things differently at some point. She began to speak differently, and words and phrases used to describe her life in the field shifted. Where once she was "going to a campus to 'do' the lesson," her emails began to indicate that she would "be teaching a new method based on one of the modeled protocols." Her confidence by the end of year one led to both praise and thoughtful inquiry regarding her own collaboration and development.

In Praise and Critique of the WITS Collaborative Program
By this time, Mary has been a coach at McKay for three years. Her insight into life as a teacher and a writer in context had grown and along with this, so has her inquiry line demonstrated a depth of thought in her readiness to continue working as a WITS coach. Throughout several interviews and informal conversations, she celebrated and asked more of WITS Collaborative. She offered several suggestions for improvement for the program, and she was heard by administrators who acted quickly on points of reference from all of the writers.

> Gender, Race, Certification and other white cap waves
>
> The field sites for the study are mostly brown and Black kids in rough areas. That's not a secret, but it isn't always talked about. WITS as a whole, can be found on some of the most exclusive campuses in the city – public and private. So, when we are in WITS Collaborative, our stories and experiences are not exactly the same. There is no real way to know that just because you are at St. Bernadette's International College Collaborative this year, that you won't be assigned to McKay next year, or even simultaneously. You know? So, I think we should talk about that more.

We shared this particular point with the WITS Collaborative's Program Coordinator, Carol (pseudonym), as one of several points echoed in our interviews with writers. She responded immediately:

> Oh yes. I feel bad because it seems like I spent the whole year ripping out sheet rock and living at the office, but before Harvey, we had discussed this very thing. One of the trainings we hope to offer them at the beginning of the year was on poverty, and another on state accountability systems because that it an unavoidable topic of discussion on the campuses we serve. We also wanted to talk about diversity as being bigger than just race.

As Carol began to open this discussion, the research team each reflected back to Mary's own discussion of "diversity":

> I am a white woman, you know. Really white and in my 40s, so even though I like to think of myself as an open and well-read person, I sometimes wonder if I bring in texts by black and brown authors, do the teachers question me since I don't have those experiences? Am I trying to teach them something about their or their kids' cultures? Some things that I think I want to check next year are really going to tough. I want to make sure I present things right. I want to be fair.

The research team was excited to see the team address these concerns in the selection of a book study for all WITS writers. The book of choice? *For White Folks Who Teach in the Hood... and the Rest of Y'all Too: Reality Pedagogy and Urban Education*, by Christopher Emdin. One member of the research team had read it and immediately celebrated the selection. She is a doctoral student in her early 30s, and her name is Velise (pseudonym).

> "The book is great." She said. "But as a Black student, I do wonder how they will use it. There are not a lot of people of color here period...More than last year, but will they be facilitating it? Will Carol?"

This brought up many thoughts for us. As a group of women with varied backgrounds, there is an oscillation among us. Whose experiences are privileged when? The project leader is nationally renowned and highly awarded. A white woman with dual citizenship and whose expertise in conducting research about school reform has extended over 2 decades in Houston's urban schools. The second author is an early career Postdoc, who identifies as black, but is of diverse lineage. Her background in public education includes positions in central administration as a curriculum director and trainer of Literacy Coaches. The third author is white, bilingual, and a Research Associate who has been a principal at a dual language school as well as an administrator at a high needs inner city high school. The long and short of it is that we interpret what we see in light of our own background and experiences and we make sense of others' comments and actions accordingly.

In the end, Tim Martindell, the consultant responsible for presenting protocols and facilitating WITS Collaborative discussions, calmed all of the thoughts running through people's minds in his address of the text. While the books had been issued during the previous monthly meeting, the WITS writers were not given a specific reading requirement. He worked with this by introducing a protocol that directed them to reflect upon words and phrases that stood out to them, no matter how far into the book they had endeavored. The following field texts capture the activity of the group:

> Tonight, the focus was on the book, *For White Folks Who Teach in the Hood*, a book of which I have ordered a copy. Tim instructed the writers to find a favorite sentence, 3-word phrase and then a word. The writers and Tim stretched the margins of the rules as is the case with all creative people (me included) .... we adhere to the hard-and-fast rather than to approximations and/or inventions with students, but perhaps tonight there would be a model presented that could shift that tide. (Researcher 1)

Another researcher wrote:

> I am still reflecting on the questions. Mary's and Velise's. I wonder how Tim will be received as he guides the WITS Writers and I wonder if it matters at all. Just a month ago, I had not thought much about perception because my focus was on the text. I was so busy thinking about the importance of the subject matter and the quality of the selection by the administration...I just didn't think about delivery immediately. As a Black person, perhaps I should have (?) (Researcher 2)

And then it was time. We entered the protocol, and the room was still in contemplation. Then there was flipping through the text and whispered conversations. Some joked about not having read very much because of the workload, and others told of reading habits that made them skip from chapter to chapter out of sequence. "I just started at the end to give myself a teaser," one voice from the back rolled forward. "That's fine." Tim Martindell said. "It doesn't matter at all where you are, just focus on what you have read and identify a phrase that moved you. We'll talk about why and share out shortly."

The following list captures phrases of impact from WITS writers as they launched the discussion connecting the reading of *For White Folks Who Teach in the Hood* by Christopher Emdin (Fig. 3).

WITS writers, including Mary, shared vignettes and personal stories. They questioned the balance of positive to negative tone in selections made, and they asked one another for help:

- Are we measuring success, knowledge of content, or compliance?
- It's about the bigger picture – not about compliance, but about engagement – right?
- How do we implement? Is it possible for us all to be Paulo Freire's in the classroom?
- We need to understand what brought the teachers to the field of education... We need to show what those reasons are – they are still there...How can we remind them?

Phrases

p. 17	The segregated American South rendered African Americans invisible
p. 33	These kids—those kids
p. 9	Imaginary white middle class ideal
p. 39	Bias justifies ineffective teaching
p. 29	Not being validated, not being taught well
p. 33	Distracted from goal to affect change
p. 26	Go beyond what is physically seen to see my behavior as the problem
p. 50	The delicate balance to self-manage structure and innovation
p. 27	Safe and trusting environment located in more psychic imagination
p. 50	Delicate balance, but also war against young people
p. 44	Pentecostal pedagogy
p. 14	Classroom colonialism, powerful conversations, co-teaching, huge gap
p. 38	Personal stories, hierarchies, barbers
p. 59	Value voices, foster families, savior complex, black twitter, infusing humor/story, delicate balance

Fig. 3. Phrases of Impact for the WITS Writers.

There was so much discussion that the protocol ran over its allotted time, which was not a problem for WITS, but they thought about how it would be an issue for teachers in the classroom. "We need to take what we need from this book and this protocol. Teachers need to be able to take what they need from us, too. They need the big takeaways. That's how we best support them," said one WITS writer.

"And what is the big takeaway from tonight's protocol?", Tim Martindell asked.

"Text renders experience." Carol responded. "That's what I got. We talked about it so much and carried the conversation so far from just a few pages when you look at it."

It was a night of rich discussion, and we came to see that every concern that Mary had expressed was addressed – and though not everyone was working on a campus like McKay, many of the standard victories and struggles were shared. Most importantly, the vision was shared. With the support of the WITS Collaborative program, the WITS writers had a safe space – that had cultivated and sustained a knowledge community – in which to navigate the complexities of the work and a place to release the STS they picked up along the way. If the torrent ocean of urban education were to pull their teacher cohorts, they seemed determined to be the surfboard that aided riding the waves.

CONCLUSION

In looking back at WITS writer Mary's interactions with McKay teachers during the school year following Hurricane Harvey, this narrative inquiry uncovered the complexities in the lives of teachers in urban schools through restoried experiences among a community of teachers. It seemed that McKay was a look forward and backward into each circumstance that the team observed. The second language issues, the high mobility, the struggle for consistency all coalesced here. There was a spirit at McKay that was hopeful and cynical, a tale to be told of policy wars, protection, challenge, and triumph – and it was the end of the road for the lower grades schools we had visited in the feeder pattern. We ended the year with a final visit to McKay and saw the teachers clinging to the collaborative for a safe space in the midst of a storm. In essence, much of what we saw was a collectivist coping system embedded in the emergent community (Ebersöhn & Loots, 2017). With that in mind, we turned back to look at our evaluation questions to take stock. It was a tale of budget and leadership change, inconsistency, and the teachers who storied themselves into living or leaving in the face of these challenges. Reflecting back on these situated experiences from a 2021 perspective, we note the perseverance and determinedness of WITS writer consultants and McKay teachers as they strived to support student learning amid often uncertain personal and professional circumstances that may have helped them, in some measure, to later navigate the unprecedented situations resulting from the pandemic. There was a sense of teacher agency developing at McKay, along with increasing resilience, confidence, and a focus on self-care for teachers and students that we continue to explore and share as the notes and dialog continue throughout the study.

REFERENCES

Amadeo, K. (2018, May 31). Hurricane Harvey facts, damage and costs: What made Harvey so devasting. *The Balance*. Retrieved from https://www.thebalance.com/hurricane-harvey-facts-damage-costs-4150087

Ballesteros, C. (2017, November 26). Hurricane Harvey victims: More than 20,000 children in Houston are Homeless, report show. *Newsweek*. Retrieved from http://www.newsweek.com/hurricane-harvey-victims-homeless-fema-722640

Blake, E. S., & Zelinsky, D. A. (2018). *National Hurricane Center tropical cyclone report: Hurricane Harvey*. National Hurricane Center. Retrieved from https://www.nhc.noaa.gov/data/tcr/AL092017_Harvey.pdf

Chan, C. K., & Pang, M. F. (2006). Teacher collaboration in learning communities. *Teaching Education*, *17*(1), 1–5.

Clandinin, D. J., & Connelly, F. M. (1999). Storying and restorying ourselves: Narrative and reflection. In A. Chen & J. Van Maanen (Eds.), *The reflective spin: Case studies of teachers in higher education transforming action* (pp. 15–23). Singapore: World Scientific Publishing.

Clandinin, D. J., & Connelly, F. M. (2000). *Narrative inquiry: Experience and story in qualitative research*. San Francisco, CA: Jossey-Bass.

Clandinin, D. J., Huber, J., Huber, M., Murphy, S., Murray Orr, A., Pearce, M., & Steeves, P. (2006). *Composing diverse identities: Narrative inquiries into the interwoven lives of children and teachers*. London: Routledge.

Cochran-Smith, M., & Fries, M. K. (2001). Sticks, stones, and ideology: The discourse of reform in teacher education. *Educational Researcher*, *30*(8), 3–15.

Connelly, F. M., & Clandinin, D. J. (1990). Stories of experience and narrative inquiry. *Educational Researcher*, *19*(5), 2–14.

Connelly, F. M., & Clandinin, D. J. (2006). Narrative inquiry. In J. Green, G. Camilli, & P. Elmore (Eds.), *Handbook of complementary methods in educational research* (pp. 477–489). Washington, DC: American Educational Research Association.

Craig, C. (1992). *Coming to know in the professional knowledge context: Beginning teachers' experiences*. Unpublished dissertation. Edmonton, AB: University of Alberta.

Craig, C. (1995). Knowledge communities: A way of making sense of how beginning teachers come to know in their professional knowledge contexts. *Curriculum Inquiry*, *25*(2), 151–175.

Craig, C. (2012). "Butterfly under a pin": An emergent teacher image amid mandated curriculum reform. *The Journal of Educational Research*, *105*(2), 90–101.

Curtis, G., Reid, D., Kelley, M., Martindell, P. T., & Craig, C. (2013). Braided lives: Multiple ways of knowing, flowing in and out of knowledge communities. *Studying Teacher Education*, *9*(2), 175–186.

Darling-Hammond, L. (2000). Teacher quality and student achievement: A review of state policy evidence. *Educational Policy Analysis Archives*, *8*(1). Retrieved from http://epaa.asu.edu/epaa/v8n1/

Darling-Hammond, L., & Bransford, J. (Eds.). (2005). *Collaborativearing teachers for a changing world. What teachers should learn and be able to do*. San Francisco, CA: Jossey-Bass.

Dewey, J. (1938). My pedagogic creed. *School Journal*, *54*, 77–80.

Ebersöhn, L., & Loots, T. (2017). Teacher agency in challenging contexts as a consequence of social support and resource management. *International Journal of Educational Development*, *53*, 80–91.

Fox News. (2017, September 3). Harvey fallout: 53 of Houston's schools have 'major' damage, at least 22 will be closed for months. Retrieved from https://www.foxnews.com/us/harvey-fallout-53-of-houstons-schools-have-major-damage-at-least-22-will-be-closed-for-months

Hall, H. R. (2007). Poetic expressions: Students of color express resiliency through metaphors and similes. *Journal of Advanced Academics*, *18*(2), 216–244. doi:10.4219/jaa-2007-355

Hydon, S., Wong, M., Langley, A. K., Stein, B. D., & Kataoka, S. (2015). Preventing secondary traumatic stress in educators. *Child and Adolescent Psychiatric Clinics*, *24*(2), 319–333.

Johnson, S. M., Berg, J., & Donaldson, M. (2005). *Who stays in teaching and why: A review of literature on teacher retention*. Cambridge, MA: Harvard Graduate School of Education, Project on the Next General of Teachers.

Keyes, D., & Craig, C. (2012). Burrowing and broadening in the storied places of teacher education. In E. Chan, D. Keyes, & V. Ross (Eds.), *Narrative inquirers in the midst of meaning-making: Interpretive acts of teacher educators*. Bingley: Emerald Publishing Limited.

Meier, D. (1992). Reinventing teaching. *Teachers College Record, 93*(4), 594–609.

Musanti, S. I., & Pence, L. (2010). Collaboration and teacher development: Unpacking resistance, constructing knowledge, and navigating identities. *Teacher Education Quarterly, 37*(1), 73–89.

Ollerenshaw, J. A., & Creswell, J. W. (2002). Narrative research: A comparison of two restorying data analysis approaches. *Qualitative Inquiry, 8*(3), 329–347.

Richardson, V. (2003). The dilemmas of professional development. *Phi Delta Kappan, 84*(5), 401–406.

Schön, D. A. (1987). *Educating the reflective practitioner*. San Francisco, CA: Jossey-Bass.

Schön, D. A. (1991). *The reflective practitioner: How professionals think in action*. New York, NY: Basic Books.

Schwab, J. J. (1954/1978). Eros and education: A discussion of one aspect of discussion. In I. Westbury & N. Wilkof (Eds.), *Science, curriculum and liberal education: Selected essays* (pp. 105–148). Chicago, IL: University of Chicago Press.

Shulman, L. S., & Shulman, J. H. (2004). How and what teachers learn: A shifting perspective. *Journal of Curriculum Studies, 36*(2), 257–271.

REFLECTIONS ON PRINCIPAL LEADERSHIP AND WRITERS IN THE SCHOOLS

Michael Curl and Cheryl J. Craig

ABSTRACT

In this chapter, we discuss how an outside writing program was able to assist the stakeholders at a local middle school and the story behind the leaders involved in the process. This program was part of a larger system of "interventions" geared toward improving student success and teacher efficacy. Traditional interventions (after-school tutorials, grouping by state assessment scores, test-taking strategies) were viewed as lacking when it came to their impact on the campus's mostly students of color. Knowing the potential impact of a solid reading and writing program on urban youth, the faculty on the campus teamed with a Writers in the Schools (WITS) writer who proposed several promising practices. The contributions of a professional writer, real-world examples, and ongoing teacher professional development with support contributed to creating a knowledge community of writers that, in addition to creating more scholarship for students and staff, manifested itself in more minority students performing at the highest levels on the state accountability assessments.

Keywords: Writers in the Schools (WITS); principal leadership; personal practical knowledge; principal images; knowledge communities; alternate certification; students as writers; student success

THE STORY BEFORE THE STORY (CHERYL J. CRAIG, AUTHOR 1)

Cheryl Craig: *As a teacher in Canada, my personal experiences with six principals as school leaders over a 15-year period were mostly positive. I felt each did what* they could to support my classroom work with K-6 children. They also encouraged me to connect theory and practice (policy was not on my radar screen at that time) through teaching concurrently in the public schools and the local research-intensive university. Before accountability agendas were politically conceived and mandated, these principals wrote rich evidenced evaluations of my practice that detailed how I met the needs of students along the learning continuum. At that time, evaluation was not a zero sum game where one teacher's gain necessitated another teacher's loss with principals having limited points to allocate to whole-school faculties.

Later, when conducting my dissertation research with Tim (research participants), I discovered something else about principals that I have long-remembered. As a beginning teacher, Tim happened to be placed on a campus where a former head of the province's principal association was the school leader. Every time I would arrive at the school to observe or interview Tim, I could not get past the principal's office. After three unsuccessful attempts, I came to the realization that Victor, Tim's principal, was just as lonely as Tim, the beginning teacher, was. Victor also had no one with whom he could share his narratives of experience (Connelly & Clandinin, 1990). Hence, I began a parallel inquiry with Victor to facilitate my dissertation study with Tim. Because I attended faculty meetings with Tim, I gained first-hand insights into Victor's personal practical knowledge (Clandinin, 1985) – his on-the-ground sense of knowing – concerning how to be and how to get things done as he worked alongside teachers and students at Meadowlark School, which was a K-6 campus. At one point, the school district wanted teachers to "clock in" each work day. Victor was adamantly opposed to this edict. He believed this would not be treating teachers and prospective teachers like Tim with the dignity of their profession. Also, when extracurricular activities on his campus started to overwhelm teachers, Victor was willing to reduce noon hour and after-school obligations to ensure that out-of-school activities did not overshadow in-school teaching and learning. These situations and others like them showed that Victor was more aligned with the teachers with whom he worked than he was with school district mandates flowing down the conduit (Clandinin & Connelly, 1995; Craig, 2002). The fact that principals and teachers belong to the same union in Alberta also may have contributed to Victor's stance.

Ultimately, I wrote a chapter about Victor that was published in Connelly and Clandinin's (1999) book on professional identity. I argued that Victor embodied and enacted the image of principal-as-rebel based on his ongoing circumvention of school district policies that subtracted from teachers' professionalism. When I approached Victor with the first draft of the developing chapter, I was unsure as to how he would respond. After all, I had cast the leading principal in the school district – the one with connections stretching well beyond the province (equivalent to an American state) – as a "rebel."

When I returned to Meadowlark School about two weeks later to solicit his feedback, I found Victor tossing files from a cabinet into an unceremonious heap on the floor. He then wheeled his chair around and told me that the files were his school district principal evaluations. He then looked me directly in the eye: "And you have understood me, you have portrayed me, you have 'got me' – in ways my evaluators have never previously done…" (Craig, 1999). My research with Victor taught me that principals hold and express personal images of the principalship and that they, like teachers, develop knowledge from their experiences lived in context over time.

At this juncture, I moved to the US and began researching the $60 million Houston Annenberg Challenge (HAC) reform movement. As a faculty member at a local university, I was invited to be the formative researcher for five of the 11 lead HAC campuses and was chosen to do the summative evaluation of a sixth campus in a third district. This meant I conducted research in two elementary schools, two middle schools and two high schools. Two of the campuses in two different districts had more experienced principals (Brianna Larson, Henry Richards) who shared the same kind of respect for teachers that Victor had exemplified in Canada. Brianna Larson, the first principal, worked on a 1500-student campus located in the inner loop of Houston. She often shared how her championing of teachers left her "on the short end of the stick" where her school district was concerned. Henry Richards, the second principal, led a high school the size of a small city (3,500 students). He was explicitly known for the "circle of protection he placed around… teachers so [they] could work with students" (Craig, 2004, p. 1238). However, both principals' relationships with their respective school districts ran amuck, probably due to Texas putting high stakes accountability mandates into place in the state before the US's No Child Left Behind Act (NCLB, 2002) became law. Against this policy backdrop, Brianna retired early. As for Henry, he left his urban campus and transferred to a school in the suburbs with a high performing student body whose scores would not affect his employment. These two principals' recognition of the primacy of teachers came from their personal moral stances. However, Brianna and Henry, unlike Victor in Canada, did not belong to the same union as their teachers, which made Canadian teachers' issues the same as Canadian principals' issues. This was because the Houston area unions were broken into smaller units when desegregation happened. This deliberate act ensured that no principal/teacher group would ever again have enough power to participate in the overturn of a state-authorized practice (separate, but equal schooling).

At this point, I began to work with different principals in Greater Houston. Some had the same orientations held and expressed by Brianna (US), Henry (US) and Victor (Canada); others did not. For example, the male principal who replaced Brianna at T. P. Yaeger Middle School started by mirroring her behaviors. However, he quickly learned that he needed to pay more attention to students' test scores than the quality of their instruction. Consequently, he began to force reforms "down the throats" of Yaeger's literacy teachers (Craig, 2013). This led me to publish articles about teachers' high stakes accountability experiences bearing titles like "Butterfly under a pin" (Craig, 2012), "Learning to teach in the 'eye of a storm'" (Craig, 2013) and most recently "Data as [G]od" (Craig, 2020). Concurrently, experienced and beginning teacher attrition was on the rise in Houston. By 2014, 80% of the largest urban school district's teachers had five years or less of experience and 50% of its principals had five years or less of experience. Consequently, when I was chosen to do the formative and summative evaluation of the Writers in the Schools (WITS) project with Chestin, I knew that the experience level of local teachers and principals was dangerously thin in some schools and school districts. I also knew that how principals aligned themselves (or not) with the *writing reform project would be key to its impact on teachers and, in turn, students. Given these challenging circumstances, it was fortuitous that I was given the opportunity to work with Principal Michael Curl, a school leader who championed the WITS project like Victor would have done in Canada and Brianna and Henry also would have done "during the halcyon days of school reform" in Houston (Craig, Curtis, Kelley, Martindell, & Perez, 2020)...*

INTRODUCTION

Michael Curl: You can't improve test scores simply by practicing for the test. It does not work that way. Teaching and learning need to improve. The teachers at Suburban East Middle School wanted to become involved in Writers in the Schools (WITS). When teachers are behind something, I listen. As a principal, I know they really need to be engaged for change to happen with students in their classrooms. I invest time and funds in projects that advance quality teaching and learning. WITS fit what we were trying to achieve.

When Michael Curl (first author) opened our Zoom discussion with this statement, Cheryl Craig (second author) was relieved to know that she would not need to dance around the master narrative that practice testing massively improves student learning. As Principal Curl made clear in his opening remark, he and the teachers at Suburban East Middle School recognized that the practice testing approach does not work, although it is a convenient cover story (Clandinin & Connelly, 1995; Olson & Craig, 2005) that most around them frequently tell.

Michael Curl and the Suburban East faculty, it seems, had chosen a less traveled path. The approach they were taking, they claimed, was "the right thing to do by students." This sounded uncannily like what the Eagle High School faculty and principal, Henry Richards, had told Cheryl Craig two decades earlier.

In this chapter, we (Michael Curl and Cheryl Craig) detail how the WITS Project unfurled at Suburban East Middle School, what the principal and teachers liked best about it, how the teens on campus responded, where Michael Curl and Suburban East's teachers and students would like to go from here, and the influence that the program has had on students' high-stakes accountability test scores – with WITS being Suburban East's only literacy "intervention," as the school district would define it.

Before we share this chapter's literature review and explain our research method, we introduce Michel Curl's story before the story in order to learn about his background and the career trajectory that brought him to Suburban East Middle School and ultimately to participation in the WITS program.

THE STORY BEFORE THE STORY (MICHAEL CURL, AUTHOR 1)

Fresh off the stage at George Washington Carver University with a Bachelor of Arts degree in Criminal Justice, I would have never thought that being a secondary school principal would be in my future. As I was searching for a Master's program in Criminal Justice, Chestin, my soon-to-be spouse, shared how she was going to teach while she looked for a law school program. She had discovered the Alternative Certification Program (ACP) and found that after being accepted into the program, one was able to serve as the teacher of record in a public school. This meant full benefits and a salary that was more than the starting pay I would receive for any local law enforcement position. With her knowledge and her record of never steering me astray in our years together, I applied, was accepted, and walked into the local high school – the campus I had graduated from as a student – just four years prior.

As I think back on my interview, I find it almost comical that I was able to secure a teaching position. I had no knowledge of pedagogy, curriculum, or instruction. I knew nothing about the state assessment approach of the day or anything else having to do with teaching and learning other than referencing my personal experience. I spent the interview time talking about being involved in extracurricular activities in high school and my academics and leadership experience from college. You see, although I had been accepted into the Alternative Certification Program, my classes did not start until several weeks after my school classes officially began at the high school campus. With the help of an outstanding master teacher, a woman who started teaching after retiring from a full career at the Social Security Administration, I was able to metaphorically "build the plane while flying it" and find success in teaching high school. I taught several subjects as the new person on faculty who received all of the "stray" classes that the veterans did not want. They earned their single preparation periods and I was able to hone my skills with all grades from freshman to seniors during my time at the campus. I strove to build relationships with my students, to learn as much as I could, from whomever I could, whenever I could. Fresh out of school with fewer responsibilities than I have today, I was able to work late, attend games, and volunteer at events. Part of this was my way of making up for not having the conventional education background held by my peers. I never wanted to feel that I was not doing my part due to not being classically prepared as a teacher. This played a significant shaping role in my work as my career progressed. Attempting to make up for my atypical preparation drove me to participate in more professional development sessions than required. I felt a level of comfort with asking questions not afforded to everyone and a drive to ensure that I was only utilizing the things that worked while setting aside the things that did not work with the students in my care. Working at a Title I school, I found that the practices that showed some gains at other campuses were not effective with our underserved students. I sought out practices and policies that were proven to work with students from all backgrounds. I also sought sound knowledge among my peers as we discussed and collaborated on the needs and goals of the campus. I had a significant background in criminal justice (which helped with classroom discipline), but was flying by the seat of my pants when it came to education, pedagogy, and teaching.

My skills improved and I was afforded opportunities to participate in various decision making committees and leadership opportunities during my years at the campus. The more I learned about how traditional decisions were made, the more

I realized that these decisions had not consistently yielded anticipated results for the students before me. I found that I was very interested in new positions or initiatives that were presented. I believe this was tied to my not having the "we've done this before" appreciation for past initiatives and the fact that I did not have a long history of teaching that would lead me to be pessimistic about possibilities based on my experience. It was also important to me to have solutions that worked for these kids (low income, minority, and full of often unseen potential) because these students not only looked like me, they also grew up in the same area as I did, and attended the same feeder pattern schools. They faced the same low expectations from the system and the lack of human and financial investment in their schools. These students walked the same neighborhoods where they could travel blocks without seeing someone with a college degree much less the doctors, lawyers and professionals that others could see as living examples of what was academically, socially and economically possible. They navigated the same narrative of "Where are all of the young adults?" You see, most families starting out did not choose these areas to plant roots so much of our view entailed our peers or older people. Again, it was important for me to find solutions that worked for these underserved students who were flying beneath education's radar. I knew for a fact that they were not only capable of being college ready but were capable of graduating from college, attending graduate school, thriving in the workforce just as my peers and I were doing.

As time went by, we were afforded positions on campus that were collectively known as the Teacher Leadership Corp. These positions were teaching units that had periods during the day reserved for training, data analysis, and peer collaboration. These leadership training sessions provided by the curriculum department varied from the leadership classes I would attend later when I was pursuing a midmanagement certification. These sessions focused on letting the student data lead the conversations opposed to the opinions of the adults being the driving factor. I learned early about disaggregating data, running reports, and collaborating with peers as a fellow teacher providing instruction in the same subject area. This was different from the role of the assistant principal who supervised a content area and brought down pages of data from the latest assessment for us to review. The assistant principal may have or may not have a background teaching in the subject they supervised. Having never taught science, the data and implications meant something different than they did to a veteran science teacher. As a teacher of that content, several factors immediately would come to mind when looking at data: The wording of the question, where we were chronologically in the curriculum, and the knowledge of the actual lesson in which the content was covered, and so forth. These additional layers of thinking play a significant role when analyzing the results. As teachers of the content, we would put into action the concepts we agreed on together and would be mutually accountable for the success or failure of the students in our care. I would be there with the team as the results came in and I would be there for the conversations that occurred afterward.

In my next role as department chair, I learned a new skill set as the liaison between the teachers in the department and the administration. When things needed to be communicated to the department from "above our pay-grade," I was called down to a meeting with other department chairs and provided information that would need to be relayed to our teams at our next department meeting. *I quickly found that repeating it verbatim was not going to be the most efficient way of communicating what were, at times, unpopular messages. I took to practicing the presentation, keeping my teacher hat on, and adding to/adjusting the message to ensure that it would be the most agreeable way of relaying the information when possible. As the first line of defense for the teachers in the department, I often found that confidence and candor were my allies (Auzenne-Curl, personal communication, 2012). As a vehicle of communication transporting information from campus leadership, I found the same applied. Hearing from multiple angles benefited me greatly as I progressed in my leadership journey. I took the skills obtained from gathering, processing and relaying information from students, teachers, and administrators into all the work I engaged in from then on.*

Having shared our background experiences that brought us to Writers in the School (WITS) and the writing of this chapter, we now provide an overview of the literature and the research method we use to make sense of the influence of WITS on the teachers and students at Suburban East Middle School and the perspectives we took away from it as principal (Michael Curl) and researcher (Cheryl Craig). We begin with a discussion of the primacy of teaching and learning in schools (which backs up Michael Curl's assertions), the importance of experience, and the critically important role that narrative plays in excavating teachers' and principals' knowledge from their lived stories of experience.

OVERVIEW OF THE LITERATURE

The Primacy of Teaching and Learning

"Teachers matter..." asserted OECD, the Organization for Economic Cooperation and Development, more than a decade and a half ago based on a 25-country mathematics study (OECD, 2005). "Teachers matter" trumpeted a second OECD report advocating for the stature of teachers (Schleicher, 2018) "Teaching quality matters most," chimed in Dan Goldhaber (2016) in his salute to the *Coleman Report*, the ground-breaking American policy document that came in the heels of the Brown versus Board of Education court ruling. The quality of a nation's education can never catapult "the quality of its teachers," underscored Barber and Mourshed (2007, p. 13). To cut to the quick, the teachers we put in front of students have a great deal to do with how life comes to them (Dewey, 2020) because teachers are the only people who spend the better part of the day with students (Schwab, 1983). Thus, parents, policymakers, and community members-at-large have no direct way of influencing what students are taught in classrooms except through teachers whose preeminent roles need to be acknowledged.

Experience

As prefigured, teachers are important because they bring education and life to students through the experiences they bring to them. To Dewey, each new experience grows out of the experience that came before (Dewey, 1938). Also, ongoing streams of experience develop one's capacity for future streams of experience. In the WITS project, writing is the experience on which focus is placed. It goes without saying that writing experiences can shape how students live, how they learn, and how they become literate human beings. Dewey also believed that teachers' experiences sharpen their mindedness and fuel their agency. With teachers and writers teaching and learning alongside one another, there is a compounded experiential impact on students. This is because they are moving in tandem to support students' learning. These educators (teachers and writers), "moved by their own intelligences and ideas" (Dewey, 1908/1981, p. 16), create robust synergies not only for themselves but also for their students through the modeling and teaching of writing that organically occurs.

Narratives of Experience

Teachers, writers, and students' experiences are unavoidably connected to narrative because experience can only be captured through storytelling and represented in narrative form. When we "follow... where story leads" (Craig, 2002), we unravel storied experiences pivotally important to teachers, writers, and students, which in turn affect their subsequent thinking and actions. Boiled to the essence, the sharing of "evocative stories of experience...allows [those participating] to reflect on what could be different because of what [they] learned" (Wall, 2006, p. 148). These narratives of experience indicate that they, as human beings, are homo narrans (Baboulene, Golding, Moenandar, & Van Renssen, 2019). As storytelling human beings, they "weave coherence, meaning, and beauty in the spaces between themselves and their social worlds..." (Penwarden, 2019, p. 249). They show how they have "all [they] need to come through..." (Lamott, 2018, p. 179).

Personal Practical Knowledge

Conveyed in teachers' and principals' storied experiences – within their narratives – is their practical knowledge of how things work and why. Hence, personal practical knowing changes as more experiences are interpreted in cumulative ways. Boiled to the essence, personal practical knowledge is

> in a person's experience, in the person's present mind and body and in the person's future plans and actions. It is knowledge that reflects the individual's prior knowledge and acknowledges the contextual nature of the teacher's knowledge. It is a kind of knowledge, carved out of, and shaped by, situations; knowledge that is constructed and reconstructed as we live out our stories and retell and relive them through the process of reflection. (Clandinin & Connelly, 1994, p. 125)

What teachers know and do, as well as who they are, reflects their personal practical knowledge in action. The same goes for principals. What Michel Curl knows and does, in addition to being markers of his identity, stems from his personal practical knowledge surfacing in context.

NARRATIVE INQUIRY

Description

Narrative inquiry is a research method that uses story to study storied experience. In narrative inquiry, both method and form are narrative (Clandinin & Connelly, 2000; Connelly & Clandinin, 1990). Hence, narrative inquiry research is known for its smooth flowing prose that seeks to communicate with its reading audience. It does not use language that excludes. Narrative inquiry aids decision-making instead of making generalizable knowledge claims, although some sense of transferability from one classroom or school to another classroom or school exists.

Interpretative Tools

Narrative inquiry employs three interpretive tools: broadening, burrowing, and storying and restorying. This chapter begins with broadening. In our two "story before the story" sections, the broader landscape of education is introduced as well as to how we as authors have been positioned and as well as our key interactions. Burrowing, on the other hand, is what we do when we capture elements of the WITS reform at Suburban East Middle School. We pay attention to particular experiences and transactions and their subsequent learning outcomes. Finally, storying and restorying is the way we show change. Shifts can involve teachers, students, writers, and ourselves. Storying and restorying shows these changes and actions that might not be otherwise known.

Research Backdrop

Suburban East Middle School is located in a community adjacent to the City of Houston. It had not yet been annexed during Cheryl Craig's Annenberg Challenge school reform days, but it is presently part of the US's fourth (soon to be third) largest metroplex. Suburban East has approximately 1,100 students in grades 6–8. The campus's demographic breakdown is 15% African American, 20% white, and 65% Hispanic. Seventy-three percent of its students are categorized as economically disadvantaged and 56% of its population meet the state criteria for being labeled as "at-risk" students. Furthermore, 11% receive special services under Section 504 (Section 504 requires that school districts provide a free appropriate public education to qualified students in their jurisdictions who have a physical or mental impairment that substantially limits one or more major life activities (Protecting Students with Disabilities, 2020)); 13% qualify as English language learners. Suburban East is assigned to a comparison group of schools in Texas that are similar to it. The similarities include grade levels served, size of campus, percentage of economically disadvantaged learners, students' mobility rates, the percentage of English language learners, and the percentage of students served by special education (2017 TEA Accountability Manual Appendix H – Campus Comparison Groups). In Suburban East's case, this included many Title I schools (Title I (2018) schools have large concentrations of low-income students that receive supplemental funds to assist in meeting their students' educational goals), though technically the campus is not labeled a Title I school. Thus, Suburban East Middle School has faced many of the challenges of a Title I campus but has had none of the additional resources typically available to campuses with that designation, which could be drawn on to address the middle school's challenges. Suburban East's faculty knew early on that it would be up to them as teachers and administrators to bridge the gaps for students. The fact that it is one of the non–Title I schools in its school districts led many to believe that its campus challenges were fewer and its affluence was really higher than it was. Suburban East's faculty saw a changing demographic year after year and heard of other campuses utilizing Title I funding for additional staff, programs, and interventions. Knowing that our solution for improving the academic achievement of our students was going to be in our hands utilizing the resources at our disposal, we needed to ensure the professionals in each classroom – that is, Suburban East's teachers – would play pivotal, contributing roles in the endeavor. After a few months together, Michael Curl (Author 1) and the school's established staff began conversations about how to leverage the success of students at Suburban East Middle School. Discussion of the WITS program soon moved from the edge of possibility to the center of action in the faculty conversations that took place.

THE STORY OF THE COLLABORATION WITH WITS

As a teacher, department chair, assistant principal, and building principal from 2003 to the present, my (Michael Curl's) experience with leadership in public education has evolved from a "books, butts, and busses" perspective to one of instructional leadership. The No Child Left Behind Act (2002) and new parameters surrounding high-stakes state testing caused a shift from school administration as campus management to school administrators as instructional leadership. It was no longer the most efficient use of human capital to not have the leaders fluent in the language of instruction and academic achievement. Leaders who sought to promote would do well to learn the language of curriculum and instruction as a basis for decision-making. I used this knowledge to grow myself in the area of instructional leadership by paying close attention to those around me who were excelling in the curriculum, instructions, and instructional coaching arenas. Personally I focused on becoming the most instructionally savvy assistant principal on our campus. Auzenne-Curl (2016) consistently reminded me that the title of Principal originated from the concept of the leader of the school was the principal teacher of the campus. This always stuck with me as I led and did my best to enact policies and conduct actions that were in the best interest of students and teachers. I am a firm believer that the better we take care of our teachers, the better they will take care of students. This philosophy is built up from the writing and research of Craig (1995), Freiberg (2005), Auzenne-Curl (2016), DuFour (2015), and Muhammad (2009). The teacher in the classroom has the most impact on the academic achievement of students on a campus. Second, research has shown that an effective principal has a positive effect on student achievement (Haller, Hunt, Pacha, & Fazekas, 2016; Sutcher, Podolsky, Kini, & Shields, 2017; Wieczorek, 2017).

The decision to move from classroom teacher to administrator was based on preparation meeting opportunity after having served as a team leader, a department chair, and a member of the teacher leader corps. I had recently completed my principal certification, we had a new baby girl in the house, and I was driving 45 miles to work each day. When an assistant principal position opened at the high school in my home's attendance zone, I applied. I was offered the position, accepted, and three days before the contract started, the principal that hired me let me know that he would be taking a promotion in a neighboring district. Talk about baptism by fire.

My work that first summer was indeed trial by fire as we had a new building principal. The other ninth grade assistant principal and I were new and a consultant had been hired to start us on the journey of becoming a Professional Learning Community (PLC) based on a model written about by Richard Dufour and Robert Eaker (1998). This text along with *Good to Great* by Jim Collins (2001), *The Fred Factor* by Mark Sanborn (2005), and books by Jeff Gordon (2007) had significant influence on my work as an assistant principal. I was tasked with managing discipline for a grade level and supervising a content area in which I did not have prior experience. I learned early on that my experience as a student that attended and taught at a Title I high school provided me with many skills that I do not think one can pick up from coursework or seminars. Relationship building is much easier when you have lived with building relationships with those who are seen as more difficult to connect with. Combining the skills with I grew up, the skills I learned in college, and the skills I learned professionally put me on a path that led to achieving success as an administrator. We were fortunate enough to rotate with the students as they matriculated through high school. Students I started working with in the ninth grade were able to shake my hand at their graduation four years later. Watching them grow, learning their families, and helping them to navigate high school provided another layer of skills that assisted me on my professional journey.

I was fortunate enough to start as a building principal in January of an academic school year. This allowed me most of a semester to learn about the school and its culture. I was able to meet with student leaders, teacher leaders, parents, and paraprofessionals during those first few months. The knowledge gained and trust built was exceptional. This enabled us to learn from each other, ask questions, and discuss plans for moving the campus forward as we prepared for the following school year. After spending time building a foundation of trust and transparency, of confidence and candor, we were able to have honest discussions about what we could achieve as a campus and how we could get there. After months working through the district-designed systems for instruction, we learned that this did not work well for all of our students. Some were not achieving at the same levels as their peers, though they were attending the same classes, receiving the same instruction, and interacting with the same teachers. We decided that we needed to move to a "by student by standard" way of looking at our kids. We would provide academic intervention during the school day while frequently assessing and adjusting our practices.

As we analyzed our data, we noted that reading and writing were in need of campus level improvement. After hearing of the WITS program being employed in a neighboring district, we decided to reach out and set up a partnership. Our experience with the WITS program was directly linked to our campus philosophy of operating as a professional learning community. We believed that the most impactful person in terms of student achievement was – once again – the teacher in the classroom. After all, the teacher is the only one who works with students for the better part of the day (Schwab, 1983). With this in mind, we allowed for time during the school day for these experts to collaborate with our teachers on what was best for the students in their care. We knew that a solid reading and writing program would benefit all content areas. As the saying goes: "The high tide raises all ships." Better readers make better writers and better writers make better readers. If as a campus we can improve reading and writing across the campus, all content areas will benefit. As a learning organization, we navigated away from the kill and drill test prep strategies of other schools. We built a community of trust that allowed for the common understanding that if we focus on teaching and learning, the state test results would take care of themselves (Clandinin & Connelly, 1992). This is not to say that we did not do some test preparation during a small window of time before the assessment. But we did not allow the results of the state assessment to be the primary driver of our instructional program. We lived in the space of learning, engagement, and application.

Our WITS coach had a dynamic personality with all of the writing skills we were looking for. His ability to engage middle school students who were different from him was a sight to behold. Alex connected with the youth at Suburban East in a way that put the classroom teacher at ease and left them optimistic about the skills the students would learn from him. They had real conversations, fluid interactions, and discussed writing as a tool for life, not merely something to practice for the state assessment. The students looked forward to the visits and Alex exhibited an energy that made them feel that he looked forward to working with them as well. The teachers of the writing courses were pleased with their work with WITS as well. They enjoyed discussing and collaborating about writing as a tool and not in the space of something else to be tested. Alex and the staff were able to discuss writing as the teachers wanted it to be and not how traditional systems had regimented it to be. The state described writing in a way no true writer would define it. The curriculum facilitated the teaching of writing in a way that was not agreeable to people who actually wrote for a living. Our teaching staff and Alex were able to build a bridge between real-world writing and skills students would need to be successful at school. This made everyone – from students, to staff, to WITS, to the principal – ecstatic about the opportunities that lay ahead.

The results of our partnership is a significant part of why our campus was able to achieve academic recognition from the state for multiple years in a row. In fact, our campus was the only middle school campus in our district to receive academic distinctions from the state. We went from zero, to one, to three academic distinctions from the Texas Education Agency (TEA). One of these distinctions was for closing achievement gaps on our campus between students grouped demographically. We performed in the top 25% of schools in our category in college readiness, closing achievement gaps, and academic achievement. The percentage of African American and Hispanic students scoring in the highest category doubled for each group (TEA, 2019). Given the opportunity to engage in authentic writing with a writing professional who wrote for a living, our students – across the board – were able to increase their abilities to perform at the highest levels of our state assessment, while not having been specifically prepared for "writing for the test." Given the opportunity to tell their stories, receive feedback on their stories, and make adjustments to make the narratives more clear, their abilities to communicate through writing improved significantly. Our campus received the most academic distinctions from the state of any secondary school in our district during this time frame. We shared our experience with WITS and with anyone who would listen. We found it interesting that few in our own district would ask questions regarding our academic achievements. Asking questions of successful campuses was one of the things I credit when discussing our ability to show improvement year after year (Table 1). When we were asked to discuss how we were able to achieve the results we were producing, WITS was always a part of that conversation. I have had the opportunity to present at state level conferences about our work and have a slide dedicated to the work that WITS did with our students and staff.

In addition to our campus's overall improvement, the writing scores for our African American student group increased significantly. The percentage of students performing at or above grade level increased from 22% to 38%. In reading, the percentage of African American students performing at or above grade level increased from 29% to 38%. Our African American percentage at the highest level "Masters" went from 5% to 10%, and for our Hispanic students, it increased from 8% to 16%.

Deciding to pay relentless attention to literacy as the Suburban East faculty clearly had done contributed to the significant increase in students' academic performances, especially where the scores of underserved students of color were concerned. A further boon was teachers' co-planning and co-teaching with our campus's assigned WITS writer, which would seed future years of student achievement.

Table 1. Suburban East Middle School's 2017–2019 Literacy Scores in the Texas Academic Performance Report (TAPR) Released by the Texas Education Agency.

Assessments 7th AA Students	2017–2018	2018–2019
State writing assessment At or above grade level	22%	38%
State reading assessment At or above grade level	29%	38%

REFLECTIONS

Principal Michael Curl (first author) – *What Cheryl Craig shared in her story before the story showed her awakeness to the Greater Houston school reform landscape and how difficult it is for principals to initiate changes on their campuses while conforming to school district edicts. This is further complicated by student test scores as she indicated. If high stakes accountability scores falter, more district interventions happen. Hearing about principals who previously ran against the grain was both heartening and frightening. Like me, they were highly committed to their teachers and students. However, also like me, they operate within systems and are not invincible. I need to remind myself of that and move cautiously, keeping more of what we are doing at Suburban East as a secret story. When voluntarily sharing the processes and rationale for our actions that led to success, my story often fell upon deaf ears. It would be met with statements like "we can't do that, we don't have the staff for that, my teachers won't, our kids won't, and so on." There were a few principals who were collaborative and we would often talk about what was working and what was not working. We would talk about why we were not talking about these things at the district level or at principal meetings. We realized that what we were doing flew in the face of what schools had been doing for years and was not in line with what our district leaders had experienced. It is often difficult for people to accept that others are finding success in an arena where they have experience, but no success that rises to the level of recognition by outside entities. Working at a school that utilized a program like WITS to disprove stereotypical beliefs about children of color and those who come from economically challenging situations caused a level of cognitive dissonance that was challenging. We were happy to try new things to serve our students' greater good. We knew from our observations of other schools that just hoping for the best was not going to get us the results we were seeking. We believed in rigorously enacting a process that powerfully fuses teacher collaboration, a focus on learning, and a belief that all students can learn – and achieve – at high levels.*

Cheryl J. Craig (second author) – *What stood out in Michael Curl's story before the story and his lived narrative of WITS being enacted on his campus instantiates the development of his personal practical knowledge as an administrator. Principal Curl recognized that practice testing does not work and that it presented the Suburban East Middle School teachers with a challenge to which <u>all</u> would need to seek a solution and to which <u>all</u> would need to contribute. The fact that the middle school may have acquired a story of being an underdog campus in the school district – one flying beneath the radar, so to speak – may have helped to convince the Suburban East teachers to rally around Michael Curl. Another dominant theme is Michael's keen ability to live a counter story (counternarrative) in the face of the dominant narrative of his school district and what is typically believed about his school's "population" – students whom he describes as being underserved, mostly Black and Brown, with a significant number speaking English as a Second Language. Such students remind Michael Curl of himself as a student of color, a student who also was personally filled with abilities, dreams and a desire to contribute. Michael Curl finds it relatively easy living this counternarrative. After all, it reflects his life and is consistent with his own knowing. The story he lives* as the principal of Suburban East Middle School is an outgrowth of the personal practical knowledge he has developed over time and the image of the principalship that he feels best serves Suburban East's students and teachers. Effectively being a Title I campus without the resources that come with it becomes just another challenge in the overall scenario. It is a complex cover story with which Suburban East Middle School is forced to wrestle.

The faculty at Suburban East Middle School was able to buy into the WITS project and latch onto its change story because it had curricular applicability and inspired both teachers and students. Also, Suburban East was in need of a new chapter in its school story and WITS fit with the direction where Suburban East Middle School wanted to head. There was a synergy there – and Principal Michael Curl had the acumen to capitalize on it.

CONCLUSION

Principal Michael Curl, the Suburban East Middle School teachers, and the campus's students all live stories nested individually and collectively in larger narratives of school districts that connect to the state, the nation, and ultimately to international comparison tests that reflect the current global neoliberal agenda. In the midst of this sits the WITS program which genuinely seeks to help students become better writers and assists teachers in improving their teaching of writing. As long as student test scores are on the rise, support for WITS will become strengthened and hopefully amplified as positive news about the WITS program travels from school to school both inside and outside the school district. This explains why a proposal to continue to fund the program at Suburban East Middle School has been approved. The fruit WITS bore was officially deemed worthy of continuation.

However, this does not mean that Michael Curl as Principal or WITS as an exemplary writing program are off the hook due to the overwhelmingly successful partnership we have described in this chapter. Both remain subject to the foibles of the school district, state, and nation and the peripatetic fate of those who rely on test scores as the sole means to capture student growth in terms other than those teaching them and how they ideally would capture them themselves.

Finally, Michael Curl's against-the-grain teacher preparation may have helped him sow the WITS program seed on his campus for the benefit of the teachers and students interacting there. For his entire career, he has been comfortable with out-of-the-ordinary programming. WITS, for its part, created a synergy and an energy to which everyone was attracted like a magnet. These combinatorial factors fused together to significantly impact teaching and learning at Suburban East Middle School. Whether the school district or other school districts and schools choose WITS as a promising practice in their contexts remains to be seen. This strong exemplar is not only a testimony to the success of the WITS program, but also it forms a narrative exemplar of the background thinking and the inquiry and leadership moves that brought it to fruition in mostly the principal's voice backed up by others' learning and leading at Suburban East Middle School.

REFERENCES

Auzenne-Curl, C. T. (2016). *Their exits and their entrances: Stories of coming and going from former teacher educators in the field.* Doctoral dissertation. Retrieved from https://hdl.handle.net/10657/4859

Baboulene, D., Golding, A., Moenandar, S.-J., & Van Renssen, F. (2019). You in motion: Stories and metaphors of becoming in narrative learning environments. In M. Hann & A. Kaal (Eds.), *Narrative and metaphor in education: Look both ways* (pp. 32–45). New York, NY: Routledge.

Barber, M., & Mourshed, M. (2007). *How the world's best-performing systems count out on top.* London: McKinsey & Company.

Clandinin, D. J. (1985). Personal practical knowledge: A study of teachers' classroom images. *Curriculum Inquiry, 15*(4), 361.

Clandinin, D. J., & Connelly, F. M. (1992). Teacher as curriculum maker. In P. W. Jackson (Ed.), *Handbook of Research on Curriculum* (pp. 363–401). New York, NY: Macmillan.

Clandinin, D. J., & Connelly, F. M. (1994). Personal experience methods. In N. K. Denzin & Y. S. Lincoln (Eds.), *Handbook of qualitative research* (pp. 413–427). London: Sage.

Clandinin, D. J., & Connelly, F. M. (1995). *Teachers' professional knowledge landscapes.* New York, NY: Teachers College Press.

Clandinin, D. J., & Connelly, F. M. (2000). *Narrative inquiry: Experience and story in qualitative research.* San Francisco, CA: Jossey-Bass.

Collins, J. (2001). *Good to great: Why some companies make the leap…And others don't.* HarperCollins.

Connelly, F. M., & Clandinin, D. J. (1990). Stories of experience and narrative inquiry. *Educational Researcher, 19*(5), 2–14.

Connelly, F. M., & Clandinin, D. J. (Eds.). (1999). *Shaping a professional identity: Stories of educational practice.* New York, NY: Teachers College Press.

Craig, C. J. (1995). Safe places on the professional knowledge landscape: Knowledge communities. In D. J. Clandinin & F. M. Connelly (Eds.), *Teachers' professional knowledge landscapes.* New York, NY: Teachers College Press.

Craig, C. J. (1999). Parallel stories: A way of contextualizing teacher knowledge. *Teaching and Teacher Education, 15*(4), 397–411.

Craig, C. J. (2002). The conduit: A meta-level analysis of lives lived and stories told. *Teachers & Teaching: Theory & Practice, 8*(2), 197–221.

Craig, C. J. (2004). The dragon in school backyards: The influence of mandated testing on school contexts and educators' narrative knowing. *Teachers College Record, 106*(6), 1229–1257.

Craig, C. J. (2012). Butterfly under a pin: An emergent teacher image amid forced curriculum reform. *Journal of Educational Research, 105*(2), 90–101.

Craig, C. J. (2013). Teacher education and the best-loved self. *Asia Pacific Journal of Education, 33*(3), 261–272.

Craig, C. J. (2020). "Data is [G]od": The influence of cumulative policy reforms on teachers' knowledge in an urban middle school in the United States. *Teaching and Teacher Education, 93*, 103027.

Craig, C., Curtis, G., Kelley, M., Martindell, P. T., & Perez, M. M. (2020). *Knowledge communities in teacher education: Sustaining collaborative work.* New York, NY: Palgrave Macmillan.

Dewey, J. (1908/1981). The practical character of reality. In J. McDermott (Ed.), *The philosophy of John Dewey* (pp. 207–222). Chicago, IL: University of Chicago Press.

Dewey, J. (1938). *Experience and education.* New York, NY: Touchstone.

Dewey, J. (2020). *The child & the curriculum.* Coppel, TX: Will Jonson & Dog's Tail Books.

DuFour, R. (2015). *In praise of American educators: And how they can become even better.* Bloomington, IN: Solution Tree Press.

DuFour, R., & Eaker, R. E. (1998). *Professional learning communities at work: Best practices for enhancing student achievement.* Bloomington, IN: Solution Tree.

Freiberg, H. J. (2005). *School climate: Measuring, improving and sustaining healthy learning environments.* Routledge.

Goldhaber, D. (2016). In schools, teacher quality matters most. *Education Next, 16*(2), 56–62.

Gordon, J. (2007). *The energy bus: 10 rules to fuel your life, work, and team with positive energy*. Hoboken, NJ: John Wiley & Sons.

Haller, A., Hunt, E., Pacha, J., & Fazekas, A. (2016). *Lessons for states: The Every Student Succeeds Act (ESSA) increases focus on and investment in supporting principal preparation and development*. Normal, IL: Illinois State University, Center for the Study of Education Policy.

Lamott, A. (2018). *Almost everything: Notes on hope*. New York, NY: Riverhead Books.

Muhammad, A. (2009). *Transforming school culture: How to overcome staff division*. Bloomington, IN: Solution Tree Press.

No Child Left Behind Act of 2001. (2002). P. L. 107-110, 20 U. S. C. § 6319.

OECD. (2005). *Education and training policy teachers matter attracting, developing and retaining effective teachers: Attracting, developing and retaining effective teachers*. Paris: OECD Publishing.

Olson, M. R., & Craig, C. J. (2005). Uncovering cover stories: Tensions and entailments in the development of teacher knowledge. *Curriculum Inquiry*, *35*(2), 161–182.

Penwarden, S. (2019). Weaving threads into a basket: Facilitating counsellor identity creation through metaphors and narratives. In M. Hanne & H. Kaal (Eds.), *Narrative and metaphor in education: Look both ways* (pp. 249–262). New York, NY: Routledge.

Protecting students with disabilities. (2020, January 10). U.S. Department of Education. Retrieved from https://www2.ed.gov/about/offices/list/ocr/504faq.html

Sanborn, M. (2005). *The Fred Factor: How passion in your work and life can turn the ordinary into the extraordinary*. London: Random House.

Schleicher, A. (2018). *Valuing our teachers and raising their status: How communities can help*. Paris: OECD.

Schwab, J. (1983). The practical 4: Something for curriculum professors to do. *Curriculum Inquiry*, *13*(3), 239–265.

Sutcher, L., Podolsky, A., Kini, T., & Shields, P. M. (2017). *Learning to lead: Understanding California's learning system for school and district leaders*. Palo Alto, CA: Learning Policy Institute.

Texas Education Agency (TEA). (2019, December). *2018–19 Texas academic performance report*. Austin, TX: Texas Education Agency.

Title I, Part a Program. (2018, November 7). Retrieved from https://www2.ed.gov/programs/titleiparta/index.html

Wall, S. (2006). An autoethnography on learning about autoethnography. *International Journal of Qualitative Methods*, *5*(2), 146–160. doi:10.1177/160940690600500205

Wieczorek, D. (2017). Principals' perceptions of public schools' professional development changes during NCLB. *Education Policy Analysis Archives*, *25*(8).

NAVIGATING THE ROLE OF TEACHER EDUCATORS IN THE FIELD: THE CASE FOR INCREASED COMMUNITY SUPPORT

Daphne Carr and Chestin T. Auzenne-Curl

ABSTRACT

This chapter provides a look at the experiences of two Teacher Educators in the Field (TEFs) as they work to shift writing instruction in suburban districts across the Houston metroplex. A review of the literature on most promising practices for literacy educators is provided along with narrative interspersion of restoried enactments of TEFs in public education systems serving students in grades 6–12. Our planned and lived experiences were often dissonant due to the complexity of increasingly diverse demographic populations in fast-growing districts who struggled to shift the focus of instruction in correlation to audience. Our stories present focused reflection on the need for additional supports geared toward teacher development, TEF retention, and consistent engagement from campus and district-level administrators.

Keywords: Literacy coaching; writing interventions; secondary writing instruction; teacher educators in the field; preservice teacher; peer coaching

INTRODUCTION

Many suburban areas in the Houston metroplex have become diverse and thriving mini-metropolises due to trending population growth (Klineberg, 2011, 2015, 2021; Rudick, 2012; Thomson, 2011). Over time, these suburban areas have mirrored the larger Houstonian landscape in racial and ethnic composition and socioeconomic diversity. These phenomena contribute to a view of suburban areas as increasingly "urbanized." Our experiential research and empirical observations have found that school systems have faced a sense of cognitive dissonance in serving populations with higher percentages of students from historically marginalized groups (Auzenne-Curl, 2016; Gale, 2020).

Several Houston area suburbs which were predominantly upper middle class and largely representative of Anglo populations have seen an influx of families of color, and families from lower socioeconomic earning brackets in positive correlation to gentrification efforts in historic minority wards, and following several natural disasters which displaced families who were generationally located in urban areas of the metroplex. Interviews with K-12 teachers and administrators reveal that the schools' response to such demographic shifts is often slow or without sustained focus. This leads to tensions and stress among teachers, and eventually, a rise in teacher attrition rates (National Center for Education Statistics, 2012; Simon et al., 2017).

In effort to retain and sustain quality teachers, several of the largest districts in the urban metroplex have developed positions labeled here as Teacher Educators in the Field (TEFs). These positions include titles such as instructional coach, peer facilitator, content specialist, and curriculum coordinators, but the list is not exhaustive. We have both worked in several of these positions. Each time, we were also located on a campus or in a district which was undergoing a demographic shift. The roles that we assumed were, on paper, focused on nonevaluative coaching and collaborative planning, but the lived experiences were often complicated. We had to learn to guide through influence, negotiate relationships with administrators who used evalualuation-based methods of supervision, and act as instructional anchor, and liaison for central office and campus communication.

Chestin's Motivation for Further Study

When I entered doctoral studies, I exited my role as a district curriculum program coordinator for English Language Arts, Reading, and Communication (ELAR) in grades 6–12. I consider this role to be one of TEF because it involved facilitating professional development (PD) and instructional coaching methods for campus-level ELAR TEF. While I served in this capacity, many of my fellow TEFs voiced difficulty in understanding their roles and holding strong to the ideals presented in the job description while meeting the demands of their lived expectations. This dialogic is echoed in much of the current body of literature on classroom teacher identity (Cuenca, Scheichel, Butler, Dinkelman, & Nicholas, 2011; Cutri & Whiting, 2015; Schaefer, 2013). I had seen, heard, and experienced it, and was compelled to write about it. I found myself researching teacher attrition and applying what I found to my concept of TEF. To me, they were still teachers; their students were also teachers. It was clear to me that TEF would be the topic of my dissertation. I had to write what I had been living and bring the subject to light for others who may not have had the opportunity to do so.

I chose narrative inquiry as methodology (Clandinin & Connelly, 2000; Clandinin, 2013) for its privileging of Dewey's (1938) consideration of experiential learning and because it would allow me to work closely with my identified TEF participants. As a participant observer, I not only provided them with a space in which to reconstruct their experiences but also joined them in a mutually educative journey to reflect on possible generalizations and resonant themes. I came into the community with three former TEF who allowed me to share in their journeys from the classroom to various TEF roles and eventually out of the positions due to perceived gaps in support from administration, clear expectations for the role, and adequate opportunities to learn in community with other TEFs for the development and share of knowledge. Through the study, my own experiences were inevitably restoried and validated. The role was in need of more support and additional studies, and the year following my graduation brought me the opportunity to do both through my appointment as a postdoctoral research associate/ fellow. This time the TEFs with whom I shared space were part of an organization that partnered with schools. The Writers in the Schools (WITS) Collaborative, one of many facets of the WITS Houston organization, contracts with schools to place experienced, professional writers in teacher community with classroom writing teachers and to facilitate learning experiences that move from the audience of teachers to the audience of students. Through coaching cycles that honor modeling, conferring, and gradual release of responsibility, the WITS Writers engage teachers and students in authentic writing experiences with prompts that range from photos and manipulatives to current events and formal prompts. I quickly recognized that the WITS Writers were TEFs. As field research leader, I observed and interviewed writers and teachers who affirmed my labeling, and in the field data collected, I heard many of the same tensions voiced from the WITS Writers that I heard from the participants in my study. Their role was further complicated by the fact that they were assigned a campus through interorganizational partnerships and often felt perceived as an outsider upon arrival.

While principals primarily function as building managers, they are also charged with leading and supporting campus instruction. It is often TEFs who provide the support needed to bridge the two. TEFs are often viewed as the instructional specialists in their local context whether or not their placement is on their home campus, from a district appointment or from an outside organization. In their efforts to support the overall well-being and growth of classroom teachers, they have the potential to mediate attrition for classroom teachers who leave due to "burnout" (physical and emotional exhaustion). TEFs are expected to facilitate goal setting and supports with the intention of reducing feeling of a lack of collegiality among peers, lack of administrative support, and others factors that contribute to teacher attrition (Craig, 2013, 2014; Darling-Hammond, 2010, 2014; Schaefer, 2013) by focusing on curriculum, instruction, and interpersonal relationships. While research is clear on the mediating effects of these supports, there is a deficiency in the current body of research on how to mediate attritions among TEFs. However, my dissertation participants, as well as recent conversations with WITS representatives, district- and campus-level TEF, and other personnel representatives indicate that it is becoming more difficult to retain individuals in these positions. More and more frequently, wide-scale budget constraints, the pressures of accountability measures, and leadership changes in the local bureaucratic structure of education organizations and school districts (Darling-Hammond, 2010, 2014), and the position of TEF have become an often contested complexity. With aforementioned research that aligns the work of TEF to test practices in teacher retention, I assert that the question should not be "Are these positions worth fighting for?" but "How can we best support the effective enactment of the role?".

The Case for Writing-focused TEF

According to the last publication of *The Nation's Report Card in Writing*, less than a quarter of all students tested in both the 8th grade and the 12th grade demonstrated proficiency in writing (National Center for Education Statistics, 2012). The same year *The Nation's Report Card in Writing* raised concerns about effective writing instruction at the national level, and composition results from the State of Texas Assessment of Academic Readiness (STAAR) caused similar consternation in Texas. More than 150,000 high school freshmen in Texas failed to make satisfactory progress on the new state assessment in writing during its first administration in 2012 (State of Texas Assessment of Academic Readiness: Statewide Summary Report in English I, 2012). Among the 180, 870 testers who did meet standard, only 26% wrote accomplished or highly accomplished expository essays (Statewide Summary Report in English I Writing, 2012). In 2019, the number of students writing accomplished or highly accomplished essays was 10% points lower, with only 56% of first-time testers passing the composition portion of the exam with "satisfactory" or "approaching satisfactory" scores (State of Texas Assessment of Academic Readiness: Statewide Summary Report in English I. Report in English I, 2019). Texas students also performed lower than the national average on the Advanced Placement English Language and Composition exam in 2019. Approximately, 42.3% of test takers in Texas scored 3–5 on the exam, in comparison to 54% of students in the United States who earned similar scores (AP Examination Results in Texas and the United States, 2019).

These results matter because written communication is essential to the human experience. We use writing to "learn new ideas, persuade others, record information, create imaginary worlds, express feelings, entertain others, heal psychological wounds, chronicle experiences, and explore the meaning of events and situations" (Graham, 2019, p. 279). When students lack basic competence in writing, they are essentially limited in their ability to explore and express their own humanity.

Daphne's Motivation for Further Study

In my first iteration as a TEF, I was called an instructional coach. The year was 2009, and I prepared for the job interview by reading Jim Knight's seminal work, *Instructional Coaching: A Partnership Approach to Improving Instruction*. I remember showing up to the interview feeling slightly nervous, yet eager to discuss curriculum, instruction, and coaching partnerships with the administrator conducting the interview. About halfway into the meeting, my mood shifted when I realized the interviewer's vision for the position was not the same as mine. In her estimation, "instructional coach" was the latest name for department chairs who also observed classes occasionally or mentored new teachers. Since she considered the difference between a chair and a coach to be nominal, she wanted to hire a strong leader who could set the tone for an English department at a new high school. She knew of my work as a team leader in a previous school district and believed I would be a good fit for the position. Opportunities for advancement did not come often to women of color in the district, so I downplayed my disappointment with her description of the role and accepted the offer.

I made the first (and last) attempt at renegotiating my job duties a few months later. During a weekly meeting with the principal, I shared the first draft of a coaching plan I had created with the help of a literacy coaching handbook. The plan included a list of support services I could provide to classroom teachers and a description of how they could initiate a coaching partnership with me for assistance. I thought the plan might expand the principal's perception of my role or lead to deeper conversations about building instructional capacity in teachers. To my chagrin, she flashed a smile that thinly veiled her condescension as she patted my hand and said, "Maybe later. You don't want to take on too much." From that moment on, I became increasingly aware of the tenuousness of my position. Being an instructional coach meant being whatever my direct supervisor wanted me to be – a stateswoman, a figurehead, an enforcer, a hall monitor, a last-minute substitute. There was no consistent job description or evaluation instrument for instructional coaches in the district, so job retention for most coaches depended on the ability to remain on good terms with the building principal.

It took a new principal and abysmal writing scores on the new state assessment two years later to focus district leaders on a specific area for educational reform. Students' writing outcomes on STAAR signaled a need for improvement in writing instruction. If the writing scores did not improve, our campus was one of several in the district that would receive a low accountability rating from the state education agency. In response to this concern and other budgetary issues, district leaders rebranded instructional coaches as "academic lead teachers" and assigned us the task of increasing student achievement through job-embedded PD for teachers. Though the district's expectations for academic lead teachers now reflected commonly held beliefs about instructional coaching, there was still no overarching plan for connecting staff development to student achievement on individual campuses – especially in terms of writing instruction.

For the next 3 years, I navigated uncharted waters as a lead teacher, grappling with questions about content, process, and efficacy as I tried to design adult learning experiences that would help English instructors become better writing teachers. These questions shaped my inquiries as a doctoral student in curriculum and instruction while I continued to work as a TEF. When I learned something new, I incorporated the findings into action research projects and PD sessions with teachers. Even after I graduated, I continued to read practitioner-oriented texts about teaching writing, in addition to attending writing workshops at regional service centers and conferences. Essentially, the answers to these questions became my life's work as a scholar-practitioner in secondary English language arts. These are the concerns and lived experiences I bring to the present study of writing-focused TEF, along with a firm belief in this role's potential to raise student achievement and liberate learners through the promotion of equity in writing instruction.

A REVIEW OF THE LITERATURE SUPPORTING MOST PROMISING PRACTICES

Content

As a TEF tasked with improving writing instruction in the English department, I first wanted to determine what researchers were saying about best practices in writing instruction. I was a first-year doctoral student at the time, and my thinking was heavily influenced by professors who emphasized consulting experimental studies for academic interventions. I knew strategies that had worked for me in previous years, but thankfully, I did not have enough confidence in them to assume that they would work for every ninth and tenth grade student on campus. The urgency of the need kept me humble. I did not want to steer my colleagues wrong because I was too proud to admit that I did not know the best ways to teach writing. (Daphne)

Researchers agree that understanding how writing develops is essential to delivering effective writing instruction (Graham, MacArthur, & Fitzgerald, 2013; Graham & Perin, 2007; Kaplan, 2008). By growing in their understanding of composition theory and practice, teachers increase their ability to make informed decisions in the classroom that can make a positive difference in the growth of student writers. In 2004, the National Council of Teachers of English published a position statement on writing instruction expressing what the organization believed teachers needed to understand about writing in order to help students. Some of these key understandings include: how to confer with and assess student writers; how to cultivate a sense of community and personal safety in the writing classroom; multiple strategies for approaching the writing process and the typical problems writers face; appropriate conventions for academic English; text structures and reader expectations for various genres of writing; the relationship between conventions and rhetorical effect; ways to analyze qualitative or quantitative writing assessments and provide appropriate feedback; and how to use student writing portfolios for self-assessment and reflection (National Council of Teachers of English, 2004).

Graham and Perin's (2007) meta-analysis of empirical research related to writing instruction ranked 11 elements of effective adolescent writing instruction based upon their effect sizes. Although these elements were not intended to constitute an entire writing curriculum, the authors concluded that effective classroom instruction for students in grades 4–12 should include various combinations of these elements to meet the diverse needs of student learners: writing strategies, summarization, collaborative writing, specific product goals, word processing, sentence combining, prewriting, inquiry activities, process writing approach, study of models, and writing for content learning (Graham & Perin, 2007).

Process

Once I had an idea about the content I wanted to share with teachers, I wondered about the most effective way of processing the information with them. I shared the article with teachers during our collaborative meeting time and asked where they would like to begin. We agreed to start with sentence combining, so I located resources to assist them with teaching the concept as part of their daily instructional routine. We practiced combining sentences together as a community of learners, as well as deconstructing passages from assigned readings into simple sentences that students could combine and compare to the originals. The conversations we had about different ways to connect ideas in sentences also allowed me to review grammatical terms and syntactical structures with teachers in a non-threatening way. We progressed through the school year in much the same way – experimenting with various high-yield strategies on the list and discussing our results with each other, hoping we would find the right combination of strategies to improve students' essay scores. (Daphne)

According to Croft, Coggshall, Dolan, Powers, and Killion (2010), job-embedded PD is a term used to describe teacher learning that occurs within the daily environment of a professional educator. Its purpose is to enhance a teacher's instructional delivery or pedagogical content knowledge while also keeping in mind the ultimate goal of increasing student outcomes. The instruction a teacher receives through job-embedded PD is markedly different from the traditional "sit and get" workshop. With this form of adult learning, a teacher assumes the role of an active learner who takes initiative in framing problems, finding solutions, and reflecting on instructional practice. Darling-Hammond and McLaughlin (1995) refer to this type of learning as "knowledge sharing based on real-life situations" (p. 1). It is ongoing, yet deeply rooted in the idea of connecting learning and application into daily instructional practice (Croft et al., 2010). With so many initiatives, standards, and increased accountability, teachers need safe spaces where they can work on "[integrating] theory with classroom practice" by taking time and opportunities to [explore] new learning and how it might be implemented in different domains" (Darling-Hammond & McLaughlin, 1995). This approach to PD can take several forms, such as examining student work, solving problems collaboratively in inquiry teams, analyzing assessment data with grade-level departments, or mentoring a novice educator within a triad or small group (Croft et al., 2010) because groups and associations constantly grow and change within a learning community. In this way, adult learners find themselves evolving and adapting, too, as the demands of the profession expand and change with contemporary society. This idea of school as *community* as opposed to school as a *building* is characterized by shared leadership and mutual accountability.

Reflection and Evaluation

When we did not see noticeable gains the first year, I suspected it was because we did not choose a specific intervention that addressed students' needs during the composing process, especially in timed situations. As I observed teachers in their classrooms, I noticed they were all engaging in process writing activities with students, but these processes varied by teachers and teams. We were integrating best practices into our daily instruction, but our choices needed to align more with the needs we saw present in our students' writing. The process of sharing the content and practicing how to use it during instruction had worked well. Teachers enjoyed being in the position of "the learner" as they referenced their own qualms and misconceptions to plan for challenges that students might have during instruction. They were learning and implementing evidence-based practices, but I could not consider our PD sessions successful since we had not produced the change we wanted to see in students' compositions. Neither could my boss. (Daphne)

My observations coincided with Guskey's (2014) assertion that producing the right results with job-embedded PD requires beginning with the end in mind. Just as educators plan units by first thinking of their standards and the appropriate assessments, adult learning facilitators should plan backward for campus success in the area of adult learning. Well-organized and effective job-embedded learning opportunities must be clearly tied to student achievement and offer opportunities for content-based, collaborative activities to occur on site with sufficient time provided for instructional planning (Guskey, 2003; Penuel, Fishman, Yamaguchi, & Gallagher, 2007). In regards to student writing, a critical first step in this process of backward planning is obtaining a current picture of writing instruction and student learning in classrooms, so that school leaders can evaluate more effectively the impact of PD on student achievement (Earley & Porritt, 2014). Omitting this step makes it difficult for administrators to ascertain positive differences in student and teacher behaviors that can be attributed to the job-embedded PD offered on campus. Furthermore, research studies have shown that teachers are sometimes unable to detect inconsistencies between their stated beliefs about effective pedagogy and actual classroom practice – particularly in high-stakes testing environments (Brindley & Schneider, 2002). This potential contradiction between belief and practice is a major reason why schools should not exclusively rely on self-reported anecdotal evidence or subjective postevent evaluation sheets to determine future PD needs or gauge program effectiveness (Earley & Porritt, 2014).

> After sharing my observations with teachers about our varied approaches to process writing, I consulted research studies for highly effective instructional strategies for composing essays. The most documented intervention strategy by researchers was self-regulated strategy development (SRSD), with an effect size of 0.95 (Graham & Perin, 2007; Graham & Sandmel, 2011; Harris, Graham, & Mason, 2006). This particular strategy entails a study of writing examples in a selected genre, explicit strategy instruction in generating and organizing ideas, and mnemonic devices that assist students with self-monitoring and reflection during the composition process. I introduced the strategy the same way I approached sentence combining because the process seemed to align with recommendations from researchers that stress the effectiveness of engaging teachers in active learning about their content area, preferably in groups, for an extended period of time with ongoing support and feedback as teachers work in the classroom. (Daphne, Journals 2020; McCarthey & Geoghegan, 2016)

Evidence of our success came at the end of the school year when our scores came back from the state assessment. We achieved our goal of increasing our overall passing percentage to 70% or higher by focusing on student writing. It was a tremendous accomplishment for the teachers and the students, but by then, the building principal had already requested that I not return to the campus as the lead teacher for English language arts.

THINKING NARRATIVELY ABOUT THE ROLE

Over the years, we have shared many stories with each other, and in the process, we have become part of our professional stories to live by. We never talk to one another solely in complaint, but as a trusted collaborator in finding a solution. This requires a degree of intentional restorying (cite) and active listening. In effect, we collaborate in "thinking narratively" (Clandinin, 1985; Clandinin & Connelly, 2000) about the experiences shared and about the context in which we share those stories.

Learning from what Connelly and Clandinin (1988) refers to as "personal practical" knowledge – that which teachers accumulate through experience, means that we reflect beyond the image we hold true of the event to its broader and contextualized place on the educational landscape. Finding that place means that we analyze those events in a 3-dimensional space of inquiry (Clandinin & Connelly, 2000) defined as "commonplaces":

- Interaction: The context of our experience as influenced by our conceptualization of the milieu (Schwab, 1973) which exist in all social conditions.
- Situation: "The physical, and topological boundaries of place or sequences of places where the inquiry and events take place" (Clandinin, 2007, p. 41).
- Continuity: The time of the story. Since our lives are entirely storied experiences (Dewey, 1938), the framing of temporality is the positionality of the narrative in the timeline of our lives.

In addition to these commonplaces of experience, "the person, in context, is of prime interest" (Clandinin & Connelly, 2000, p. 32). Therefore, we consider our role in the interpretations and how our lenses shape meaning-making along the way.

DAPHNE AND CHESTIN REFLECT ON TENSIONS FACED

Daphne – TEF Role Identity and Expectations from Supervisory Leadership

Just like students, teachers benefit from having multiple ways and opportunities to learn. In order for this to happen, school districts first must create time, space, structures, and support for teachers to engage in quality job-embedded PD (Croft et al., 2010). Creating time not only refers to the daily schedule of the school, but it also refers to the excessive paperwork and additional "duties as assigned" that can prevent teachers from having the energy or opportunity to learn with others. As the novelty of the professional learning communities (PLC) concept wears thin in school districts that began the journey two decades ago, I see more districts opting to discontinue "late arrival days" or "early release days" that were once protected times for teachers to meet. The typical response is that teachers can meet during their common conference periods within the school day. Yet teachers are also being pulled away to parent conferences, meetings with students' case managers, or meetings with their own appraisers during this time. Having done the work for nearly a decade, I find it especially difficult to condense learning experiences for adults into 30-minute time frames when I once had an hour or 90 minutes in the morning with no students on campus. I worked in one district where leaders abruptly ended late arrival meetings because students were getting into mischief in the community while teachers met in the mornings. Leaders decided it was better to require teachers to stay two hours after school for one day each week. Any PD facilitator who stands before teachers who have been placed in that position becomes the enemy by default. Teachers view you as part of the system – a system that disregards their feelings and their personal time with friends and family.

Administrators could work cooperatively with TEF to establish a culture of shared learning by delegating roles and responsibilities to various teachers in the learning community and sitting with teachers occasionally during learning opportunities. Doing so helps teachers see their school leaders as learners who are humble and approachable, especially when the leader creates opportunities for teacher leaders to share what they know about best practices with other teachers and administrators (Croft et al., 2010). There have been far too many times when I have facilitated sessions with English teachers while the administrator attends another meeting or stays in the room the entire time while typing on a laptop. Those were typically administrators who did not converse with me beforehand about the goals of the session or how the content related to the campus goals for the year. Teachers felt more relieved when these administrators left (or did not come at all) because to them, the leader's absence or multitasking in the meeting communicated disinterest and disrespect. If these principals had only offered teachers incentives or recognition for participating in study groups or leading inquiry groups, it would have gone a long way toward building community and motivating teachers to engage in professional learning.

School leaders who do not confer with TEF about classroom observations or collaborate with them in planning adult learning experiences make it difficult to convince teachers that their growth is valued and important. In the absence of this type of support, I have taken sole responsibility for designing, implementing, and assessing the effectiveness of departmental PD plans, only to be accused later of overstepping my bounds. And, in some cases, I would agree that I did – out of frustration and disappointment for the teachers I served. It is difficult when you are not considered to be a teacher or a principal because supervisors will quickly assign either role to you based on their needs or the extenuating circumstances present at the moment. When circumstances change, so do their expectations. A TEF rarely has the luxury or security of assuming that their past roles indicate an administrator's future expectations.

Chestin – TEF Enactment under Three Lenses: Campus, Central Office, Interorganizational Institutional

With the rise in popularity of Professional Learning Communities in K-12 Education (DuFour & Eaker, 1998; Eaker, Dufour, & DuFour, 2002), the United States has seen an increase in the development of TEF positions. At the time of this chapter, I have worked under several iterations of the role. While the titles were different, the tensions and struggles were very similar. The goal was the same: support teacher in actualizing and learning through their personal practical knowledge. I saw my work as a part of tiered service to students. They were the center of the target because their growth and well-being were the reason all of the adults were there. I had served in several capacities:

- In my content area: My first TEF assignment was Content Area Team Leader for American Literature;
- At the campus level: I served as an Instructional Coach for English Language Arts, as well as a Literacy Integration Specialist in Physics and Chemistry;
- At the district level: I served as Curriculum Program Coordinator for English, Language Arts, Reading and Communications; and
- As an independent consultant/researcher: I worked with various groups from all TEF and Administration groups.

In all capacities, I understood that my place was on an outer ring. The heart of that service was supporting teachers who, I believed, had the strongest impact on a child's learning experience.

Field Observations Regarding the Lived Experiences of Campus-Level TEF

> One thing that I found frustrating....working within my school. On our campus, working with the teachers there, it was more difficult [than with a district wide audience] because I think we saw each other every day. Since I wasn't an evaluator, I didn't do [the formal observation protocol] – but they saw me in the role kind of....I had a kind of quasi-administrative role, you know. I was part of the administrative team....So I think the teachers kind of felt that even though I was not evaluating them…, maybe I would be going back to administration and filling them in on weaknesses.
>
> That wasn't my role as a coach. But I think that there was a trust issue there. (Bernice, individual interview, June 2016)

Chestin met Bernice while pursuing her PhD. The two often share stories about their experience and ELAR TEF. A recurrent theme, as it has been with Chestin and Daphne, is the lack of clear expectations for the role.

> Just as a teacher is, in many instances, a surrogate parent, a counselor, a guide... a TEF is more than an instructional coach. I just have not seen that fully acknowledged by administrators. The job descriptions don't match the daily expectations and too often, someone can identify a strong or a struggling TEF, but have no criteria by which to explain how they recognize that to be true. (Chestin Journals 2020)

Field Observations Regarding the Lived Experiences of District-Level TEF

In revisiting the data collection from Chestin's dissertation, we noted two recurrent tensions at the district level: lack of community and uneasiness with power dynamics.

> One interviewee, Madeline who was a twelve-year educator at the time of the Chestin's dissertation focus group shared the importance that the study provided her through a call to reflect on her departure: This study has helped me realize what an emotionally charged time being a teacher leader was. Just talking about the successes and frustrations brought up emotions, good and bad, in me that I have not felt in the two years I have been out of that role. I was surprised how sad I still am to not be in the role of a teacher leader. I love my new job, and I am much happier on a personal level, but this experience has made me realize that I am missing the connection with teachers and students.
>
> It felt really good [to be a part of the focus group], it was so interesting to see how similar our experiences were even though we were in very different places. I think if I ever do go back to the role of a teacher leader I will search out to find/create a cohort of people to share challenges and successes with.
>
> One of the participants was in a role that was similar to the roles I supervised/lead at the district level. It was very interesting and thought provoking to me to hear her perception and experiences in that role. It also gave me some insight into what to do differently if I ever assume that role again.
>
> I hope that this study brings to light how powerful and challenging the job of a teacher leader is. We need to foster the support of these positions because of the change that they can bring about. I also hope that this study makes people currently in the role of a teacher leader feel less isolated and alone. (Madeline, Interview 2016)

Madeline added that the campus to campus autonomy in TEF enactment was problematic. This is something that Daphne and Chestin both experienced firsthand. It made building a community very difficult across the role. We believe that learning, especially in this role, cannot occur in isolation. So, Madeline's contribution illuminated the intrapersonal struggle of shaping a true identity among TEFs. Across the collected stories, TEF spoke about the immediate sense of community and comfort they felt in sharing with us. Daphne and Chestin believe that while conversation may not have alleviated the noted "problems," coming into the community left each of us feeling empowered. We realized that our struggles were not so unique.

"And we are just a few people who happen to have one person in common, Chestin. Imagine what is left to be said," remarked Madeline.

> I hope that in participating in this study, I can contribute something to the research. I looked and there was none out there when I was beginning the TEF job.

Another participant remarked:

> There was Jim Knight in the beginning, but that was it. Now there's Aguilar, a few others, but I hope that the administrators will listen to the research. Because they do not listen to us.

The research record next led us to a discussion on the power dynamics of relationships between TEFs and campus-level and district-level administrations, who are equipped with the tools to evaluate teachers on a level that can keep them or remove them from their posts. However, these administrators are often not degreed in the area of curriculum and instruction and function as building and system managers rather than instructional support.

> Madeline: It's tough. You are working with these people who are good managers, but they know very little about instruction. It's why they hired you. But they are under pressure and they make decisions without consulting you.
>
> Helena: Yes. You're at a meeting and the decision-makers make decisions about instruction… and those of us with degrees in instruction…Well. [gestures hands up and open palms]

Helena, another interviewee with 20 years of teaching experience and eight years as a TEF, used a hand gesture insinuating what I interpret to be a silent "what can we do." As curriculum and instruction specialists without primary decision-making "authority" in the role description, TEFs struggle to work to assist teachers in improving performance. When teachers understand that there is little consequence for failing to adhere to a TEF request, unless the administrator agrees, it becomes difficult to impact change in the classroom. In this manner, the intraorganizational power structure and administrative hierarchy hinders the productivity of the TEF. There is a trickle-down effect of going from nonevaluative to powerless.

Field Observations Regarding the Lived Experiences of Interorganizational TEF

In a 2019 conversation with WITS administrators, the increase in requests for services was highlighted. One of the directors noted that the number of partnerships indicated a need for more TEF and that the WITS Writers were ready to lead inside the organization as well as in the field:

> With the number of schools that we service, it is getting harder and harder for us to get to them like we used to. I think that some of the writers are ready to work with us. They can be coaches of coaches. Not only will they grow, it is a natural way to help split the numbers in the collaborative so that the groups have a mixed dynamic, plus we are looking at cultivating leaders in the organization that can help be a mid-level presence.

We interviewed several of the WITS Writers who were seen as potential candidates for these positions, and they highlighted some of the areas that they saw in need of address:

> If I were to assume one of these roles, then I would have to make sure that new WITS writers understood how important it is to pin an administrator to a schedule...I know that things happen and you have to reschedule sometimes, but on our neediest campuses we have the most cancellations. It hurts the group. The teachers need for us to be able to consistently provide support, so we need to consistently contact the administrators. (Writer 1)

> Teachers have so much to do anyway. I would want to just remind my group that we are there for teachers. You know? It's hard enough for them. We have to be really prepared each time we go. (Writer 2)

CONCLUSIONS: THE CALL FOR A COMMUNITY IN PARTNERSHIP

Even with unique "stories to leave by" following distinct shifts (Connelly & Clandinin, 1999) in elements of our field stories are recognizably similar to the internal and external dilemmas reported in related literature on beginning teacher attrition:

- Limitations placed on creativity and autonomy,
- The negative impact of state and federal accountability measures,
- Pressures related to standardized testing in conflict with preparing students for life (Craig, 2014; Schaefer, 2013).

Identification of these recurrent issues was phase one of our journey. We then returned to find suggestions for moving forward and categorized that data under the campus, district, and interorganizational supports.

The Role of Campus and District Administrators in Cultivating Teacher Knowledge

In revisiting our field notes and our own stories, we compiled the suggestions for a successful enactment (Table 1):

Instructional improvement does not happen by chance. Employing a TEF is a great step toward facilitating this improvement, but the presence of a TEF on campus does not ensure that teachers will grow as reflective practitioners. Scheduling dates and locations for PD sessions, coordinating the administration of district assessments, acquiring and formatting spreadsheets of student data – essentially, tasks that are about logistics or compliance – hinder TEF from accomplishing the real work of building teacher capacity. The hands and hearts of TEF are already full from carrying the load of guiding, comforting, and collaborating with teachers, and these tasks only add to the load. When administrators

Table 1. Suggestions from Teacher Educators in the Field (TEFs) (Auzenne-Curl, 2016).

Considerations for Hiring Administrators	Considerations for Beginning Teacher Educators in the Field
1. Provide a vision and working concept of what good instruction means in your campus or district community.	1. Your role is for teachers. Always consider the individual.
2. Define the role, expectation, and evaluation process for teacher educators in the field.	2. Your job means having hard conversations.
3. Communicate the purpose and goals of Teacher Educators in the Field (TEFs) to teachers.	3. Do not look for what you would do in the classroom; watch, listen, and learn.
4. Discuss confidentiality and how this positions to function with administrators and teachers.	4. Ask your hiring committee for expectations on how to enroll and enlist the teachers in partnership.
5. Make sure that there are structures in place for all of the expectations to be met, time and physical space for the work.	5. Ask to review your evaluation instrument.

provide the vision, the time, and the structures for professional learning, they are supplying their learning communities with the soil and the seed, so TEF can focus exclusively on facilitating growth.

The Role of Non- and for-profit Partnerships in Cultivating Teacher Knowledge

Organizations and consultants who are entering school communities often make the mistake of assuming that teachers do not know how or want to engage in instruction that is aligned to research-based practice. This can distance teachers and leave them feeling an object of condescension.

> [Consultants]They came all the time. We didn't even look up. There was always somebody coming in on the fly and sneaking a peek to tell us how to do "better" – Nobody that was really ever going to come back, and nobody that really cared about kids enough to ask them or us about what happens on a daily basis. (Anonymous Teacher, Chestin's Fieldnotes, 2019)

The quote above is one of many that expressed this sentiment. On campuses that partnered with organizations like WITS, for ongoing, job-embedded PD with the same TEF, feedback was largely favorable:

> By the end of the year, we were crying in PLC. Were you there when we cried? WITS was our kind of refuge, you know? We could actually talk about what we knew we were here to do. It was a support group for us. We looked forward to being in that community. (Anonymous Teacher, Chestin's Fieldnotes, Fall 2018)

Teacher groups felt in community and heard from their WITS Writer. They expressed that though they were initially hesitant to partner with someone who was not from their campus and who was not a teacher by trade, they were open to the partnership because their writer began by asking them what they needed and by observing their classes. One teacher expressed gratitude:

I felt like she wanted to help, and most importantly, was willing to learn from us. She spent time reading samples of the student writing with us and listening to our level lead guide our meetings before she ever facilitated one. So we felt like she was coming to support us instead of just tell us another thing that we needed to do. That is important because there is always another thing to do as a teacher.... In the end it felt like she was actually taking a few things off of our plates.

The Call for Bridging Pre- and In-service Teacher Education

There is a third facet of support that we have discussed with our participants and among ourselves. It is the seeming split between theory and practice. Schools and independent organizations often feel heavily evaluated by institutions of higher education, but not as supported. We assert that cross-institutional partnerships for preservice and in-service teachers, as well as PD certificate programs for TEF would be a strong unifying effort to bridge the gap. We hope that more researchers will turn their attention to the particulars (Schwab, 1973) of the role and collaborate with those who have lived it in order to design centers and certificates to fill this need.

Chestin's Reflections

There were so many times that I needed access to journals or even access to other people in my role, but I did not have it. I always felt that I was growing when I was in community with my peers. It is a large part of how I convinced myself that pursuing a doctorate was necessary. I believed that I could be the person from the outside that came back to help. To some degree, my belief was right, but there are two bothersome issues embedded there:

- *Not everyone wanting to improve and gain resources for their area has access and opportunity.* I was fortunate enough to have attained research and teaching fellowships, an assistantship, and a local scholarship. I also had a spouse who worked in the same field and was an administrator. He saw my growth as part of his growth. These are not supports that everyone has. Universities that provide site-based course offerings in their partner districts, and that work with districts to develop grants for cohorts make TEF and those who they guide more effective by bringing resources closer to home.
- *I am only one person.* Universities have a greater reach and more resources. We need more scholarship of service to those in the field. I have often advocated for and recently increased my research on Master's Degrees centered on induction, and preservice and in-service certificate programs that offer reflective practice and action research course selections. We have to work together to make things work.

Daphne's Reflections

Chestin's point about wanting access to resources resonated with me as I read her reflections. I had access to research databases in university libraries when I was a graduate student and a dual credit instructor. Once I no longer held either position, I lost my connection to research studies and articles about writing instruction and PD. Policymakers and university professors are quick to say that teachers in schools should incorporate evidence-based practices without considering how teachers or TEF can retrieve these resources without subscriptions. Could an institution of higher education partner with schools in providing that? Typically, educators inadvertently learn about research studies through practitioner-oriented books from "educational gurus." But, the lag time between published research and widespread dissemination of its findings in schools can be 2–3 years, in my experience. That's 2–3 cohorts of students in our schools, struggling with writing concepts or practices that research could help us address. I remember learning about self-regulated strategy development (SRSD) as a writing intervention strategy in graduate school in 2014. I only discovered a month ago that there is an entire website (thinkSRSD.com) devoted to introducing the strategy and supporting teachers with its implementation. The site's copyright date is 2018.

I think Graham's (2018) writer(s)-within-community model best encapsulates the level of support I look forward to experiencing as a TEF some day. In describing it, he says its basic organizing structures are

> (a) writing community (components of the social/cultural context within which writing takes place) and (b) writers and their collaborators (cognitive architecture, capabilities, and physical actions applied by members of the writing community). (pp. 258–259)

All writers need community, whether they are student writers, teachers as writers, or writing-focused TEF. We need the feedback, and we need the pushback.

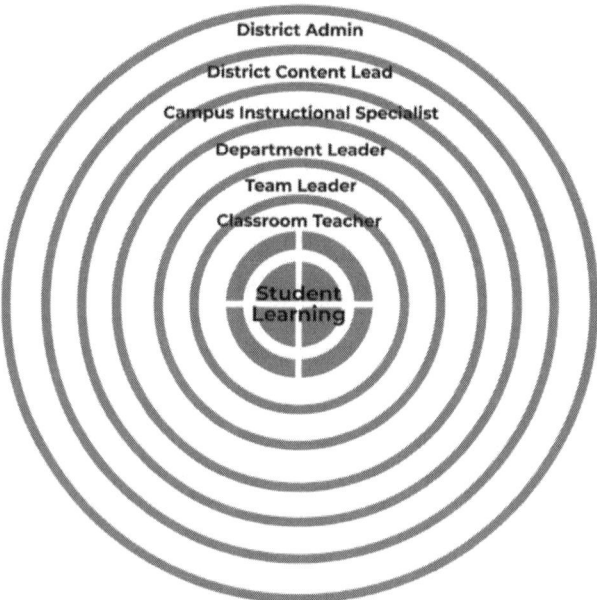

Fig. 1.   Concept of Roles Targeting Teacher Education in the Field.

We need the cognitive dissonance produced by divergent perspectives, and we most certainly need the compassion and empathy of fellow workers. Students are at the center of the concentric circles illustrated in Chestin's model (Fig. 1), and rightfully so. But, what we also have sought to prove through our shared stories and reflections is that each sphere of support for students needs its own community for inspiration, direction, and replenishment in sustaining the work.

REFERENCES

AP Examination Results in Texas and the United States, 2018−2019. (2019). Retrieved from Texas Education Agency Website https://tea.texas.gov/sites/default/files/ap_tx_and_us_2018-19.pdf

Auzenne-Curl, C. (2016). *Their exits and their entrances: Stories of coming and going from former teacher educators in the field*. Doctoral dissertation, The University of Houston.

Brindley, R., & Schneider, J. J. (2002). Writing instruction or destruction: Lessons to be learned from fourth-grade teachers' perspectives on teaching writing. *Journal of Teacher Education*, 53(4), 328–341.

Clandinin, D. J. (1985). Personal practical knowledge: A study of teachers' classroom images. *Curriculum Inquiry*, 15(4), 361–385. doi:10.2307/1179683

Clandinin, D. J. (Ed.). (2007). *Handbook of narrative inquiry: Mapping a methodology*. Thousand Oaks, CA: SAGE. doi:10.4135/9781452226552

Clandinin, D. J. (2013). *Engaging in narrative inquiry*. Walnut Creek, CA: Left Coast Press.

Clandinin, D. J., & Connelly, F. M. (2000). *Narrative inquiry: Experience and story in qualitative research*. San Francisco, CA: Jossey-Bass.

Connelly, F. M., & Clandinin, D. J. (1988). *Teachers as curriculum planners: Narratives of experience*. New York, NY: Carnegie Corporation.

Connelly, F. M., & Clandinin, D. J. (1999). *Shaping a professional identity: Stories of educational practice*. New York, NY: Teachers College Press.

Craig, C. (2013). Teacher education and the best-loved self. *Asia Pacific Journal of Education*, 33(3), 261–272. doi:10.1080/02188791.2013.788476

Craig, C. (2014). From stories of staying to stories of leaving: A U.S. beginning teacher's experience. *Journal of Curriculum Studies*, 46(1), 81–115.

Croft, A., Coggshall, J., Dolan, M., Powers, E., & Killion, J. (2010). *Job-embedded professional development: What it is, who is responsible, and how to get it done well*. National Comprehensive Center for Teacher Quality. Retrieved from http://www.gtlcenter.org/

Cuenca, A., Schmeichel, M., Butler, B. M., Dinkelman, T., & Nicholas, J. R., Jr. (2011). Creating a "third space" in student teaching: Implications for the university supervisor's status as outsider. *Teaching and Teacher Education*, 27(7), 1068–1077. doi:10.1016/j.tate.2011.05.003

Cutri, M. R., & Whiting, E. F. (2015). The emotional work of discomfort and vulnerability in multicultural teacher education. *Teachers and Teaching: Theory and Practice*, 21(8), 1010–1025.

Darling-Hammond, L. (2010). *The flat world and education: How America's commitment to equity will decide our future*. New York, NY: Teacher's College Press.

Darling-Hammond, L. (2014). Want to close the achievement gap? *American Educator*, 38(4), 14–18.

Darling-Hammond, L., & McLaughlin, M. W. (1995). Policies that support professional development in an era of reform. *Phi Delta Kappan*, 76(8), 597–604.

Dewey, J. (1938). My pedagogic creed. *School Journal*, 54, 77–80.

DuFour, R., & Eaker, R. E. (1998). *Professional learning communities at work: Best practices for enhancing student achievement*. Bloomington, IN: National Education Service.

Eaker, R. E., DuFour, R., & DuFour, R. B. (2002). *Getting started: Reculturing schools to become professional learning communities*. Bloomington, IN: Solution Tree Press.

Earley, P., & Porritt, V. (2014). Evaluating the impact of professional development: The need for a student-focused approach. *Professional Development in Education*, 40(1), 112–129.

Gale, T. (2020). *Gentri-migration: A contextualized journey into the urbanization of suburban schools*. Doctoral dissertation, Texas A&M University. Retrieved from https://hdl.handle.net/1969.1/191639

Graham, S. (2018). A revised writer(s)-within-community model of writing. *Educational Psychologist*, *53*(4), 258–279.
Graham, S. (2019). Changing how writing is taught. *Review of Research in Education*, *43*, 277–303.
Graham, S., MacArthur, C., & Fitzgerald, J. (Eds.). (2013). *Best practices in writing instruction* (2nd ed.). New York, NY: Guilford.
Graham, S., & Perin, D. (2007). A meta-analysis of writing instruction for adolescent students. *Journal of Educational Psychology*, *99*(3), 446–476.
Graham, S., & Sandmel, K. (2011). The process writing approach: A meta-analysis. *The Journal of Educational Research*, *104*(6), 396–407.
Guskey, T. (2003). What makes professional development effective? *Phi Delta Kappan*, *84*(10), 748–750.
Guskey, T. (2014). Planning professional learning. *Educational Leadership*, *71*(8), 10–16.
Harris, K., Graham, S., & Mason, L. (2006). Improving the writing, knowledge, and motivation of struggling young writers: Effects of self-regulated strategy development with and without peer support. *American Educational Research Journal*, *43*(2), 295–340.
Kaplan, J. (2008). The national writing project: Creating a professional learning community that supports the teaching of writing. *Theory into Practice*, *47*(1), 336–344.
Klineberg, S. (2011, February 11). Rice professor Stephen Klineberg predicts Houston's ethnic future. *Culturemap Houston*. Retrieved from http://houston.culturemap.com/news/city-life/01-26-11-stephen-klineberg-ethnic-future/
Klineberg, S. (2015, October 20). John Jacob and Stephen Klineberg talk on the human and natural diversity of greater Houston. Retrieved from https://www.classy.org/houston/events/john-jacob-stephen-klineberg-talk-human-natural-diversity-greater-houston/e60831
Klineberg, S. (2021). *Prophetic City: Houston on the cusp of a changing America*. New York, NY: Avid Reader Press.
McCarthey, S., & Geoghegan, C. (2016). The role of professional development for enhancing writing instruction. In C. MacArthur, S. Graham, & J. Fitzgerald (Eds.), *Handbook of writing research* (2nd ed.). New York, NY: Guilford Press.
National Center for Education Statistics. (2012). *Writing 2011: National assessment of educational progress at grades 8 and 12 (NECS 2012-470)*. Institute of Education Sciences, U. S. Department of Education, Washington, DC.
National Council of Teachers of English. (2004). NCTE beliefs about the teaching of writing. Retrieved from http://www.ncte.org/positions/statements/writingbeliefs
Penuel, R., Fishman, B., Yamaguchi, R., & Gallagher, L. (2007). What makes professional development effective? Strategies that foster curriculum implementation. *American Educational Research Journal*, *44*(4), 921–958.
Rudick, T. (2012, April 26). City in transition: Sociologist Stephen Klineberg examines Houston's rich/poor divide & what it means. *CultureMap Houston*. Retrieved from http://houston.culturemap.com/news/city-life/04-26-12-kinder-surveys-chart-three-decades-of-change-in-houston/
Schaefer, L. (2013). Beginning teacher attrition: A question of identity making and identity shifting. *Teachers and Teaching: Theory and Practice*, *19*(3), 260–274. doi:10.1080/13540602.2012.754159. Retrieved from http://tea.texas.gov/staar/rpt/sum/
Schwab, J. (1973). The practical 3: Translation into curriculum. *The School Review*, *81*(4), 501–522.
Simon, B., Craig, C. J., Evans, P., Bott, S., Stokes, D., & Abrol, B. (2017). Attracting, preparing, and retaining teachers in high need areas: A science as inquiry model of teacher education. In *A companion to research in teacher education* (pp. 455–470). Singapore: Springer. doi:10.1007/978-981-10-4075-7_30
State of Texas assessment of academic readiness: Statewide summary report in English I writing. (2012). Retrieved from Texas Education Agency website http://tea.texas.gov/staar/rpt/sum/
State of Texas assessment of academic readiness: Statewide summary report in English I. (2019). Retrieved from Texas Education Agency website https://tea.texas.gov/sites/default/files/ap_tx_and_us_2018-19.pdf
Thomson, S. (2011, February 7). Rice professor Stephen Klineberg predicts Houston's ethnic future. *CultureMap Houston*. Retrieved from http://houston.culturemap.com/news/city-life/01-26-11-stephen-klineberg-ethnic-future/

PART II

SEEING SMALL: THE CALL FOR A CLOSER LOOK AT THE WRITERS IN THE SCHOOLS COLLABORATIVE

In her 2009 TED Talk, "The danger of a single story," Nigerian Author Chimamanda Ngozi Adichie reminds us that "Many stories matter. Stories have been used to dispossess and to malign. But stories can also be used to empower, and to humanize." Consequently, any topic of research in education should not be seen small, but too often topics are treated that way. Greene frames this approach as seeing "from the perspective of a system" (2000, p. 10) as detached observers. Seeing small risks the development of an oversimplified and single story when our view of the subject should be considered through more than one iteration and presented by more than one narrator. In this manner, we unearth more of the particulars. Part II is a sieve through which we deconstruct a single image of the Writers in the Schools Collaborative professional development program. In Part I, we heard from members of the organization in terms of structure and goal setting foundations, but here we amplify the voices of participants in various programmatic and partnering roles.

Chapter 6 by Former Executive Director Robin Reagler, *Reflection on WITS history and the challenges of change*, presents a narrative history of the organization's work in establishing "The WITS Way" of professional development offering and the challenges of change inside and outside of the organization. Her focus on the goal of the program to act as "a personal trainer at the gym" by entering into a supportive and consistent partnership with classroom teachers provides a foundation for the job-embedded, relationship centers approach that has evolved into the program we see today.

In Chapter 7, *In search of a trellis: A principal's perspective on the need for cross-institutional literacy partnerships*, high school principal, Terri Osborne, shares the journey of a leader in search of support. Terri reached out to WITS during her first year as the principal of a school that was low-performing on state assessments and where the language of discourse regarding students in it was "those kids." A review of the data and the schools in neighboring areas led her to believe that what had been offering was not working. High turnover rates on the campus and at the district level left the English department and "those kids" underresourced and underperforming. So, Terri "took that language and owned it, but we did not see them as 'those' kids. They were 'our' kids," and forming a partnership with WITS was an opportunity to better serve them.

What follows the principal's anticipatory success with the program is Chapter 8, *Tough Turf: Restoried moments in the dissipation of an urban knowledge community.* Here, Abdulkader Mokhtari, Chestin T. Auzenne-Curl, and Kaleah Hicks present a collective restorying of Mokhtari's participation in the Writers in the Schools Collaborative on two campuses in one more urban and one less urban community setting. His perspective on the Collaborative as a space for relationships among teachers shed light on the ability of interorganizational partnerships to build a community of practice that is sustainable and which transcends the physical proximity of its members.

We then proceed to Sarah Jerasa's Chapter 9, *The beauty of petals and thorns: Negotiating identity as a writer-teacher*, in which she recounts the shifting perceptions of self and associated behaviors that she adopted in the field. Working as a WITS Writer on multiple campuses provided her with a window of reflection on what defines coaching as her best loved self.

Last in Part II is Chapter 10, *Reflective conversation on the value of longevity as collaborators in education*, which is guided by the transcribed interview of P. Tim Martindell by Cheryl J. Craig. The pair, along with Chestin T. Auzenne-Curl, revisit key coaching moments in the Zoom meeting and contextualize the topics of discussion with narratives from the field and relevant images. Tim reflects on his CFG® coaching role during the three-year evaluation of the program by Cheryl's research team (Chestin T. Auzenne-Curl Project Lead), and as the restorying takes place, the Critical Friends (CFG®) protocols, which are referenced as important tools for supporting the WITS writers for their field work, seem an active presence in the construction of the chapter.

REFERENCES

Greene, M. (2000). *Releasing the imagination: Essays on education, the arts, and social change.* San Francisco, CA: Jossey-Bass.

Ngozi Adichie, C. (2009, July). *The danger of a single story.* Retrieved from https://www.ted.com/talks/chimamanda_ngozi_adichie_the_danger_of_a_single_story?language=en. Accessed on February 2, 2020.

REFLECTIONS ON WITS HISTORY AND CHALLENGES OF CHANGE

Robin Reagler

ABSTRACT

This chapter is a personal account of the development of the Writers in the Schools program by immediate past-Executive Director, Dr. Robin Reagler. She notes the roots of the organization and the challenges of internal and external growth from 1998 to 2020.

Keywords: Writers in the Schools; literacy education; collaborative professional development; writing instruction; teaching writing; instructional coaching

When I became the Executive Director of Writers in the Schools (WITS) in 1998, the pedagogy used with students was already set, but there was no established "WITS Way" of providing professional development (PD) for teachers. WITS was modeled after Teachers & Writers Collaborative (T&W) in New York City, and the WITS founders, Marv Hoffman and Phillip Lopate, were leaders in that influential movement. When T&W writer Kenneth Koch published *Wishes, Lies, and Dreams* (1970), the book documented what it meant to be a teaching artist. In addition to its activity in schools, T&W launched a publishing company that provided an inspiring pedagogy for organizations doing similar work across the nation. Books such as *Poetry Everywhere* by Jack Collum and Sheryl Noethe (2005), *Sing the Sun Up* by Lorenzo Thomas (1998), *Luna, Luna* by Julio Marzan (1997), and *When Stories Come to School* by Patsy Cooper (1993) were useful how-to-teach books, and they legitimized our approach to teaching for the larger educational community.

Why did our approach need legitimizing? What was unique about this way of teaching? Here are a few key differences:

- We were practicing writers and not necessarily certified teachers.
- We used mentor texts that were not "age appropriate," meaning that we brought into the classrooms literature that was linguistically playful and that used imaginative leaps and fantastic imagery. It may or may not have been ranked at the Lexile level recommended in standard pedagogy, but the presentation of these texts was often suggestive, even dramatic, and drew students into a world of word-making.
- We assumed that the story, poem, or essay the students produced in an hour was a first draft rather than a finished product.
- We did not give grades. Instead, we responded to student writing with praise and interested questioning.
- We made it fun. (Obviously teachers are often fun, and also, this was easier for a weekly guest than a daily instructor.)

This list describes some aspects of WITS teaching. Within this framework, however, no two WITS Writers were alike. In our hiring, we selected creative people who could relate to students and use their originality and creative practice to make reading and writing an adventure.

When schools signed up to partner with WITS, they were getting neither a set curriculum nor a standardized test prep program. Although the data from outside evaluators did demonstrate improved test scores, the WITS messaging to schools was that the program would focus on student writing and reading skills. Rather than a quick fix, schools received a relationship with "their" writer and a customized, year-long commitment to student improvement. Schools did pay a per-classroom fee for the WITS program on a sliding scale. Based on federal standards, the percentage of families qualifying for free lunch was the determining factor. In cases where funders stepped in and paid the school fee, we found that programs were less effective. The phrase "buy-in" turned out to be quite literal. The school fee represented between 1/8 and ½ of the total cost of the program and was subsidized by grants and other funding. The school buy-in tended to enhance the success of the program.

While the student-focused program followed the model inherited from T&W, WITS lacked a standard approach to PD for teachers. WITS offered help to teachers when it was requested, but the PD approach varied according to the requests of each campus. As an educator, I could observe our services for students improving over the years, and outside evaluators confirmed that hunch by providing unbiased data and documentation. But we did not have a set pedagogy when it came to PD for classroom teachers.

Back in the 1980s, when Hoffman moved to Houston, he founded two programs. WITS, a program for writers who wanted to teach, was based at the University of Houston, and the School Writing Project, a program for teachers who wanted to write, was housed at Rice University. For many years, WITS experimented. Hoffman's model, which was similar to work done by the National Writing Project, excelled with teachers who were motivated to write and publish their own stories and essays. In an email, Hoffman explained,

> Each session was a mix of writing to a prompt and sharing, talking about applications of these writing activities to working with students, reading articles about writing with students, etc. In short, it was very practice-based. (M. Hoffman, personal communication, January, 19, 2021)

WITS went on to create new models that were more closely aligned with the WITS model for students. These sessions, like the student model, guaranteed successful writing, even for teachers who were dubious about WITS, PD in general, or themselves as writers. These workshops broke down the writing process into steps that encouraged specificity and prewriting without being obvious. They framed the project in a way that encouraged vivid memories in original language. Sometimes teachers and administrators would cry while sharing their stories and poems. They surprised themselves. This approach gave educators the experience of being successful as writers, but it lacked the practice-based conversation that Hoffman's method incorporated. My dream for many years was to devise an approach that was effective in helping teachers become both the writers and the writing teachers they hoped to become.

The steps to creating WITS Collaborative unfolded over a period of years. The first step was gaining more insight into school culture. In our training program for the WITS Writers, I often had used the analogy that walking into a school was a bit like entering a foreign country. Schools have their own rules and customs, and as newcomers it was important to observe and ask questions. As guest instructors, we tried to avoid offending our hosts at all costs. The first step in creating WITS Collaborative came from this knowledge. I decided we needed to hire a seasoned teacher to join our staff, become our thought partner, and help us understand school culture so that the new pedagogy worked for the teachers and enabled administrators to observe and recognize its value, as well.

Our second step was hiring Tina Angelo, a WITS teacher, parent, former Board member, and trainer. She had also been a literacy administrator in the school district. So in addition to her familiarity with the culture, she had personal connections with many leaders in public education. I asked her to spend a year studying WITS, observing the writers teaching, conducting experiments, and talking with principals, teachers, stakeholders, and competitors. The goal was to use that year in research and design mode to come up with a recommendation for the best way that WITS could provide PD training for and with classroom teachers. And she did.

As Angelo began a series of "small experiments of radical intent," I explored potential funding partners who might be interested in launching a new program. Since the new program was still undefined, we needed a known partner for whom we had already proven our ability in taking on a substantial new endeavor. We approached our most established partner, the Houston Endowment, and eventually, when we arrived at our plan, they agreed to partner with WITS.

What makes WITS Collaborative unique is that it is both job-imbedded and relationship-based so that a teacher learns and makes discoveries *with support* over the course of the school year. The WITS Writers spend 50 hours over the course of the school year with their teachers. They are there for both for the difficult moments and the celebrations. The analogy I use to describe the WITS Writer's role is that of a personal trainer at the gym. The WITS Writer is there for the teacher once or twice weekly, meeting during the planning period. The writers lead teachers in writing exercises, facilitate demonstration classes, observe the teachers, provide immediate feedback, comment on student work, assess student progress with the teachers, and devise next steps. This cycle of activity can be repeated 6–10 times throughout the school year. The combination of student-focused pedagogy and personalized support for teachers throughout the process is what makes the program so successful.

Overall, WITS Collaborative has shown both measurable and anecdotal success beyond what I imagined for it. And yet, as a conscientious educator in this particular moment, I am aware that there is more that can be done. Much more.

One of the WITS taglines explains the motivation for WITS' work this way: "because writing is revolutionary." In framing the work of WITS as revolutionary, I see two mandates. First, WITS Collaborative must make sure that our methodology does not become formulaic. Writing and teaching are both arts. As writers and teachers, we must master formulas and quickly move beyond them, addressing our students' particularities, as well as our own. Second, WITS Collaborative must incorporate more of the lessons we are learning from the prescriptive lens of equity, diversity, access, and inclusion. Within the last few years, WITS has been making an organizational push to reevaluate all our work through a lens of equity, diversity, inclusion, and access. This has affected hiring, placement of writers in the classrooms, the makeup of our library, our training, and all aspects of our model. When I retired, this process was still in progress. Change is slow, and the goal of becoming truly anti-racist will continue to be a focus in the years to come, one that requires continuous work and refinement based on feedback from students as well as peers.

In doing this kind of work, one important question I often contemplate is: *how* does change happen? The WITS Collaborative provides ideal learning conditions for students, teachers, and writers, and these conditions make change possible. But *how* this change happens is not as precise a science as some would wish. According to Michele Kotler, founder and Executive Director of Community Word Project in New York City, their Teaching Artists often begin and end their WITS sessions with students using this chant:

I have a voice.

My voice is powerful.

My voice can change the world.

The idea that young people might grow up with the deep understanding that their words make them powerful – this is the way that WITS hopes to bring about change for a more just and equitable world. When people are nurtured to recognize their own agency, change is much more likely to occur. Consider

Amanda Gorman, the 22-year-old inaugural poet for President Joe Biden and Vice-President Kamala Harris. Gorman came of age in Get Lit, a WITS program in Los Angeles, and she brought hope to the forefront with her poem, "The Hill We Climb." Without question, she is an amazing woman. And she is also a product of inspired, supportive WITS teaching.

In a speech Angela Davis made at University of California Santa Cruz (2008) about how change happens, she says that change becomes possible when people become aware of themselves as part of a group and as agents of change. Interestingly, Davis also discusses the role of imagination. To create change, we must first be able to imagine it. Within the model of WITS Collaborative, this is yet another important element. The writer models, observes, and celebrates the teacher as she fulfills her goals and dreams. But students are the ultimate beneficiaries in the classroom, learning the skills they need to fulfill their own.

REFERENCES

Collom, J., & Noethe, S. (2005). *Poetry everywhere: Teaching poetry writing in school and in the community*. New York, NY: T & W Books.

Cooper, P. (1993). *When stories come to school: Telling, writing, and performing stories in the early childhood classroom*. Washington, DC: Distributed by ERIC Clearinghouse.

Davis, A. (2008, March 7). The prison: A sign of democracy [Video]. Retrieved from https://www.youtube.com/watch?v=Q25-KJ55k_0

Koch, K. (1970). *Wishes lies and dreams: Teaching children to write*. New York, NY: Harper and Row.

Marzán, J. (1997). *Luna, luna: Creative writing ideas from Spanish, Latin American, and Latino literature*. New York, NY: Teachers & Writers Collaborative.

Thomas, L. (1998). *Sing the sun up: Creative Writing ideas from African American literature*. New York, NY: Teachers & Writers Collaborative.

IN SEARCH OF A TRELLIS: A PRINCIPAL'S PERSPECTIVE ON THE NEED FOR CROSS-INSTITUTIONAL LITERACY PARTNERSHIPS

Terri Osborne

ABSTRACT

This chapter explores the complexities of leading the improvement of literacy instruction at a secondary school populated by a majority of culturally diverse, at-risk, and low-income students. The principal's narrative charts the journey to evaluate the campus' comprehensive needs and human capital. In an effort to build teacher capacity and foster authentic learning experiences, the school leader partners with an instructional specialist and a nonprofit organization, WITS Houston (WITS), Houston. The unique professional development program designed by WITS allows teachers to connect directly with writers in order to cultivate their own voices as authors and create more culturally relevant writing instruction for students. After navigating the challenges of program implementation and the COVID-19 pandemic, the campus successfully launches the WITS Collaborative as a multitiered approach to school improvement and literacy intervention. To catalog the experience, the principal details the objectives of the partnership, preparatory considerations, tensions regarding enactment, and the implications for the field.

Keywords: Principal leadership; writing workshop; culturally relevant pedagogy; literacy; high school; diverse learners

INTRODUCTORY NARRATIVE

Of all positions across the K-12 public education spectrum, the role of campus principal is quite possibly the most complex, comprehensive, and taxing. The school leader negotiates the political landscape, strategic vision, instructional goals, and development of people while being a culture builder, spirit captain, counselor, therapist, financial and human capital manager, parent whisperer, grievance mitigator, and student advocate. Most astounding to me, as an early career principal, is that at a high-need campus, it is often necessary to be all things within a 60-minute span of time. Even with all these responsibilities, and that is not by any means a comprehensive list, experiential discourse has taught me that most principals seek to have some fun on the job, too. Above all, the principal maintains a daily record of the success and functionality of the school while exerting all efforts to assess whether or not the metaphoric ship is still journeying toward its intended destination. Point blank: it is tough work.

I moved into my first principalship with just eight years of experience as an educator. I spent four years in the classroom and four years in a variety of administrative leadership positions: Dean of Students, Assistant Principal, and Early College High School Director. With less than a decade of experience under my belt, I was highly committed to filling my gaps by reading as much and as often as I could. I read about time management, leadership, organizational behavior, communication, and high-performance habits. I desired to be a great leader, and after a few years, my drive developed into a mission to be known for building outstanding teams and a thriving organizational culture. More than anything, I wanted to be a part of transforming a school into an educational environment that allowed at-risk students to thrive. While I was certainly limited in years of experience, I was fueled by passion and establishing a reputation for being a little bit dangerous based on the tools I had in my belt from independent study and a sense of youthfulness that made me relatable to my high-school-aged clientele.

These facts may have scared other district leaders; in fact, the school to which I was headed had seen much leadership turnover in recent years. This is part of the reason that I was hired by a risk-taking talent scout who I believe saw much of himself in me. In Fall of 2018, I found myself as the first African American female high school principal in a fast-growth suburban district outside of Houston. While it all sounded amazing, and it truly was, I quickly came to understand that my new school was on the cusp of failing. By my standards, it was already a failing school. In my discussions with peers and colleagues district wide, I could tell that the expectations for students were low. Our feeder pattern was a Title I feeder and the language of discourse regarding students in it was "those kids." I took that language and owned it, but we did not see them as "those" kids. They were "our" kids, and for our kids, academic performance was subpar in most areas and abysmal in English. The athletics programs were average at best. Parent participation was miniscule. The tiny glimmer of hope that did exist was the rich tradition and history of the school. It was the first high school in the district and the namesake high school. The campus was a fixed property on the road that led to the heart of the town, facing the downtown water tower that was proudly branded with the high school's logo. Unbeknownst to me, the mission of restoring a campus to glory on behalf of students had landed in my lap. I accepted the call, and I set out to do the work.

As many principals do, I inherited my entire team of leaders, except for a few positions I was able to recruit and hire for myself. The staff of approximately 260 people included 9 assistant principals, 4 instructional coaches, and 4 area coordinators who would be under my direct supervision. My instinct was to make every campus deficiency a priority, but my research told me that people and culture came first. In *Good to Great*, Jim Collins (2001) contends that improving an organization starts by the leader determining "First Who, Then What" (p. 41). My first order of business was discerning whether the right people were in the right seats on the bus. My administrative team and I used *StrengthsFinder* by Tom Rath (2007) to explore our innate talents and *Power of a Positive Team* by Jon Gordon (2018) as a framework for how our administrative team would lead. We had a good foundation. The administrative team was passionate about student success and each of them loved the school, but there was much to be done to develop our collective instructional leadership capacity. In my assessment of the campus, I also learned that there was not a clear framework for improving instruction because there was not a clear vision for how students should be served by our school. Together, we had several key questions to answer:

- What caliber of student did we hope to cultivate by graduation?
- What did we believe about students' pathways and life after high school?
- With which nonacademic skills did we want the school to equip students in order to ensure their long-term success?

We needed to have a vision that was on a mission, a grounding belief that would constantly remind us where we were going and why we were going there (Gordon, 2018). After a comprehensive needs assessment of the school and a thorough evaluation of our own beliefs about education, we determined that our North Star, or guiding landmark, would be

> Every day, Renaissance High School will provide a challenging and innovative college, career, and life readiness experience that equips students to succeed in the future endeavor of their choice.

It was a sound and noble vision for the future of our school, and to attain it, we had to take a tough look at where we were currently. As Jim Collins (2001) also asserts, we had to face the brutal facts about the state of our academic organization. There was an abundance of work to do and many, many mindsets (Dweck, 2008) to shift before the real work could even begin. The brutal facts also revealed immense deficits in our students' ability to read and write on grade level. We embraced the idea that the shortfalls in literacy were the linchpin in solving an array of academic, culture, and socioemotional challenges for our students. Although the role of principal made me the primary instructional leader of the campus, I was quick to recognize that my background as a secondary math teacher made me a passive (and underskilled) participant in the community of educators who would take on mitigating the widespread literacy gaps. Despite my own inadequacy as a literacy educator, improving literacy at my campus was not a passive goal. It was *the* goal. Therefore, I had to be savvy enough to accurately evaluate the needs of our students and teachers, and I also had to be humble enough to recognize when solutions fell outside of my scope of knowledge.

OBJECTIVES AND RATIONALE FOR THE PARTNERSHIP

While the principal role certainly means wearing multiple hats, I quickly realized that the greatest service I could do for my campus was learning to be an effective unifier of the work, a sort of trellis that served to bring together the vines that might otherwise grow in different directions. A critical adjustment for me was learning to envision, orchestrate, and analyze the work being done as opposed to getting in the trenches and getting my hands dirty every day. Now do not get me wrong here, that does not under any circumstances mean doing nothing or delegating everything. In my quest to incrementally shift the campus toward our North Star, I spent long hours disaggregating, reflecting, and planning to ensure the strategies we implemented were solutions to our core issues.

My reflections and analysis left me with a litany of areas of opportunity. The campus was suffering from a curriculum, instruction, and capacity crisis. As a high-need school inside of a highly decentralized district, the previous leaders, like myself, were charged with improving multiple areas of deficiency with only so many minds and hands to get it done. Philosophically, I believed that the instructional planning process was, and still is, the gateway to improving teaching and learning, so we were in desperate need of an instructional framework. I was not in search of an extraordinary, overly complicated system; we needed a structure that indicated we believed in objective-based teaching with aligned activities that included a focus on reading and writing. Furthermore, the framework needed to emphasize that literacy stretched beyond the basic agreement that students should read consistently. I introduced *Fundamental 5* by Sean Cain and Mike Laird as our core message about high-quality instruction. This text resonated with me because its content was pointed yet simple, and the length of the book was not intimidating for first-time readers. The context was relatively self-explanatory: the perfect formula for high-quality instruction includes an actionable learning objective, teacher-student proximity, specific and encouraging feedback to students, strategic use of class time, and a clear emphasis on literacy (Cain & Laird, 2011). At my campus, we would use the Fundamental 5 as the basis for evaluating the effectiveness of our lessons. We would frame the lesson, teach in the power zone, use precise praise to recognize and reinforce student success, chunk lessons with purposeful student talk in small groups, and elevate learning with critical reading and writing. I envisioned that every teacher should also be able to answer a few related questions during the instructional planning process:

- What I am teaching, and why?
- Do my activities facilitate and assess the intended learning?
- How do I physically interact with students in my classroom?
- How do I bring out the best in students and affirm their growth?
- How can I integrate relevance and engagement through listening, speaking, reading, and writing?

With an instructional framework in place, my hope was that a more critical and thoughtful planning would take place among teachers. In addition, the Fundamental 5 would serve as a guidepost for improving the instructional capacity of the leadership team. We all needed an instrument to calibrate our evaluation of teaching and learning.

Beyond refining the instructional planning process, we needed to solve our challenges around teacher capacity. Over a 10-year span, the campus demographics had drastically changed from a majority white super school to a moderately sized, majority at-risk population. The radical shift was a result of attendance rezoning and construction of several new high schools in the district. Like so many other high-poverty, majority-minority schools, teacher turnover was an ongoing problem that firmly embedded itself as the campus demographics changed. The consequence of hiring upwards of 30 teachers, year after year, had resulted in a large population of brand new teachers as well as many teachers who were alternatively certified. There was a lack of foundation in educational best practice, not to mention a lack of depth of knowledge in each content area. Nevertheless, what we were not deficient in was passion about helping underperforming, underserved students. We had something to work with among our teachers much like we had a rich tradition to rebuild our school culture upon.

Because the administrative team was busy evolving from a loosely coupled group to a team dynamic, while playing whack-a-mole with campus operations, I leaned on my assistant superintendent for support in bringing on an instructional consultant. About midway through my first semester as principal, I was able to hire an academic specialist to support our vision for improving our instructional systems. Yes, instruction is system, and Dr. Chestin T. Auzenne-Curl was well versed in transforming instructional vision into forward-marching boots on the ground. All the more important, she was familiar with the campus and the district. About 5 years prior, Dr. Auzenne-Curl served as an instructional coach at the school, and she also spent a few years working in the teaching and learning department of our central office. I viewed her as the right combination of talent and historical context. At that time, I still needed to hire an associate principal for academics, so Dr. Auzenne-Curl would facilitate the cohesion of the instructional coaches, help develop a framework and common language for our professional learning communities (DuFour & Eaker, 1999; DuFour, DuFour, & Eaker, 2006), and outline a professional development plan to build teacher capacity. It took us most of the Fall semester to get a real grasp on the needs of the campus, to look under all the rocks, shall I say.

We established that we had to prioritize teacher development in order to have the greatest impact on students' experience in the classroom. One of the approaches that Dr. Auzenne-Curl proposed was the Writers in the Schools (WITS) Collaborative. She described WITS as a twofold support system. Their methodology would provide consistent and focused teacher development to increase pedagogy and also supplement the curriculum to engage students in relevant learning experiences. I did not have any knowledge of the program or its effectiveness, but, again, I was willing to recognize my principal responsibility to extend trust to those with wisdom and experience. Great leaders hire people into their strength zone for them to shine and add value, not to shoot down ideas that are unfamiliar or daunting (Collins, 2001). Furthermore, what the WITS program presented aligned my knowledge that the workshop approach to literacy education had proven impact with culturally diverse students (Graham, 2018; Graham & Perin, 2007; Hammond, 2014). Even with the consistent and well-monitored integration of the *Fundamental 5*, we were struggling to see this workshop-based approach to literacy in our classrooms, so piloting the WITS model, even at a small scale, was another step in the right direction for students and teachers.

The unexpected introduction to the program left me feeling hopeful about building teacher capacity and integrating fresh and relevant methods of writing instruction. Our initial meeting with WITS in late February 2020 was equally exciting and inspiring. Tina Angelo, the Education Director, was focused on understanding the vision I had for elevating instruction while being deeply passionate about presenting how WITS could be a promising partnership. I was able to convey some of the needs that had been uncovered in the evaluative work being done by Dr. Auzenne-Curl and myself. Through our conversations with teachers, we had learned that students needed support in multiple areas of the writing process. Our students struggled with basic writing structure, brainstorming, developing ideas, and metacognition, just to name a few. I also shared that turnover and a new teacher crisis drastically limited our campus-wide tools for increasing literacy. Essentially, Dr. Auzenne-Curl was correct. The WITS partnership was an opportunity to accomplish three of our major goals:

(1) expose students to authentic learning experiences and effective writing practices,
(2) develop a culture of collaborative professional learning for teachers, and
(3) fill the gaps in content knowledge and objective-aligned literacy instruction that existed among teachers.

There are always multiple approaches that can be taken to solving a problem, so WITS, of course, was not the only strategy that we could have implemented to begin to turn the tide. This one, however, was important because we believed that through literacy instruction, we would be reaching our students in a communicative pathway. Another factor that weighed heavily in my decision to move forward with the WITS partnership was the idea that support could be provided without adding any additional responsibilities to my leadership staff. As I mentioned, improving instruction was only one of many priorities for transforming the school. Independently, we would have been hard-pressed to be able to disrupt the literacy education space in my first year as principal. Our resources were finite, and the support from the central office was not as consistent or deep as we truly needed.

The move to partner with an out-of-district organization meant that we could get assistance prescriptive to our campus' needs above and beyond the district's vision, strategies, and time. I also understood the importance of having different voices address our institutional challenges. The students would get a more authentic and fresh learning experience, but it would be powerful for the teachers to have such an unconventional professional development encounter.

Through the initial meeting with the WITS team, I learned that the organization had a clear vision for providing in-class coaching, feedback, and collaborative writing experiences. The writing workshops provided by the WITS Collaborative would address the needs of diverse learners through culturally relevant instructional practices. Students would participate in innovative writing classes with a professional mentor who designs and co-teaches lessons with the classroom teacher. Most important to our unique student demographics, the mentors would expose students to culturally relevant texts and authentic writing tasks in a way that built on students' background knowledge and generated enthusiasm for writing. These culturally responsive practices, combined with explicit strategies for revision during the writing process, would give our diverse learners and striving writers the support necessary for improved writing outcomes (Graham & Perin, 2007). WITS also had very structured roles for the individual participants in the overall process. The WITS writers and administration, the teachers, and the campus administrators each had well-delineated responsibilities in meeting the writing needs of students. The well-designed system allowed every stakeholder to understand their part in implementing and advancing the program.

PREPARATORY CONSIDERATIONS

With a clear understanding of the program's value, structure, and goals, I felt confident in proceeding with the next steps. There were several preparatory tasks to execute before the partnership could launch. The campus certainly had the financial resources to secure the partnership; however, the logistical nuances of school finance and purchasing had to be prioritized and executed. As always, my first question was "are you a vendor?" At the time, WITS had not previously partnered with our district, so Tina worked with our campus accountant to complete the vendor paperwork, including submission of W9 forms, a quote for services, and a request for proposal (RFP). Our timeline for implementation was April 2020, giving time for paperwork processing and school board approval of the RFP. We left for Spring Break thinking that our partnership was moving full steam ahead.

Then, there was a pandemic, and the best laid plans went awry.

We quickly shifted our campus focus to launching a virtual school. For our campus, that included prioritizing the acquisition of laptops for students and online instructional resources for teachers. We did not, however, give up hope on forging the partnership with WITS. Dr. Auzenne-Curl applied for a grant through our district's education foundation in hopes that we could fund the project in a different manner. Being awarded the grant would also allow us to have earmarked funds for the subsequent school year, thereby keeping our hopes alive. Fast forward a couple of months: We survived the drastic pivot to virtual learning in Spring 2020, and the tumultuous restart of school in the Fall. To our pleasant surprise, the WITS grant request was fully awarded by the education foundation.

Ultimately, our planned experience looked quite different than the lived experience because of the pandemic school closures and the change in our funding source. Although the money was free, anyone who knows anything about grants knows that there are some extra hoops to jump through for gifted funds. Some of the requirements of the education foundation included developing a detailed budget, attending mandatory grantee meetings, providing ongoing grant reporting, and sharing post-program outcomes. While we were quite fortunate to have received the money to keep the project going, the grant-driven processes for funding the project were far more involved than my normal routine of just signing a purchase order and approving the budget entry in our financial management system. I would recommend the use of campus-based funds if at all possible.

We were able to lock in our WITS partnership and move forward with the collaborative in Fall 2020. Logistics looked much different. We originally planned to implement the WITS Collaborative with our sophomore-level English teachers and students; however, when the fall semester got started, there was a greater need for teacher support on our English 3 team. The group of four teachers, one of whom was teaching fully online from home, was struggling with curriculum development and forging a relationship with the new English instructional coach. My assessment led me to believe that they could benefit most from the collaborative process, structured writing cycle, and an outside coach. Despite some of the challenges they were experiencing as a team, they were connected by a shared passion for providing students with learning experiences that were relevant and captivating.

The WITS organization had made a few pandemic adjustments as well. The primary shift was that our writer would no longer be working with the teachers and students in-person on campus. Instead, interactions and coaching sessions would be conducted through Zoom, Google Meets, or Microsoft Teams. In our November reconnect meeting, Tina was accompanied by a new program manager who would facilitate our partnership launch and ongoing support services. The format and structure of the program remained fundamentally unchanged. Students would still take part in the unique workshop model with the writing mentor. Teachers would still collaboratively plan writing lessons and develop their student conferencing skills through the professional development process. The school administration was still responsible for providing infrastructure, resources, and time so the teacher-writer collaborative model could take shape.

TENSIONS REGARDING ENACTMENT

Once we were able to retool, I introduced the WITS project to the key players from our campus: the English 3 team lead, the English instructional coach, and the two administrators who supervised the English department. Fortunately, everyone on the team was optimistic and open-minded about the program being implemented.

Perhaps, after navigating the pandemic school closure, we all felt a little more capable of managing anything new and different in stride. The implementation team coordinated the initial planning meeting with the WITS staff via email. Following a flurry of two-way communication, a date was set for the week prior to Christmas break.

At this point, oversight of the program shifted to my administrators and instructional coach. In the planning meeting, the team was able to make their first real connection with the WITS staff. The teachers were provided an opportunity to report their perceptions of student needs and discuss how the writing cycle could be integrated into the next unit of study in the Spring. Our English 3 students would be reading *The Hate You Give* upon returning from break, and the program offered a chance for authentic writing to occur in conjunction with high-interest reading. As a passive participant in the process, I received ongoing updates through a tight feedback loop between myself and my leaders. Through one-on-one meetings with the administrative team and our biweekly instructional leadership team meeting (instructional coaches and administrators), I was able to remain connected to the process, ask questions, and help troubleshoot. The WITS staff did an excellent job providing me with detailed notes from the planning sessions as well. They knew I would no longer lead the project yet remained aware of my general need to know the project happenings. In order to fill the communication gap, they consistently kept me copied on email communication between them and my team. In short, the systems were in place to keep us all connected, aligned, and moving toward the vision.

Although the teachers were open to trying something new for themselves and for their students, they did have one major point of contention – planning time. As a non-EOC subject, the English 3 teachers only had one conference period per day and no common planning period. The lack of aligned planning time was the catalyst for their struggles with curriculum development and collaboration with the instructional coach. They essentially put their foot down about not having a common planning period when the WITS Collaborative was proposed, and I am okay with saying, rightly so. A direct responsibility of our administration was ensuring that issues of equity, resources, and time were mitigated to the benefit of the teachers who were doing. I often describe my role as principal as being the resource captain – like being the sergeant in the helicopter flying above the troops on the battlefield. I am wearing the headset, maintaining direct communication and a clear visual on the mission and current battle. As the resource captain, I drop supplies to the ground, scoop up injured troops, and provide timely strategic adjustments when I see change is necessary. This time, the soldiers were requesting more resources.

One of the administrators working with the WITS project was also the lead for the master schedule, so we were able to quickly evaluate how to shift classes around and provide the English 3 team with a common planning period. These changes are often impossible midstream; however, we were able to make the adjustment with relative ease because we were approaching the end of the semester. It also helped us that approximately half of our student population was now learning virtually; it is pretty simple to close and combine classes with less than 10 students in them.

We made the necessary changes to honor the teachers' request and enhance the possibility of successful implementation.

Having experienced a complete inversion of our original plan as a result of the pandemic, I know remaining flexible will be important as we move forward. This is an ideal I will continue to convey to my team. While we are very hopeful and positive about the outcomes of the innovative instructional endeavor, we learned that during a pandemic, many factors existed outside of our locus of control. There is a real possibility of having another drastic pivot now that the program has launched but the pandemic, its accompanying uncertainty, rages on. Unfortunately, such setbacks have the potential to influence the program sustainability we hope for, but it does not keep us from standing strong on original vision. The goal is to perfect a replicable model of the workshop approach to writing instruction and spread a culture of collaborative and intentional planning among teachers. I believe this remains possible because of the English 3 team and their influential capacity as teacher leaders with strong voices. Successful launch and implementation of the WITS Collaborative with this team in particular will serve as a cornerstone for the future of professional learning communities across the campus.

IMPLICATIONS FOR THE FIELD

At the time this narrative was written, we were yet in the beginning stages of launching our collaborative. Hopeful and optimistic, preparing for the return from Christmas break. Although not much has been completed in the way of actual in-class execution, it is still very possible for myself and my team to reflect on the implications of our initial experience. What would we do if there was a button to rewind to that introductory meeting took place?

Let me make it clear, I do not believe that any educator would rewind to the beginning of the pandemic. However, there were many lessons to be learned regarding holding loosely to one's plans and remaining adaptable. The pandemic presented a radical shift in the campus' immediate priorities. We became more centered in the affective domain. Our students' basic needs had to be met before we progressed to typical academic discussions. Still, it did not shift us away from our vision of improving student learning experiences. I believed deeply that keeping the North Star in front of the troops was my core responsibility as the principal. Although administrators are no longer classroom teachers providing direct instruction on a daily basis, it is still our work to model for our staff how to be resilient and flexible through adversity. In the case of enactment of the WITS Collaborative, this meant revising our expectations about "how" or "when" things should be accomplished. Such considerations are very different from steering away from "what" should be accomplished. Through these complexities, I learned to manage my expectations as well, including my expectations for myself, for my team, and for the campus. There is really something to be said about being vulnerable enough to grieve one's original expectations, ambitions, goals, and action plans and then model to the staff a willingness to press forward.

Despite our midstream adjustments, the objectives of our partnership were still the same. I am reminded of when I put a destination in the GPS, and it gives me three or four options for how to get there. Human nature prompts us to select the fastest route or maybe the most comfortable if taking toll roads and highways are not the preference. In either case, traffic jams and road closures do not constitute changing the destination, and that has to be the principal's message during implementation adversity. I would have originally said that my role was to orchestrate the logistical components of the program (personnel, financial resources, time, etc.) and then release the work to my leaders and teachers. The pandemic certainly challenged me to consider what my real role is in ensuring that our vision is achieved. Under the given circumstances, my responsibility was to stay committed to the vision, jump the hurdles, and find a way to make the original plans come to life – even if we had to take the long way.

REFERENCES

Cain, S., & Laird, M. (2011). *Fundamental 5: The formula for quality instruction.* North Charleston, SC: Createspace.

Collins, J. C. (2001). *Good to great: Why some companies make the leap ... and others don't.* New York, NY: HarperBusiness.

DuFour, R., DuFour, R., & Eaker, R. (2006). *Professional learning communities at work plan book.* Bloomington, IN: Solution Tree.

DuFour, R., Eaker, R., & National Center for Education and Innovation. (1999). *Professional learning communities at work: Best practices for enhancing student achievement [motion picture].* Bloomington, IN: Solution Tree.

Dweck, C. (2008). *Mindset, the new psychology of success: How we can learn to fulfill our potential.* New York, NY: Ballantine Books.

Gordon, J. (2018). *Power of a positive team: Proven principles and practices that make great teams great.* Newark, NJ: Wiley.

Graham, S. (2018). A writer(s) within community model of writing. In C. Bazerman, A. N. Applebee, V. W. Berninger, D. Brandt, S. Graham, J. Jeffery, ... K. C. Wilcox (Eds.), *The lifespan development of writing* (pp. 271–325). Urbana, IL: National Council of Teachers of English.

Graham, S., & Perin, D. (2007). *Writing next: Effective strategies to improve writing of adolescents in middle and high schools.* Retrieved from https://media.carnegie.org/filer_public/3c/f5/3cf58727-34f4-4140-a014-723a00ac56f7/ccny_report_2007_writing.pdf

Hammond, Z. (2014). *Culturally responsive teaching and the brain: Promoting authentic engagement and rigor among culturally and linguistically diverse students.* Thousand Oaks, CA: Corwin.

Rath, T. (2007). *StrengthsFinder 2.0.* New York, NY: Gallup Press.

TOUGH TURF: RESTORIED MOMENTS IN THE DISSIPATION OF AN URBAN KNOWLEDGE COMMUNITY

Abdulkader Mokhtari, Chestin T. Auzenne-Curl and KaLeah Hicks

ABSTRACT

This chapter is guided by Abdulkader Mokhtari's reflections on participation in the Writers in the Schools Collaborative. As a member of the professional development program on two campuses in the Houston Area, Mokhtari recalls the program model as part of a structured enactment of DuFour and Eaker's (1998) Professional Learning Community concept and an organically nurtured, portfolio-based knowledge community (Craig, 2007). During what he recalls to be a difficult time on campuses seeking to engage learners in a fresh approach to literacy, Mokhtari recounts pivotal moments of success and struggle to Chestin T. Auzenne-Curl and KaLeah Hicks, both former high school teachers and contributors to research on teacher development programs.

Keywords: Knowledge communities; urban teacher education; professional development; literacy education; peer coaching; writing instruction

BACKGROUND

All three of us worked in the same district at one point in our career. Chestin and KaLeah have since worked on various professional development programs and supplementary learning materials, while Abdulkader (Mokhtari) has extended his teaching career across multiple contexts. Chestin met him in her role as

Postdoctoral Research Fellow and Field Team Lead with a Texas A&M University/Writers in the Schools (WITS) partnership for programmatic review and evaluation. We supported Mokhtari in his reflection and in linking the stories he shared to theory by probing with questions and burrowing in and out of the experiences which drove his story to live by (Connelly & Clandinin, 1999) and, eventually, his story to leave by.

CONCEPTUAL OVERVIEW AND METHODOLOGY

After years of informal conversation, we invited Mokhtari to share a more structured version of his journey of sustaining on a campus with long-term efforts for reform. In this chapter, we use narrative inquiry (Clandinin, 2013; Connelly & Clandinin, 1990) to study the impact of knowledge communities (Craig, 1995, 2007) in his story to live by. We frame our reflections using Schwab's (1973) concept of curriculum commonplaces for a holistic view of each story as an educative experience (Dewey, 1938) – that is, an experience that sets the stage of learning yet to come.

Narrative inquiry supports meaning-making by reflecting on stories of experiences in a three-dimensional space aligned with the Deweyean concept of experience involving time (past-present-future), place (context), and social interaction (connections) (Connelly & Clandinin, 1999). It is Schwab, however, that guides our description of context and our frame for understanding the impact of restoried tensions and victories. Schwab asserted that through deliberation we learn about meaning-making as an intersectionality of places: student, teacher, subject matter, and milieu as the desiderata or commonplaces of curriculum.

CONTEXTUALIZED COMMONPLACES

Teacher

Though we previously worked in the same district, we were not collaborating teachers. We knew of Mokhtari because of his reputation for high student engagement and collegiality on his high-school literacy team. In this district, a Black male English teacher was a rare sighting and, therefore, of frequent mention. We were finally able to observe this collaborative spirit and high energy when we were collecting field data for the WITS review on the campus of Claude McKay HS in Houston, TX.

I was riding high after five years of relative success in the classroom, multiple trainings led, and the confidence from one of the new school's administrators that not only could I teach "these kids" but that I could also lead the department in our endeavors to "turn the school around." I was ready to step outside of my carefully cultivated cocoon and make a name for myself in another community in the Houston area that was near and dear to my heart. My step-father was born and raised in the community that recruited me, and I had spent a lot of time in this particular neighborhood in my youth. I was determined that if the school failed, and the state took it over, it would be in spite of the English department – not because of it.

And then on August 25, 2017, disaster struck: Hurricane Harvey unleashed a consistently slow-moving deluge on the Houston area. Living walking distance from Brays Bayou, I was not spared. My partner and I got five feet of water in our home. I had been in a flood before, but this water – as my students would say – "hit different." When my house flooded in 2001, the process was much slower – more dramatic. The water would seep up ever so slowly from beneath the house's foundation to where it would create little wet spots in the carpet. Then squishy puddles. Then pool. Then finally it was ankle deep. With Harvey the water was ankle deep within minutes.

After the initial days of Hurricane Harvey passed, we ended up living on the third floor of my partner's cousin's house. We were extremely blessed to have a place to stay rent-free while our home was being renovated, but this situation was hardly ideal. Imagine the frustrations of dealing with insurance and contractors, and the pressures of starting any new job, let alone a job as department head at a school that has exactly one year to turn scores around or face a state take over, and you have my new reality.

Students

According to state data reports for the past five years, the student population at McKay HS has been 75%–80% African American, 20%–24% Hispanic, and 1%–3 % White/other. The at-risk population averages 80%, 11% are limited in English proficiency, and 99.9% of the students are economically disadvantaged. The campus was listed on the Texas Education Agency's "watch list" and faced the possibility of a state facilitated restructure in effort to provide additional support in hope of increasing student achievement.

Subject Matter

The WITS Collaborative is a professional development program based on the belief that students learn to write most effectively when their teachers are experienced writers. The WITS Collaborative has been partnering with schools as a service provider that places published authors with a partner teacher in order to enact a job embedded coaching model that "engages teachers and students in shared writing experiences" (witshouston.org). In Texas, writing scores on the state assessment are consistently low at grade level requirement, making partnerships for professional development in writing instruction increasingly popular. Mokhtari was a high school English teacher in a large Houston area school district when he first engaged with the program. When he left that campus, he moved to a campus that was beginning a partnership with the program. Chestin observed him on the new campus as he referenced the protocols used by the WITS writer. He also shared some of the strategies from McKay with his new team.

Milieu

McKay High School proved to be a rich campus for our study into shifting teacher identity and student achievement. Every meeting there stood at the intersection of policy and practice. McKay also proved to be both a challenge and a reward for the research team. Of all our field sites in the three-year study, this campus presented the highest number of rescheduled meetings and cancelations. Yet it remained the site of insightful meetings that extended beyond the practice of teaching literacy and into the essence of the lives of teachers. During early observations of protocol and Professional Learning Community (PLC) (Dufour & Eaker, 1998) time, teachers at McKay seemed to tune out the numerous announcements, disruptions by administrators, and double-booked meetings to engage in discussions of student work, but there was stress everywhere.

Mokhtari's Reflection

McKay was labeled an "IR" school. That means improvement required. When a school in the state of Texas has received a failing grade from the state for a certain number of years, the Texas Education Agency can take over not only the school but also the Board for the entire district. With so much on the line, we all expected walkthroughs from "important" people, but I was naïve to think that they wouldn't have a drastic impact on my ability to lead our team.

These walkthroughs were not simple and unobtrusive. They were ostensibly designed to foster anxiety among administrators and teachers alike, which, of course, trickled down to our students. Imagine anywhere from 3 to 10 White people in suits, with laptops and notepads, walking into your classroom in a straight line and surrounding the back row of your students in an intimidating "U" formation. "What, are we zoo animals or something?" A student's question, raised indignantly, caused my heart to sink a little. "How are we going to get these students what they need if they can never be observed in an authentic learning environment?" I mused to myself.

After a few months of countless walkthroughs by everyone from TEA – to the school board, to principals and teachers from other schools – we, as an English department, were not fed up or angry, but tired and drained.

> By the end of the year, we were crying in PLC. Were you there when we cried? WITS was our kind of refuge, you know? We could actually talk about what we knew we were here to do. It was a support group for us. We looked forward to being in that community. (Chestin's, Field Journals, Fall Y2)

Mokhtari shared the quote above with Chestin during their reunion after his resignation from McKay. He had been hired by another campus that also enlisted WITS Collaborative for professional development support. Chestin had been contracted for leadership coaching and curriculum support there. He continued, "Here it's easier for me than it was there because we were pretty much in survival [mode] there. The whole department is gone. WITS was our 'one thing,'" he recollected.

Our research record revealed that he was not alone in that feeling. Many others found the WITS Collaborative to be an important part of their community; its sustenance was the only shining moment for McKay. The team at McKay HS shared freely about how WITS provided a consistent healing space for them even though the time was not always protected. Early on, the teachers' discussion was heavily influenced by the need for higher student attendance and for less pressure related to the accountability measures of the state exam. "We have about 65 % of our ninth graders not reading on a third grade level. I don't want to hear about a test until we can figure out how to get them here and give them an opportunity to make some Lexile gains," one teacher said (Correspondence 2018). These struggles were, and continue to be, valid points of concern at McKay. Though these concerns were not eliminated during the program enactment, the teachers developed increasingly complex questions regarding how to help students increase performance as the program progressed. The research record indicated that the language of instruction became more specific and explicit. The group even self-identified conferring with students in a workshop approach to secondary genre study as its next area for improvement.

AN INTERVIEW ON TEACHER EXPERIENCES REGARDING TEACHER SUSTENANCE IN URBAN ENVIRONMENTS

Because I (Mokhtari) believe that the best way to understand the effects of our pre-WITS PLC time is to interview the people on the front lines, I interviewed a former colleague. He was the only other African American male teacher in our Writing Collaborative.

Recounting Reactionary Administration

The converse of practical wisdom is simply natural instinct, which issues in impulsive activities that are both unreasonable and uncontrolled. Such people are easily provoked to anger and their leadership style is...erratic. (Paris, 1995)

Ninth-grade classes at this inner-city school were huge, with well over 30 students. One of the many "consultants" had observed all the English/Language Arts (ELA) classrooms and concluded there was only one master teacher on the ninth-grade team. She, of course, shared her opinion with the head principal. The teacher I interviewed taught ninth grade, but he was not the "master teacher" identified by the consultant. The principal met with the whole ELA department and told everyone what the consultant said. She then decided to combine *all* ninth-grade classes into one classroom. That meant over 70 ninth graders with behavior issues all in one classroom.

What does this do to the morale of the team as a whole? Bigger problem: what does this do to the morale of the other ninth-grade teacher, Arthur? Arthur became upset in the meeting room after the principal left, but there was still an administrator in the room. She surreptitiously sent a text message on her phone. Minutes later, the head principal came back. Arguing ensued, but to no avail. The ninth-grade classes would be combined the following week. Arthur showed up to work every day feeling hurt, embarrassed, and ultimately indignant. Not wanting to get in the way of the "master teacher," he took a back-seat in a class of 70 plus students.

When asked to reflect here is what Arthur had to say:

"*I felt undermined. I am originally from California, originally trained in Common Core Curriculum, and I needed time to get aligned to Texas TEKS. I showed up to a classroom where two teachers had quit before I arrived. Leadership allowed me to observe the class for two days before takeover. I realized the issue: students were not engaged. They did not trust what they were being fed.*

As a black male, working in the inner city, a female leader who decided to make me a second class teacher attacked my confidence. I felt she had issues with my strong presence. She was a dominant figure, and so was I.

We clashed.

It made me question who I was as an educator, and if this is something I wanted to do long-term. When I showed up, the students told me that they were going to make me quit. But they did not. I was unlike the other two teachers prior. I needed support, I needed strong leadership, yet I felt the leaders turned on me. I came to [this school] with the idea that I was going to help those that looked like me, only to realize some of those that look like me did not believe in my ability. So, I checked out. I said, 'If I'm not good enough, do it your way'.

Shortly after, my students were returned to me in my class. I never agreed with the (initial) decision, and I never agreed with the actions that followed. The administration never apologized or recognized their wrongdoing. They never explained why they returned classes to their original state, and I never felt like the school leaders believed in my ability. I am working at a school that has been on IR for over five years, and you question my ability, in my opinion, in a disrespectful manner. I felt morally obligated to stay at this school. I wanted to stay. Black children in America needed to be served by someone who genuinely cared about their success. I knew students lacked what I provided. A strong Black male, who had never been arrested, who knew how to navigate the American system. I felt bad for them. When I saw them and spoke to them, I treated them like I would my own children. I believe in their untapped potential. I am someone who cares about their success.

Yet I left because I knew I could not work under the leadership of people who questioned my ability and motives. I struggled with the decision to leave. I really did not want to, but I did for my own sanity. I went to a new location and made an immediate impact. I remember thinking about the kids, but I was not willing to go back working for those who did not believe in me."

Mokhtari's Reflection

I was part of this environment for too long. It breeds erratic leadership styles, which are not necessarily the fault of the leaders, but rather a symptom of a larger problem: When administrators are stressed to the point of losing their jobs due to accountability measures, they will often do whatever a consultant deems necessarily. The problem in Arthur's case was that we had so many consultants – all with different opinions. That problem, combined with an overly stressed and reactionary administration, resulted in a diminished capacity to serve the students.

Notes from Chestin and KaLeah

Mokhtari and Arthur echo what the research team heard from other struggling campuses: too many consultants. To address this concern, the WITS partnership sent the same writer out to the campus for years. There was not the feeling of someone dropping in and making decisions for teachers. Instead, through established relationships and a consistent presence, the WITS writer became a facilitator of discourse and aided teachers in making decisions for themselves. This space of autonomy seemed to be a recurrent and freeing theme in our notes.

The absence of voice in the direction of efforts toward improvement is rooted in an authoritarian form of leadership which operates in a "Knowledge-for-Teaching" stance as opposed to a "Teacher Knowledge" stance (Craig, You, & Oh, 2017). As we reviewed the images, recordings, and transcripts from McKay, it became clear that teachers strongly disliked the numerous initiatives enacted to improve student performance. One teacher shared, "We see people come in, and it feels like we're in a zoo. Before we can really figure out why they are here, they are gone and the next one comes." Even when we attempted to approach the administration for interviews, we received no response, nor did the campus administrators respond to the annual surveys for the collaborative.

In taking the anecdote and our field notes into further examination, the teacher's knowledge was largely absent from decision-making. Teachers voiced a concern that "whoever is choosing these consultants thinks we don't know what to do. I wish they would just ask us." The consultants who were selected seemed to disregard the knowledge born of experience on that campus, and the divide and tensions increased. This was echoed by Mokhtari in correspondence (2021):

> ...treat us like professionals and respect the fact that we eventually have too much on our plates, which causes burnout and resentment. Teachers also need to be given the chance to practice and plan their craft. Forcing teachers to go to PDs all the time takes away from the time they could use in quality PLC with their teams.

MOKHTARI ON WITS

I taught at McKay for one year. It was an inner city school that was 94% African American. We were one year away from being taken over by the state, and we were desperate to get the students' writing scores up. We were willing to try anything. It was clear that having numerous consultants was ineffectual, so WITS became one of those "anythings."

I remember our first PLC with our WITS coach. In walks this tiny, older, white-haired, Caucasian woman. My immediate thought? *My students were going to eat her alive.* My students. They were 18- and 19-year-olds in the 10th grade, some with ankle monitors, accustomed to walking out of class to go to work, pick up their kids, or "take care of other business." During that first meeting, she modeled a fantastic writing lesson, and we completed the assignment. We then decided which days we would like for her to teach our classes. When the day came, I was terrified for her.

But I was the one who got a lesson in humility.

This tiny white woman came in and commanded my class better than I had all year. I was astounded and a bit embarrassed. The students were engaged and many even completed the entire assignment. This was an example of getting it right. I found out later that one of the teachers on our team knew this particular instructor, her background, experience, and heart – but also knew our kids. Both the instructor and the teacher on my team knew that these students needed to be listened to. It did not matter if the listener looked like them, and many had not been listened to by someone that did not look like them. They seemed inspired to succeed by someone that in their mind "wasn't just doing this for a paycheck."

Administration, in this case, listened to the recommendation of a master teacher, and we successfully implemented a Writing Collaborative on our campus. It allowed for a deeper well of shared knowledge and experience among our team. It gave us tangible, quantifiable writing samples from exceedingly reluctant writers. This was the first time I experienced a quality Writing Collaborative. This is where the professional relationship can flourish – through the shared experience and the removal of ego.

The PLC time in collaborative was only successful if:

- Administration and team/level leaders ensured that certain criteria were met.
- Everyone on the team was on board, not only with the initial PLC where the lesson is modeled, explained, and then completed by every teacher on the team but also for an actual writer to lead the class.
- The expectation was clear that the collaborative would not work if the teachers did not participate.
- Every teacher had a product to share by the end of the lesson.

These things can help build any PLC.

OUR RESPITE: EACH OTHER (MOKHTARI)

If there is one thing I know for sure, it is that the bonds that are forged in fire are the hardest to break. My team members leaned on each other constantly, and we were always there to support one another because at the end of the day, we knew what our team and our students were up against. We developed friendships through the hardships of working together at a school on the brink. We bonded over the successes and setbacks alike, and we are still in contact with each other to this day.

WITS is a unique collaborative experience between experienced writers and former teachers with current teachers who are attempting to get the best out of their students' writing. We do this through creative writing assignments that inspire students to not be intimidated by the blank page, which as most English teachers will tell you, is one of the most difficult aspects of teaching writing.

One particular assignment was called "Memory Blueprint." In short, we were required to read two mentor texts, meditate on a familiar place, and then draw that place in the form of a blueprint in as much detail as possible: familiar objects, feelings of joy, feelings of sadness, things that you learned about yourself, landmarks, etc., and then share if you felt comfortable.

The stories of my colleagues were personal and compelling, but they are their own; I have no right to share them. It was only through our shared experience of working together in a failing school that we were even comfortable enough to share it with each other. I will; however, share mine – not for self-aggrandizement or applause, but so that one can see the benefit of a quality PLC for professional educators with students who are taught that expressing emotion is a weakness. The location I chose was my grandparents' home:

My grandfather was a dignified man, a product of WW2 where he served as a medic. Every morning he had the same routine. First, he would wake me up to go use the restroom (I had a bedwetting problem...) Then he would shave with the same DE razor that he used in the war. I still remember the smell of the canned Colgate shaving cream. He would talk to me as he did it – I think he knew in the back of his mind that my father was never going to teach me. "Against the grain and then with the grain," he would say. The sound of the razor like sandpaper against his skin. After the shave he would retreat to his bedroom to get dressed for the day. He had long been retired and had no reason to put on trousers, a short sleeve buttoned down shirt, long socks, and loafers, but he did. Every morning. Then to the kitchen, where he would reach in the freezer and get a frozen can of concentrated orange juice, squeeze it in the same pitcher he used every morning, shake it up, sit at his spot at the head of the table, and read the newspaper while I watched cartoons. This was our time as my grandmother would often sleep until 11 and my sister wouldn't get up until around 9. This was our time; simple consistency that I adored in stark contrast with the tumult of my mother's home. Other than the African masks that hung above the kitchen that as a child I found "scary," this house was my refuge – my place of peace. Sometimes later we would go to the backyard and pick plums from the tree, peppers, and tomatoes then ride around the neighborhood and give some to our neighbors. If the lawn needed mowing, he would put on his straw hat and mow. If cars needed washing, he would wash them, and then he would prepare lunch. Towards the end of his life though, he stopped being able to shave himself; that was my job. He stopped having to get me up to use the restroom; that was my job. He stopped being able to mow the day he collapsed in the backyard; that was my job...to pay someone to do it for me. One day when I was helping him get dressed, he, out of the blue, looked at me and said: "Abkader, don't get old." It was then that I felt he had lost his dignity. But in my eyes he never would – he had taught me so much. You don't have to live in excess to enjoy life. Buy nice clothes, but not the whole rack. Eat good food, but not the whole plate. Drink good whiskey, but not the whole bottle. Love....

And that was when our time to write was up. Everyone shared their story and at the end, everyone was in tears. The Writing Collaborative provided a much needed therapeutic session for drained teachers working at a school on the brink of collapse.

From a pedagogical standpoint, the Memory Blueprint lesson provided much in terms of craft and literary technique in a 15-minute first draft: parallel structure, metaphor, compare/contrast, quotes in context, and imagery. Admittedly, this first draft came from an educated adult, but if I can do this in 15 minutes, imagine what our students could do?

Notes from Chestin and KaLeah

The research team was present when writing instruction came to a halt after the STAAR EOC I, and EOC II tests were administered. All the teachers were called to the auditorium. Even the team that was in a WITS PD session. We did not know what was happening, but it seemed urgent and department representatives were walking the halls to make sure that every English teacher made it there quickly. We would find out minutes later that while urgency may have been debatable, the subject would have a great impact on the partnership with WITS, and thus the community of teachers and their classroom practice. Each teacher returned with a series of worksheet packets to use for the duration of the school year in order to support testing and retesting in the content areas of social studies and science.

For many teachers on the campus, that act was the final straw in reduction of morale. Several had found refuge in WITS PD, and even with the promise of focusing more on workshops in the next school term, they were lost without a classroom in which to practice. It was difficult because the WITS Collaborative coach wanted so badly to intervene. One of the other teachers we interviewed stated that the program was the one thing that kept her at McKay. It was tough for the coach, but neither the teacher collective nor the coach as an outside support was able to reverse the decision. It was the exposition of a co-constructed story to leave by (Clandinin, Downey, & Huber, 2009). In the last meeting we observed on campus, teachers cried and vowed to see one another at happy hour for drinks and to continue corresponding after the school year ended. Many revealed they had accepted new positions. Others had job offers pending.

Throughout this chapter, Mokhtari and his colleagues faced tensions related to their experiences "on the brink" as he described it. This phrase brought the editors to Parker Palmer's (2018) *On the Brink of Everything* in which the same sense of culmination resides:

> *Looking back, I see why I needed the tedium and the inspiration, the anger and the love, the anguish and the joy. I see how it all belongs, even those days of despair when the darkness overwhelmed me ... without which the fabric of my life would be less resilient.*

The "tough turf" of McKay enabled Mokhtari to grow into a more confident and reflective contributor in PLC at his new campus. He was immediately seen as a leader and a source of valuable experiences.

MOKHTARI'S CONCLUDING REMARKS

We were definitely a knowledge community. I do not recall a single originating event, but having WITS as a part of our PLC time was a big part of cultivating it. After Chestin invited me to reflect on my time at that campus, she shared two articles with me: "Braided Lives: Multiple ways of knowing, flowing in and out of knowledge communities" and "Teacher Education and the Best Loved Self" (Craig, 2013). Both the articles address how shared experiences and accepting our "best loved selves" go a long way toward conveying to our students and our colleagues that we are more than the subjects we teach. We had that at McKay. These articles addressed the fact that quality instruction and learning outcomes occur when teachers accept and incorporate all aspects of their identity and training in their instruction. For example, you cannot teach nonfiction or argumentative essays without addressing the political and social context of the time. Furthermore, a teacher cannot remove their training or lived experiences from the content. These articles elucidate the importance of "…teachers as knowledge creators" as opposed to "teachers as curriculum implementers" (Curtis, Reid, Kelley, Martindell, & Craig, 2013). McKay, with all of its efforts to be a better place for student achievement, was losing the teachers they needed. It became what was a consistently shifting landscape (Curtis et al., 2013), and that was hard to navigate. So many left.

One significant factor that much of the numeric data from research on urban education neglects is the function of communication and shared experiences among both professionals and students. Students need quality teachers. Quality planning comes from quality teams that know and trust each other on a fundamental and professional level. Communicating our experiences and being honest with ourselves in terms of where we excel and where we struggle is key to quality learning outcomes, and to get to that level, we need a safe and consistent space that is free from the attack of random consultants and erratic "…decisions that affect us, but neglect us" (Chestin T. Auzenne-Curl, personal communication, 2021). We need community.

REFERENCES

Clandinin, D. J. (2013). Chapter 4 Personal practical knowledge: A study of teacher's classroom images. In C. J Craig, P. C Meijer, & J. Broeckmans (Eds.), *From teacher thinking to teachers and teaching: The evolution of a research community. Advances in research on teaching* (Vol. 19, pp. 67–96). Wiley. doi: 10.1108/S1479-3687(2013)0000019007

Clandinin, D. J., Downey, C. A., & Huber, J. (2009). Attending to changing landscapes: Shaping the interwoven identities of teachers and teacher educators. *Asia Pacific Journal of Teacher Education, 37*, 141–154.

Connelly, F. M., & Clandinin, D. J. (1990). Stories of experience and narrative inquiry. *Educational Researcher*, *19*(5), 2–14.

Connelly, F. M., & Clandinin, D. J. (1999). *Shaping a professional identity: Stories of educational practice*. New York, NY: Teachers College Press.

Craig, C. (1995). Knowledge communities: A way of making sense of how beginning teachers come to know in their professional knowledge contexts. *Curriculum Inquiry*, *25*(2), 151–175.

Craig, C. (2007). Illuminating qualities of knowledge communities in a portfolio-making context. *Teachers and Teaching*, *13*(6), 617–636. doi:10.1080/13540600701683564

Craig, C. (2013). Teacher education and the best-loved self. *Asia Pacific Journal of Education*, *33*(3), 261–272. doi:10.1080/02188791.2013.788476

Craig, C. J., You, J., & Oh, S. (2017). Pedagogy through the pearl metaphor: Teaching as a process of ongoing refinement. *Journal of Curriculum Studies*, *49*(6), 757–781. doi:10.1080/00220272.2015.1066866

Curtis, G., Reid, D., Kelley, M., Martindell, P. T., & Craig, C. J. (2013). Braided lives: Multiple ways of knowing, flowing in and out of knowledge communities. *Studying Teacher Education*, *9*(2), 175–186. doi:10.1080/17425964.2013.808062

Dewey, J. (1938). My pedagogic creed. *School Journal*, *54*, 77–80.

DuFour, R., & Eaker, R. E. (1998). *Professional learning communities at work: Best practices for enhancing student achievement*. Bloomington, IN: National Education Service.

Palmer, P. J. (2019). *On the brink of everything: Grace, gravity, and getting old* (16pt large print edition). Oakland, CA: ReadHowYouWant.

Paris, P. J. (1995). *The spirituality of African peoples: The search for a common moral discourse*. Minneapolis, MN: Fortress Press.

Schwab, J. (1973). The practical 3: Translation into curriculum. *The School Review*, *81*(4), 501–522.

Writers in the Schools (2014). WITS collaborative. Retrieved from https://witshouston.org/wits-for-teachers/

THE BEAUTY OF PETALS AND THORNS: NEGOTIATING IDENTITY AS WRITER-TEACHER

Sarah Jerasa

ABSTRACT

To be a writer, one must write. Research shows when teachers write and identify as writers, they transfer their writing practice into their classroom, positively impacting their students' writing development. Shifting instructional practices or identities requires educators to self-determine a gap in order to take on transformative learning experiences, such as mentoring, professional development, or modeled learning. Often professional development is chosen by administrators for educators to shift their instructional practice, ignoring a teacher's curriculum-maker role, and best-loved self identity. This narrative inquiry analysis details one teacher-writer in a creative writing professional development residency as she supports educators with a goal to transform educators into teacher-writers. This chapter includes the small step successes and systematic struggles the author faced as she modeled the writer's craft and writer's workshop strategies with her teachers. The chapter concludes with a discussion on the important role teachers have to decide, navigate, and discover their own best-loved self-teaching identity.

Keywords: Teacher-writer identity; best-loved self; literacy professional development; transformative learning; stories of experience; literacy coaching

I left the classroom in 2015, taking a pause to reexamine what brought joy to my work. I began a new journey as a creative writing instructor and professional development coach with Writers in the Schools (WITS), a nonprofit organization whose core mission is to inspire and engage children from all demographics and ages in the power and joy of writing. Through school, community, and professional development programs, WITS has been an arts presence in Houston, Texas, for over 35 years, fostering and engaging students and teachers through authentic writing practices (Writers In the Schools, 2014). Rather than focusing on state assessments or mandating a set curriculum, the WITS program encourages writers to use inspiring, noncanonical mentor texts and creative prompts as the invitations for writing with students.

WITS Collaborative is a professional development program that provides an opportunity for teachers to be mentored as writers to improve their writing instruction. For school administrators, better teacher instruction equates with student success and stronger assessment scores. Therefore, school leaders are willing to spend valuable budget dollars on external professional development programs, like WITS Collaborative, in the hopes to support teachers and ultimately to improve student achievement data. In states like Texas, assessment scores are not just attached to the individual student but instead are vital data sets connected to a school's rating and performance, ultimately impacting school and district funding (Texas Education Agency, n.d.). Although school administrators who contract with the WITS Collaborative program for their teachers may voice a desire for teachers to write, they usually want improvement in their school data and assessment scores. The program's overarching goals are focused on engaging teachers and students in authentic writing, but administrators too often ignore that messaging in hopes of achieving a one-stop professional development solution for their schools. In other words, they want a silver bullet for success.

WITS Collaborative's core objectives center on professional development to support teachers as writers to impact their instructional practice. Through weekly team meetings, teachers are asked to engage in writing exercises and written reflections to experience writing as their students might, providing an opportunity to collaboratively discuss and amend the lesson as it suits their individual classes. WITS writers also model and teach the lessons in the teachers' classrooms, adding an additional layer of modeling and collaboration for a teacher's professional development. In this way, WITS Collaborative engages and invites teachers to reflect, respond, and create as writers.

THEORETICAL FRAMEWORK

As a professional development coach with the WITS Collaborative program, my role was to inspire and engage classroom teachers as writers, through a collaborative and reflective process. My work and approach aligned with the theoretical framework of transformative learning theory (Mezirow, 2000) which suggests that realizing a "disorienting dilemma" (p. 22) or personally significant experience can trigger learners to reframe their way of knowing and seeing the world (Kagan, 2000). In this way, transformative learning is not simply accomplishing a new task or obtaining new knowledge. Rather, it is the shifting of an individual's "frame of reference" which includes "habits of mind and point of view" (Kagan,

2000, p. 52). In my past experience, establishing a writer identity was triggered by a problem I saw within myself, my instruction, and my writing community. My transformative learning experience ultimately changed not just how I taught writing to my students, but the way I viewed the world.

Writing has multiple outcomes as a process of discovery of self, knowledge, and identity. In a study on the impact of the National Writing Project (NWP) Summer Institute on teacher-writers, Whitney (2008) examined how teachers gradually identified as writers and experienced transformative learning through the act of daily writing practice. Whitney (2008) suggests that the very act of writing is, in fact, transformative. In this way, the WITS Collaborative professional development model intended for teachers to have a new frame of reference to develop a writing identity through the transformative act of writing (Mezirow, 1991; Whitney, 2008). Ultimately, this new lens would positively impact their writing instruction for students. This mission was cultivated through weekly Professional Learning Community (PLC) meetings (Darling-Hammond, Hyler, & Gardner, 2017; DuFour, 2005; Fountas & Pinnell, 2020) with a WITS Collaborative professional development coach/writer. A PLC meeting, unlike a grade-level team meeting, is intentionally designed for collaborative opportunities between teachers that might include modeled lessons, reflective writing opportunities, and discussions (Darling-Hammond, Hyler, & Gardner, 2017; DuFour, 2005; Fountas & Pinnell, 2020). During a 50-hour coaching residency at a school, I was the expert writer assigned to a grade-level team to support, guide, and mentor teachers' writing instruction.

I joined the WITS Collaborative team in 2016 and was excited to share my love of writing with other teachers. I wanted to be a mentor and shift teachers' identities into writers, just as I had experienced through collaboration and active learning as a classroom teacher (Darling-Hammond et al., 2017). I wanted to excite teachers and reveal a new way to see their writing instruction through reflection, shared writing, and collaboration. I wanted to envelop teachers in a writing community, where they could thrive and grow in their own writing practice (Lieberman & Wood, 2001). I personally had experienced what Mezirow (1991) describes as transformative learning through my own experiences with graduate-level coursework and the NWP's Summer Institute professional development (Whitney, 2008). Therefore, I wanted teachers to see writing, not as a part of the school day lesson, but as a powerful tool for their own reflection, learning, and communication. Becoming a writer had such a positive change for me as both teacher and person. I wanted my teachers to have a similar, transformative experience.

Most professional development is determined for teachers by administrators based on a school's assessment data results. Often, low assessment scores require schools to respond with remediation or additional instructional support. As a result, professional development opportunities at the school level are often chosen *for* teachers and not *by* teachers, ignoring the specific and unique needs individual teachers have to grow and develop in their instruction (Lieberman & Wood, 2003). When teachers are mandated to participate in required professional development, often there is resistance, resentment, and rejection. Traditional professional development positions teachers as passive consumers of information and asked to compliantly apply strategies, interventions, or lessons into their teaching (Cochran-Smith & Lytle, 2001; Lieberman & Wood, 2003; Little, 1993). According to studies on effective professional development, when teachers engage together as experts using their own practical knowledge, shared knowledge is constructed and is more likely to produce a fruitful learning experience, impacting long-term instructional change (Lieberman & Wood, 2001).

Teachers need to view themselves as curriculum-makers rather than curriculum-implementers (Clandinin & Connelly, 1992; Connelly & Clandinin, 1988). This means if teachers are not at the helm to determine gaps in their own professional growth and development, any professional development experience will likely produce minimal impact for a teacher's practice. Craig (2013) suggests that a key component of teacher as curriculum-maker (Clandinin & Connelly, 1992; Connelly & Clandinin, 1988; Craig, 2013) is the teacher's vision of their best-loved self and "how they desire to teach" (Craig, 2013; Schwab, 1954/1978). Thus, an educator's vision of their best-loved self is the wheel and motivator to engage in curriculum and shift their own practices. Craig (2013) suggests, "no enactment of curriculum would be complete without [a teacher's] active engagement" (p. 264). Seeking a change in teacher practice cannot be forced or mandated. Rather, a teacher needs to see the necessity in order for a change to take place (Craig, 2013). When professional development facilitators attempt to improve or grow a teacher's skills or knowledge, they should consider coaching roles that support a teacher's view of their best-loved self. In this way, coaching has the potential to highlight the importance of a teacher's individual voice, response, and community to effectively develop teacher knowledge and practice.

METHODOLOGY

In this narrative inquiry analysis, I will take the stance as both researcher and participant to examine my own understandings, responses, and reflections as a WITS Collaborative professional development coach, teacher, and writer. This chapter will chronicle my experience as a writing coach for WITS where I provided professional development to teachers across various schools in a southeast Texas city. I will highlight snapshot stories from yearlong residencies at Brown Elementary School, St. Leo's Catholic School, and Rodrigo Elementary School. These vignettes will illustrate how classroom teachers can negotiate their own teacher-writing identities and how my work as a coach supported those identities. In these anecdotal stories, I will describe how my identities (teacher and writer) guided me to respond, reflect, and raise teachers' writing development.

Narrative inquiry is the choice of analysis due to its nature and focus on story as the source and frame of understanding. Connelly and Clandinin (1988) suggest that people are storytellers and the story is the pathway to understanding the reality of lived experience (Mitchell, 1980). My frame of lived experience as a teacher, writer, and professional development coach shifts my lens of understanding and my interpretations of how my WITS Collaborative residencies were received and considered. The goal of this analysis is not to find a right or a wrong or a statistical level of significant impact. Rather, this analysis unpacks how transformative learning and a teacher's view of their best-loved self took shape within the context of a writing professional development experience. My ability to analyze these vignettes from a new perspective, as a researcher, serves an additional layer of analysis as I am able to see these situational snapshots from a wider perspective.

Data Collection

The vignettes for analysis were collected from my personal notes, email communication, and lesson plans throughout my WITS Collaborative residencies. Part of my work as a writer was to take notes on teachers' responses, commentary, and my own reflections, and then share them during WITS monthly staff meetings. These vignettes were selected from the many stories and experiences within my residencies because they captured unique takeaways for me as a WITS Collaborative professional development coach.

Data Analysis

Analysis for my narrative inquiry will take place by first examining my response to each vignette as a teacher-writer. I will consider how my own teacher and writer identities take shape within each unique residency and how these identities played an important role in my reactions and responses. In addition, my analysis will consider the teachers' perceptions of their transformation and the identity of their best-loved selves. A key component of my analysis is to ask the question, how did teachers view themselves in this snapshot moment? Was the teacher's best-loved self realized within that moment? As a researcher, my analysis will also ask me to step back as a variable and to question how transformative learning theory takes shape and what the developments mean for a teacher's professional development journey toward teacher as curriculum-maker and teacher as writer.

Limitations

Analysis in this way has several limitations, namely the specific recollection of details, quotes, and reactions. Many of these school snapshots took place many years ago, and like any story, the interpretation is held in the hands of the storyteller. My attempt to recreate the sentiment, quotes, and reactions from each WITS residency were drawn from multiple sources (i.e. lesson plans, email communication exchange, text communication, written reflections) to provide as much objectively accurate detail as possible.

NEW WRITER, WHO DIS?: ACTUALIZATION OF MY WRITING IDENTITY

Finding my identity as a teacher and a writer was a personal journey. My identity transformation as a writer evolved because of multiple intentional experiences from my own ambition to change. My realization as a writer was not an overnight transformation. It took many years of reflection, purposeful writing experiences, and engaging in authentic writing habits with a community of writers.

When I began most residencies, curious students would ask if I was legit and qualified enough to be called a writer. While I lacked a *NY Times* best-seller published book, my answer to these curious students was always a confident "yes." I am a writer because I see myself as a writer, I have stories and opinions to share, and I consistently return to the page to write them down. I am a writer because I see the value in my words and how they impact others. I am a writer not because I have achieved a great feat or accomplished an inconceivable goal, rather, I am a writer because I have a notebook with words and a community that helps me grow. I have grown from seed to bloom, transformed into my own best-loved self as a writer with a new frame of reference.

LAYING THE FOUNDATION; SOIL, SEED, SUN

All WITS Collaborative residencies begin with planning meetings. In these meetings, writers meet their team of teachers, review the goals of the program, and teachers share their hopes for their writing instruction for the year. I remember my very first residency planning meeting: I was so excited to share with teachers my love of writing, and I was confident that it would be only a short matter of time that they would be converted to my "church of writing." I anticipated meeting teachers who were thrilled to have the *opportunity* to work with me and like sponges, ready to soak up all the knowledge I was about to share. But, my first meeting was totally different from what I had envisioned.

I stepped into a conference room, known as the "Data Room" where large posters of assessment scores hung on the walls, stacks of binders placed across the tables, and groups of teachers sat hunched over papers, planning out the following week's assignments and assessments. This school was not unlike many schools across Texas who face the immense pressure of annual high stakes tests to measure growth and determine school funding. The pressure is felt from all corners from a school; administration, teachers, even classroom decor, all emphasizing the importance of meeting the high-pass rates on the annual state-wide assessments. The conference room door opened, and I stepped into heavy silence, immediately feeling my presence was impeding on teachers' precious planning time. I was not what the teachers asked for. I was another thing added to their already long to-do list.

As a writing coach, providing professional development ultimately meant that I had to redefine what success meant and what it would look like. My fantasy had to be altered. I quickly learned that each school and each grade-level team was unique with its own needs and goals. Success could not look the same at every school, and it was dependent on what teachers brought. And while I was hopeful to transform each teacher into a magnificent writer and writing instructor, I knew that *my* transformative experience into a writer might not be possible for all of my teachers. I worked in many schools across southeast Texas, some urban, some magnet, public and private, spanning grades 2nd to 8th. I learned that many things were out of my teachers' control such as last minute administrator meetings, teacher absences, school closures, and testing requirements. Through these many experiences, I had to adapt, be flexible, and reimagine how coaching moments would be beneficial for my teachers. Despite all of these challenges, what remained consistent at all my schools was that I wanted my teachers to *feel* like writers and to experience how their writing growth could transfer into their writing instruction. I wanted all residencies to be some kind of transformative experience for my teachers. I wanted teachers to take ownership of their writing instruction. The question still remained, did my teachers see a need to be transformed?

WITS RESIDENCY VIGNETTES

Brown Elementary – Silver Bullet for Test Scores

January 7, 2017

I arrived at Brown Elementary for my weekly 3rd grade team meeting. It was our first meeting after winter break and the start of a new semester. As I signed in, I saw brightly colored numbers illuminated on a sign on the foyer walls: 98 school days until state testing. This countdown was a visual reminder of the reason we were all here: the STAAR test, the mandated high stakes end of year state assessment given to all Texas public school students. Brown Elementary historically had not performed well on these Texas state tests. According to the Texas Education Agency, reports indicated that at Brown Elementary 49% of 3rd grade students passed the 2016 reading test and only 36% of 4th grade students passed the 2016 writing test (Houston Independent School District, n.d.). *My WITS Collaborative focus with the 3rd grade team would be to help lay a foundation for writing in order to support upcoming 4th grade test scores for the following year.*

Today's team meeting was to engage everyone in personal writing for teachers to connect their writing with their instruction. Using group engagement protocols from the School Reform Initiative (SRI), I wanted the teachers to reflect through writing around a successful moment in their teaching. I arrived at Ms. Bosworth's classroom door as her class was lining up to go to their ancillary class. Students smiled and waved as I quietly entered, trying to avoid being a distraction. A barrage of questions from the student line were shouted in my direction, "Are you here for us today?", "Ms. J what writing are we doing?", "I wrote a new story yesterday!". In a hushed response, I whispered I would see them the following week with an exciting lesson to share. And soon Ms. Bosworth led her class down the hall and I was left alone to set up for our PLC meeting. I distributed copies of our writing prompt, "The Success Analysis Protocol" and set up pencils and pens for teachers to use. And then I sat. Our meetings were set to start at 10:30 am when students went to their ancillary classes, on the other side of the school building. I sat and waited, watching the time dwindle down. We only had 45 minutes for our meetings but in order to have time for the teachers to pick up their students on time, go to the bathroom, take attendance, we were lucky to get 25 minutes together. And today, it was looking like our meeting time would be much less.

It was 10:48 am by the time all three teachers came in for our meeting. Each apologized breathlessly as if they had run several laps around the building before arriving at our meeting location. I reassured the teachers, "No worries, we have plenty of time" however I knew that was not the case. I knew that writing shouldn't be rushed and today we were doing reflective writing. I wanted our writing to drive the meeting, to deepen our discussion, and time to write is the only way to get there. I quickly glanced at the protocol plan for the day to see what could be quickly cut to make more time available.

*I began and handed out pens and paper since several teachers realized they forgot their materials. "Today we are going to reflect on our past successes to gain insight into the conditions that lead to those successes as teachers, so you can do more of what works when providing writing instruction. I want you to think of a successful moment you have had as a teacher this year. I would like for you to think about your successful moment and describe the specifics of the success and answer 'What made **this lesson different** from others?'. Perhaps choose a successful moment that is unlike others."*

I set my timer as we all began to write. Soft piano music played, pens scribbling away in black and white marbled composition notebooks. All three teachers were writing, the entire time. There was a sense of accomplishment in seeing teachers engaged as writers: writing down their words, telling the stories of their most successful teaching moments from the year. I was encouraged and eager to hear what they would share.

As the time drew to a close, I said, "Now take a moment to tell us what you wrote about. You don't have to read exactly what you wrote but try to let us know what made this successful teaching moment different." I sat still and patiently waited for a teacher to gain the courage to speak. I never wanted to force someone to share. I let the silence be the heavy pressure for volunteers.

A nervous silence fell in the room. Eyes were down on papers and I heard the tick of the clock moving.

Ms. Bosworth went first, quietly sharing a moment from a previous year when she taught a lesson on how to tell time to 2nd graders. She noted how she had never taught this math concept before and explained she had no idea how to do it. "I got the idea to make my lesson very interactive, like a game and I was so surprised at how excited the kids all got." She explained how this moment stood out because of all the fun she had planning and teaching this activity for her students. She felt like because she had enjoyed doing the lesson, that her students learned more and remembered the concept better.

Another teacher, Ms. Alwin, also shared a lesson she prepared when a Texas Education Agency (TEA) appraiser was coming in for an observation. "I was so nervous for this observation visit. I'm usually a good teacher in front of students but to have another adult watching from such a high position, watching my every move, made me feel different." Ms. Alwin explained she usually just goes along with the district's curriculum pacing guide, using the lessons the district provides. But this lesson was different because it was completely designed by her. She shared how she planned every single component: text, examples, materials, and even included how long each part of the lesson would take. Ms. Alwin shared that often she doesn't put this much energy into her normal everyday lesson. But this lesson had to be different because her reputation was at stake. Her lesson stood out because every component fit together and she felt like a rockstar. Ms. Alwin noted that her hard work really paid off because the TEA gave her glowing remarks and her students were the best they ever had been. She shared that this probably means she should plan in this way for more lessons, but it just takes too much time.

These real stories had such implications for the teachers' practice. I could have easily told them how these stories could be used to support their writing instruction. But this was a collaborative meeting, where I didn't need to have the answers. I wanted the teachers to make these discoveries on their own. So I asked, "How can we take these successful moments and apply them to our current practices?" I wanted the teachers to connect their past experiences to support their student writers. The stories they had just shared were such gems and could easily turn into applied lessons for future instructional practices. I wanted the teachers to make connections with their best lessons and their current writing instruction. I waited for the teachers to respond. Silence. I looked at my watch, three more minutes before the teachers had to dash. I knew it wasn't enough time but I still patiently waited for them to try to connect their experiences, hoping it would be done before they had to leave.

Ms. Alwin started to share. I smiled, thinking this would be the link, where I could see the teachers making important steps toward growth in their own writing development. "I'll be honest, Sarah," she began, "we are getting a lot of pressure right now from school admin to amp up how we are teaching reading. Our kids are taking the STAAR reading assessment and the data from the last district assessment wasn't good, at all. I can't even think about teaching writing because I need to focus on my students and their reading."

In thinking about this snapshot, I remember initially feeling defeated. No connections or discoveries were made. Teachers didn't link their great writing to their teaching. None of it. The teachers quickly saw that it was time for them to go, and I quickly packed my bag, so I could walk alongside them to wrap up and talk about our next meeting. I remember feeling rushed as I tried to think on my feet, suggesting we do a modeled lesson that supported the students' reading and writing levels. In that moment, I just wanted to please the teachers and be a support, rather than keep pushing for what I felt was best. I reflected on my own previous experience as a classroom teacher, remembering the data meetings, the administrative pressure, and the urgency to meet impossible assessment goals. I remembered feeling helpless and overwhelmed as a teacher, wanting to be better but just trying to make it through the end of each quarter, week, day. My response that day was to give the teachers what they needed, and support in reading and literacy skills for their students. Rather than push my own agenda, I shifted my plan to integrate reading and into my writing lessons to meet their request and urgency to increase reading test scores.

Examining the Brown Elementary teachers, I remember how they engaged in writing the entire time during our meetings. While our meetings were rushed due to time restraints, the teachers showed up most weeks, ready to write. Our meetings were led by me and my determined agenda. The teachers did not often bring dilemmas or triggering issues to our WITS Collaborative meetings beyond their administrator's concerns around data and assessment scores. It often felt like the teachers were waiting to be told or given a lesson that would be the solution. In this way, teachers viewed their role as curriculum-implementers. The examples that Ms. Bosworth and Ms. Alwin shared, however, were glimpses of teachers attempting a shift to a new frame of reference as curriculum-makers. Ms. Bosworth shared her joy to plan and teach her lesson and alluded to a best-loved self-experience as a curriculum-maker. Ms. Alwin noted that she planned a lesson entirely by herself, knowing that she would be observed by a state education official, and felt confident that her ability to execute a well-planned lesson could be repeated. In these examples, both teachers noted that they knew this was a successful moment because of their students' responses, not just because of assessment scores.

Through the Brown Elementary teachers' writing, they were starting to gain realization of their best-loved selves and what components of their successful lessons could be replicated in future lessons through their written reflections. Without our collaborative group discussion, I was left to wonder if these moments emerging as curriculum-makers would be revisited by the Brown Elementary teachers again or nurtured to continue growth. These writings, I believe, are early self-actualizations of teachers' own frames of reference. However, when faced with a school culture that demands uniformity in instruction and results-oriented mindset, I believe the teachers quickly shifted back to a curriculum-implementer role as they were directed to focus only on State of Texas Assessment of Academic Readiness (STAAR) reading related activities. What is significant to me was that teachers who often are suppressed in a curriculum-implementer role can have moments of transformation through writing where they can consider how they might change or evolve as a different kind of teacher.

St. Leo's Catholic School: How Teachers Value, View, and Apply Writing
Ms. Caine, 5th Grade Teacher
February 9, 2017

I arrived at Ms. Caine's classroom door a few minutes early for my lesson with her rambunctious 5th grade students. I would be teaching a class lesson on name poetry I had previously demonstrated during my grade level team meeting earlier that week. Teachers wanted new ways to engage students to write poetry. In our team meeting, teachers created a chart and brainstormed nicknames, meanings, symbols, and memories associated with their names to create a poem or narrative to explore their self-identity. Typically after our PLC team meeting ends, so does the writing. Rarely are notebooks opened or used until the next meeting. But I realized this lesson was going to be different as Ms. Caine pulled me aside before the classroom lesson began.

Ms. Caine, an energetic yet quiet teacher, whispered, "I kept writing after our meeting. I worked on my poem over the weekend. I'm not very good at writing on demand but I wanted to keep working on it. Can I share my poem with the class during the lesson?" Ms. Caine asked somewhat nervously.

My heart beamed. She wanted to participate and share with her students. Most teachers sit back and let me take over the class, fearful of stepping on toes or relieved to have a momentary break. Rarely do teachers want to co-teach or engage in the lessons when I come. I certainly had never had a teacher ask to include her own writing. "Absolutely. How about we use your writing as our modeled text instead of mine? Can you project your poem on the smart board?"

As my lesson took place, the students were compliant and engaged but a new tone occupied the air when Ms. Caine announced she wanted to share her writing. A hushed silence took over as all 5th grade eyes were on the board, reading their teachers' words and poem. I stepped aside as Ms. Caine took the floor and explained how her brainstorm helped her think about her ideas. Students' heads nodded as she openly admitted how difficult it still is for her to think of ideas to write about. "When I was younger, I used to get in trouble because I would spend all of my writing time thinking instead of writing. I just couldn't come up with something that was good enough to put down." Ms. Caine then showed how her brainstorm chart connected and inspired parts of her poem about her name, Donna. She pointed out memories, explaining their significance and meaning to her. Student hands shot up, eager to ask Ms. Caine questions and hear more about her writing.

When it was time for the students to write, there was a different energy in the room. Often when I lead lessons and share my notebook, students see my work as "expert" or "too good to be done." When Ms. Caine shared her words and her writing process it felt very different. A new intensity was ignited as students wrote their own name poems. A figurative door was opened that hadn't been there before. A teacher took the risk to be vulnerable with her students, sharing stories she hadn't shared before through her writing. Ms. Caine's students saw her writing process and confirmed that her writing mattered.

During our final team meeting later that year, Ms. Caine explained how sharing her writing that day was an eye opening experience for her. Ms. Caine said that experience made her feel more empowered to write alongside her students and share her progress. She said, "I felt more willing to make mistakes and show students how messy writing really can be." She didn't think it would have the impact it did. She didn't think it mattered that her students heard her talk about her writing struggles. I asked her, "What made you decide to share your notebook that day?"

Ms. Caine responded, "I put myself in the shoes of one of my students who struggles with writing. I personally struggle writing 'on demand' pieces and I considered there are likely other students in my class that struggle in the same way. The brainstorming strategy really helped me, I wanted to share that with my students."

In reflecting on Ms. Caine's actions that day, I recalled a dramatic shift that normally didn't take place within my WITS Collaborative residencies. Ms. Caine took ownership of the lesson to model her authentic writing practice. I didn't have to be the coach or curriculum expert. Rather, Ms. Caine and I were sharing a collaborative space together as teachers and writers. During a classroom writing lesson with students, I typically would spend a significant time making my process visible. Traditionally, students often only see finished products of writing that have been polished and published. As a writer, I always try to make that messy work visible, to make the reality of writing attainable for reluctant writers. Rarely did my residency teachers want to engage in this work in front of the students until Ms. Caine took the courageous step to ask permission to be vulnerable and share her own unpolished writing.

Ms. Caine brought her writing life into her classroom as a result of meeting a specific student and classroom need. She shared at our final PLC meeting that she was motivated to share her writing because she has students who struggle to draft and brainstorm. She moved beyond her own comfort zone and shared her writing process because of the value it might hold for her students. In that moment, I believe, Ms. Caine saw the potential for how her visible writing process could be beneficial for her and her students. Whether Ms. Caine felt like a true writer, she was applying her own successful strategies and authentically modeling those strategies for her students as a curriculum-maker. Luckily, Ms. Caine took this step *with* me, coaching and coteaching the lesson together. The students were eager, excited, and beyond motivated to write and engage with their teacher. In this positive moment, I believe Ms. Caine experienced her best-loved self, moving toward a curriculum-maker mindset, realizing that she has the writing knowledge and potential to step away from a lesson plan and that her own lived writing experience can be curriculum for her students.

As I consider Ms. Caine's transformative experience, her triggering moment or dilemma revolved around her concern for her students. She saw something in her students' writing that was pushing her to change or shift. This, I believe, was the start of a transformative learning process. Ms. Caine took the challenging step and addressed a writing issue she witnessed in herself and her students, writing on-demand pieces. This dilemma was big enough that Ms. Caine pushed herself out of her comfort zone and attempted writing on her own. As Mezirow (2000) suggests, a path of transformative learning includes "provisional trying of new roles" (p. 22). The way Ms. Caine spoke about the result of that move makes me wonder if she felt confident to keep that transition going? While this moment may not have transformed Ms. Caine fully into a new identity as a writer that day, she took valuable steps toward moving in the direction toward self-realization of her best-loved self.

Ms. White, 3rd Grade Teacher
October 12, 2017 and January 26, 2018

It was my second year at St. Leo's Catholic School and while the hallways and the classrooms were familiar, my teams of teachers were drastically different: some were new to the school, new to the profession, or just new to teaching writing. It was the halfway point of my residency where I had been in classrooms working with students, modeling lessons, and engaging 2nd, 3rd, and 4th grade teachers in writing exercises at St. Leo's Catholic School, a private parochial school serving a southeast Texan city for grades PreK-8th grade. My team meetings went in cycles; a modeled lesson with teachers, in-class demonstration, reflection protocol to write as writers. This year, team meetings that focused on lessons for students always seemed to be a bigger hit with the teachers: they were engaged, they loved to add ideas to the lesson to individualize for their classes, and appeared to enjoy creating modeled examples to use with their students. For some reason when the meetings focused on teachers' writing practice, the engagement fell flat. Teachers rarely shared their writing and seemed reluctant to participate. There felt like there was a huge disconnect between the writing teachers did for themselves and the writing teachers did for their lessons.

Ms. White was a new, yet experienced 3rd grade teacher at St. Leo's. From the beginning of the year she was reluctant and noticeably irritated that her grade level was participating in WITS Collaborative professional development. During our meetings, she declared that she already knew everything there was to know about teaching writing, implying she didn't need my support or guidance. Once during a one-on-one meeting she pulled out her binder of writing lessons to prove to me how well she knew writing instruction. Ms. White's behavior was so different from every other writing teacher I had met. She didn't show any ways she wanted to grow in her craft or practice, she didn't engage in personal writing, she didn't see any value in new lessons or ideas beyond her lesson binder.

I remember early in my residency at St. Leo's, I sat down with Ms. White to see how I could adjust my lessons or plans to best support her. I could feel the struggle. Her administration told her WITS Collaborative was mandatory. I could tell she didn't want to take any more time to meet, talk, or write with me. Attempting to crack a hard nut, I asked how she uses her writing in her classroom, thinking this could be a good segue to start a conversation about authentic writing practices. She opened a notebook to a "personal narrative" tab and showed a xerox copy of a handwritten paragraph she had previously written. "Here is my writing. I use this to show students what I write about for writing a personal narrative."

"That's great," I started, "but I'm also thinking about how you show your own writing life to your students. Like what do you write about right now for you, not just what you have written in the past for a student example?"

Ms. White's eyes narrowed in my direction and she pointed to an anchor chart and declared "I write this anchor chart with my students and show them what it has to look like and what they have to include." She closed her notebook and laptop. That was her final answer and I quickly got the silent message that our meeting was over. It was time for me to leave and reassess how I might support a teacher who does not want to be helped.

Ms. White and I were not on the same page. I thought I was being clear but my words weren't being understood. I realized I was speaking with a frame as a writer yet she was hearing me in the frame as a teacher. I assumed that my language of authentic writing, writing practice, and modeling a writing life was common jargon. But one thing I knew was that I was in no position to prove or show Ms. White that she needed to transform herself into a writer. Ms. White felt she didn't need to be a writer in order to teach writing. To Ms. White, she had the lessons, the mentor texts, the anchor charts, and sampled writing expectations all ready to go. To Ms. White, she didn't need to change anything.

Establishing a writing community was a primary goal for my PLC teams. I wanted to provide a space for teachers to engage in writing, share their work, and receive praise and feedback as writers. To facilitate this, I always began each meeting with a quick write or written connection for teachers to ground themselves into the work we would do together as teachers and writers.

It was January 26, 2018 and it was my first meeting after a long hiatus from the holiday season. I was excited to bring the St. Leo's teachers back together and reunite together as writers. I wanted to start right away with writing about a lesson that the teachers learned when they were growing up. This writing would be used to anchor some co-planned lessons together. In my mind this reflective meeting was going to be perfect. That is until Ms. White interrupted to say, "So, why do we have to write about it?"

I felt like the wind had been punched out of my lungs and I tilted my head, signaling my confusion in her question. I thought to myself, "Of course we would write, that is why we are here. This is how we always begin our meetings. Why would we do it any other way?" I let my silence hang in the air as my mind raced for the right words to respond.

Ms. White continued, "I'm just saying, we take so much of our time during our meetings to write. Can't we just tell you our lesson or memory and discuss it? I think we all would find that to be easier and I like hearing what people have to say." Ms. White looked around to the other teachers, seeking their approval.

In reflecting on this snapshot, I remember feeling conflicted. I wanted to comply and honor Ms. White's request but I struggled with the intention behind her words. While some may argue that Ms. White's suggestion was valid, it also negated the entire reason we were gathering together as writers. So much research has found that writing deepens understanding, constructs new knowledge, and makes meaning and connections more than oral discussions or reading alone (Bazerman, Simon, & Pieng, 2014; Knipper & Duggan, 2006). As Blau (1993) suggests for "most learners writing is actually (literally) the most powerful available instrument for making meaning and constructing knowledge for oneself" (p. 17). The act of writing is what brings a writing community together. Without writing, how are we writers? Analyzing my interactions with Ms. White, it was pretty clear that I struggled to fully grasp her frame of reference. I saw our work through the lens of a writer and that writing was the necessary act to help us process, create, and collaborate. While she viewed our writing work as perhaps a hindrance or obstacle because she already had what she needed: the binder of lessons.

In thinking about Ms. White and her viewpoint from these interactions, I consider her resistance from our writing, meetings, and professional development work as declaring agency for her own best-loved self. And while I disagreed with her approach for teaching, Ms. White was set on the way she had always taught writing and ran her classroom. It was very clear that she was confident in her approach, and she felt it worked. In many ways, Ms. White viewed herself as a curriculum-maker, using the tried and true lessons she held closely in her binder. From the beginning of our work together, she made it clear that she did not have any dilemmas with her teaching nor any ways she wanted to receive help. She did not want to be transformed as a writer to be a better writing teacher. In many ways, Ms. White did not view herself as curriculum-implementer, blindly following scripted curriculum. Rather, in many ways, Ms. White exhibited traits of a teacher as curriculum-specialist, viewing herself as the expert of writing when she told me she had all the lessons and everything planned out perfectly. No amount of nudging or coaching was going to change her viewpoint.

This meeting was a low point for my residency and my work with Ms. White. I felt like a failure. I could not force Ms. White to see how her personal writing could be transformative in her own life as well as her instructional practice. I also didn't want to waste her time. I realized that I came to find writing and see myself as a writer because I was *open and willing*. No one forced me. I had to swallow my pride and admit my failure. Ms. White left our PLC team, and a new teacher joined the group.

My work with Ms. White forces me to pause on how professional development often assumes a dilemma with a teacher's practice. But, when a teacher is confident in their pedagogy and instruction, how can transformative learning take place? Mezirow (2000) notes that much of the transformative learning needs to begin with the dilemma of practice or triggering moment (p. 22). But, if a teacher is not willing or is forced to make an unwanted change, as Craig (2013) suggests, it is often met with resistance. In many ways, I wish Ms. White's administration had given her choices rather than ultimatums to participate in the WITS Collaborative where it would better serve her and her students in meaningful ways. Perhaps Ms. White needed a different approach to see how teaching writing from a writer's frame of reference could benefit her students. This would be a self-realization to take place on Ms. White's terms and not mandated from her administration.

Rodrigo Elementary: Inquiry Focused Collaboration

January 23, 2019

It was my third year with the 3rd grade team at Rodrigo Elementary. Walking up to the main office I was excited to spend time with this group of teachers. My placement at Rodrigo Elementary was unique in many ways, not just because it was a school I had worked with for the longest period of time. As an International Baccalaureate (IB) school, the school's instructional focus is based on inquiry learning and integrating content, literacy, and mathematics into their curriculum. The school had a very teacher-focused culture, where the teachers had significant voice and input for support services and professional development they received. My WITS Collaborative residency was paid using dollars exclusively raised by the school's Parent Teacher Association (PTA). The 3rd grade team had made WITS Collaborative a priority because they valued the professional experience and felt it positively impacted their students. Rodrigo Elementary is located in a wealthy neighborhood in the city, having a highly active PTA that raises well over $250,000 each year for the school and its teachers. Rodrigo Elementary has also performed well on state-wide assessments, often with passing rates above 90% in reading, writing, and mathematics tests. My conversations with Rodrigo Elementary teachers rarely focused on student test scores or meeting achievement gaps. School leaders or administrators did not attend our PLC meetings to "check in" on our progress. At this school, teachers had the luxury of wanting authentic experiences for students to be writers.

On this day I was particularly looking forward to my team meeting as we would be co-planning a writing unit together. I remember how excited I was when the team leader, Kaitlyn, asked for my input and if I could pull resources for their upcoming unit on realistic fiction. In my other residencies, teams made requests for specific lessons or test-prep strategies to support their students. But this was not a request for just lessons, rather it was an invitation to be a part of the team's planning. I would not be "the expert" but rather an equal voice of the community. This was a shift I celebrated mostly because it came from the request of the teachers, not me and not from an administrator.

I did not plan an agenda or lesson for this meeting. Instead I brought mentor texts, unit calendars, and personal writing that might be helpful during the discussion. Kaitlyn even said, "You don't need to plan anything. We just want to hear what you think and have to say about our ideas." This gave me permission to take a backseat and reassess my role in the meeting. I didn't have to lead it or outline every minute. My only goal for the meeting was to listen.

We all gathered together in Kaitlyn's classroom sitting at student desks as I laid out mentor texts of realistic fiction and picture books. Another teacher, Elisa, started distributing copies of a unit calendar that had been used in years before as she explained, "This is what we've done in the past. What do you think?"

Instead of responding with thoughts and opinions, I started with questions, "What did you feel has been successful for students in the past? What do you think this unit lacks?"

Teachers who had taught the unit before shared their comments:

- The students all wrote the same type of piece.
- Their stories lacked an arc of transition.
- Characters weren't believable.
- Some students got confused about the genre and ended up writing fantasy stories.

I then asked, "Let's think about being a reader of realistic fiction. What do you like about the books you read in this genre? What engages you as a reader?"

These questions guided the discussion for the teachers to reframe their thinking not as teachers but as readers or consumers of writing. I wanted the teachers to think less about the standards or curriculum they were planning and concentrate on the components that made writing really good to read. If they thought about what they liked and how real authors of realistic fiction wrote, that could transfer into powerful lessons for their students. During our discussion, teachers shared their favorite books, authors, and the realistic fiction stories they loved. They noted how realistic fiction had problems that felt real and relatable even if the setting or characters were unlike themselves. The teachers all identified how a character's authentic voice came alive and how dialogue moved a realistic fiction story.

> *From that brief conversation, the teachers all took out their pens to mark up the unit calendar, inserting possible lesson ideas, strategies, or craft moves to introduce to their students. One teacher suggested connecting the writing unit to their science inquiry unit on natural disasters, which could be the setting or problem for the realistic fiction stories. This work was all unprompted from me and felt like a natural progression of work for the teachers. There was a sense of urgency, not for time, but to get all the ideas out before they were forgotten. The energy was fierce in the room and we all left energized. I said and did very little during this team meeting. But by actively listening, I knew how I could provide to help the teachers to develop a unit and which writing experiences might connect to the genre in order to teach their students.*

My response to this snapshot ultimately is through the role of neither teacher nor writer but as a professional development coach. For over three years, I had worked closely with this group of teachers modeling lessons and collaboratively planning. But, this moment stood out because it was the first time I was able to step back and actively listen rather than having to lead actively. My role had ultimately shifted from expert to participant and from having answers to asking guiding questions. Cochran-Smith and Lytle (2001) suggest that professional development through inquiry means can result in teachers engaging in conversation toward constructing knowledge (p. 53). Through asking simple questions like "What do you enjoy most about reading realistic fiction?", the teachers were able to construct criteria that would be used to later create writing lessons for their unit.

The Rodrigo Elementary teachers in that moment were actively viewing themselves as curriculum-makers and likely had this viewpoint for quite some time. Their school's culture supported teachers to develop their own lessons and curriculum, with minimal administrative input. As a group, these 3rd-grade teachers had identified areas of concern and luckily had support, like WITS Collaborative, to guide them through inquiry toward solutions. Lieberman and Wood (2003) suggest that teachers learn best when they collectively bring their own valuable experiences and knowledge rather than have an expert deposit knowledge to educators (p. 181). In this snapshot, everyone included in the discussion was an equal voice and contributor of knowledge. In this way, teachers were able to construct curriculum that best fit their understanding and meet the needs of their students. Additionally, because of the teachers' frame of reference, they also did not view my role as curriculum-specialist or simply as the expert. Rather, they wanted my *input* and support, so they could do their work to construct their curriculum and lessons that fit the needs of their students.

Reflecting as a researcher leads me to consider how these teachers at Rodrigo Elementary were in the process of transformative learning. Whitney (2008) suggests that when teachers identify areas of concern or instructional practices that aren't working, it can be the groundwork for transformative learning opportunities (p. 157 as cited in Mezirow, 1991). Teachers had asked for specific support to meet their instructional needs. As a professional development coach, my pulled back stance allowed for the teachers to construct their understanding and knowledge. This exchange was beneficial for teachers on multiple levels: supporting the immediate need as well as developing collaborative skills to be used for future curriculum constructing discussions.

DISCUSSION: RESULTS AND REFLECTIONS FROM COACHING RESIDENCIES

I was a writing coach for WITS Collaborative for over five years. I had worked in six different schools with over 10 residencies. Over these experiences, no residency has ever been the same. A successful residency depended on the following factors: teachers' willingness to participate in professional development, how they viewed the role of writing in their lives, and the dynamics of the grade-level teams. These factors heavily contributed to the overall success and/or struggles in a WITS Collaborative residency.

When teachers participated in the WITS Collaborative professional development, teachers either began to engage in writing habits or behaviors that supported their writing instruction. Participation, however, is not a passive activity as it requires teachers to identify areas of growth and be willing to make changes. I have found that the teachers that used writing to tap into their inner fears about teaching, openly admit failures, or seek opportunities to grow were those teachers who gained the most from a WITS Collaborative residency, perhaps shifting their frame of reference into curriculum-maker or teacher-writer. However, as a result of the marketing to schools and the program structure, most teachers are mandated to participate and, therefore, simply comply with the activities, lessons, and PLC meetings. In many cases, teachers do not realize gaps in their writing practice or instruction (Whitney, 2008). When schools like Brown Elementary mandated teachers to attend training and workshops to resolve low assessment data, these efforts did not support or grow a teacher. If teachers are reluctant to participate or engage with professional development, they can at best comply.

Writing is at the core of the WITS Collaborative model. The majority of the teachers I worked with during professional development did not write beyond their day-to-day tasks of emails, lesson plans, and student feedback. For many teachers in my residencies, writing was what the students completed, not teachers. When teachers took the time to write for *themselves* and removed their teacher hat temporarily, they were able to share and learn from one another. Writing became the vehicle to connect and communicate stories, experiences, and ideas. Too often, teachers were reluctant to be vulnerable and expose their struggles through writing. And so, many times writing completed during WITS Collaborative team meetings was a facade, written only for student or classroom use. The way teachers valued writing impacted how effective WITS Collaborative could be. If teachers understood the professional development work as *only* a support for their students' assessment scores, they were often disappointed. The work of reflective writings, SRI protocols, and discussions served to develop a writing community, not a silver bullet for state assessments. When teachers opened up about their authentic writing practices, struggles, and achievements, students' writing was also positively impacted. Teachers made realizations about their writing practice and instructional choices as a teacher (Whitney, 2008). This attitude about the value of writing is essential for transformative learning to take place (Mezirow, 1991).

A community of writers requires mutual respect for other members in a group. This respect is more than just a formality. It is essential for group members to feel safe enough to be vulnerable to share their writing to others. Additionally, a writing community must have equally valued voices, where there isn't a single "expert" in the group. When teachers gather together as a team, the dynamics they bring to a professional development program can deeply impact the effectiveness of the writing community. During PLC meetings, we wrote together to share their words and provide feedback to push the writing. When teachers felt agitated, threatened, or judged, the writing often fell flat. Additionally, the way teachers spoke to one another was also greatly impacted. Too often, there would be no discussion, just awkward silence as teachers opted to be reserved and safe rather than speak their truth. This is to say that much of what I needed to spend more time on was in order to build the community and interactions with the teacher teams to create a safer and positive space to write, share, and critique.

FUTURE STEPS: MY JOURNEY AS A WRITER CONTINUES

In 2019, I began a PhD program at the University of Houston in the Curriculum and Instruction Department to pursue working in higher education and support preservice teachers. Despite my best efforts to help teachers through the WITS Collaborative professional development program, I always felt like I was coming up short of my initial goals because of limitations and restrictions. I wanted to have some level of authority to tell my teachers, "This is meant for you. You may not think that right now. But it will help you. Trust me." I wanted my teachers to have a transformative learning experience and to see beyond their teaching identity to see themselves as writers, their best-loved selves as teachers. My role in WITS Collaborative wasn't allowing me to fully engage in those dialogs or work. I had to make a move.

WITS Collaborative allowed me to gain a wider understanding of what immense stress teachers are facing today. I was able to work in many different schools and support a diverse group of teachers. I saw what worked, what didn't, and what could be improved in literacy instruction. I had a better understanding of reasons why teachers are reluctant to teach writing or engage in writing themselves. It is hard work, and I learned from numerous discussions that many teachers have negative attitudes about their writing that still impacts them today. I learned that when administrators mandate training or professional development, it may not be at the personal interest of the teacher. I also learned that being a writer can mean very different things to teachers, depending on their narrative, experience, and personal identity.

In reflecting on my experience as a WITS writer, many components of the professional development worked. WITS staff members were up front with schools and administrators that the purpose of the professional development program is to lift up the teachers' writing by working with a writer in order to positively impact writing instruction. The WITS organization has always been a supportive presence in low-income and at-risk schools through grants and arts initiatives. The 50-hour residency is intended to provide long-term support and develop a writing community within a PLC team of teachers. The ingredients are there, but the recipe was sometimes inconsistent.

My definition of success could not look the same for each school and residency I had with WITS Collaborative. Much of the progress was completely dependent on the school and team of teachers I had in a residency. Many times administrators wanted WITS Collaborative to ultimately improve assessment scores in writing, and this meant that most times WITS writers were assigned to grade-level teams that would be taking a statewide writing assessment (i.e. 4th grade, 7th grade, and high school). WITS Collaborative was selected *for* teachers and not chosen *by* them to support their professional development goals. When teachers were mandated and required to comply with professional development, WITS writers were often in an uncomfortable position of who to support.

CONCLUSION

I am a teacher, but I am also a writer. I did not come to this transformation easily. I had to allow this shift to take place over many years. I had to take deep reflection of my faults as a writing teacher, realizing I wanted a change to take place. I sought out help, and as a result, I discovered much more than just quick tips and helpful strategies. Taking writing classes and being a NWP fellow fostered a voice and self-confidence I didn't know I had. My identity as a writer manifested not just because I wrote and engaged in writing habits; it ultimately shifted my identity because I had peers and writing colleagues that encouraged me to see myself as the writer *they* saw. My writing mattered to me and to the people around me.

I took this positive and personal transformation with me as a WITS Collaborative professional development coach. I had sincere hopes to help the teachers I worked with to help them see their own potential as writers. But unlike myself, many teachers I encountered during my residencies weren't always ready for that shift to be writers or change their frame around writing instruction. During my residencies, I faced circumstances out of my control and ultimately had to meet teachers where *they* were in their writing journey. This sometimes meant abandoning my own goals to meet their specific classroom needs.

In thinking about this analysis, I am left to wonder how might professional development efforts allow for teachers to transform their identities? To begin to answer this question, I think about time, process, and development. Too often in professional development for educators, teachers and administrators want to see immediate results, change, and transformation. But, true transformation and growth must take shape organically and be given time and space to evolve. The teachers at Brown Elementary started their reflective work as a curriculum-maker through their writing, but their school's data-driven culture limited their ability to view themselves as anything but curriculum-implementers. Growth requires trust. Schools and administrators and even teachers need to have the trust that they know their best-loved selves, know what benefits their students, and know when to seek guidance for support.

When thinking about transformative learning for teachers' identities, it is important to consider how teachers can shift into identities of curriculum-makers? To answer this, I think about both Ms. White and Ms. Caine at St. Leo's Catholic School and the teachers at Rodrigo Elementary. In both schools, these teachers exhibited transformation as curriculum-makers but driven mostly by their own self-realization. Ms. Caine and the Rodrigo Elementary teachers identified a dilemma of practice independently and made conscious decisions to act in response to those dilemmas. In this way, these teachers experienced transformative learning opportunities to reveal their best-loved self through establishing agency and ownership of their instruction and curriculum. While I did not witness Ms. White transform during our WITS Collaborative professional development, I do believe a shift did still take place for her. She firmly stood on her approach, beliefs, and pedagogy as a teacher, and clearly viewed herself as curriculum-maker as well as curriculum-specialist. I believe that she already owned her instructional practice and used the WITS Collaborative professional development to further confirm her best-loved self as a teacher. Transformation or self-realization of identities cannot be mandated by external forces and needs to come from within a teacher. Schwab suggests that teachers are more than just the subject matter they teach (Craig, 2020; Schwab, 1954/1978), and when teachers are forced or mandated to teach in a way that does not reflect them, resistance, resentment, or even worse compliance will take effect.

I recall wanting my work with WITS Collaborative professional development to be a certain way, for teachers to transform just like I did. But, what I discovered was that I couldn't expect that to happen. My journey to identify and transform as a writer took shape because I allowed it to happen and I sought guidance and support to resolve my own teaching dilemma. No one mandated I fix my problem, it was my own journey and my own transformation. Looking back I was naive to think that transformative learning could be as easy as osmosis. I neglected to consider what do the teachers see as their *real* need and how do I fit into that equation. With these lessons in mind, I see how I could have given teachers space they needed, honored their requests, and asked more questions to guide their learning process.

Growing a teacher to realize their best-loved self requires giving space for the teacher to negotiate their own identities, what fits best for them. Professional development cannot have a set agenda to mold or "fix" a teacher to be in a certain way. Teacher as a curriculum-maker means giving teachers agency and honoring ownership of their development. This means allowing space for them to reflect and determine their needs and dilemmas. Professional development is not the silver bullet or the vaccine to a pandemic. Rather, professional development is guidance and coaching to support teachers along their journey. The journey cannot be time limiting. Development takes time and can wind and bend in many different ways. Teachers need to be afforded the time to meander and find their best-loved selves.

REFERENCES

Bazerman, C., Simon, K., & Pieng, P. (2014). Writing about reading to advance thinking: A study in situated cognitive development. In G. Rijlaarsdam (Series Ed.) & P. D. Klein, P. Boscolo, L. C. Kirkpatrick, C. Gelati (Vol. Eds.), *Studies in writing: Vol. 28, writing as a learning activity* (pp. 249–276). Leiden: Brill.

Blau, S. (1993). Constructing knowledge in a professional community: The writing project as a model for classrooms. *Quarterly of the National Writing Project and the Center for the Study of Writing and Literacy*, *15*(1), 16–17. 19.

Clandinin, D. J., & Connelly, F. M. (1992). Teacher as curriculum-maker. In P. W. Jackson (Ed.), *Handbook of curriculum* (pp. 363–461). New York, NY: Macmillan.

Cochran-Smith, M., & Lytle, S. (2001). Beyond certainty: Taking an inquiry stance on practice. In A. Lieberman & L. Miller (Eds.), *Teachers caught in the action: Professional development that matters* (pp. 45–58). New York, NY: Teachers College Press.

Connelly, F. M., & Clandinin, D. J. (1988). *Teachers as curriculum planners: Narratives of experience*. New York, NY: Teachers College Press.

Craig, C. (2013). Teacher education and the best-loved self. *Asia Pacific Journal of Education*, *33*(3), 261–272.

Craig, C. (2020). The best loved self. In *Curriculum making, reciprocal learning, and the best-loved self*. Cham: Palgrave MacMillan.

Darling-Hammond, L., Hyler, M. E., & Gardner, M. (2017). *Effective teacher professional development*. Palo Alto, CA: Learning Policy Institute.

DuFour, R. (2005). What is a professional learning community? In R. DuFour, R. Eaker, & R. DuFour (Eds.), *On common ground: The power of professional learning communities*. Bloomington, IN: Solution Tree Press.

Fountas, I. C., & Pinnell, G. S. (2020). Literacy leadership from the classroom: Learning from teacher leaders. *The Reading Teacher*, *74*(2), 223–229. doi:10.1002/trtr.1945

Houston Independent School District. (n.d.). Research and accountability. Retrieved from https://www.houstonisd.org/Page/63696. Accessed on August 1, 2020.

Kagan, R. (2000). What "form" transforms? A constructivist-developmental approach to transformative learning. In J. Mezirow (Ed.), *Learning as transformation: Critical perspectives on a theory in progress* (1st ed., pp. 35–69). San Francisco, CA: Jossey-Bass.

Knipper, K. J., & Duggan, T. M. (2006). Writing to learn across the curriculum: Tools for comprehension in content area classes. *The Reading Teacher*, *59*(5), 462–470.

Lieberman, A., & Wood, D. (2001). When teachers write: Of networks and learning. In A. Lieberman & L. Miller (Eds.), *Teachers caught in the action: Professional development that matters* (pp. 174–187). New York, NY: Teachers College Press.

Lieberman, A., & Wood, D. (2003). *Inside the national writing project: Connecting network learning and classroom teaching*. New York, NY: Teachers College Press.

Little, J. W. (1993). Teachers' professional development in a climate of educational reform. *Educational Evaluation and Policy Analysis*, *15*(2), 129–151. doi:10.3102/01623737015002129

Mezirow, J. (1991). *Transformative dimensions of adult learning* (1st ed.). San Francisco, CA: Jossey-Bass.

Mezirow, J. (2000). Learning to think like an adult: Core concepts of transformative theory. In J. Mezirow (Ed.), *Learning as transformation: Critical perspectives on a theory in progress* (1st ed., pp. 3–33). San Francisco, CA: Jossey-Bass.

Mitchell, T. M. (1980). *The need for biases in learning generalizations* (pp. 184–191). New Jersey, NJ: Department of Computer Science, Laboratory for Computer Science Research, Rutgers Univ.

School Reform Initiative. (n.d.). *Protocols*. Retrieved from https://www.schoolreforminitiative.org/protocols/. Accessed on July 26, 2020.

Schwab, J. J. (1954/1978). Eros and education: A discussion of one aspect of discussion. In I. Westbury & N. Wilkof (Eds.), *Science, curriculum and liberal education: Selected essays*. Chicago, IL: University of Chicago Press.

Texas Education Agency. (n.d.). *Assessment scoring and reporting*. Retrieved from https://tea.texas.gov/texas-schools/accountability/academic-accountability/performance-reporting/assessment-scoring-and-reporting. Accessed on July 26, 2020.

Whitney, A. (2008). Teacher transformation in the national writing project. *Research in the Teaching of English*, *43*, 144–187.

Writers in the Schools. (2014). *Our story*. Retrieved from https://witshouston.org/about/our-story/. Accessed on July 26, 2020.

REFLECTIVE CONVERSATION ON THE VALUE OF LONGEVITY AS COLLABORATORS IN EDUCATION

P. Tim Martindell, Cheryl J. Craig and Chestin T. Auzenne-Curl

ABSTRACT

This chapter revolves around a Zoom conversation between Tim Martindell and Cheryl Craig to which Chestin T. Auzenne-Curl added field-based evidence and reflective comments. The exchange between Martindell and Craig had to do with how Tim facilitated the Writers in the Schools (WITS) writers in conjunction with Tina and Maryann who led the WITS Collaborative. The embedded snapshots and excerpts stemmed from the field notes we accumulated during the life of the project. The conversation discusses some of the fine points of facilitation as well as the boundary areas where what unfolds fringes on the unknown. Near the end, hope for the future is discussed.

Keywords: Literacy coaching; Writer's workshop; professional development; Critical Friends (CFG®); Critical Friends (CFG®) protocols; peer facilitator

BACKGROUND

Cheryl and Tim enter the aforementioned conversation with shared experiences in both the Houston A+ Challenge, and in working with personnel from the Writers in the Schools (WITS) professional development collaborative. Cheryl's research in the Houston area spans three decades and includes field-based research on school reform, teacher knowledge, and using the narrative inquiry method to gain insight into the development, exchange, and communal establishment of teachers' stories of experience. She first encountered Tim as a middle school teacher at Hardy Academy during the Houston Annenberg Challenge. Tim then became a Houston A+ Challenge employee as a program coordinator over the literacy coach project in the Houston schools for a New Society initiative and concluded his career in the public education sector as the Supervisor for Literacy and the Language Arts at a Greater Houston school district. After that, he officially retired and became a middle school literacy teacher on a private campus in Houston. Tim also completed his master's degree and an Ed.D. with Cheryl Craig as his advisor. Their professional relationship has resulted in previous work seeded by the Portfolio Group with the recent book, *Knowledge communities in teacher education: Sustaining collaborative work* (Craig, Curtis, Kelley, Martindell, & Perez, 2020) being Tim's initial suggestion. Despite their shared past, Tim Martindell and Cheryl Craig entered this conversation, having lived two different plotlines in association with the WITS Collaborative's professional development review.

CONTEXTUALIZING RELATIONSHIPS AND KEY TERMS
Cheryl

Cheryl J. Craig, a professor and the Houston Endowment Endowed Chair of Urban Education at Texas A&M University. She was chosen from a competitive pool of applicants who had submitted proposals to undertake the evaluation of the WITS Collaborative Program. Craig had previous experience researching and evaluating grants from the US Department of Education, Texas Education Agency, Houston Annenberg Challenge, National Science Foundation, and projects connected with other smaller philanthropies. She has an internationally recognized research reputation where teacher identity development, the image of teacher-as-curriculum-maker, and teacher knowledge communities are concerned. Her prior experiences in the literacy arena were strong; however, that background initially stemmed from her early years of working in Canada. More recently, though, she had conducted a 20-year study of curriculum reform in a literacy department in the United States. Recognizing that the Texas literacy context would come into play in this work, she invited Dr. Chestin T. Auzenne-Curl to work as a Post-Doctoral Associate and the Program Lead alongside her where the WITS change effort was concerned. Cheryl participated actively in the majority of the activities associated with the WITS Collaborative with a noted exception happening when her teaching schedule occasionally collided with project activities. This meant she wrote field notes and interviewed writers and teachers like Chestin and other members of the evaluation team did. She, like the others, turned her field notes, archival documents, and photos over to Chestin who entered them into the WITS research record. This was how the centrality of teacher voices and the voices of writers formed the foundation of the WITS project research.

Chestin

As presaged, Dr. Chestin T. Auzenne-Curl served as the project lead for the WITS field-based researcher. She was a former doctoral student of Cheryl Craig who offered the post-doctoral research fellow position that she accepted. Chestin collected data, fieldnotes, conducted interviews, and co-authored reports with Cheryl Craig and other team members about the WITS Collaborative. She was in charge of the research record. All entries were dated, assembled, and managed by her.

Critical Friends Group

Critical Friends Groups (CFGs®) are teacher professional development communities that use structured questions, usually referred to as protocols, to help to equalize voices in the discussion of critically important classroom and school issues and in service of student learning. As conversations deepen, CFG® leaders strive to maintain a safe space within which reflections and actions can be deliberated with the greater good in mind.

Houston Annenberg Challenge/Houston A+ Challenge

Houston A+ Challenge was the successor to the Houston Annenberg Challenge reform initiative which extended the school reform work beyond the original five years of the Annenberg funding. This allowed the nonprofit organization to continue to work in the areas of high school reform, literacy, numeracy, and teacher empowerment.

Tim

Dr. P. Tim Martindell was a program coordinator for high school literacy and critical friendship during the initial Houston A+ Challenge years who worked alongside Tina Angelo in a project to embed literacy coaches into 32 Greater Houston high schools. The successful project continued for seven years until a change in leadership took the schools in a different direction. Tim then left Houston A+ for a curriculum leadership position in a neighboring school district. After Tina Angelo retired, she became the Education Director for WITS and started the WITS Collaborative with an initial startup grant funded by a well-known local philanthropy. She brought long time collaborator and colleague, Tim, into the Collaborative as an external coach to embed critical friendship into the practice of the writers.

Tina

Tina Angelo, Education Director for WITS, had a long-standing relationship with Tim Martindell who was her mentor and friend during the original Houston A+ Challenge years. Her successes at the high school level were well known. She spent over 20 years teaching literacy in high schools in Greater Houston and nine additional years as a central office administrator who worked with literacy teachers on 44 middle schools and 36 high schools. Tina's theory of action is that teachers who resonate with images of themselves as writers are more likely to find success as teachers of writing. Tina and her WITS colleague, Maryann Gremillion, contributed a chapter to this book.

Maryann

Maryann Gremillion worked for 15 years as an elementary school teacher. She joined WITS and worked as a writer-in-residence and then as a WITS program director, alongside Tina Angelo, for a total of 12 years. Maryann Gremillion's writing can be found in many publishing venues, including her co-authored chapter in this volume with Tina Angelo.

Writers in the Schools Collaborative

The WITS Collaborative is a cross-institutional collaboration that places experienced authors in classrooms to partner with teachers. With the goal of increasing engagement through workshop approaches (Graham, 2018) to integrated reading and writing instruction, the collaborative writers worked with Tim to increase authenticity of voice and craft in classrooms. Tim worked with the writers monthly. Each meeting provided them with a model for their approach to sharing instructional strategies with classroom teachers, as well as points of discussion for following their lesson cycles with teachers.

Interview

Cheryl: Let us start at the beginning. How did you come to be the facilitator with the WITS group?

Tim: Tina was my counterpart in the literacy coach project in HISD when I was with the Houston A+ Challenge Head Office. She was one of the original literacy coaches at one of the high schools. She was in the original cohort. Later, she became the literacy person for the district. We developed a coach-mentee relationship that was a very tight relationship and we still have that relationship to this day. Therefore, what she did was she went over to WITS and the whole WITS Collaborative was her brainchild.

Cheryl: So the Collaborative was built from the ground up?

Tim: Yes, I was brought on to the WITS Collaborative Project for the implementation years. However, Tina and I had been doing this type of coaching, and her model for the Collaborative is based on my model of the literacy coach which was based on my CFG and Abydos Project work (see Fig. 1)... Her model was a continuation of that work, just in a different kind of context...

Cheryl: So there is a real comfort zone between Tina and you...

Tim: Absolutely. We work very, very well together because she is a fine-detail person and I am a global one. We are sort of Yin and Yang because she will have the tightly planned agenda, and I will show her how to turn on a dime, depending on the needs of the people with whom we are working.

Cheryl: I see... So when you started working with the writers what is one of the first things you did to get the project started?

Tim: We began early on using the CFG® protocols and some of the icebreaker techniques. We were modeling what we wanted the writers to do in the schools because the writers in the Collaborative were charged more with working with the teachers than the traditional WITS model of working with classes of students. .. It was always about modeling and then it was about gradual release. (I do. We do. You do).

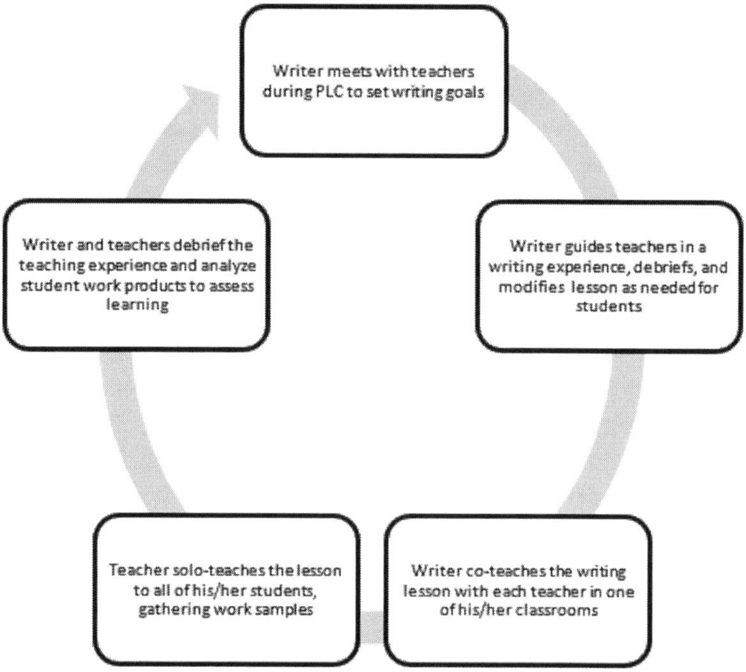

Fig. 1. Writers in the Schools Coaching Cycle.

(Continued)

Cheryl:	When did [the members of the Collaborative] meet?
Tim:	The meetings were originally on Saturdays. The initial meetings were four hours monthly on a Saturday and later switched to a monthly two-hour evening meeting on weekdays. We would come in and model what the writers would then do in their professional learning communities on the campuses. Therefore, we would not give them a prescription... However, we would give them a tool or multiple tools for doing something... Initially, it was the icebreakers. How do you build trust, how do you build the collaborative? How do you build relationships? How do you do a needs assessment?

Reflections on Segment 1

This introductory segment highlights the importance of trust that exists in the relationship between Tim and Tina. Their history includes a positive coaching relationship. As Tim reflects on the dynamic of "yin and yang," we come to see peer appreciation and recognition for Tina's gifts as well as his own. This "knowing and being" of self was evident in each monthly collaborative meeting. The writers, Tim, Tina, and Maryann shared in community a respect for what we noted as "knowing differently," not "knowing better," than one another. We believe that this degree of mutual respect for the work and value of diverse contributions created a context that was welcoming to vulnerability and truth speaking.

We witnessed both acts in every meeting. In order to make the monthly meetings more accessible, opportunities for attendance existed by the time the program review occurred. On Saturdays and on a weeknight after Hurricane Harvey, when the study was launched, each session started with an agenda item called Connections. Connections was an intentional sharespace facilitated by Tim, so that before engaging in the school-based topics of the day, each writer, along with Tina, Maryann, and Tim himself, had the opportunity to speak a truth about something outside of their lives and symbolically leave it on the table. The activity did not invite others to speak during the share. Instead, listening intently to understand rather than to respond was the key.

> This activity. I'm so glad that Tim is giving us that time. We don't have to share, and I was not going to share. My plan was to just listen to whoever decided to. But there is something about really being called on to listen to the other people at the table that has you actually connect to them. (Laughs) I guess that is the name. (Anonymous WITS Writer, Spring 2018)

This verbatim quote is one writer's response to the Connections activity. Chestin sent an email out after one meeting and one of the writers who shared that evening responded first. This writer shared less frequently than the others, but that evening she opened up about her professional gains. She said that she had brought a story of how much farther she had to go in her work to the table, but after another writer shared about a tragedy in her family and the weight she was happy to leave on the table, the negativity seemed "small and petty." Furthermore, she stated in a follow-up conversation with Chestin that the lines between personal and professional could not be clearly defined. These connections drew them into the universal roles and struggles that educators have as human beings.

The recollection that all of this is embodied knowledge and experience among them creates narrative threads. Later, in the official protocols, they shared experiences from work and reached out, jokingly or with sincere emotion, including information shared during Connections. "As the continuity of experience unfolds, 'what you see (and hear, feel, think, love, despise, fear, etc.) is what you get…' (Craig et al., 2018, p. 330) in relationship to the work that is done in the program."

In listening to her peer share, our responding author realized that she may have been projecting the personal on the professional. "It really helped me open up my mind for the protocol."

Protocols

Cheryl: Tim, please explain the protocols. Let us talk about the paper plate protocol, for example.

Tim: Yes, it happened at the beginning of the year. I made that one up. Everyone made their own dishes based on certain prompts. I asked each of them to fill up their plates with the main course and three side dishes… You know, tell something about yourself, tell something you would want others to know about you, your favorite novel, people you already know in the group, etc. Then, we moved to the buffet table. Everybody sampled from the others' paper plates. Some even stopped by for second helpings. The idea was that you would go and you would look at other people's plates, and you would see their skills, hidden talents, interests, and so forth, and you would network and get ideas as you moved from one writer to another.

Reflective Conversation on the Value of Longevity 159

(Continued)

	Along the way, people would get to know everyone better… Do you remember the playwright? For example, I learned that I could talk with her about script writing or playwriting, or something like that. However, truthfully, I just totally made that protocol up. That is the beauty of the Critical Friends work. If you do it long enough and it becomes ingrained enough, protocols – the original protocols – sort of fall away, and you create new things in the moment. I guess that was one of those moments (Fig. 2).
Cheryl:	Another question I wanted to ask: How far ahead did you figure out the protocol you were going to use (in any given session), or did you wait until the events of the meeting before?
Tim:	We would debrief after each meeting just casually, and we would talk about where we want to go next time. Tina was good at capturing the ideas, and she is really good at the needs assessment of the group. She and I would look at what the group needs. We would have an idea of where we are going two months out. We would also talk about each evening. You know, here is what is going to happen tonight…Also, here is what makes sense as the next step. We did not have a long-range plan at the beginning of the year, but ideas emerged based on the feedback of the group. What we did was really driven by that….
Cheryl:	Did Maryann participate as well or was everything communicated to Marianne through Tina?
Tim:	Oh yes…absolutely Maryann was a part of it. Maryann was part of the original cohort of WITS writers. I think for two years. Then, she was brought in when they expanded the program. She was brought in to help Tina. So, there was a coaching relationship there as well. Yes, Maryann was integral as well. Absolutely.
Cheryl:	So can you remember some of the things that worked really, really well with the WITS Collaborative?
Tim:	One of my favorites was free form discussion when an idea emerged that called for a global protocol. I would start with a question, and what would come out of it would be the needs of the group…For example, when working with the school district literacy coaches a few years back, there was a week when a young white teacher had gone to a lecture by Spike Lee and

Fig. 2. Paper Plate Protocol.

(Continued)

came back to the Group and said she did not understand some nuances of Black culture. She felt free enough to say that. Also, the trust level was high enough in the group that she could ask a very, very potentially loaded question, but she could go in with this honesty about wanting to understand something. It was probably the most difficult work I have ever experienced as a facilitator. I had to make sure that the African American members were comfortable enough and safe enough to be able to explain whatever it was... I would ask a general question and then suddenly, there would be an outpouring, and they would build upon each other's ideas. It was as if the floodgates opened.

Cheryl: Hmm...

Tim: Those protocols are the ones that I like best because on those occasions, the best conversations happen... Because the protocols make the conversations safe to have. I guess safety is the key...

Cheryl: Yes. There are emergent, "on the spot" questions. You cannot predict where they are going to go as a facilitator.

Tim: My role as a facilitator is to make sure people are safe, without jumping in and taking control... I am just traveling with you and just getting into some unknown territories as I call them. Because the last thing that we would ever want to happen is for something from that room to get out. However, sometimes you just have to; you just have to ask those questions. Within the Collaborative is the safest space to do it.

Cheryl: Let us talk about a safe protocol you used...

Tim: The Gallery Walk (Fig. 3). We use that one at least once a year. There are two levels of participation. The Writers get a lot out of it. It is very interactive when questions or artifacts are discussed. Then there is silent time (which is never completely silent). That is when they really have to listen to each other because they are reading the others' stuff. However, it is also good for Tina, Marianne, and I as facilitators. It is a great way for us to read the temperature of the group to find out what different needs were emerging. It is a good check in.

Fig. 3. Gallery Walk and Paper Plate Activities.

(Continued)

Cheryl:	Yes, I was thinking you were always gauging the group. It was almost like the taking of a temperature.
Tim:	Well, when we would do activities, even the small group activities, I would always sort of be like a butterfly bouncing around the room, trying to pick up the little snippets because it is the work of a facilitator. You know my work was to facilitate them having the conversations, their actual conversations were not necessarily going to be that impactful on my professional work, you know, as a teacher, although I was always getting ideas that I could take back to my classroom. I think that the role changed a little bit when I did return to the classroom because that also gave me a little bit more credibility than I initially had. I already had the credibility of having been an administrator in a curriculum position. But I was back in the swampy lowlands of practice (Schön, 1983) when I chose to go back to the classroom. I think that gave me more street credibility.
Cheryl:	Absolutely…
Tim:	Teaching happens best, you know, when the teaching is not about the teacher, it is about student learning.

The protocols that were modeled in each meeting were modified from the School Reform Initiative (SRI). As Tim stated, the team would debrief after each session's meeting results. Reviewing writers' responses and the outcome of the protocol which had been visited on that evening, Tim, Tina, and Maryann would compare the stories of work in the field to the products rendered in response to the protocol and leave Tim with guidance for his next protocol selection.

Reflections on Segment 2

The protocols (Fig. 4) that Tim used with the team moved practice forward in the community by revealing more about each member's growth to WITS administrators. Discussions highlighting the team's contributions in revising and differentiating curriculum in the field led to organizational restructuring and additional positions. Tim often paired the teams more experienced coaches with those newer to the team. Tina and Maryann made note of Tim's effective pairing of "mentors and mentees" within the group and extended the focus of partner share. There were many writers who surfaced as "Strong coaches who need more than being a mentor. They are ready for the next step. Whatever that is" (Recorded conversation, Fall 2018). As the year progressed, more specifics surfaced:

> With the number of schools that we service, it is getting harder and harder for us to get to them like we used to. I think that some of the writers are ready to work with us. They can be coaches of coaches. Not only will they grow, it is a natural way to help split the numbers in the collaborative so that the groups have a mixed dynamic, plus we are looking at cultivating leaders in the organization that can help be a mid-level presence. (Field notes, Spring 2019)

WITS moved forward in developing job descriptions for and hiring additional positions for the following school term. Such development affords members of the collaborative the chance to self-identify or be recognized for the potential to be a leader in the group. Administrators, as well as the research team were eager to see the differentiated learning pathways and field structure that would come from tiered learning targets, and the inclusion of new roles in the collaborative under Tim's guidance.

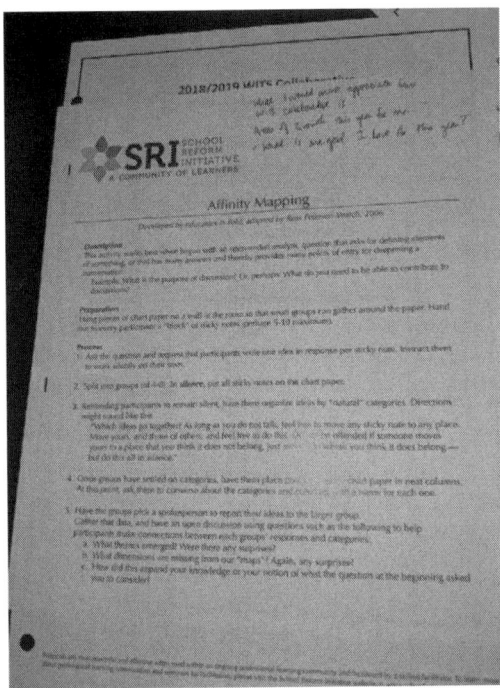

Fig. 4. Sample School Reform Initiative Protocol.

Facilitation

Cheryl: It is like your facilitation, I think. I am hearing that you are not the centerpiece of the facilitation.

Tim: Really, I just introduce the topic and the people to one another and create the conditions for them to come together and I just step back and see what happens. It is very much the workshop style of teaching. You know, the Readers and Writers Workshop, which I am doing in my school. I teach those courses at the university too. The fact that I am a classroom teacher doing them, and I can show what I did today…And I think, the other thing that worked was my connections to things like the Texas Council of Teachers of Language Arts (TCTLA) and people at the Texas Education Agency (TEA). In districts in Greater Houston, the information does not get down to the classroom teacher often – not even the nuances of it. The first couple of years I was in Greater Houston and active on the state level with curriculum updates. I could bring the innovative stuff back to these writers and explain it. You know we have all the education jargon and the writers are not all former teachers. I could translate the jargon as well. Also, I think through the facilitation, the writers became mentors and teachers.

Cheryl: I think it was both with and through your guidance. It was all about your modeling and you are assuring them of these different roles that they would have not seen themselves in.

Tim: Absolutely. The writers began to say my classroom and my teachers. You know they left their place of being somebody who just happens to visit this place (school) and they became very connected with it, and I think the language over time. You are right. The language changed the way people would talk about their work; it became very different from the beginning. For

Reflective Conversation on the Value of Longevity 163

(Continued)

	example, in one cohort, the poet laureate for Houston was a member. In addition, other dynamite writers were movers and shakers from the Latinx literacy community and the African American literacy movement in Greater Houston. We had some real movers. That was exciting because that was one of the things that I took back to my classroom: my knowing of these folks and what they wrote about and what I was able to share with my students, my diverse audiences of students. I mean Houston's Poet Laureate was commissioned by the British Broadcasting Commission to write a poem about Hurricane Harvey. Moreover, she performs it because she is a spoken word poet (https://www.bbc.com/news/av/world-us-canada-41140999).
Cheryl:	I remember her – and I remember the impact of Hurricane Harvey on everyone.
Tim:	I use that poem/performance at the beginning of the year now, every year with my eighth graders when we start literary analysis, and we do it like the first week of school. In addition, what a piece to begin with because we have experienced the hurricane. I end with an incredible poem she wrote about the church shooting in Charleston and performed as well (https://www.youtube.com/watch?v%3DbQHGvd6cSCY). She has been gracious because, if my students have a question about something, we email her and we get a message right back. I think through that relationship I learned how I could interact with the other writers as well. That is something I learned from Tina along the way, too. We have become more peer coaches than anything else.

Reflections on Segment 3

Tim's intentionality is highlighted in this segment. In the previous segment, we come to understand more about how he sets the path for each meeting through purposeful selections and modification of protocols. Here, we see more on how he models the role of facilitator as each protocol is enacted among the group.

Cheryl and Chestin reflected on this in a conversation (2021):

Chestin:	Tim's leadership reminds me of my teaching English. I had fun and learned with them. I was always encouraging my students to think about their thinking. The first word of the year was metacognition. They felt important with a "big" word to learn so early on, and when we read, they always responded from their viewpoint and the viewpoint of the speaker, or character that we were reading.
	Tim does that with the writers. He puts them in the position of guide in their own groups and asks them to interact as coaches. He also asks them to consider the teachers' reactions and responsibilities: How might this be changed? How might this be difficult? How might it be improved? He also never forgets to ask them questions about how the teacher might approach the work with students. This, I think, is key to his effective coaching of coaches. He calls upon them to consider many perspectives through intentional inquiry circles.
	You have known Tim for a while. I am sure that this is similar to what we would see in his classroom. The "I do, We do, You do," and a little extra to see where you go. Is that so? Does his work in the classroom mirror his work in WITS?
Cheryl:	Yes in many ways. Tim always created the conditions for students to write; he never prescribed how many sentences they would write or anything like that. With his support, his students often wrote more – not less – than what was expected of them. Also, Tim knows that people enter writing in different ways. When the Portfolio Group members took up writing in journals, Tim was accustomed to writing sideways on paper bag like material. From his own experience, he knew that writing conditions and materials are different for each person. He knew that these things matter.

Major Influence of Writers in the Schools

Cheryl: So now when you have shared one of the benefits or one of the influences of WITS, that is, certain writers having a profound effect on you and others. What other major influences do you see happening as WITS moves into the field?

Tim: I think the WITS program itself. This was a new experimental idea. It was not just creative writing. I think the program was growing exponentially until the pandemic.

Cheryl: People were seeing the value in bringing authentic writers into the classroom.

Tim: Yes. Even with the state testing. When you introduce authentic reading/writing workshop work, such as Abydos at Hardy Academy (my former campus), students see themselves as writers and then the state testing is nothing. We saw that at Hardy, which was located in a historically underserved African American community. A workshop-based literacy workshop program worked well with Hardy's predominantly students of color because they were motivated to write about topics of concern in their lives (i.e., Hurricane Harvey, church shooting in Charleston). Tina and I built on the early work at Hardy Academy with funding from the Houston A+ Challenge. I am tracing the narrative threads of the work here. I am sort of the conduit, so to speak. It links to reflective practice and the classes I teach as well...

Cheryl: And it is in your dissertation.

Tim: Yes, yes. It was all of these things and they came together into one. It was what graduate school did for me. It took all the things that I was experiencing and created this internal combustion. All of a sudden, I had all of these things going on and suddenly there was clarity. They could have influence and influence one another. I think that has been happening to me again...

Challenges in Writers in the Schools Facilitation

Cheryl: Let us shift to another topic. Were there some things that did not work well with the CFG work and the WITS Collaborative?

Tim: Occasionally, there would be a protocol that would just bomb. Then, the beauty of a relationship would step in. Over time, with the cohort, you know, because they saw me, as their coach was that, if something was not working, we could turn the conversation on a dime. "Hey, this isn't working. Let's, let's regroup and try something else?" "Absolutely." Moreover, you know, at the end of the evening, we always ended with an oral debrief or written debrief. I would ask them about what moves I made when something did not work out. I would ask: "What moves would you see me modeling?"

Cheryl: Yes, pedagogical moves are so important...

Tim: Because sometimes you go down blind alleys that are not quite meeting their needs and where they need to go. However, what a lesson it is to be able to say, "Hey, you know this, this isn't working, let's think of someone else." It is such an important thing when you are modeling with teachers/writers, especially newer teachers/writers.

Cheryl: Yes, you hit one of those dead ends. Moreover, you do not know what to do.

Tim: You are about two seconds away from crying because it is just not happening. You know and I know that we make those mistakes all the time as experienced teachers. Something happens that we did not hope would happen.

Cheryl: But you know how to spin it, Tim...

Tim: Yes. I know how to do something different, which is an important skill.

Reflections on Segment 4

Dr. Martindell's candor was also a factor in his influence on the group. Sharing his experience as a classroom teacher, an ABYDOS trainer and prior CFG work with the Houston A+ Challenge Initiative enables him to coach the group into deep and fluid conversation about the needs of teachers, students, and the metacognitive duality of being both teacher and student in varied contexts. Fueling his openness and readiness to meet the needs of the writing coaches is his present position as a classroom teacher.

> When it was Tim's turn to speak, he said that he was very proud that the meeting would cohere around a protocol that Tina developed for the evening. He furthermore acknowledged that there was a writer in the group...who came from the school where protocols began as part of the National School Reform Faculty initiative.
>
> Tim then said they would follow the agenda (Appendix 1) and begin with Connections. The importance of connections, he explained, is to clear your mind of things that might interfere with your work. It is a place to "get things out." (Field notes, Researcher 1, November of Year 2)

Another researcher noted his consistency and impact:

> Tim's presence and even temperament is a gift. He is a knowledgeable "expert" while actively learning and growing as he shares. It's evident that the writers feel heard and valued. Every protocol presented seems to be selected with intention and explained thoroughly in terms of what writers can expect to yield from teachers and how the protocols can be adapted for classroom use for students. I am a silent guest and the young teacher in me feels heard, drawn in, and connected. (Field notes, Researcher 2, January of Year 3)

Lessons to Take Forward

Cheryl: Now if we are going back to the Wits work....If you were doing it again, if you were going to facilitate again. Is there anything that you would do more of, or anything that you would do less and explain?

Tim: Well, we developed a CFG planning curriculum. And at the end, it worked. Now I had to adapt. I think I would want to add more icebreaker type activities at the beginning. Also, when conversations went deep, I would allow more time for the discussions. These are the things that I would do if I had to do it over again. Also, I was a paid consultant. If I were to do it over again, I would do it for free because there were so many benefits for me as a teacher.

Cheryl: Say a bit more...

Tim: I am sad that it is over. They no longer had money for an outside person. I miss the collegial relationship with Tina. I miss the regular relationship with Maryann and her. Also, there is work that still needs to be done. People are feeling the absence. The project had so much richness. It brought like-minded people together, each of whom brought something to the table. The Critical Friends aspect allowed us to see that.

Cheryl: Yes, and your facilitation of the conversations left spaces for all their voices and all the special areas they were interested in to be discussed.

Tim: As a facilitator, it was always interesting because I had to always be in the moment and figure it out. I am a loose facilitator. So I will, I will be fine with extended conversations. Frankly, I do not care how long they go. Yes, I know there are some people that stay stop. I am more

(Continued)

	global, which is probably why I have had so much trouble doing some of the writing lately. I have to percolate a lot.
Cheryl:	Then it comes out...
Tim:	It is all consuming, but on the other hand, I love the work. It is an energy generating activity. After a long day of school, I might be exhausted. Nevertheless, I'd get to the WITS meetings and the conversations were so rich. I got pumped up, and it was not what I personally was doing. Personally, it was so nice to be with colleagues that are so excited about teaching writing.
Cheryl:	You really spearheaded it, though... You were not dominating the conversation but you opened up the conversation and they flew.
Tim:	Well, that facilitation skill comes to some of us over time.
Cheryl:	It does not come to everyone. It does not appear on demand.
Tim:	I have read that to be an effective leader of a group you have to be the best follower. In addition, when I am facilitating, it is all about those people in the room, not about me (Fig. 5). I do not think people understand that it is not a take-charge role. Especially at this point in my career. I am all about building the next generation. I have had my time in the sun. Therefore, for me, it is for the writers and the teachers to carry the love of writing to students in the school. It is about them and for them and not me. Absolutely.

Fig. 5.   Tim Facilitating Discussion on Culture and Reality Pedagogy Based on Chris Emdin's Work.

Reflections on the Road Ahead

Texas A&M's team was brought in as the program evaluation team in years 4–6, a period of time that started with Hurricane Harvey and concluded with the COVID-19 pandemic. The idea that the project began with a flood and ended with a plague has biblical connotations galore, and the challenges were daunting. These two disasters frame the complexity of that unpredictable period of time.

–Robin Reagler, Former Executive Director of WITS

As former Executive Director Reagler indicated, Tim's work with WITS and our own work as well was bookended by Hurricane Harvey and the COVID-19 Pandemic. As we ended this interview, we remained in the midst of the uncertainty of compounded pandemic responses. Just as a need for new roles and approaches to professional learning surfaced in Greater Houston schools, the momentum became sluggish due to pandemic-related disruptions in the allocation of resources and partnerships. The WITS administrators also noted a number of new positions in partner schools. One shared, "There is a need for us to reach the campus leaders. Not the managers, but the instructional lead teachers and coaches that the districts employ." These positions are often designed to provide mentorship and instructional support to teachers on a daily or weekly basis. They have the potential to carry on the work of WITS alongside, or in between visits from, WITS writers.

Providing professional development in this capacity would require the help of highly specialized WITS personnel and a newly structured curriculum and CFG (CFG®) protocol series. Without such scaffolding, the fidelity of the model would be left vulnerable in the field. This area of growth is projected to become an essential focus of requests from field sites and partnering institutions. Still, a level of uncertainty remains. Even with WITS's swift response to calls for virtual coaching and supplementary workshops, schools are also in the throes of a restructure that complicates consistent enactment of the coaching model. Tim's hope is that the needs that have been amplified by the onset of school responses to COVID-19 will call districts and nonprofit agencies to value long-term collaborations with an eye toward building a more sustainable future.

REFERENCES

Craig, C., Curtis, G., Kelley, M., Martindell, P. T., & Perez, M. M. (2020). *Knowledge communities in teacher education: Sustaining collaborative work*. New York, NY: Palgrave Macmillan.

Craig, C. J., You, J., Zou, Y., Verma, R., Stokes, D., Evans, P., & Curtis, C. (2018). The embodied nature of narrative knowledge: A cross-study analysis of embodied knowledge in teaching, learning, and life. *Teaching and Teacher Education, 71*, 329–340.

Graham, S. (2018). A writer(s) within community model of writing. In C. Bazerman, V. Berninger, D. Brandt, S. Graham, J. Langer, S. Murphy, … M. Schleppegrell (Eds.), *The lifespan development of writing* (pp. 271–325). Urbana, IL: National Council of English.

Schön, D. A. (1983). *The reflective practitioner: How professionals think in action*. New York, NY: Basic Books.

PART III

SEEING MORE: SOMETHING TO PURSUE

In "*Imagining Futures: The Public School and Possibility*" (2000), Maxine Greene presents a case for educators to engage "in the name of something to pursue." She draws upon the need for school leaders and teacher educators in the field to engage in "active learning, critical questioning, and the construction of meanings" infused with a sense of imagination that would draw deficiencies in our daily struggles to a close. For this purpose, section three presents five chapters that are born from such behaviors. Each was inspired by issues which challenged our perception of what our work was in the field, but to begin with an address of these issues is to invite discussion and imagination toward a resolution.

In Chapter 11, *Gentrimigration: Two tales, one city's story of a changed community*, Tenesha Gale unpacks two female teachers' perceptions of their peers' responses and attitudes toward students at various points during a defined period of demographic shift. Gale's parallel stories bring about questions related to factors such as teacher attitudes based on the race, socioeconomic background, and linguistic diversity of their students in contrast to their expectations for their students and the implications of these behaviors on equitable educational opportunities. Gale reflects on the bias that she encountered in her high school English class and shares that story alongside the experience of an English teacher that provides a classroom environment that she perceives to be more inclusive than the one that she endured as a student. More so, she "wanted to know about Larami's time teaching at Hope High School and how other teachers were affected by the change in demographics" in order to devise a plan for preparing future teachers to maintain high expectations and sensitivity to the needs of students from all backgrounds.

In Chapter 12, *Poetry is not a luxury: Engaging learners in multiple literacies through creative poetics*, Lobat Asadi examines poetry performance through the lens of multiple literacies. As Asadi interviews student participants in performative expression, she becomes an active participant in learning about the nature and impact of multiple literacies among marginalized student populations. The collected interviews revealed that the students' "interest in reading and writing was significant because CCPD helped her develop literacies in a way that her K-12 schooling had not." Therefore, Asadi's work challenges common means of expression used in K-12 classroom (prompt-based writing) and standardized essay writing by presenting a review of the literature and narrative interspersion to demonstrate the alignment of multiple literacy theory and increased engagement by the participants of her study.

Chapter 13 *"After a trip, the suitcase stays full till I need something": Unpacking narrative truths from the field* is a revisitation of two interviews. Chestin T. Auzenne-Curl constructs a narrative centered on meaning-making and the construction of self through stories from the field. Auzenne-Curl's reflections on how each interview called her to restory her experiences and add to her meta-analysis of personal practical knowledge reveal how the participant observer contributes to the expansion of individual and collective understanding through storytelling. The study envisions autobiographical narrative inquiry as a "portal through which a person enters the world and by which their experience of the world interpreted and made personally meaningful" (Clandinin, Pushor, & Orr, 2007, p. 375).

We then enter Chapter 14, which provides an examination of social media discourse among Black womxn who are literacy teachers and coaches during the COVID-19 pandemic. Titled *The implications of social media scholarship on knowledge communities in black cyberculture: A co-constructed narrative*, the chapter is a facilitated reflection on what Chestin T. Auzenne-Curl and Daphne Carr deem an organically derived knowledge community in cyberspace. The authors note recurrent experiential tensions related to underrepresentation of Black women scholars in academia and assert that entering into a virtual community of knowledge sharing on the Twitter platform acts as a mediating factor against impostor phenomenon. The imaginative presentation of unrolled threads as courses facilitated by those who made the initial tweets opens in a new venue that is characterized by an inclusive call and response nature of scholarship shapes our consideration of social media scholarship exchange as an accessible and inclusive e-portfolio that amplifies the voices of Black womxn scholars who may feel excluded in higher education. Finally, Chestin T. Auzenne-Curl and Cheryl J. Craig reflect on the impact of not one, but the four pandemics that rocked the Greater Houston area during their work with the WITS Collaborative and how *Research across four pandemics – their reflection along the continuum of time –* shaped the educational landscape and brought them to the completion of this volume with many dangling questions left unanswered.

REFERENCES

Clandinin, D. J., Pushor, D., & Orr, A. M. (2007). Navigating sites for narrative inquiry. *Journal of Teacher Education*, *58*, 21–35.

GENTRIMIGRATION: TWO TALES, ONE CITY'S STORY OF A CHANGED COMMUNITY

Tenesha Gale

ABSTRACT

Written as a parallel story, this article explores two teachers' perceptions of their peers' responses or attitudes toward students at various points during the defined period of demographic shift from the perspective of two Black female employees at the largest high school in Hope City District, Hope High School. As the community became more ethnically, socioeconomically, and linguistically diverse, the school climate began to change. So did teachers' attitudes. The purpose of this second article is to explore how shifting racial, socioeconomic, and linguistic demographics impact teachers' perceptions of students' achievement and students' ability in a suburban context. This narrative inquiry examines the narrative resonances across the parallel stories of two teachers of color who worked through a demographic shift on a suburban campus. Their perceptions of White teachers' attitudes toward non-White students, as well as the echoes of their own stories of experience, are presented to promote discourse on future narrative inquiries concerning stories to live and leave by (Connelly & Clandinin, 1999; Craig, 2015).

Keywords: Literacy education; diversity; parallel stories; marginalized students; gentrification in education; demographic shift

INTRODUCTION

I was a social worker for one of the nation's largest dropout prevention agencies, and while I was working at Hope High School, I felt what the students felt: unwelcomed. The teachers that passed my office daily seemed to be so full of negativity. What initially appeared to be passing conversations about how students no longer had school spirit opened the floodgates to a much larger inquiry into teacher attrition due to changes in the school's student population demographics. My role as a case manager required me to advocate, broker relationships, and teach hidden rules to an underbelly of poor, historically disenfranchised, mostly Black and Brown students now enrolled there. I wanted to give them opportunity. I realized my role on the campus was not needed 10 years prior because the school did not have a large population of students who needed such services. Conversations about how much the school had changed were constant during my time at Hope High School. At first, I attributed this to the new zoning boundaries drawn by the school district. The boundaries placed most of Hope City's poorest students at Star High School. However, I soon realized that Hope City itself had undergone a massive change. Once known as a booming predominantly White suburb, it had become a mostly poor, Hispanic and Black community resembling the inner city. I began to wonder what caused this transition, how did people not see the change happening, and what has been done to address the change?

I recognized the teachers' coded language; hearing these complaints had become my norm at Star High School. It was not uncommon for me to hear teachers say things like, "These kids just don't have the same school spirit as the kids in the past. It's like they do not care. This will be my last year here," or "I hate when students speak in Spanish. They should only speak in English at school. It hinders participation" or "This school is so dangerous now that we can't even have pep rallies on a regular basis. It wasn't always this way; these kids are out of control." The conversations about how much the students had changed were a normal part of my day. Most of the conversations between teachers about students carried racial and classist undertones that left me wondering why these teachers remained at Star High School.

It was clear to me that many of my professional peers longed for a time when their interpretation of an ideal student attended Hope High School and struggled to comprehend their new reality. This became the backdrop to my research. For three years, I witnessed teachers masking the struggles they were living as secret stories (Clandinin & Connelly, 1996) by blaming students and highlighting how disinterested they were. Many teachers experienced tensions as they attempted to reconcile their "stories to live by" (Connelly & Clandinin, 1999) – their identities in narrative terms – as teachers with the reality of their teaching landscapes.

Many teachers left Hope High School in search of old Hope City at the district's newest high school. What they found there were similar conditions. I then witnessed teachers leaving the profession altogether because they could no longer relate to the social changes and the changing classes of students. There were other teachers, however, who did become better teachers as the schools grew more diverse. Larami (a pseudonym), my main participant, was one of them. During my second year, I met a woman named "Larami" who had attended schools in the area and who had begun to teach in that region several years before I arrived. Larami helped me contextualize what had happened in Hope City. She had grown up in this city and had only moved away to attend college. She then moved back to teach there. She had seen the transformation first-hand as a student and a teacher.

COMING TO THE INQUIRY

Part of my inspiration for becoming a teacher came from my experiences as a social worker in one of the largest suburban areas of the nation's third largest metropolitan area. During this time, I was responsible for building meaningful relationships with students to help them achieve their educational goals. I was an advocate and broker for my students and, eventually, teachers at Star High School. Most of my students were students who were at risk of dropping out for various reasons. I made it a goal to create a safe place for them to come and seek help with issues varying from tutoring to drug addictions. Larami and I often discussed campus happenings, student needs, and her relationship with her students, which was unlike most of those I had witnessed. She was able to build meaningful relationships with her students as evidenced by their willingness to work their hardest in her class. The year I met her (2009), her students had performed exceptionally well on the state assessments.

Based on my first-hand observations, Larami's success as a teacher stemmed from her positive relationships with her students and her ability to keep them motivated. I asked her why she thought that others were not achieving the same perceived success working in the same fluctuating environment. As we talked, she used the term "gentrimigration" to describe the shift in population demographics of her hometown. My immediate interpretation of the term conjured up thoughts of the migration patterns of urban residents of low socioeconomic status due to gentrification, and I wondered whether the teacher's mentioning of it would hold a similar understanding. In a recent conversation, we revisited the concept:

TG Remember when we talked about the reason that the teachers on your campus had trouble building relationships with their students? The term "gentrimigration" was brought up. Why did you use that term?

L   During that time, we were living in a bubble in Hope City. The teachers wanted the student population from 1999, but it was 2009 and a lot had changed. To me, it was the gentrimigration factor.... when people from urban areas in Houston made their way to campus. It had been happening slowly, but things were amplified in the cultural aftermath of Hurricane Katrina... all of the movement/migration, from New Orleans and from Houston, as it became gentrified, made Hope City a lot more financially accessible for a lot of people. The Section 8 housing was here.

I wondered about so many of the things that Larami described and what she herself had observed during this critical time of change. I wondered what might be learned from other teachers working in the same area about their teaching experiences as student demographics changed. After working in the same community in what I considered to be the midst of this phenomenon, I wondered about why certain teachers stayed and others left.

As a witness to the aftermath of the demographic changes in the Hope City schools, I experienced several reactions to the changes, including teachers leaving the profession, teacher apathy, as well as some teachers staying and remaining diligent in instruction. While I watched the various responses of many teachers, the stories of staying with those who remained intrigued me the most. I wondered what kept these teachers in the field. What were their motivations as the environment around them so radically changed in Hope City? This narrative inquiry will focus on better understanding the influence of gentrimigration on teachers' attitudes as their work milieu shifts. As I story and restory my and Larami's story alongside each other, I center on common experiences we had working with a predominately White faculty at Star High School.

Context

Hope City is located southeast of one of the nation's largest city and is home to two of nation's largest producers of oil. Hope City was known as a city of prosperity for most of its history. It maintained its top-of-the-pile status until a major shift occurred in the early 2000s that resulted in the urbanization of this suburban city. Because schools represent a cross section of the community, any changes that occur in the community are first experienced in the schools. Hope City is part of Hope City School District.

In 2000, the Hope City School District was composed of 17,837 students whose student demographics consisted of 17.6% African American, 39.2% Hispanic, and 42% White (Texas Education Agency, 2018). Of those students, about 51% were eligible for free or reduced lunch, meaning their households were living at or below the poverty line. Hope City School district data gathered by the Texas Education Agency (2018) demonstrate a much different picture of its student population by the 2017–2018 school year with the school district educating 23,701 students, with 15.4% being African American, 19.7% being White, and 61.8% being Hispanic. About 66.7% of these students are eligible for free and reduced lunch. For students to receive free or reduced lunch, they must come from homes that are considered low-income households, meaning the families of four earn less than $47,000 or less per year (Texas Education Agency, 2018). As can be seen by the Figs. 1 and 2 below, Hope City experienced an unprecedented demographic shift captured in Hope High School's demographics.

The graduation rates at Hope High School in 2000 were considerably higher compared to those in 2018. In 2000, 98% of African Americans, 98% of Hispanic, and 99.1% of White students graduated, and 98.9% of the economically disadvantaged students graduated. In 2018, 88.7% of African American, 88.7% of Hispanic, and 91.1% of White students graduated, whereas 72.4% of the economically disadvantaged students graduated. The drop in Hope's graduation rate is alarming but also telling. Hope City School District had a major shift in demographics. It appears the district did not take measures to keep up with the change (Fig. 3).

The most dramatic drop in student achievement and attainment was the graduation rate of African American students and the economically disadvantaged. The African American population decreased in size. At the same time, their graduation rate decreased the most (11.7%). Nearly one out of every 12 Black students enrolled at Hope High School would fail to matriculate. This raises questions such as: Was the district and school paying attention to that segment of the population? What reforms were going on at Hope High School at that time? Why did they not benefit Black youth? The district saw a 15.7%

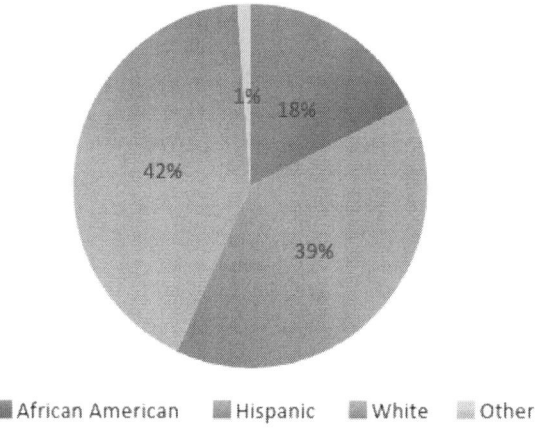

Fig. 1. Hope Demographic Composition in 2000.

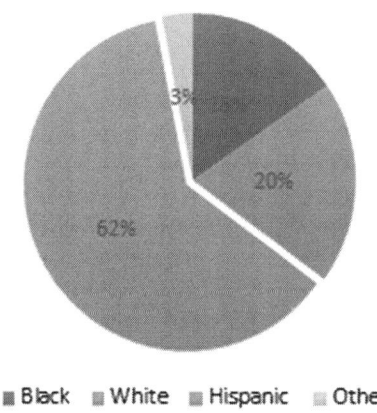

Fig. 2. Hope Demographic Compositions in 2017–2018.

increase of economically disadvantaged students and a disturbing 26.2% drop in graduation rate. The Hispanic population almost doubled from 2000 to 2016, and their graduation rate fell by 9.3%. It appears the district did see an increase in English language learner (ELL) students, but ultimately their efforts were not effective.

By the year 2030, possibly 40% of students in K-12 schools will be children whose first language is not English (US Census Bureau, 2015). Teaching ELLs is

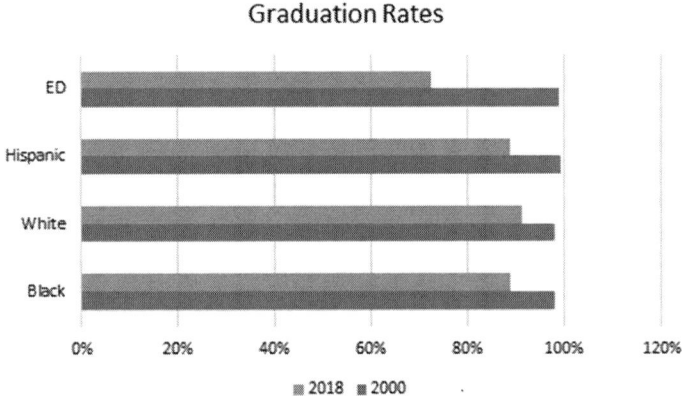

Fig. 3. Hope City School District Graduation Rates from 2000 to 2018.

often broadly categorized as teaching "teaching diverse students"; however, ELLs require more than cultural understanding from their teachers (Hallman & Meineke, 2017). Cultural as well as linguistically responsive teachers are needed to address the increase of ELLs in the United States (Lucas & Villegas, 2013). Students and parents who are ELLs are often faced with feeling isolated because of language barriers, the negative perceptions from educators in schools, and the challenges of understanding academic content (Gaitan, 2012; Lucas & Villegas, 2013).

INTRODUCTION OF CO-RESEARCH PARTICIPANTS

Larami: A Veteran Teacher

Larami is a woman in her mid-30s of Afro/Latino descent. She identifies as African American but acknowledges her Latina heritage. Coming from an ethnically and socioeconomically diverse family, Larami has been able to see a full spectrum of what life can be in Hope City. She grew up there and can recall a time when Hope City was known as a wealthy suburb. Her upbringing was that of a traditional middle-class family. Her father was employed by Exxon Mobil; her mother worked as a deaf education interpreter. At the time of this report, her mother and father have been married for 40 + years. She has one younger brother.

Larami was identified as *gifted* and *talented* early in her schooling and excelled in Hope City School District. She attended Star High School and earned her B.A. in Literature and Composition at a college within the state. Larami wanted to be an attorney, but decided to move back home after graduation to teach and save money before entering law school. Larami returned to Hope City and became a high school English teacher at Hope High School where she experienced great classroom success. Upon completion of her master's degree in Curriculum and Instruction, she was assigned to coach struggling teachers and became the chair of the English department. Larami exited the classroom when she was offered a job as a district level Director of English in another suburb of the metropolis. Later she resigned from that job to obtain her PhD in Curriculum and Instruction. After completing her doctoral degree, Larami launched her own consulting firm where she continues to work with English teachers. She has two daughters and a husband who is an educator and middle school administrator.

Tenesha: Novice Researcher/Novice Teacher

I am an African American woman who was born in Memphis, TN, a city plagued by poverty. I was subsequently raised in Arlington, TX, a suburb of Dallas, TX. Having spent time in both contexts has had a strong impact on the person I have become. My experiences have fueled my passion for equality, equity, and social justice due to my insight into both lifestyles. I excelled in school despite having to deal with several instances of educators making assumptions about me and my ability based on race. I participated not only in athletics on a varsity level but also in orchestra, National Honor Society, Junior Optimist Club, and several other organizations. I went on to receive the Gates Millennium Scholarship[1] which allowed me to attend any university of my choice for free for a 10-year period. Hence, the scholarship also paid for my master's degree education as well as my doctorate degree program. After my undergraduate education, I began working at Hope High School in Hope City School District as a case manager for Advocates on Campus (pseudonym), the nation's largest and most effective nonprofit dropout prevention organization. The mission of this organization is to surround students with a community of support, empowering them to stay in school and achieve in life (Advocatesoncampus.org).

After determining that the biggest issues with which Star High students struggled were educational, I enrolled in an alternative certification program[2] to become a teacher and a master's program at a local university to further my academic education. I started teaching science at a Title I[3] Junior High School in Hope City School District that was the lowest performing junior high school in the district. Over time, my department became the highest performing science department in the district. I eventually left my position to pursue a doctoral degree in curriculum and instruction with a focus in urban education and teacher education, which led me to conducting this research.

Purpose of the Inquiry

As I progressed through school, I witnessed teachers who were not prepared to work on campuses that were highly diverse. My experiences lead me to wondering about how teachers respond to the demographic changes. As a student I attended a school that was in a suburb of a major city. However, this suburb was highly populated and included residents who were ethically, linguistically, and socioeconomically diverse. As new schools were being built, school boundaries become more and more important. The school board and parents wanted to control which type of student went to each school. I recall attending a school board meeting to listen to a discussion about the new boundaries to be drawn for the upcoming high school. A parent stood up in the meeting and angrily shouted, "I don't want my kids going to school with those south-side kids."

I myself was a south-side kid from my hometown. The high school the parent mentioned would have been the high school I would graduate from. The south side of town was the most diverse. The experiences in that high school have lingered with me through my adult years. There were several times when I felt othered because of my race or had to deal with teachers' lack of cultural understanding because they were not prepared to work in such a diverse school. For example, my junior year in Advanced Placement (AP) English. We were reading *Huckleberry Finn* (1884) aloud in class. As many are aware, the book contains the word "nigger" over 200 times. With each occurrence we became more and more uncomfortable. The White students did not seem to feel comfortable saying the word, so they would replace it with "n-word." The Black students became increasingly upset. We often asked why we had to read this book, and the teacher, a White woman, would reply "It is an American classic." Her cultural disconnect was apparent. She did not care how the book affected the Black students in class. She did not understand our pushback because she felt the book was an American classic. Our behaviors were foreign to her. After becoming a teacher, I came to know that the approved reading list had over 50 books she could have chosen, but at the time I thought it was "required" reading because of her. One day a Black girl finally had enough of the book. She asked the teacher "Ms. – What is a nigger?"

Without hesitation, the teacher said, "A Black person."

Everyone was shocked by her truncated response. The student asked another question, "Well, am I one?"

In a matter-of-fact way, the teacher responded, "Well you're Black, aren't cha?"

My class sat motionless for a few seconds; each student with a shocked expression. I, along with several others, walked out. I went directly to an administrator who had taken me under her wing. I talked to her about how it felt wrong to even read the book – aloud, nonetheless. I added how upset I was about the teacher's remarks. The school leader looked upset but stuck to her role as an administrator and convinced me she would "look into it."

I cannot say whether that teacher was reprimanded at all, but she was definitely not suspended. However, we did stop reading the book. One of my coaches told me that the administrator I talked to had no control over teacher suspensions or discipline. Those things were in the hands of the head principal, an older White man. In my opinion, this teacher had gotten away with damaging students and damaging teacher–student relationships.

As an educator, I have had new experiences with teachers not being culturally aware, especially during my time at Star High School. These experiences have fueled my wonderings and lead to my research questions. I now wonder:

- What are the narrative resonances in parallel stories of teachers' perspectives on school climate during a socioeconomic demographic shift?
- How do teachers of color examine the residence of White teachers' attitudes toward non-White students during the demographic shift in a suburban high school?
- How do shifting racial and socioeconomic demographics impact teacher perceptions of student achievement and ability in suburban contexts?

REVIEW OF RELATED LITERATURE

Students of color represent the majority of students in public education for the first time in history, and nearly half of the students in public school are classified as low income based on federal guidance for free and reduced lunch (National Center for Education Statistics, 2017). While the student population has grown more diverse, the teacher population remains White, middle class, women (Geiger, 2020). It has recently been determined that America's Black and Brown students are now twice as likely to be taught by a White teacher. Many of these teachers are not prepared to work in diverse classrooms and have a major disconnect from their students (Boutte, 2012; Castro, 2010; Ladson-Billings, 2001). Many teachers have not had experiences with students who are ethnically, linguistically, socioeconomically, and culturally different from them, yet they are expected to successfully teach these students (Banks, 2001; Castro, 2010). They often hold negative misconceptions about their students as well (Banks, 2006; Castro, 2010). With this knowledge we know that something must be done to better prepare teachers for a diverse student population.

Suburban neighborhoods nationally have undergone rapid demographic changes (Holme, Diem, & Welton, 2014). The suburbs now consist of at least 35% of people of color (Fry, 2011). Sometimes called "melting pot" suburbs, Houston, Las Vegas, San Francisco, and Washington D.C. consist of a majority of people of color opposed to being mostly White (Fry, 2011). As the nation's population grows more diverse, historically White middle-class communities are also becoming more ethnically, socioeconomically, and linguistically different (Kneebone & Garr, 2008). Suburban communities surrounding major metropolitans represent the new face of poverty. The effects are first seen on school campuses as schools are a cross section of most communities (Kneebone & Garr, 2008). Also, all communities have schools, some of which are dedicated to other purposes or have been torn down.

Methodology

Pulling from the narrative forms of telling stories (Craig, 1997) and parallel stories (Craig, 1999, 2003), individual teacher narratives are represented and interpreted using my researcher narrative to help move the inquiry (Curtis, 2013). The parallel stories reveal challenges, growth, transformation, and the "intentionality and concreteness of everyday life" (Greene, 1995, p. 10). Using Craig's (1999) parallel stories method, I incorporate "the narrative of a school as an institution" (p. 401) with "the stories of a teacher's experiences within that institution." Because of my ties to Hope City and Star High School, I act as a co-participant with Larami. Together we will not only recreate the narrative landscape for Star High School, but we will use our experiences to tell and retell our stories of a particular sequence of time and a shared place within which we worked.

Narrative Inquiry

Narrative inquiry is a method of research used to explain lived and told stories (Johnson & Christensen, 2014). This exploratory study takes the experiences of teachers and investigates their internal and existential condition, through storying both backwards and forward. Narrative inquiry allows for the teacher participating in this study (Larami, me [Tenesha]) to restory their experiences and allow me to identify miseducative and educative happenings (Dewey, 1938; Mitton-Kukner, Nelson, & Desrochers, 2010). Narrative inquiry is, for me, the best way of understanding experiences because it attends to teacher experiences (sociality) that occur in context (place) over time (temporal) (Clandinin & Connelly, 2000). These three aspects of inquiry: sociality, place, and temporal form a three-dimensional inquiry space.

Broadening, burrowing, storying and restorying are the three analytical tools I will use to analyze Larami's story (Connelly & Clandinin, 1990). Using broadening, I situated Larami's experiences against a change being felt in many metropolitan cities (Fry, 2011). To investigate what major themes would come to the surface, I burrowed into Larami's personal experiences. Using the last analytical tool, storying and restorying, I was able to highlight Larami's personal and professional feelings about working in a community that experienced an ethnic, socioeconomic, and linguistic change.

INTRODUCTION OF CO-RESEARCH PARTICIPANTS

I (Tenesha) met Larami, an English teacher at Hope High School (pseudonym) in Hope City School District in Hope City. At this time, I was a social worker with a bachelor's degree from Baylor University. As a social worker, I saw and heard the issues students were having with their teachers as well as the issues the teachers were conversely having with the students. I worked with students who had hardships that were hindering them from academically achieving in school. Larami and I talked regularly during this time because many of the students I worked with were also in her English classes. She was often given the students who were labeled "low achievers," and she was able to help them make great academic strides on standardized tests. I felt Larami would be the best participant for this study because she had insights about the Hope City School District from the 1990s to the 2000s. She had been a student and a teacher in the school district. Her firsthand narrative account helped me to identify the changes that occurred in the district and what it was like to be a teacher during this time of great social, economic, racial, and educational transition.

Larami's Early Years

Larami's father graduated from college with a degree and worked in the oil and gas refinery plants in Hope City as many males did during this time. Her mother was a stay-at-home mom. They lived in a middle-class neighborhood, but Larami attended Wilkins (pseudonym), a school outside of her zone. Her mother registered her using her grandmother's address so that Larami could be enrolled in a school that was considered the best in Hope City School District. During her time at this school, Larami recalled being the only Black student in her classes. She remembered there was one Indian student as well. Most of the students in her class were white and from upper middle class to affluent families with their parents either owning businesses or working in the local chemical plants during the energy booms.

Her words stood out to me because the area Larami grew up in had changed dramatically. Now, it was predominantly lower middle class, whereas when she lived there, it was considered a prime suburb of the larger metropolis. Larami described Hope City as a "big-small town" because the town had a large population of about 100,000 but had a small-town feel to it.

During her time at Wilkins, Larami only recalled one instance of racism. Although schools were segregated by color, she felt that class as a social marker was most notably important in Hope City. The only person at the school who made race an issue was a "poor student" – an impoverished student – whose mother told her she could not play with Brown students.

L   I remember there was a girl who I played with a lot when I was in the 2nd grade. She had always wanted me to come to her house and play after school. My mom said that would be fine once she met the girl's parents. Well, I met her mother at a Valentine's Day party. While we played, everything seemed fine. The next day, however, the little girl told me that her mother said she could not play with me anymore and that she wasn't allowed to have brown people at her house.

As Larami told this story, she seemed unbothered by the girl's comments. As I asked more questions, Larami revealed why.

L   I felt sorry for the girl. She was poor. I noticed her clothes were often dirty, and the other kids would not play with her. I didn't really notice these things until her mother pointed out that I was Brown. I was trying to befriend her when the other kids would not. She did not hurt my feelings because I thought her mother's reasoning was sad. I grew up in a multiethnic family, and we recognized differences without placing value on them. I now realized others did.

Larami's teachers initially noticed that she belonged in the Gifted and Talented (GT) program. She was tested and admitted; however, during this time, the district housed the program for elementary students at a school that was predominantly Black and in an impoverished area of the city. Larami's mother did not want her to go to this campus because she was approached by three people on drugs before she made it to the front door when she went to visit. She considered it unsafe for Larami to attend. Larami did not know the exact reason the GT program was housed there, but she suspected it was to help the school district seem more equitable where school programs were concerned. "It could have also been Hope's own suburban gentrification attempt to diversify the area," she pondered aloud.

During junior high and high school, Larami was tracked into Pre-AP courses. She noted that she was one of the five Black students who participated. As a student at Hope High School, she was well known and very active in school activities. She participated in the school's dance group, track team, and National

Honor Society. During this time, she wanted to be a lawyer. When asked about college, she recalled no one talking to her about the admission process. Her private voice instructor helped her get a vocal performance scholarship to a college. "So that became the college I attended," she said. Larami did receive scholarships from other universities, but because her vocal teacher actually talked to her about the college, it was her choice. Hope High School was known as the district's best high school during this time.

The Teaching Years

I wanted to know about Larami's time teaching at Hope High School and how other teachers were affected by the change in demographics. She also was very aware of the changes that had happened to Hope City and Star High School.

L   As a teacher, I knew the anticipated shift had happened because four years prior, I had been the only Black in several classes and now I had classes where there was only one White. Most of my classes were diverse, but some were largely Hispanic which was very different. I also understand that my experience was different due to tracking placement.

I asked about her own practice as a teacher. Larami saw great success in areas the other English teachers did not. She attributed some of this to her being able to see herself reflected in her students.

L   I had the ability to see myself in every student. I thought I was just like everybody. I often asked myself, "What would I want?" or "What would I need?" if I were one of my students. If I could not relate to the particular struggle of a student, I found some part of the student I could relate to.

Larami did not cite an instructional technique that helped her students but did note that community was important in her classroom.

L   My students would often say "we talk to people in the class we don't ever talk to and might never have without it." I felt I created a sense of community with them and that kept me going. I would think about what would happen if they did not have a teacher like me. I would think about the bad teachers I had, and I did not want to leave them with that.

Larami explained that she did not have many issues as a teacher. Her students always performed well, so much, so, she was accused of falsifying passing rates by a colleague. "She didn't understand that engagement and compliance were two different things." Larami said of this peer. "I told her that active engagement can be loud and messy and still yield learning. She only backed down on her feelings of my grade "padding" when the state scores came back and my students passed at the highest rate in the district." Larami did her best to make all her students feel important and valued. She even started several school programs that embraced multiculturalism.

Larami felt the other teachers were not used to having to teach their students because before the students were self-directed and did not need much assistance.

She perceived the teachers she worked with were afraid to teach Black or poor students because of accountability and a general lack of understanding.

L Many of the teachers who worked in Hope City School District did not have to work. Their spouses had well-paying jobs that provided enough income for them to stay home, so their money was viewed as disposable income. There were teachers who were able to put most of their money towards retirement and just live off their husbands' income. When the population shifted, these teachers were not prepared. They had been told, and many held the belief, that students of color could not perform.

The Black and Brown students at Hope High School became a challenge that most teachers were not prepared to endure. Their normal teaching methods were not engaging to the new population, and they were faced with teaching students who were ELLs. They were used to working at a school that did not have to worry about diversity or poverty. Many of the teachers who witnessed the change harbored resentment for the students and had a hard time adjusting to the change. Hope High School administration did try to change the climate of the school as the student population changed, according to Larami.

Larami continued to explain that these teachers felt the students did not care, and education became mediocre. The teachers felt the students did not belong, and a sense of helplessness filled the school's atmosphere. When asked if teachers left the school or stayed, she responded:

L Teachers did a little bit of both. Some stayed if they could teach "AP kids." They believed that this meant the kids were "better," more behaved, and smarter. That was not the case, of course. But AP became a place for teachers' kids, and kids who had active and vocal parents. It was an attempt to recreate the bubble that I grew up in, but unsuccessful because when I was there [as a student], you had to test, have a teacher referral, and a previous years' average of 95 or higher in that subject area. The College Board removed room for those tracking patterns and that opened AP up to anyone.

The teachers attempted to recreate classrooms that resembled the old Star High School, by separating students based on ability. The perceived ideal was that the students in Pre-AP courses were better behaved; however, as ideas surrounding tracking began to change, they could no longer avoid having diverse classrooms. According to Larami, the administration at that time did attempt to react to the increase of Black, Brown, and impoverished students by hiring a more diverse staff.

L New administration ran many sour teachers to early retirement or transfer. The new principal was also very vocal about hiring a faculty that mirrored the diversity of the student population. And he did it.

She continued:

When I was hired in 2003, there was just me and a male history teacher... perhaps an assistant coach, too... But in the next three years, the Black and Hispanic teacher count was up. So, the old teachers did not really change, but the new teachers had different attitudes. They were often hired from places with a large or majority minority population. So, the tide shifted as the staff did.

The new teachers were more understanding and felt the original teachers did not want to step up to the challenge.

L   They [new, diverse group of teachers] thought that suburban poverty and the demographics were a walk in the park. They voiced that the teachers who had been there longer than they had did not realize how lucky they were to be teaching there. Some voiced that the teachers complaining were just lazy and used to kids coming in and being compliant. I agree with most of that. There was not often a discussion of compliance versus engagement until the new crop came in.

Larami further explained:

That is again tied to leadership. The new principal had also come from a high poverty school and himself had grown up in poverty. He also had ADHD and was always thinking of what he needed when he was in school. So that was the lens that he used during casual walk-throughs. "Who would have reached him?

Larami only left the classroom after she felt her identity as a teacher was changing because of an assignment change. She was appointed to be department chair as well as a specialist. For the assignment, she spent half the day teaching and the other half coaching struggling teachers. This dual job status made it difficult for her to focus on the one thing she loved, building relationships with students.

L   I found myself being pulled in two different directions, and I did not like that. I think that if I could have been a full-time Literacy Coach or a full-time English teacher, I would have stayed at Star High School. I was in a space where my identity was not clear... was I a teacher of students, well sometimes.... was I a peer coach... sometimes? I just did not like it.

After two years of a dual status role, Larami left Hope City School District. She worked as a campus Instructional Coach and then a district level English curriculum director for a neighboring school district. At the start of her third year in that district, Larami began pursuing a terminal degree in curriculum and instruction at a tier one research institution.

These interviews with Larami were very insightful. Her experience was unique because she was always a part of this community. I entered the community as an outsider. My views of Hope City are similar to those of an observer. I found that I only knew of the changes because of the action of teachers and students. Larami experienced the changes within the community as an active member.

RESEARCHER REFLECTIONS

I entered Hope High School as a case manager in 2009 two years after the school district rezoned the students from the poorer side of town to Hope High School. Hope High School also had a new principal. The previous principal who took actions such as hiring a group of diverse teachers to adjust to the demographic changes had been moved to the new high school across town. Many of the teachers he hired followed him to the new school, leaving a less diverse teacher population. After speaking with Larami about how the teachers and administrators responded to the demographic changes, I realized Hope High School had undergone yet another major change – a change in administration. It was also the year a brand-new high school opened, which caused Hope City School District to rezone its feeder pattern communities again. The new rezoning left Hope High School majority Hispanic as many of the historically Black and Hispanic neighborhoods, as well as most of the Section 8 apartment complexes, were zoned to the new high school.

Teachers

During my first year at Star High School, there seemed to be dissension among the staff. Many of the teachers with whom I interacted had a negative view of the changes made at the school, and of the nonprofit I worked for. It appeared they did not understand why such a program was needed in their school and believed the students I worked with only wanted to skip class. They did not realize that many of these students were dealing with hardships that most adults in the building had never encountered. The teachers at Hope High School were used to a certain type of student and were having a difficult time adjusting to their student population.

In my view, Larami was seen as a person in the storm with the teachers, whereas I was alongside the "at-risk" students who were viewed as the storm itself. Our positioning at Hope High School was vastly different. Larami recalls the new administrator's direct address of negative behaviors by teachers. This time, they were replaced with a new group of teachers. They were more diverse ethnically, racially, and in age than those who departed. However, as the school underwent changes in administration and teacher population, conversations in my office suggested there was a widening gap in cultural understanding. This could have been because of what my presence in the school represented. Needing a dropout prevention program to assist "at-risk" students meant there were students in the school who fell outside of the traditional norm for the school. Whether those students came from the school from across the tracks, the inner city, or were Katrina evacuees, they were not the representation of the school the teachers wanted, the school with which the teachers had previously identified.

Administration

The new principal was not charismatic; he was a very serious, no-nonsense person. He did not like conflict and would easily cave into the wants of certain school personnel. I had the opportunity to learn more about him, and how he felt about students during a meeting about issues we were having with an after-school program tied to the nonprofit agency I worked for. During this meeting, he chastised the leader of that group and made a statement about wishing he could pour a slab on concrete outside for this program to keep the students from meeting inside of the school. I had to remind him several times during this meeting that the students in the after-school program were the same students who attended his school during school hours. During the principal's second year as the school's leader, two of Hope City School District's Black female students were murdered. One of the girls attended Hope High School and was a student who was on my caseload. I found out Sunday about the incident and quickly alerted the principal. Monday when I walked into the building, a group of students had already started forming at my office. I expected counselors to be notified and for a grief room to be available for the students to have a safe space to cry. The principal did not notify anyone. He did not have a room set up for the students, and he did not understand why I would request a moment of silence for a student who had only attended the school for three months. He was not aware that the student was popular and had family members who also attended the school. I had to fight for a moment of silence and a safe space for the students at the same time as I dealt with my grief and the grief of all my students. I believe the principal handled this situation poorly, in part, because it was a Black student. He was not responsive to the climate in Hope High School and lacked the cultural sensitivity needed to improve the campus's climate.

This school leader was drastically different from the one Larami described. Whereas the previous principal was intentional about his actions and used a culturally responsive method to address the diversity on Star High School's campus, the new principal did not continue the same efforts to help teachers adjust to the changes of Star High School. His actions or lack of actions aborted the previous progress made in improving the school climate.

MAJOR THEMES

After interviewing Larami, I was able to identify three major themes. Through Larami's experience at Hope High School, she was able to build a community for her students because it was the thing she longed for as a student. Larami's experience with the teachers at Hope High School during the demographic shift was varied. Most teachers were afraid of the accountability that came along with teaching diverse students. However, the teachers who refused to embrace the change were removed from the school by an administrator who understood what was best for students. This leads to the third major theme, the impact leadership has on the culture and climate in schools.

Larami's Experience

Larami did not fear the change in demographics. She believed in her students and decided to teach every child instead of giving in to the helplessness others may have felt because Hope High School exhibited a major shift in the social class of its students. Being able to build community led to Larami's success in the classroom. Her students had a place where they all belonged and that kept them engaged. Throughout Larami's story, community or belonging was a major theme in her life. As a child, she played with the only students who did not have friends, during school she built her community around the students by creating programs for them to participate in, and as a teacher she left the profession when she felt she had no community because her identity was split between teacher and administrator. Community sustained Larami in the classroom, and she worked hard to create a sense of community for her students.

Teachers' Experience

Larami spoke of the fear other teachers felt due to accountability. They believed their scores would decrease if their classes were full of Black and Brown students, and they would lose their value as a teacher. For years teachers have been told that minority students do not perform well academically, so when faced with a classroom of minority students, teachers made assumptions about their students. I found that many of the teachers I spoke to would say "How can you make students care who just don't?" or "How am I supposed to teach students who just can't learn?" The teachers feared diversity because they had accepted that it was a helpless situation.

Larami stated that the first wave of teachers left because they felt forced out by the administration. I had a different experience. During the second wave, I heard the things teachers were saying about the students. I can recall a teacher telling me she would not return next year because the kids "lacked school spirit," and the overall atmosphere of the school was just different. These were sentiments I heard from many other teachers as well. I believe they were just uncomfortable and afraid of teaching students who were completely different from themselves. Larami knew some teachers held racist beliefs, but she mostly noted that they just did not want to be accused of poor teaching when students did not perform as well academically. Teachers were now living in a world of high stakes testing and had been told over and over again that African American students struggle with reading and math. As their classroom became more diverse, they were forced to deal with this "issue."

Most of my conversations with teachers had a racist undertone, similar to the ones mentioned before, but they also were laced with a classist undertone. Many of the teachers were not used to having students who struggled to have their basic needs met. When I started working at Star High School, I would deliver food to families in need. Larami's childhood neighborhood started as a middle-class neighborhood, but it too had become one of those places on my food delivery route. Economic status, according to Larami's account, determined which school you attended, what activities you could participate in, and how teachers treated you.

The Impact of Leadership on Climate and Culture

From Larami's interviews and my encounters with principals and administration, I find their role to be pivotal in calibrating teachers' identities amid the dramatic school landscape change. Star High School, before my entry in 2009, had a leader who was focused on the positive climate of the school. He took actions to ensure that all students felt welcomed and that teachers were prepared for the new type of students they were encountering. The administrative team provided professional development for the teachers and allowed teachers like Larami to create spaces and organizations for students of color. Larami is able to speak about a time that appears to be more progressive than my time at Star High School.

On my first day at Hope High School, I was greeted by a principal who had just been hired the year prior. My interactions with him were limited. However, they often left me feeling that he did not understand the students who were in his school. This was evident in the comments he made about laying a slab of concrete for the after-school kids and his reluctance to acknowledge the death of Black students. Through his leadership style, he changed Hope into a place that was oblivious to the needs of students of color and the needs of students living in poverty, many of whom were suffering from food anxiety.

CONCLUSION/FUTURE STUDIES

In revisiting how teachers react to demographic changes, I learned that there are teachers who are able to maintain their image of their best-loved self and grow from their experience of a demographic paradigm shift. Larami was able to better navigate the change of demographics because she was able to see herself in all her students. After many conversations, it was clear to me that Larami's background and upbringing prepared her to teach all students, especially with her family being ethnically and socioeconomically diverse. Larami also practiced being a culturally responsive teacher, by having a cultural knowledge base, by being caring as she created organizations for the Black and Brown students, and by building community in her classroom. From her interview, I could see how her humility allowed her to be a better teacher to all students. In the future, I will look for that quality in other teachers I interview.

From the interviews, I identified many other issues I would like to explore in the future. One major one is the intersection of race and social class. In the United States, race and class are inextricably linked because of the historical oppression of people of color, especially Black people. Now that more Black people are moving into the middle class, assumptions about social class are now being challenged. No longer is it safe to assume that Black people are living in poverty or that they reside in urban centers. With the changes that are occurring in shifting suburban communities, I wonder if educators are willing to adjust their assumptions and biases as well? Not all Black and Brown students in suburban classrooms are living in households that are impoverished. Some of these families are middle-class and similar in socioeconomic status to Larami's family. This also leads me to wonder how other teachers would have viewed the changes if it were White students of poverty moving into their communities? How would their reactions have changed, if at all?

Being culturally responsive is not just important for teachers, but for administrators as well. At Hope High School, most of the culturally responsive actions were taken by an earlier administrator who recognized the importance of changing with the community. However, once that administrator moved to another assignment, the positive attitudes of the teachers changed. I believe the school climate starts with leadership. From talking to Larami, I now understand how the principal's attitude trickled down into the teacher population. Leadership sets the tone of Star High School. Is this a common theme for other schools facing similar demographic and human challenges?

I am interested in how schools in suburban areas adjust to the changes in their community as well as schools. If schools are going to become mixed demographic schools, in what way can we better sustain teachers? How will these new faces challenge teachers? Will teachers continue to react as the teachers in Hope High School did or will they grow into more culturally responsive educators? And, if they are able, how might the transformation best be accomplished?

Ongoing Theme

As I continue writing, a major overarching theme has emerged: a teacher's ability to maintain an image of their best-loved self (Craig, 2013; Schwab, 1954/1978) as their classrooms become more diverse. If teachers' ideas of their best-loved self are confirmed in their classrooms, they are more likely to be sustained in their careers. As shifts happen and they move away from their perceived best-loved self, they are more likely to become dissatisfied in their role as educators and leave the profession. This leaves me with the lingering question: How can teachers' best visions of themselves be sustained during times of dramatic demographic transition?

NOTES

1. The Gates Millennium Scholars (GMS) Program, funded by a grant from the Bill & Melinda Gates Foundation, was established in 1999 to provide outstanding African American, American Indian/Alaska Native*, Asian Pacific Islander American**, and Hispanic American students with an opportunity to complete an undergraduate college education in any discipline area of interest. Continuing Gates Millennium Scholars may request funding for a graduate degree program in one of the following discipline areas: computer science, education, engineering, library science, mathematics, public health or science (GMSP.org).

2. Alternative or nontraditional teacher certification was initially introduced to fill critical teacher shortages (Ingersoll, 2001).

3. "Title I, Part A (Title I) of the Elementary and Secondary Education Act, as amended by the Every Student Succeeds Act (ESEA) provides financial assistance to local educational agencies (LEAs) and schools with high numbers or high percentages of children from low-income families to help ensure that all children meet challenging state academic standards" (National Center for Education Statistics, 2019).

REFERENCES

Banks, J. A. (2001). Multicultural education: Historical development, dimensions, and practice. In J. A. Banks & C. A. McGee Banks (Eds.), *Handbook of research on multicultural education*. San Francisco, CA: Jossey-Bass.

Banks, J. A. (2006). Improving race relations in schools: From theory and research to practice. *Journal of Social Issues, 62*, 607–614.

Boutte, G. S. (2012). Urban schools: Challenges and possibilities for early childhood and elementary education. *Urban Education, 47*, 515–550.

Castro, A. J. (2010). Themes in the research on preservice teachers' views of cultural diversity: Implications for researching millennial preservice teachers. *Educational Researcher, 39*, 198–210.

Clandinin, D. J., & Connelly, F. M. (1996). Teachers' professional knowledge landscapes: Teacher stories—Stories of teachers—School stories—Stories of school. *Educational Researcher, 25*(3), 24–30.

Clandinin, D. J., & Connelly, F. M. (2000). *Narrative inquiry: Experience and story in qualitative research*. San Francisco, CA: Jossey-Bass.

Connelly, F. M., & Clandinin, D. J. (1990). Stories of experience and narrative inquiry. *Educational Researcher, 19*(5), 2–14. doi:10.3102/0013189x019005002

Connelly, F. M., & Clandinin, D. J. (1999). *Shaping a professional identity: Stories of educational practice*. New York, NY: Teachers College Press.

Craig, C. J. (1997). Telling stories: Accessing beginning teacher knowledge. *Teaching Education, 9*(1), 61–68. doi:10.1080/1047621970090109

Craig, C. J. (1999). Parallel stories: A way of contextualizing teacher knowledge. *Teaching and Teacher Education, 15*(4), 397–411. doi:10.1016/s0742-051x(98)00062-6

Craig, C. J. (2003). Characterizing the human experience of reform in an urban middle-school context. *Journal of Curriculum Studies, 35*(5), 627–648. doi:10.1080/0022021032000145732

Craig, C. J. (2013). Teacher education and the best-loved self. *Asia Pacific Journal of Education, 33*(3), 261–272.

Craig, C. J. (2015). Complexities of teaching and learning: Contexts, orientations and interpretations. *Teachers and Teaching, 21*(2), 127–130.

Curtis, G. A. (2013). *Harmonic convergence: Parallel stories of a novice teacher and a novice researcher*. Unpublished doctoral dissertation, University of Houston, Houston, TX.

Dewey, J. (1938). My pedagogic creed. *School Journal, 54*, 77–80.

Fry, R. (2011). *Melting pot cities and suburbs: Racial and ethnic change in metro America in the 2000s*. BROOKINGS. Retrieved from https://www.brookings.edu/research/melting-pot-cities-and-suburbs-racial-and-ethnic-change-in-metroamerica-in-the-2000s/

Gaitan, C. D. (2012). Culture, literacy, and power in family–community–school–relationships. *Theory Into Practice, 51*(4), 305–311.

Geiger, A. W. (2020). Public school teachers much less racially diverse than students in US. Retrieved from https://www.pewresearch.org/fact-tank/2018/08/27/americas-public-school-teachers-are-far-less-racially-and-ethnically-diverse-than-their-students/

Greene, M. (1995). *Releasing the imagination: Essays on education, the arts, and social change*. San Francisco, CA: Jossey-Bass.

Hallman, H. L., & Meineke, H. (2017). Addressing the teaching of English language learners in the United States: A case study of teacher educators' response. *Brock Education: Journal of Educational Research and Practice, 26*(1), 68–82.

Holme, J. J., Diem, S., & Welton, A. (2014). Suburban school districts and demographic change: The technical, normative and political dimensions of response. *Educational Administration Quarterly, 50*(1), 34–66.

Ingersoll, R. M. (2001). Teacher turnover and teacher shortages: An organizational analysis. *American Educational Research Journal, 38*(3), 499–534. doi:10.3102/00028312038003499

Johnson, R. B., & Christensen, L. (2014). *Educational research* (5th ed.). Thousand Oaks, CA: SAGE.

Kneebone, E., & Garr, E. (2008). *The suburbanization of poverty: Trends in metropolitan America, 2000–2008*. Washington, DC: Brookings Institute. Retrieved from http://www.brookings.edu/~/media/research/files/papers/2010/1/20-poverty-kneebone/0120_poverty_paper.pdf

Ladson-Billings, G. (2001). Multicultural teacher education: Research, practice, and policy. In J. A. Banks & C. A. M. Banks (Eds.), *Handbook of research on multicultural education* (pp. 747–759). New York, NY: Macmillan.

Lucas, T., & Villegas, A. M. (2013). Preparing linguistically responsive teachers: Laying the foundation in preservice teacher education. *Theory Into Practice, 52*(2), 98–109.

Mitton-Kukner, J., Nelson, C., & Desrochers, C. (2010). Narrative inquiry in service learning contexts: Possibilities for learning about diversity in teacher education. *Teaching and Teacher Education, 26*(5), 1162–1169.

National Center for Education Statistics. (2017). Fast facts: Public school students eligible for free or reduced-price lunch (898). Retrieved from https://nces.ed.gov/fastfacts/display.asp?id=898

National Center for Education Statistics (NCES), a part of the U.S. Department of Education. (2019). *Digest of education statistics-advance release of selected 2019 digest tables.* (n.d.). Retrieved from https://nces.ed.gov/programs/digest/2019menu_tables.asp

Schwab, J. (1954/1978). Eros and education: A discussion of one aspect of discussion. In I. Westbury & N. Wilkof (Eds.), *Science, curriculum and liberal education: Selected essays.* Chicago, IL: University of Chicago Press.

Texas Education Agency. (2018). *Snapshot.* Austin, TX: Author. Retrieved from https://rptsvr1.tea.texas.gov/adhocrpt/Standard_Reports.html

US Census Bureau. (2015, July 16). *Statistical abstract of the United States: 2007.* Retrieved from https://www.census.gov/library/publications/2006/compendia/statab/126ed/population.html

POETRY IS NOT A LUXURY: ENGAGING LEARNERS IN MULTIPLE LITERACIES THROUGH CREATIVE POETICS

Lobat Asadi

ABSTRACT

This study explores the experiences of five high school–aged youth involved in creative writing and poetry slam performances operated by a nonprofit organization in the city of Houston, Texas. Seeking to understand how poetry may have helped the youth in this study, Multiple Literacies Theory (MLT) (Masny & Cole, 2007) is used as an interpretive tool in this paper. In addition, the literary writing style of bildungsroman, *or writing that reflects on one's worldview and personhood through lived experiences, is discussed as part and parcel to the poet's process because of the personal narratives used in their poetry. Narrative inquiry methodology was used in this longitudinal study because it allowed fluid ways of analyzing emergent sociocultural issues faced by the participants, who identified as Black, LGBTIQ, Asian American and also indicated intersectional, marginalized life experiences. It is hoped that this study will outline some of the benefits of art-based education and bildungsroman for marginalized learners, as well as inspire further research into art-based pedagogies and assessments, which may better reflect multiple literacies.*

Keywords: Poetry; bildungsroman; arts-based education; multiple literacies; culturally relevant pedagogy; spoken word poetry; performance arts

> Poetry is not a luxury. It is a vital necessity of our existence. It forms the quality of the light within which we predicate our hopes and dreams toward survival and change, first made into language, then into idea, then into more tangible action. Poetry is the way we help give name to the nameless so it can be thought...
>
> –Audre Lorde (as quoted by Popova, 2020)

INTRODUCTORY NARRATIVE

Poetic knowledge is born in the great silence of scientific knowledge.

–Aimé Césaire

I interviewed Oasis. Oasis believes poetry has saved her life. "This poem only lived on stage for one night, but it saved me," she said when I interviewed her as a participant in a research study about creative writing and poetry slams, operated by Classroom Collaborative for Professional Development (CCPD) and Innovation. Oasis continued, "There were things that I could not say, and express to people close to me. Like things that have happened to me, but it just comes out in a poem when I sit down to write" (personal interview, 2018). I was reminded of a line from Oasis's poem, which she performed when I was an audience member at a poetry slam she competed in: "His arms were around me in an uncomfortable hold…" I began putting the pieces together. She had just said to me in our interview, "This poem only lived for one night on stage, but it saved me," meaning, poetry was a kind of weapon. In this instance, Oasis, who self-identified as a Black woman, also identifies poetry as a remedy.

I proceeded gingerly when I asked Oasis how she felt about writing and sharing personal experiences on stage during poetry "slams," which are a type of spoken word competition in which poets perform their own original poetry in front of judges and an audience. Oasis, a 17-year-old high school student at the time, grew wide-eyed and said, "I like to perform," adding that since she joined CCPD, a nonprofit run by teachers and writers in their spare time, she found herself reading and writing more than ever before. "Toni Morrison made me realize I could write about anything." Oasis eagerly continued, "Now I want to go to college, and I never wanted to do that before!" She said she had shocked everyone, including herself, when she became interested in a degree in English.

Oasis' interest in reading and writing was significant because CCPD helped her develop literacies in a way that her K-12 schooling had not. Poetry was also a source of her emotional well-being, and it was notable that she also likened her personal experiences to another woman of color, Toni Morrison, who may be considered a self-defining, coming of age writer of *bildungsroman*. Oasis' impassioned response to writing seemed, to me, reminiscent of the joy in self-expression of Aimé Césaire. Despite Césaire's (2001) resistance to French colonial structures, he responded to his mental and physical oppressors by writing in French, the colonial language of his country, Martinique: "In the end, Discourse was never intended to be a road map or a blueprint for revolution. It is poetry and therefore revolt" (p. 28). In this sense, poetry was a way to speak out or revolt against oppressive experiences for both Césaire and Oasis.

I conducted one in-depth interview with five of the young poets who were involved with the poetry slam sponsored by the CCPD and Innovation. I was also an audience member at several of the poet's poetry slam performances over a two-year period. This study explores how the process of writing poetry and participation in poetry slams impacted the five participants, who all self-identified as belonging to marginalized demographic groups, specifically Black, Asian, and LGBTIQ. Their stories prompted me to consider why reading and writing poetry and arts-education may be part and parcel to the development of multiple types of literacies among learners who may be considered members of marginalized youth populations. Finally, I make pedagogic recommendations for educators in formal and informal learning programs.

CONTEXT

Multiple Ways of Knowing

Educators have asked traditional schooling to incorporate more languages (National Council of Teachers of English, 2013), lived personal experiences (Clandinin, Caine, & Lessard, 2018), ethnic studies (Valenzuela, 2019), culture (Ladson-Billings, 1995), ethnographic research (Bhattacharya, 2009), ethnographic theater (Saldaña, 2016), and the arts (Greene, 1995) for decades. Multiple-award winning scholar Dr. Gloria Ladson-Billings was consulted about providing better education for already marginalized and vulnerable learners in postconflict spaces, including the aftermath of COVID-19:

> I think the pandemic has taught us a lot about education. We are all in the same storm, but not on the same boat. Yes, we are all facing a pandemic, but we also know Hurricane Harvey and Hurricane Katrina were also encountered very differently, based on race and economic status. What I hope is that we don't go back to the way things used to be in education before the pandemic. (Ladson-Billings, Personal Interview, January 27, 2021)

As previously mentioned, the study is centered in Houston, Texas, which felt the impact of Hurricane Harvey's disruption to scheduling and the trauma of natural disasters. The prophetic City (Klineberg, 2021) is also known to be demographically representative of the shifting population demographics of the United States as a nation. This means, among other things, that there is an increasing population of historically marginalized populations.

For these reasons and more, this study looks to arts-education and, by extension, to the literary writing style of bildungsroman (Morgenstern, 1819 as cited in Swales, 2015) for their relationship to writing poetry and performative poetry slams such as that by CCPD. Like the poetry undertaken by CCPD, bildungsroman it is a creative literary genre in which a youth undergoes psychological and moral growth until reaching adulthood. Similar to the learner identity and academic achievement-boosting benefits of arts-education (Bowen & Kisida, 2019), in bildungsroman, the protagonist's character change is important because they examine their relationship to their society and environment (Boes, 2012).

LITERATURE REVIEW

In response to the expanding notion of literacy to encompass the changing landscape of the 21st century, new frameworks, pedagogies, and perspectives are needed. Bildungsroman allows for personal narratives to answer the bigger questions about race, society, politics, culture, and more. Bildungsroman should entail the writer's realization of their own capacity to make a personal or social difference through their writing (Boes, 2012). Thus, reading, feeling, writing, research, examinations of society, and other factors involved in bildungsroman serve as the sources of literacy. Literacy, once defined as simply reading, writing, and communicating, is thereby viewed from a broader lens. One lens is multiple literacies, a pedagogical framework by a scholarly group, the New London Group (1996). Literacy has been expanded to include "the ability to understand, respond to, and use those forms of written language that are required by society and valued by individuals and communities" (i.e., multiple literacies) (Ministry of Education, 2003, p. 13). Literacy attained through nontraditional schooling is pertinent to people of color and other marginalized groups such as immigrants because like nontraditional learning, they are also under the surveillance of normative discourses (Campano & Ghiso, 2011).

Furthermore, literacy can be performative in the sense that when learners read, write, or and embody the text, such as in a poem slam, they are not only imparting meaning but also they are interpreting it. To explain, when students respond to knowledge performatively, they are demonstrating their knowledge, but also their abilities as "literary critics" (Sipes, 2008, as cited in Enriquez, Johnson, Kontovourki, & Mallozzi, 2015, p. 44). Learners are performing as they are disrupting normative understandings and assumptions (literacy) through their own critical performances of literacy (Enriquez, Johnson, Kontovourki, & Mallozzi., 2015). In this way, poetry can be performed in a transactional sense because the performance displays the learner's understandings.

Reading can inspire writing poetry because bildungsroman and multicultural texts can stimulate as they may relate to the learner's own personal lived experiences. In addition, multiple ways of knowing, such as reading, researching, analyzing, interpreting, and creating, are involved in the process. In the case of CCPD, the process of reading poetry to write poetry, transferred to a performative literary product that made the learners, poetry slam performances (CCPD teacher, personal communication, 2019). Knowledge or meaning-making in the poet-participants' lives depended on their prior life experiences, just as bildungsroman, or coming of age writing, relies on lived experiences that propel the writer to grow, and even inspire social change (Boes, 2012). Marginalized people are faced with challenges such as language barriers, immigration, gentrification, ostracization, and other challenges. This indicates marginalized people inherently possess and readily attain more multiple literacies, but their literacies remain underdeveloped and underappreciated in their environment.

Culture

Unfortunately, multiple literacies, culture, and bildungsroman are not commonly accessed in traditional schooling. For example, Texas has been embroiled in social instability and educational controversies because of its English-only education and practices since its inception (Blanton, 2007). Likewise, formal schooling in the United States tends to subtract culture from the curriculum, which is an extension of one's family history and lived experiences (Valenzuela, 2019). This lack of representation and understanding in the education system and curricula impacts people of color negatively (Ladson-Billings, 1995). However, cultural understanding and representation can be activated by educators through youth participatory action research (Cammarota & Fine, 2008), bildungsroman, and creative writing (Anzaldúa, 1987) that stems from the lived experiences of people of color and otherwise marginalized people.

Research methods that generate counter-story telling might also involve aspects of bildungsroman. To explain, Lather (2018) also encourages the researcher to restory participants' stories, by using literature and their own imagination to meet their knowledge with verisimilitude. Counter-story telling, a form of narrative inquiry methodology (Clandinin & Connelly, 1999; Craig, 2020), may also support understanding of one's of lived experiences that may run counter, or opposite to the larger more dominating "mega-narratives" (Olson & Craig, 2009). To critical race scholars, counter stories can be "racial micro-affirmations through narratives as a response to racial microaggressions" because they create a counter space to the common narratives about people of color (Solórzano, Huber, & Verjan, 2020).

In this study, I use narrative inquiry methodology (Connelly & Clandinin, 1990) because it was devised for educational research, and it allows for counter-story telling (Craig, 2020), among other narrative forms, to explore lived experiences. In narrative inquiry, as in bildungsroman, the writer (or researcher) can become literate or informed, by using narratives that run counter to the mainstream, as opposed to negating nontraditional ways of learning and knowing. In this study, I hope to demonstrate how literacy can be encountered in a nonformal setting vis-à-vis lived experiences. Lastly, I warn how the rejection or scrutiny of literacy, in any form, be it by traditional schooling, dominant society, or positivist research, is hindering education, multiculturalism, and diversity in the United States.

In this chapter, I reflect on how multiple literacies, which, like marginalized peoples, are outside of the traditional framework of learning and literacy, may benefit learners. To explain, after I attended three different poetry slam performances as an audience member, I noted that the poets expressed emotional, cultural, and political lived experiences. The poetry they had written and performed demonstrated their literacy about the world around them, as they actualized, interpreted their lived experiences. In this way, I realized that the process of personal narratives performed in poetry slams had become part and parcel of the learner's literacy.

Multiple Literacies

Just as there are multiple cultures, races, languages, and other multiplicities, there are multiple ways of knowing. Multicultural learners need education that allows for a convergence of their culture and cognition to inform their literacy (Hammond, 2007). Education is often considered to be a purposeful, constructed process taking place in a carefully designed exclusive space for learning – most commonly thought of as a school. Yet, Morris (1997) asserts that the language (of learning) is itself immersed in social and cultural contexts. "Language is not a neutral medium that passes easily and freely into the private property of the speakers intentions; it is populated - overpopulated with the intentions of others," (Bakhtin, cited in Kramsch, 1995, p. 27). Bakhtin states a universal linguistic code that acts as one voice for all speakers cannot exist because language use is related to history and power (Kramsch & Widdowson, 1998). Morris (1997) believed that history itself is an internal drive that produces states of language, which in turn, produces conflicting forces. By extension, we can assume that one can explore their personal history by looking backwards into their lived experiences.

Neimeyer and Sands (2011) studied learning across space and time in an analysis of letters written by women in the 1700s–1800s to understand "informal learning" of the marginalized gender. They concluded that space-times of education are not limited to certain places. Instead, they open up in the course of history whenever the relation of individual and society, self and world, enters in a process of transformation. Therefore, a learner can reflect upon their own life and learn in various informal ways, across different moments in time, if their personal experience identifies with that historical rendering in time. In this analysis, the marginalized people were women, who, among other restrictions in the 1700s, were not able to attend schooling as openly as men were, but they were able to learn by writing letters and reflecting upon their experiences in the writing sharing of these letters. Likewise, with CCPD, we can see how writing and self-reflection may be particularly beneficial for people who may be "voice-less" and under presented in education, and overall, in society. Through such reflection and self-study, poets and other writers can build, or bildung in German, meaningful writing – bildungsroman.

Learner Identity

The concept of bildungsroman is in the constant endeavor to understand how a subject and his or her surroundings, the self, and the world, are interrelated in a writing style which allows for continuity and personal growth and change. The individual is understood as capable of political impact because writing bildungsroman is dependent on knowledge about the relationship of oneself and their environment (Boes, 2012). These pieces of writing can be described as coming of age novels, poetry and other forms of non-fiction. Harper Lee's *To Kill a Mockingbird* is a bildungsroman in the classic sense because it is about the pains of growing up and understanding the different people and issues in your environment. The writings of James Baldwin, Gloria E. Anzaldúa, are also considered bildungsroman because they analyze oneself in relation to their problems and learn about their own identity in the process.

Other writers such as Richardson (1999) have called for writing as a method of knowing and inquiry. To elaborate, reflecting on oneself through writing that explores personal, historical narratives are outlined by scholars in various ways, and oftentimes the writing style has its own focus. What is different about the concept of bildung is that it builds a personal biography, and as the writing develops, its beings shift the focus to the individual transforming as an autonomous subject (Boes, 2012). Bildungsroman places emphasis on the writer as a human being having transformative experiences (Kim & Zimmerman, 2017).

Arts-based Education

While the aesthetic is frequently considered something of minimal value, but from time immemorial, we can see how human beings have looked to music, theater, poetry, the visual arts, and other aesthetics, for both learning and pleasure. The arts often offer processes and pathways to the imagination (Greene, 1995), as well as learning and research (Barone & Eisner, 2012). To elaborate, artists can choose to challenge audiences about their perceived social and political inequities in society. Critical thinking, writing, and the arts can be combined for a variety of political, social statements that protest oppressive or otherwise dominant standards (Bagley & Castro, 2012).

Furthermore, using the arts in education as well as art education in K-12 may benefit cognitive functions and hold keys to developing a society that has increased empathy and understanding. For example, the arts benefit learners far beyond what achievement tests display in areas such as advanced thinking (Hargrove, 2012), the ability to cope with stress, enhanced self-awareness (Autry & Walker, 2011), and life skills (Clinton & Hokanson, 2012). Participation in community-based art therapy demonstrates that art making can empower people with difficult, often racialized realities by transporting learners into a realm that allows for free "speech" and expression (Lee, 2013).

THEORETICAL

The concept of multiple literacies is based on the Multiple Literacies Theory (MLT), the work of late philosopher Gilles Deleuze, which looks at the role of multiplicity in literacy instruction. MLT allows for this learning to take on a natural and organic quality by providing a means for students to integrate and work within contexts, authentically (Bogue, 2009). This is because MLT expands the concept of literacy instruction from that of a linear, sequential process to one where "communication abilities form feedback loops and aggregate internal and external ways" (Masny & Cole, 2007, p. 3). In order to assess the impact of poetry and poetry slam performances in tandem with multiple literacies, I use MLT (Masny & Cole, 2007) as an interpretive tool. While other ways of looking at literacy have been identified by other theorists, I have chosen MLT because the theory had the most accurate overall reflection of the cultural, emotional ways of knowing, alongside the reading and writing outcomes expressed most by participants. MLT outlines these literacies: (1) Cultural Literacy, (2) Digital Literacy, (3) Emotional Literacy, (4) Environmental Literacy, (5) Numerical Literacy, (6) Political Literacy, (7) Scientific Literacy, and (8) Visual Literacy (Table 1). Like MLT, writing bildungsroman also calls for and seeks out lived experiences as sources of knowledge.

Table 1. Multiple Literacy Theory – Definitions.

Cultural Literacy	"The ability to read and interpret culture in its many manifestations (cultural artifacts) by applying skills and knowledge inherent to literary and cultural studies, opening up the possibility to modify such artifacts or one's attitudes toward them, to the benefit of everyone involved in a given situation" (García Ochoa, McDonald, & Monk, 2016).
Digital Literacy	"The awareness, attitude, and ability of individuals to appropriately use digital tools and facilities to identify, access, manage, integrate, evaluate, analyze, and synthesize digital resources, construct new knowledge, create media expressions, and communicate with others in the context of specific life situations..." (Pow & Fu, 2012, p. 288).
Emotional Literacy	The ability to demonstrate resilience that supplements the cognitive performance of a learner by aiding in self-regulation, thus character development (Van der Kolk & McFarlane, 1996).
Environmental Literacy	The capacity of a person to successfully engage in society and natural systems by taking the appropriate environmental considerations about sustainably in daily decision-making about consumption, lifestyle, career, as well as taking civic action (Masny & Cole, 2007).
Numerical Literacy	The ability to use mathematical concepts in learners' lives, not just limited to the use of mathematical operations. (Kramarski & Mizrachi, 2006).
Political Literacy	"Understand party differences and know basic political concepts and facts" (Cassel & Lo, 1997, p. 317).
Scientific Literacy	The "...knowledge and understanding of scientific concepts and processes required for personal decision making, participation in civic and cultural affairs, and economic productivity" (National Research Council, 1996, p. 22).
Visual Literacy	Visual literacy is the ability to interpret and create "visual representations of ideas and information" (Silverman & Piedmont, 2016).

Fortunately, neither mode of literacy, MLT or bildungsroman, nor my chosen method or narrative inquiry seeks to silo skills or isolate one's personhood from meaning-making.

Theoretically, when equipped with the ability to read, write, and communicate across multiple literacies, students are able to tap into an affective domain that permeates future decision making. In a world rapidly changing in response to social, technological, and economic developments,

> ...the central question for each of us is not "How do we teach children to be literate?" Instead, the central question is... "How do we help children learn to learn the new literacies that will continuously emerge?" (Leu, 2001, p. 568)

Schooling is not done in isolation, just as coupling texts with other literacies, such as visual, cultural, and political, is an integral part of the learning process. Masny (2012) explains, "Within MLT, discourse is taken up as an assemblage of texts that come together as sensation (affects) and resonate becoming" (p. 126). For example, under MLT theory, understanding multiple languages and being bicultural indicate that the learner has multiple literacies. Yet, unfortunately, in the United States, where bilingual education is not the norm, and educators continue to fight for the right to teach ethnic studies (Cabrera, Milem, Jaquette, & Marx, 2014; Valenzuela, 2019), a monocultural curriculum and monolingual pedagogy dictates who and how one is deemed literate. While MLT has expanded notions of literacy, unless these literacies are acknowledged and accepted within our K-12+ pedagogies and curriculum, nuanced ways of meaning-making are still left out of schooling.

METHOD

In this study, I selected theories and methods that converged culture, personhood, and knowledge because I believe them to be the least invasive to the already vulnerable population of learners involved in this research. Fortunately, since political and social issues continue in the 21st century for people of color, the LGBTIQ community and others, more research methods which benefit people of color, as they permit their stories to be told, have taken flight. Some research methods include testimonio (Huber, 2012), which emerged among Latinx people, and ethnography (Cottom, 2018), which has been recommended for African American populations. Yet, testimonial and ethnography were sufficient for this study as they focus mainly on culture and social interactions among one group of people rather than on experiences of different marginalized people in a larger, shared space.

To elaborate, the narratives that run counter to larger, grand scale narratives, or mega-narratives (Olson & Craig, 2009) are often the stories of the marginalized people, who may live in the periphery of society. Like the performance of an original poem derived from lived experiences, in narrative inquiry, life stories that are lived are re-told, reconstructed, and re-lived (Connelly & Clandinin, 1994). In addition, different dimensions, temporality, sociality, and spatiality are incorporated into narrative inquiry's research space (Clandinin & Connelly, 2000). Thus, the researcher may interpret emergent key issues in relationship to time, culture, and lived experiences (Riley & Hawe, 2005). In this paper, I use narrative inquiry as a qualitative method because of its effectiveness, noninvasiveness, and fluidity over time, culture, and society when exploring the poets' lived experiences as learners, performances.

Researcher Positionality

As time, culture, and people are considered important aspects in narrative inquiry, the relationship of the researcher must also be specified when analyzing participants' stories. As a researcher, I conduct field-based narrative inquiries with marginalized learners, such as immigrants and people of color (Asadi, 2020; Suárez et al., 2020). To explain, Craig (2000) states

> ...the researchers' personal thinking and narratives become revealed. This is because our wonders and ponders inform our inquiries and our relationships with participants are essential to how research puzzles become understood. (p. 355)

For these reasons and more, I pay close attention to narrative inquiry methodology's capacity to uncover the experiences of socioculturally marginalized learners.

Participants

As previously stated, there are five participants. I have changed their names for anonymity, albeit none of them asked me to do so, and I have included their self-identification in reference to gender or orientation because they expressed their marginalization was related to their identity in many instances.

DISCUSSION

In Table 2, some of the quotes the participants shared in unstructured interviews were selected for their cultural and emotional implications. It is important to note that I did not specifically ask participants about literacy, nor did I ask for any specific cultural or emotional narrations. The last column, Bildungsroman, highlights statements that indicated the participant reflected on their personal history and lived experiences in order to grow and overcome any challenges. This potentiates bildungsroman as a beneficial and congruent writing style with MLT because their experiences either informed their writing or their writing informed their personal growth and "coming of age."

Table 2. Literacies and Bildungsroman

Name and Self-identification	Emotional Literacy	Cultural Literacy	Bildungsroman (Personal Identity Development through Writing)
Edward White male, gay	I'm really interested in work that is able to speculate anything existing in a space and this weird place in time.	We see so many people sometimes put in a position or told that they're in a position where they're powerless at the ability to create spaces even imagined it to be really powerful.	My grandmother as a librarian I think is one of the pivotal people in my life that led me toward writing. When I told my grandmother I was writing poetry, she told me when she was a librarian, there was conflict around books Baptist preachers and very religious people were trying to get Harry Potter books banned for promoting witchcraft. And so my grandmother was fighting to keep the books in her school's library.
Emily Asian female	Sometimes whenever we feel really strong emotions, it's really hard to say what we're thinking and what exactly it is that's bothering us because these emotions are so overwhelming, but, through poetry, I not only		I had a very difficult time conveying my anger growing up as a kid. Uh, so poetry was a good way to express myself and find the words to convey that anger without using insults without hurting other

Table 2. *(Continued)*

Name and Self-identification	Emotional Literacy	Cultural Literacy	Bildungsroman (Personal Identity Development through Writing)
	break down the problems that I was facing but also allow other people to understand me.		people's feelings and generally just getting to the point, in a more direct way. It also helps me convey my sadness.
Michelle White female, queer	If I just had some sort of big events in my life in any direction, if it's really exciting work, it's, it's traumatizing somehow. I don't usually like to write about that very immediately because I don't. I think when it's fresh, we aren't able to think as critically about it.	I was reading some texts about foreign languages, and I read about a tribal language in which directions are always cardinal. So, instead of right and left hands, it is east and west. When you shift where you're facing, it then becomes a different direction. So, they are constantly perceiving the world as a moving compass. It is also very stationary because the directions never change where their bodies are. The things around them change. That's really amazing, and I was thinking that we too can access a type of language or a specific way of directing our language to pursue the world around us.	Like the banking system of the classroom as it generally is set up is to, for students to be very receptive and, it almost feels, I would say dehumanizing, but it just feels, um, very degrading to, to that application that will be no nothing. And we are only here to receive from these teachers who are sometimes put in a light of this amazing, like almost omnipotent power, like, you know, all, all of the information that I need, and I'm only here to receive it from you.
Celine Black female	So like I control reality. So then that's really dark, but the tissue is writing. I think a lot of times I put myself in a position of being a creator.	I remember I was writing one poem, and the text is all about my ability to control the world. So I'm saying like, my blood is honey… and through my perception I am able to call things even grander than they may be if I wasn't using this language.	I feel like poetry is my chosen medium mostly because like I said earlier, I don't tend to go to a lot of other people with my problems and I'm mostly voiced throughout poetry. And um, I feel like it is the way that I become more honest with myself.
Oasis Black female	I find that being able to do poetry helps me work through a lot of emotions and stress that I may be feeling from my school life.	I think it's challenged me in the classroom. I keep thinking I being taught this? What is the purpose? I think about how that information can be more engaged, and I wonder if the curriculum is even intended for me.	Now, a lot of my work with poetry is combined with my school life, whether it's doing performances at school, participating in the black history show via poetry, or just doing any kind of school-related event where I'm representing my school's poetry team.

Organically, many other literacies including political and environmental were indicated in the interviews, and oftentimes the multiple literacies were interlinked. Meaning one literacy seemed to lead to another, or several literacies were indicated in the same statement. Yet, for an in-depth discussion, as well as consideration of these literacies to coming of age writing – bildungsroman, the scope of this study and length of the chapter was limited to just two literacies – cultural and emotional. The next section discusses cultural and emotional indicators of literacy using the interpretive lens of MLT. As a pedagogic tool, bildungsroman is highlighted because the literary genre is similar in outcome to the benefits of growth and self-development that CCPD poets derived from writing about their life experiences. Lastly, visual literacy and performance arts-based education are discussed.

Cultural Literacy

In this study, I opted to look at cultural and emotional literacies in detail because I wanted to identify and consider any relationship between multicultural people (cultural literacy), marginalized people (emotional literacy), and MLT. Ignoring racial creolization of people's personhood as well as their knowledge in literacy in traditional schooling has initiated a crisis of cultural transmission, which continues to oppress already vulnerable populations. Emily said it was very eye opening for her family to learn a little bit more about Emily through poetry:

> It has helped me connect with my parents as well because my dad is also a huge fan of poetry. And so that helped us kind of come back together and rebuild our relationship. Getting into poetry actually helped me come to terms with my identity as an Asian American, a girl who is the daughter of two immigrants.

In addition, the cognition of one's surroundings can vary based on the privilege one has in that space (Allen, 1999). The emergence of transnational spaces in North America and elsewhere has created cultural hybridity (Anzaldúa, 1987; Bhabha, 2012). Emily explained:

> Bloodline about coming to terms with my heritage: Whenever me and my mother talk, especially like whenever we get heated, I'm sometimes, like we'll say things that the other person doesn't necessarily understand. And so it makes it hard to convey our feelings, but if we were writing things out, if I had time to sit and write things out, in Vietnamese, maybe it'd be easier for my mother to understand my feelings because when I'm talking to her, just saying things right off the top of my head, I don't necessarily have all the words I need at the time.

Michelle, a White female, discussed her new found fascination with other cultures and how what she has learned about an African tribe has helped her in conceiving of new ways to write and use language:

> I was reading some texts about foreign languages, and I read about a tribal language in which directions are always cardinal. So, instead of right and left hands, it is east and west. When you shift where you're facing, it then becomes a different direction. So, they are constantly perceiving the world as a moving compass. It is also very stationary because the directions never change where their bodies are. The things around them change. That's really amazing, and I was thinking that we too can access a type of language or a specific way of directing our language to pursue the world around us.

When imagination and creativity are granted alongside the technique of reading and writing poetry, things related to personal lived histories and time-space related contexts, emotions, culture, and challenging life experiences can collide, but they also help the learners grow and learn in ways that compartmentalizing learning cannot. "I'm a very emotional person, so I felt like it was a good outlet for me to sort of control those emotions and find a way to express them without any widths. Destructive to myself or other people," explained Emily. In these ways, permitting the poet's entanglements with aspects of life such as sociocultural, familial, political, sexual, and other matters can influence learners to dig deeper than standardized methods of reading and writing may afford.

Emotional Literacy

Writing poetry versus performance of their origins poetry may have added additional aspects of learning and literacy to the learners' expressed forms or knowledge and personal development. Yet, through exploration of their feelings about family, love, race, and gender, the learners all said they were able to transcend prior beliefs about themselves as well as their most challenging life experiences such as coming to terms with sexuality and race. For instance, through poetry slam pedagogy, Oasis found her voice about an otherwise shunned topic, sexual harassment:

> When it comes to writing very vulnerable pieces, I tend to pull from my own life experiences because I'm not there to tell anybody else's story. I find a lot of breathing room and closure in being able to be that vulnerable. I wanted to comfort people who have gone through a very frightening moment in life, so they know there are other people who have gone through and that can help them heal.

Edward said he found emotional acceptance and awareness about his sexuality as a queer man through writing poetry:

> I, as a queer person, met somebody who is saying it was very easy for them to be queer, and that it (queerness) should be a celebration, but I became very angry when hearing that because I had to work so hard to reach that point. If this is the way it should be for people and why am I holding so much resentment? I was extremely angry when I found out and I don't know, I don't think queerness should be something that needs to be worked towards, but to me it felt like I had to, and in a way I feel like I earned my right to feel good about myself, somehow, through poetry.

I recollected being an audience member at a poetry slam in which Edward presented a poem about being queer: "It was beautiful to witness your performance about claiming your sexuality at the Space City Poetry Slam, but I also felt sad because when I was in high school, my friends and I were not afforded such an opportunity to reconcile sexuality, our identities." What I did not tell Edward is how learning about his development of self-awareness made me wonder if one of my high school friends, who we lovingly called Puffy Shawn, because of his fluffy, curly blond hair, would have benefited from writing poetry, too. I suspect if Puffy Shawn would have been able to develop enough emotional literacy and self-love, to accept and talk about his sexuality, which he hid from his family, he may not have taken his own life at the age of 15.

Bildungsroman

Poetry and performativity seems to have supported emancipatory self-expression for the performers, who were at the brink of making career and life decisions for themselves. These memories capture the moments or periods in one's personal history (or bildungsroman), when the relation of self and surrounding – subject and world – is ultimately transforming (Boes, 2012). Emily elaborated:

> One of the most beautiful things about the human race is that we always find ways to communicate with each other. I want to become a writer because you can put emotions and feelings into words and other people will be able to understand what you're feeling in a moment by reading what you've written about it.

Overall, the poets often referred to their struggles and how restoring them or replacing them in a different space and time in front of an audience impacted their perceptions of those challenging life experiences related to identity, sexuality, or race. Michelle explained how creative writing supports her emotionally:

> Language kind of helps put it out there in a way that is not as it doesn't make you feel as vulnerable even if you're writing about something that's sensitive to you. Adding a little bit of creativity to it and making it into something that tells a story and instead it's like, it's like that in itself, like you're telling a story instead of putting yourself out there.

Lynn echoed this sentiment:

> There is always a space where you feel like a teacher because you have to guide your audience through your world. Um, and it, I think it is very empowering in that sense to say that, that I know more than anybody else on this topic or whatever it is.

Morris (1997) explains that in order to create meaning out of language, we process the historical connotations and genre conventions embodied therein. Thus, the poets' feelings and recollections will vary across space and time. For example, Edward described what his grandmother encountered when she was a librarian, and how she impacted him:

> She was working in a community that sought to ban literature such as Harry Potter because they had magic, which that community considered as being against their religion. She really fought against this and risked losing her job. I see how much she influenced me, just in terms of sign language, literature, and freedom of expression. So, I'm really interested in language right now in terms of its inability to shape the way we perceive the world.

Within their writing practices, the poets seemed to have developed the language, creativity, self-awareness, and overall intellectual capacity to construct affirming ways of orienting themselves in their respective environments and lives. Edward elaborated:

> Capturing the self as flawed can be something very difficult to do. It's very easy as a writer to write yourself or your eye as this amazing human being who is doing all these wonderful things, but then to interrogate the ways in which I am flawed or my speakers are flawed can be really difficult. Or even, what am I trying to say? Like very complex emotions that come from different positions.

Evidently, the learners had devised literary ways and cultivated the necessary strength to distribute their history, knowledge, and feelings through their writing indicating that a narrative space (Clandinin & Connelly, 2000; Jackson, 1995) was created when writing. These multiple ways of affirming, knowing, living, and reliving can expand literacies and build upon literacy projects that are embedded in different spatial memories of the learners. Michelle illustrated how relying information through poetry can shift awareness when it also is performed:

> Performing time either was slower or faster than you are, so time is not under control for me in a sense. The connecting with an audience is odd for me. It sounds like that comes naturally, but I like when you're up on a stage performing, the impact is different than individual impact. This is a sort of responsibility because you have to convey something to everyone in the audience and to do that. The writing world isn't all about what your words are like, a lot more of it has to do with planning and sometimes hosting events and getting along with people.

Like narrative space, performative, or creative spaces may feel like symbolic or imaginary realms to the performance artist, or poetry slam artist, yet they provide concrete guidelines for how thought can become action. Spence explains that narrative truths permit lived experiences to fortify one's future by having a "story to live by" (Spence, 1984, as cited in Craig, 2020). Michelle, who believes time, history, and poetry have impacted her in both concrete literacies such as reading and writing, and in other imagined ways through relationship-building, elaborated:

> I've always loved Emily Dickinson, I just, I tend to like historical writers because especially ones that leave a little mystery to them. I was such a superstitious kid and I don't know why but I believe in all kinds of magical things, so whenever I read Emily Dickinson, I would always imagine her with me because and no matter how you read it, you are always playing a trick on you, like a fairy would.

Be it through mystical, familial, or cultural or other forms of inspiration, the participants indicated that writing poetry and developing multiple forms of literacy has helped them build relational experiences that surpass time and space. Hooks (1994) argues for educators to "celebrate teaching that enables transgressions - a movement against and beyond boundaries. It is that movement that makes education a practice of freedom" (p. 12). Likewise, rather than placing hybrid, multicultural, or alternative learners at constant conflict because their ways of meaning run counter to traditional schooling, curricula, structures, and/or dominant societal stories, education in the 21st century must find ways of supporting them. Based one on the work of CCPD and what was expressed by the poets, this may not be as complicated as traditional schooling would have us believe. Oasis articulated the sentiment:

> Poetry is like that you're telling a story instead of putting yourself out there. Now, I tend to think critically about the curriculum in school. Is the structure of this classroom conducive? Adding a little bit of creativity to it and making it into something that tells a story has made me want to learn more about English and go to college.

Clearly, pedagogic and linguistic innovation is a necessity if we are to have variable ways to look out for marginalized learners. When given a chance to explain their understanding of the world around them, the poets prefer their own analysis over that of a formal curriculum. Furthermore, in analyzing the poets' interviews and having heard their poetry, it is clear that their experiences with traditional schooling, which separated their culture, lived experiences, as well as their emotions, from learning, meant these learners had to rely on other people for interpretation of meaning in their lives. Yet, this enforcement of normativity and normative learning and preordained knowledge segregated learners from their internalized knowledge, personhood, and their own lived emotions.

This ostracization from the self further marginalized already oppressed learners who identified as being queer, sexually minoritized, sexually harassed, and oftentimes culturally marginalized. The learners in this study all said they were unable to express their multiplicities before having come to CCPD and learning to read, write, and express themselves vis-a-vis poetry and poetry slamming. Upon completion of this analysis about multiple literacies, it is clear that literacy can emerge as dependent upon one's personal lived history, as well as the space and time continuum, but it is also vital to afford learners, especially marginalized learners, the credibility to determine what is put into text.

RECOMMENDATIONS

Visual Literacy and Arts-based Education

An important finding was that multiple literacies accessed through arts-based education may advance the skills of monocultural and monolingual learners. Given the results of this study show overwhelmingly positive support for learners in conflicted spaces derived from creative writing and performance arts in education, which aligns with the notion of arts being able to support traumatized learners (Appleton, 2001), more research studies are needed to explore the benefits of the arts in education, as well as the benefits of arts in education for marginalized learners. In performing their poems and honoring their personal multiplicities, the learners also affirmed their ways of knowing, thinking, and existing in the world. All of participants said they deliberately faced some of their most difficult life challenges, through the artistic process of writing, reflecting, and performing. This study indicates that multiple literacies may be more evident through nontraditional, arts-based pedagogies. Overall, the arts-based performative outcomes of the CCPD participants' original poetry seem to have encouraged multiple literacies, which was affirming to the poets, which self-identified as being from marginalized groups.

Culturally Relevant Text

Previous notions of language, writing, and imagination need to be renegotiated because people should not be confined to culturally dominant discourses that limits the validity of their lived cultural, emotional, political, environmental and other literacies, or experiences. These grand narratives may seem phony to marginalized people who are at odds with conformity. Cesáre rightly coins hegemonic narratives as "omniscient and naïve conquers" (as cited in Sartre & MacCombie, 1964, p. 15). Clearly, marginalized people are not comfortable with the large scale stories or "mega-narratives" because they are unable to map their relational positions within those hegemonic confines.

Overall, the poets said they put their tensions into their poetry in order to overcome them, whether the poems culminated in a performance or not. This is similar to the process of bildungsroman in which the writer conquers the gap between this normative expectation and tension, through joy of validating their knowledge in personal narrative-style writing or poetry (Kim & Zimmerman, 2017). Furthermore, the sharing of a final product, or poem, which I have entangled with multiple literacies, could easily be transferred into assessments by educators, which may further benefit anxiety-ridden test takers and nontraditional learners – of all backgrounds.

Bildungsroman and Identity

The fact that humankind has globalized, and sociocultural issues have multiplied in the 21st century, yet educational praxis lacks recent insights into how culture (Hammond, 2017) and emotions (Lin, Liew, & Perez, 2019) influences learning and cognition, is nothing short of problematic. In fact, bildungsroman seems to offer multiple benefits of culture, literacy, and self-development, which Boes (2012) explains:

> ...each person and each culture strive to find its own individual response to a universal formative drive. Viewed through this new interpretive lens, the ultimate question confronted by every Bildungsroman is not how the protagonist might actualize some hidden ideal, but rather how a multiplicity of individual developments might be combined into a meaningful whole – how a number of diverse stories might yield to the imperative of a singular "History" writ large.

The relationship of bildungsroman, poetry, and multiple literacies is drawn in efforts to impart the benefits of all of these forms of learning since this study with CCPD poets revealed the learner's experienced personal identity development, confidence, and deepened their literacies. Whether they were reading, writing, or performing poetry, the poets reported experiencing personal development alongside literacy.

> Personally I find a weird kind of comfort on stage. I am a person who's grown up, very anxious, and scared to participate in most things. It's different for me to project into a room rather than one on one with because I feel like the more kind of intimate space is, the more afraid I am to express those emotions. When it comes to poetry performances, you still have that intimacy, but it's kind of dispersed throughout the crowd.

Many times, poets said they put their tensions into their poetry in order to overcome them, whether the poems culminated in a performance or not. Likewise, in bildungsroman, the writer conquers the gap between this normative expectation and tension, through the joy of validating their knowledge a personal narrative-style (Boes, 2012). Given that the participants in this study all self-identified as being from marginalized groups who benefited from being able to write using personal reflection, it would appear that bildungsroman could be a useful pedagogic response to the struggles that minorities may face.

Further Study

Unless we address the needs of marginalized learners and update pedagogy to meet the globalization of today, transcultural incommunicability will be worsened when the educational foci are segmented and looks at literacy but misses the multiplicities involved in literacy, and we must respond as educators and policy makers. Further study into the benefits of performance art (i.e., poetry slam performances) is needed. To elaborate, being able to place oneself in relationship to social issues that may leave one feeling marginalized, and facing issues of equity all emerged in this study through a reflective form of creative writing, namely poetry, which culminated in a performance seems to have supported all of the participants in this study. For instance, I wonder would MLT-related educational experiences that may be especially well suited for people of color because they can access their cultural knowledge, be transferable to other marginalized learners? Inquiries such as; how might MLT be a more culturally relevant way to look at educational learning outcomes for people of color, may provide additional educational methods and identify more benefits for marginalized learners, among others. This study also indicated that there may be considerably beneficial educational aspects of MLT, art-based education, and bildungsroman that warrant further research and can benefit multiculturalism and interethnic alliances. For example, multiple literacies may have been attained by audience members, who were introduced to social, political, and cultural ways of knowing through the lived experiences of the poetry slam artists.

CONCLUDING REMARKS

Unfortunately, meanings of words are enforced by dominant ideologies and controlled by educational institutions that are often unwilling to incorporate alternatives like arts-based pedagogies and multiple literacies, as demonstrated in this study. The findings of this study, as well as the theories and participants' statements, which align with my own research observations as an immigrant, multilingual, and multicultural person, and educator of over 15 years, indicate that we can support a healthier society. Foremost, institutionally, education can open up moments or periods in one's personal history or lived experiences through diverse, multicultural, and all other personal narratives, as demonstrated in poetry, and bildungsroman. Through this "time travel," the learner may alter and even reformulate their understanding of situations that once vexed them, and as such learners can fly above and beyond oppression.

Arts stimulus funds under the Obama administration and the creation of the National Arts Policy Committee was stamped out by the Trump administration in 2016 that dismantled these arts objectives (Americans for the Arts). CCPD's funding was also cut by their benefactors and caused them to close their doors. Regardless, since studies many have found that alternative, arts-based pedagogies, which tend to include or permit the expression of culture and personal experiences, may improve a student's relationship to schooling (Bowen & Kisida, 2019), arts-based education, art education, and creative writing need to be accessed more by traditional schooling and educators alike. These reasons and more are why instead of repeating the pedagogies that seem to perpetuate racial wars, and suppress diversity and impose monocultural practices on the youth of the United States – we must activate creativity and respect personhood.

REFERENCES

Allen, R. L. (1999). The socio-spatial making and marking of 'us:' Toward a critical postmodern spatial theory of difference and community. *Social Identities*, 5(3), 249–277.

Anzaldúa, G. (1987). *Borderlands la frontera*. San Francisco, CA: Aunt Lute Books.

Appleton, V. (2001). Avenues of hope: Art therapy and the resolution of trauma. *Art Therapy: Journal of the American Art Therapy Association*, 18(1), 6–13.

Asadi, L. (2020). Casting the researcher as actor. In L. Asadi & C. Craig (Eds.), *Truth and knowledge in curriculum making* (pp. 105–134). Charlotte, NC: Information Age Publishing.

Autry, L. L., & Walker, M. E. (2011). Artistic representation: Promoting student creativity and self-reflection. *Journal of Creativity in Mental Health*, 6(1), 42–55.

Bagley, C. C., & Castro-Salazar, R. (2012). Critical arts-based research in education: Performing undocumented historias. *British Educational Research Journal*, 38(2), 239–260. doi:10.1080/01411926.2010.538667

Barone, T., & Eisner, E. W. (2012). *Arts-based research*. Thousand Oaks, CA: Sage.

Bhabha, H. K. (2012). *The location of culture*. London: Routledge.

Bhattacharya, K. (2009). Negotiating shuttling between transnational experiences a de/colonizing approach to performance ethnography. *Qualitative Inquiry*, 15(6), 1061–1083.

Blanton, C. K. (2007). *The strange career of bilingual education in Texas, 1836–1981* (Vol. 2). College Station, TX: Texas A&M University Press.

Boes, T. (2012). *Formative fictions: Nationalism, cosmopolitanism, and the bildungsroman*. Ithaca, NY: Cornell University Press.

Bogue, R. (2009). Preface. In D. Masny & D. R. Cole (Eds.), *Multiple literacies theory: A Deleuzian perspective* (pp. vii–viii). Rotterdam: Sense Publishers.

Bowen, D. H., & Kisida, B. (2019). Investigating causal effects of arts education experiences: Experimental evidence from Houston's arts access initiative. *Research Brief for the Houston Independent School District*, 7(4).

Cabrera, L., Milem, J., Jaquette, O., & Marx, R. W. (2014). Missing the (student achievement) forest for all the (political) trees: Empiricism and the Mexican American studies controversy in Tucson. *American Educational Research Journal*, 51, 1084–1118.

Cammarota, J., & Fine, M. (2008). Youth participatory action research. *Revolutionizing education: youth participatory action research in motion*, 1–12.

Campano, G., & Ghiso, M. P. (2011). Immigrant students as cosmopolitan intellectuals. In S. Wolf, K. Coates, P. Enciso, & C. Jenkins (Eds.), *Handbook of research on children's and young adult literature* (pp. 164–176). New York, NY: Routledge.

Cassel, C. A., & Lo, C. C. (1997). Theories of political literacy. *Political Behavior*, 19(4), 317–335.

Césaire, A. (2001). *Discourse on colonialism*. New York, NY: NYU Press.

Clandinin, D. J., Caine, V., & Lessard, S. (2018). *The relational ethics of narrative inquiry*. New York, NY: Routledge.

Clandinin, D. J., & Connelly, F. M. (1999). Storying and restorying ourselves: Narrative and reflection. In A. Y. Chen & J. Van Maanen (Eds.), *The reflective spin: Case studies of teachers in higher education transforming action* (pp. 15–23). Singapore: World Scientific.

Clandinin, D. J., & Connelly, F. M. (2000). *Narrative inquiry: Experience and story in qualitative research*. San Francisco, CA: Jossey-Bass.

Clinton, G., & Hokanson, B. (2012). Creativity in the training and practice of instructional designers: The design/creativity loops model. *Educational Technology Research and Development, 60*(1), 111–130.

Connelly, F. M., & Clandinin, D. J. (1990). Stories of experience and narrative inquiry. *Educational Researcher, 19*(5), 2–14.

Connelly, F. M., & Clandinin, D. J. (1994). Telling teaching stories. *Teacher Education Quarterly, 21*, 145–158.

Cottom, T. M. (2018). *Thick: And other essays*. The New Press.

Craig, C. J. (2000). Stories of schools/teacher stories: A two-part invention on the walls theme. *Curriculum Inquiry, 30*(1), 11–41.

Craig, C. J. (2020). Generous scholarship: A counternarrative for the region and the academy. In C. J. Craig, L. Turchi, & D. M. McDonald (Eds.), *Cross-disciplinary, cross-institutional collaboration in teacher education* (pp. 351–365). Cham: Palgrave Macmillan.

Enriquez, G., Johnson, E., Kontovourki, S., & Mallozzi, C. A. (2015). *Literacies, learning, and the body: Putting theory and research into pedagogical practice*. London: Routledge.

García, O. G., McDonald, S., & Monk, N. (2016). Embedding cultural literacy in higher education: A new approach. *Intercultural Education, 27*(6), 546–559. doi:10.1080/14675986.2016.1241551

Greene, M. (1995). *Releasing the imagination: Essays on education, the arts, and social change*. San Francisco, CA: Jossey-Bass.

Hammond, Z. (2017). *Culturally responsive teaching & the brain*. Thousand Oaks, CA: Corwin, Sage.

Hargrove, R. (2012). Fostering creativity in the design studio: A framework towards effective pedagogical practices. *Art, Design & Communication in Higher Education, 10*(1), 7–31.

Hooks, B. (1994). *Teaching to transgress education as the practice of freedom*. New York, NY: Routledge.

Huber, L. P. (2012). Testimonio as LatCrit methodology in education. In S. Delamont (Ed.), *Handbook of qualitative research in education*. Cheltenham: Edward Elgar Publishing.

Jackson, P. W. (1995). On the place of narrative in teaching. In H. McEwan & K. Egan (Eds.), *Narrative in teaching, learning, and research*. New York, NY: Teacher's College Press.

Kim, J., & Zimmerman, A. (2017). Bildung, bildungsroman, and the cultivation of teacher dispositions. *The Teacher Educator, 52*(3), 235–249. doi:10.1080/08878730.2017.1315624

Klineberg, S. L. (2021). *Prophetic City: Houston on the Cusp of a Changing America*. Simon and Schuster.

Kramarski, B., & Mizrachi, N. (2006). Online discussion and self-regulated learning: Effects of instructional methods on mathematical literacy. *The Journal of Educational Research, 99*(4), 218–231.

Kramsch, C. (1995). The cultural component of language teaching. *Language Culture and Curriculum, 8*(2), 83–92.

Kramsch, C., & Widdowson, H. G. (1998). *Language and culture*. Oxford: Oxford University Press.

Ladson-Billings, G. (1995). Toward a theory of culturally relevant pedagogy. *American Educational Research Journal, 32*(3), 465–491.

Lather, P. (2018). Within and beyond neoliberalism: Doing qualitative research in the afterward. In M. Spooner & J. McNinch (Eds.), *Dissident knowledge in higher education* (pp. 102–120). Regina, SK: University of Regina Press.

Lee, N. P. (2013). Engaging the pink elephant in the room: Investigating race and racism through art education. *Studies in Art Education, 54*(2), 141–157.

Leu, D. J. (2001). Internet project: Preparing students for new literacies in a global village. *The Reading Teacher, 54*, 568–572.

Lin, B., Liew, J., & Perez, M. (2019). Measurement of self-regulation in early childhood: Relations between laboratory and performance-based measures of effortful control and executive functioning. *Early Childhood Research Quarterly, 47*, 1–8.

Masny, D. (2012, February). Multiple literacies theory: Discourse, sensation, resonance and becoming. *Discourse: Studies in the Cultural Politics of Education, 33*(1), 113–128.

Masny, D., & Cole, D. R. (2007). Applying multiple literacies in Australian and Canadian contexts. In A. Simpson (Ed.), *Future directions in literacy: International conversations conference proceedings* (pp. 190–211). Sydney, NSW: Sydney University Press. Retrieved from http://ses.library.usyd.edu.au/bitstream/2123/2336/1/FutureDirections_Ch11.pdf

Ministry of Education. (2003). *Effective literacy practice in years 1–4*. Wellington: Learning Media.

Morris, P. (1997). The Bakhtin Reader. Bloomsbury Publishing PLC.

National Council of Teachers of English. (2013). *The NCTE definition of 21st century literacies*. Urbana, IL: National Council of Teachers of English.

National Research Council. (1996). *National science education standards: Observe, interact, change, learn*. Washington, DC: National Academy Press.

Neimeyer, R. A., & Sands, D. C. (2011). Meaning reconstruction in bereavement: From principles to practice. In R. A. Neimeyer, H. Winokuer, D. Harris, & G. Thornton (Eds.), *Grief and bereavement in contemporary society: Bridging research and practice*. New York, NY: Routledge.

New London Group. (1996). A pedagogy of multiliteracies: Designing social futures. *Harvard Educational Review, 66*(1), 60–92.

Olson, M. R., & Craig, C. J. (2009). "Small" stories and meganarratives: Accountability in balance. *Teachers College Record, 111*(2), 547–572.

Popova, M. (2020, October 18). Audre Lorde on poetry as an instrument of change and the courage to feel as an antidote to fear, a portal to power and possibility, and a fulcrum of action. Retrieved from https://www.brainpickings.org/2020/10/18/poetry-is-not-a-luxury-audre-lorde/. Accessed on February 18, 2021.

Pow, J., & Fu, J. (2012). Developing digital literacy through collaborative inquiry learning in the web 2.0 environment: An exploration of implementing strategy. *Journal of Information Technology, 11*(1), 287–299.

Richardson, L. (1999). Feathers in our cap. *Journal of Contemporary Ethnography, 28*(6), 660–668.

Riley, T., & Hawe, P. (2005). Researching practice: The methodological case for narrative inquiry. *Health Education Research, 20*(2), 226–236.

Saldaña, J. (2016). *Ethnotheatre: Research from page to stage*. Abingdon: Routledge.

Sartre, J., & MacCombie, J. (1964). Black Orpheus. *The Massachusetts Review, 6*(1), 13–52.

Silverman, K. N., & Piedmont, J. (2016). The big picture: A visual for today. *Knowledge Quest, 44*(5), 32.

Solórzano, D. G., Pérez-Huber, L., & Huber-Verjan, L. (2020). Theorizing racial microaffirmations as a response to racial microaggressions: Counterstories across three generations of critical race scholars. *Seattle Journal for Social Justice, 18*(2), 10.

Suárez, M. I., Asadi, L., Scaramuzzo, P., & Slattery, P. (2020). Using photovoice as arts-based instruction for Grieving: LGBTIQ+ students and the pulse nightclub shooting. *International Journal of Qualitative Studies*.

Swales, M. (2015). *The German bildungsroman from Wieland to Hesse*. Princeton, NJ: Princeton University Press.

Valenzuela, A. (2019). The struggle to decolonize official knowledge in Texas' state curriculum: Side-stepping the colonial matrix of power. *Equity & Excellence in Education, 52*(2–3), 197–215.

Van der Kolk, B. A., & McFarlane, A. C. (Eds.). (1996). *Traumatic stress: The effects of overwhelming experience on mind, body, and society*. New York, NY: Guilford Press.

"AFTER A TRIP, THE SUITCASE STAYS FULL TILL I NEED SOMETHING": UNPACKING NARRATIVE TRUTHS FROM THE FIELD

Chestin T. Auzenne-Curl

ABSTRACT

In this chapter, I trace instances of meaning-making through fragments of two interviews. Using restorying and the construction of parallel stories to interpret resonances across the participants' stories and my own stories of experience, I draw strong personal connections with elements of each semi-structured interview. In a revisitation of the narrative threads of identity, community, and change, the image of Black women as literacy educators who co-construct meaning in and out of the classroom is rendered.

Keywords: Black literacy educators; storied experience; parallel stories; teaching in pandemic; instructional coaching; literacy education

NARRATIVE BEGINNINGS

In all aspects of my life, I plan. Professionally, I spend weeks constructing a syllabus complete with rubrics and resources before it leaves my hand. Writing is not different. Some 90 percent of my thoughts are coded and parceled before they leave my headspace. They trickle out as plot points on paper first, and then to the keyboard in a stream of consciousness challenge to connect the dots. As my daughters say, there are many things that "live in my head rent-free." The unpredictability of life, especially the personal aspects, makes these behaviors both gift and curse, yet there are times that my thinking is a point of crippling exhaustion. It leaves me with a full suitcase at all times.

Research Is Travel

For five years, I worked as an education consultant and traveled alone from state to state. I learned to pack quickly, efficiently, and methodically. I cannot remember a time that I arrived somewhere ill-prepared, though many unpredictable things happened on each trip. My preparation included watching the weather for days ahead of my journey, using GPS maps to plot the timing of my departure, refilling medications, and making sure that I had cash, and a host of other checklist items that became second nature to me after a few trips. I felt that I would be less stressed when met with unforeseen circumstances such as plane delays, and blizzards, if the basics were accessible in a single, meticulously organized suitcase that never left my side.

It was post-trip behavior that I never mastered. My suitcase often remained full until I needed something. I came home, tossed the worn laundry in the bag for laundering, and zipped the suitcase back up.

There were days when I would think, *where is my yellow cardigan*, or *I know I just bought a new pair of trouser socks*, and out of necessity, I would go to the suitcase and retrieve only what I needed; nothing more. I did not have to search for the item in question. Everything was tucked away neatly and with the care I had originally placed it. This is the same intentionality and retrieval method under which I have found myself functioning as a researcher. Interviews are quite a trip, and planning questions that are semi-structured and open enough to allow participants to share a narrative that I follow rather than lead requires preparation and flexibility that yield a mental suitcase of compartmentalized anticipation.

METHODOLOGICAL UNDERPINNINGS

I began my career in education as a high school English teacher. I taught 11th grade American Literature most consistently, and like many literature teachers, I had a favorite unit. It was the didactic literature unit. The impact of the literature I compiled influenced my pursuit of coursework grounded in qualitative research methods when I pursued my doctoral degree. That unit sparked joy for me because the students seemed engaged in the brief and educative stories. I often share versions of a fable that stays with me, though the origin has escaped me. The irony is that the gap in my memory makes the moral ring loud and true. It is centered on an owl and a fox running for office in the forest:

> ...[T]he animals tirelessly prepared to address their voting constituency, and when the day came to speak, the fox was certain that he would out smart the owl by demonstrating his trustworthiness and wisdom.
>
> He approached the audience with an impressive collection of data in charts and recounted statistics that supported his stances on issues and why he would be the best candidate for the job. However, before he was done with the presentation, he looked up to discover that the audience had fallen asleep. Even the owl did not know what to do next. They looked at each other and at the sleeping audience, but suddenly, AESOP appeared. He asked, "May I?" indicating the podium, and they nodded yes. Then he stepped up, cleared his throat, and began,

"Once upon a time there was a fox, and an owl running for office." Immediately the audience began to sit up, straight-backed and alert.

While they stretched and focused, the owl leaned in and asked, "How did you do this?" to which Aesop responded, "It's easy. Information touches the mind, but story sinks into the heart."

Narrative Inquiry

In their 1990 article, Michael Connelly and Jean Clandinin presented a view of inquiry as a storied experience that posited researchers as "storytelling organisms who individually and socially lead storied lives" (p. 2). Through story, meaning is rendered and explored. Engaging in experiential construction of knowledge makes narrative inquiry a humanistic approach to research that draws the inquirer in to understanding phenomena, solving problems, and asserting meaning at the intersection of story plotlines.

Narrative Tools

In a 2015 interview with my mentor and former doctoral adviser, Cheryl Craig, she provided a description of tools for meaning-making, noting that however natural the occurrence of narrative may be, when narrative is methodology, some specific terms are conceptualized as tools for the journey of interpretation. I used three of them in the development of this chapter:

- Broadening, which is indicative of painting the landscape; reaching outward from the specifics of the narrative,
- Burrowing, by which the inquirer digs deeply into the experience in order to figure out where the journey may lead, and
- Storying and restorying, as an active and repeated revisitation of narratives to retelling them purpose.

Context

As stated above, my doctoral adviser was Cheryl Craig. I remain a student of her work. As a student of Jean Clandinin and a postdoctoral scholar working with Michael Connelly, Cheryl's scholarly roots run deeply into the soil of inquiry, and my passion for storytelling and collecting brought me to her, eager to expand my knowledge of applying the methodology to field work. As I prepared for graduation and pondered my next professional endeavor, Cheryl was forming a partnership with Writers in the Schools Houston (WITS). While the organization provided many community and school-based programs for literacy education, they were seeking a review of one program in particular: WITS Collaborative. Funding for the review included support for a field research lead, and when offered, I quickly accepted.

"This will be a perfect fit for you," Cheryl said. "The organization is looking for a project evaluation lead for their literacy coaching collaborative." Again, my adviser was correct. It seemed a perfect fit. I had served as a literacy coach, as a curriculum coordinator who acted as coach of coaches, and my dissertation was centered on the life cycles and stories to live and leave by (Schaefer, Downey, & Clandinin, 2014) of teacher educators in these field-based (TEF) roles. In addition to the established knowledge base, I wanted to extend my understanding of the experiences of TEF. WITS Collaborative presented a new dimension of role enactment in that it would be my first experience working with TEF who were working with teachers through interorganizational partnerships.

The three years we spent following the WITS Collaborative sparked the production of several papers, presentations, and this volume – all of which are rooted in the stories of experience of TEF, researchers, classroom teachers, and administrators who hope to support student engagement and positive learning experience by building strong communities of practice among the adults who guide them. In this chapter, I broaden from, and burrow into, key points from the two final interviews of our field work. Each served as a disruption from the primary interview topic and led me to my mental suitcase, to retrieve parallel stories of experience from which I rendered meaning alongside the participant transcripts here.

REVISITING THE JOB AND THE WORK

> These places of possibility within ourselves are dark because they are ancient and hidden; they have survived and grown strong through darkness. Within these deep places, each one of us holds an incredible reserve of creativity and power, of unexamined and unrecorded emotion and feeling. (Lorde, 1985/2015, p. 1)

Through stories from the field, I was able to draw upon memories from my time in the K-12 classroom and as a literacy coach. I made connections across these stories of experiences and one strong theme among the interviews of the WITS writers was the development of self as a writer and teacher. Many of the writers voiced a desire to help teachers see themselves as writers, but somehow overlooked the aspect of themselves as not only writers but also teachers. As the quote above references, both teachers and writers seemed to hold a view of themselves in the dark, too often, but for a few, like Jasminne Mendez, the connection was strong, and it was evident in her approach to the work and in her sharing of the creativity and power the duality of this presence could yield.

The Interview in Context

I first met Jasminne[1] in a monthly meeting for the WITS Collaborative. I quickly recognized her to be one of few women of color in the group. As it was an early year meeting, post-hurricane Harvey, many of the field sites were still inactive. Many of the partnering districts had delayed the start of classes due to the extensive damage from the floods that came along with the storm. While many schools and homes had been destroyed, the campus on which Jasminne served was active, and she was happy to share a strategy that she incorporated as a model. She described using lotería cards (traditional Mexican game, similar to bingo) as creative prompts for writing and explained that the idea was modified from an activity she had previously used in theater. As she continued to explain her method for planning and executing the lesson, I knew that she held a strong image of herself as curriculum maker (Craig, Ross, Conle, & Richardson, 2008), and that culture and engagement in the arts were underlying elements of her craft.

The research team observed her work in the field on two different campuses and noted high engagement in the facilitation of coaching cycles by the teachers with whom she partnered. In addition, Jasminne and I began to follow one another on social media. After the research team's project with WITS came to a close, we learned that Jasminne had moved on from the collaborative following the birth of her child. She had become more focused on her own writing, though she still contributed to the WITS organization in other projects. In the Spring of 2020, following a mass shutdown of public schools due to social distancing safety measures, WITS created virtual programs and facilitated e-lecture and a YouTube streamed literacy series. Jasminne participated in these events and we wanted to interview her about her journey as a literacy educator without a classroom. In this final interview with Jasminne, facilitated by research assistant Lobat Asadi and me, I found myself reflecting deeply on the impact of her identity and personal story on how she approached the work of educating young people.

I related to much of what she shared and was called into reflection regarding her preparation for entering the field, her path to seeing herself as a writer, and her views on storying as an act of liberation and connection. Below, you will find elements of her story followed by a restorying of experiences which I found a strong connection and echoed truths.

On Identity

Lobat:	Tell us about yourself and anything that you feel is important for us to understand about you (race, ethnicity, gender/preferred pronouns, etc.)?
Jasminne:	I am the daughter of Dominican immigrants. I was born and raised here in the United States. I'm a military brat, so I grew up everywhere...but I mostly have lived in the South, which is a new identity for me. Being Southern is something that I had not reflected on until recently, but it's a different layer to my Dominicaness, and there are many I feel connected to Texas – to Houston. I do identify as Afro-Latina, or Afro-Dominican. I have a complex relationship with the Term Latinx or Latina as of late. I switched my bio to Afro-Dominican...I'm a poet. I'm a writer. I'm an educator... I'm she, her, hers – those are my pronouns. (Laughs) That was a lot, huh?
Chestin:	It's good. We want to hear all that you want to share. How did you arrive at WITS?
Jasminne:	I got my undergrad in English Literature and my Master's in Curriculum and Instruction, and I taught with a couple of organizations, but I struggle with a chronic illness and I'm open about it. One of the reasons that I was drawn to WITS is because, as you know, teaching full-time is exhausting. It's a lot to juggle If you want to do a good job. You have to worry about the kids. You worry about assessments and all that comes with a full time teaching position. So I started working with and training teachers on how to integrate technology in the classroom. I was on the front end of the whole blended learning movement, you know – here's how you use iPads, and all of that. The new technological boom that happened from 2010–2015 or so. It was online and I could do that professional development and WITS.

On Being a Writer

Chestin: I have been following your work through the pandemic. You seem to be very busy now. Can you tell me more about that?

Jasminne: The time for my story is now. I do think that for stories by marginalized communities, the time is now and I really want to take advantage of that and be heard.

I feel a little guilty saying that because the world is burning in front of our faces, but like I said before the story of my writing is a love of language and art. I need it to survive. I've always been obsessed with language and storytelling – of how stories are connected and how they are told.

I remember one of the earliest things that I wrote – it would be problematic today, horrible – but it was to write our own version of the *Indian in the Cupboard* and that was it. That was the first time that someone asked me for MY story, and I was so excited. From then on, my dad would bring these huge ledgers home. They had hard green covers and blank pages and I would fill them with stories.

Having an immigrant father, those ledgers came with the stories of things like *some people in my country 'weren't allowed to learn to read'* and how *back home they could not afford books*. We couldn't afford a lot of books, either and so we went to the library often. My father was this huge inspiration for me reading, and through reading, I think I became a better writer....

It was in middle school that was the first time that I was introduced to Black writers in school, though – or any writers of color, actually. They were "the two" you know – they exposed us to Maya Angelou and Langston Hughes and I thought WOW people who look like me. They write. So I continued journaling, again, to survive. It was angsty in my teenage years as I continued to draw on how my household wasn't oppressive, but my parents were more strict and seemed to have more rules than my American friends' parents. But I never thought that I could be a writer. I had no concept of what being published could look like for me. It wasn't until I was an adult that telling the story of my chronic illness became my solace and that I knew my story had to be heard.

I had a great response from turning my journal into a blog. People needed to hear the story of my identity. I was Black woman navigating medical racism, chronic illness, generational trauma. I was writing to answer these questions I had about myself, but the question was not *Why me?* It was *What now? Can I share a story to connect others?* I didn't want others to feel alone in their experience the way that I did. I felt disconnected when I was first diagnosed. It had me reflect on other aspects of who I was. I write stories for survival and I write the stories I want to read.

On Being a Teacher

Lobat: You have touched on this a little, but how do you see yourself as a teacher?

Jasminne: It's still something that I'm very passionate about and I would love to do more. I know how important it is to my students – especially students of color: Black, Hispanic, Indigenous…to see someone who looks like them and sounds like them as a teacher and a writer. They need someone who believes and listens to their story.

I believe that my job as a writing teacher is to just help students believe that their stories matter, and to give them the tools to tell the stories they want to tell…. So much of school teaches them otherwise, especially in early grades. I wanted my students to feel free, curious and creative.

I'd always start all of my WITS classes with the orange folder that says, "I'm a writer on it" When I went to church camp as a kid, every session would start with us all saying "God is good one day at a time. One day at a time, God is good." So I modified that and I would start class with them saying, "I am a writer one word at a time. One word at a time, I'm a

After a Trip, the Suitcase Stays Full 221

(Continued)

> writer" – and the page can seem so daunting sometimes. I have to give myself that pep talk. The kids look and think I have to fill this whole page with words?! There's no way. I would tell them just a couple of words become a sentence and a couple of sentences become a paragraph. A couple of paragraphs become an essay, or a poem, or a play. Providing low-stakes opportunities for kids to take chances is what I would do. Everyone has something to say and in that, everyone is a writer. As a teacher, I just give you the tools to learn haiku, onomatopoeia, similes and the terminology. I facilitated the discussions that hopefully made that language more accessible, you know?

I did know. What Jasminne said there was an indication of using "the job" to do "the work." The job of teaching, when we are fully invested in the work of life. I tried to do the same. In seeing that transcript, and hearing say that, I unpacked more memories of the words of our final project interviewee.

MEANING-MAKING ACROSS NARRATIVES OF EXPERIENCE: REFLECTIONS ON AN INTERVIEW WITH GLORIA LADSON-BILLINGS

> Academia is a job, but the work is so much bigger. And if you're a Black scholar, an Indigenous scholar, a Latinx scholar, an Asian/Pacific Islander scholar, you have work to do for life. Don't get job and work confused. Dr Gloria Ladson-Billings (from Ladson-Billings et al., 2021)

The quote above was recounted from a round table discussion that occurred three weeks after the contributing authors of this book were invited to interview Dr Gloria Ladson-Billings and share our chapter topics with her. I had already been inspired by her previous lecture on the four pandemics through which we are navigating. There is no doubt that the words on this page will live longer than any of us, but the sound of "2020" will be louder – the images that it will evoke, a global pandemic. Everyone was aware of it, but Dr Ladson-Billings illuminated our views on how complex life was becoming. We were only beginning in reflecting on COVID-19. That was the first pandemic. The second was the pandemic of racial injustice which took a global stage in the summer after the murder of George Floyd. It brought international attention to the movement to address America's history of police brutality and violence and the domestic terrorism faced by Black Americans. In addition to these were the increasing climate-related disasters, which had heavily impacted the Houston area, and finally, what Ladson-Billings referred to as the impending economic crisis. In my attempt to remain productive and to subvert the impact of primary and secondary traumatic stress, I had oversimplified the weight of the time. Again I was called to unpack.

Just days before the submission of the volume, I find myself revisiting this chapter and field texts in order to reframe and restory alongside the quote above, because what I hear in Jasminne's and in Dr Ladson-Billings' voices, I hear in my own recounting. The work is so much bigger. The job has become complicated by new constraints in our lives, but the work remains the same – in the classroom or out.

Broad Truths

Truth 1: Marginalized People Have Been Here
Lobat asked Jasminne to elaborate on an insular feeling in a COVID world and Jasminne responded with, "It's a hard line. There is a tension that I have been trying to navigate. I feel like a lot of what the world is experiencing right now, this anxiety, the waiting for a cure...I've been here for twelve years."

As the conversation continued, I listened to her truth about the lack of understanding able-bodied citizens exhibited in a statement that I heard all too frequently, "when things get back to normal." Jasminne's discussion about the impact of her diagnosis spoke to a truth that I had recently discussed with many scholars from marginalized backgrounds: we have arrived at a point in which we are called to rethink normal. Normal has never served us well.

Jasminne continued, "There is no going back to normal. There is going to be a new normal, but there's no going back to before. So many people seem stuck in this space of waiting for lives to go back... I don't know if that is necessarily an option – or it shouldn't be. Why can't we rethink the way that our normal is going to look, to help everybody?" While Jasminne's experience with chronic illness was at the core of this discussion, I was reminded of the insurrection at the nation's capital and the response of many Black Americans to seeing such radicalism and violence in response to the ratification of presidential elections results. As white Americans took to social media to express disappointment through the phrase "This isn't America," the response from many members of the Black community was "This has always been America to us." The response was so strong in the community that major news outlets reported on the trending #BlackTwitter. Following the upon hashtag, thousands of responses from Black Americans presented the same sentiment heard in Jasmine's "I've been here."

Truth 2: Literacy Education Can Be a Pathway to Engaging in an Expression of Social Discourse
What is evident in this situational parallel in the dichotomous situational response of able-bodied versus those with disabilities with COVID-19 and Whites versus non-Whites with domestic terrorism and violence was predicted in Maxine Greene's *Imagining Futures: The Public School and Possibility* 20 years ago. She called upon Mikhail Bakhtin's conceptualization of *heteroglossia* as an act of "becoming more aware of the diversity of horizons in the discourse, and the danger of reducing what is know to a single consciousness, rather than a multiplicity of voices" (p. 269). It seemed that we had indeed arrived at a prime opportunity to act on the amplification of these voices through literacy education. In Greene's consideration, the school's primary

function would be to abandon its historic existence as a ground on which to teach children from marginalized background to assimilate toward ideals that would see them as more "Americanized" and to become a safe space to the language, music, and other cultural cues that allowed them to act as their truest self. In pointing to this, I think of the canon and of the traditional values which it reflects, the voices that drive it.

Unpacking Personal Experience
As a student, I was given a curriculum and it was often accompanied by a required reading list. There was little choice in text or assessment. Much of the lecture-driven pontification, which seemed to me as a vindication of the wonders of white men by white men – consequently delivered by white women, was what pulled me toward teaching American Literature. My classroom did not function the same way. It was not normal. However, I would later find that this was not anomalous in schools with larger numbers of teachers of color. Where I was teaching, I was the only teacher of color in the English Department and one of six in the building though our student population demographics were nearly inverse with non-white students at 68% and rising.

Unpacking Field Observations
There have been two recent movements toward creating a more equitable literacy environment. One, covered heavily in social media through the hashtag "#DisruptTexts" (Auzenne-Curl & Carr, 2021; Stoultzfus, 2019), is centered on a critical reconsideration of the texts and the lens with which students engage with the texts they read in K-12 classrooms. It calls upon literacy educators to approach literature through the core principles of (Ebarvia, German, Parker, & Torres, 2020):

- Self-examination of biases,
- Centering Black, Indigenous, and People of Color's (BIPOC) Voices,
- Applying a critical lens, and
- Work in community.

Through these principles, Tricia Ebarvia, Lorena German, Kimberly Parker, and Julia Torres call upon educators to consider the voices and experiences of students from diverse backgrounds. This call to action does not, as some critics assert, lean into the cancel culture or banning of books. Rather they call upon a more sophisticated negotiation of space in which teachers and students analyze and center counternarratives presented by BIPOC who are often characterized as present, yet silenced – or spoken on behalf of, in traditional canonical texts. In this manner, teachers, as curriculum makers, "respond imaginatively to an educational deficiency" (p. 278) and lean further into acceptance of reality as a complicated and co-constructed experience to be interpreted through claims to truth. In a trip to Suburban East High School, I observed well-meaning teachers acting outside of these principles in a conversation on text selection for an upcoming novel unit:

> I entered the team lead's classroom and the conversation had already begun. The teacher with red hair suggested that "in honor of next month being Black History Month, we should have all of the kids read The Hate You Give. I think we have enough copies." The blonde sitting across from her suggested that, instead, students should read Dear Martin, as it was less violent and tragic. The red head countered. "I just think that THUG is better because using a novel with all Black key characters will be more appropriate for February."
>
> "Why do you think the key characters aren't Black in *Dear Martin*? Did I miss something?" the team lead asked. "Well the best friend is Manny Rivera. That's a Hispanic name, right?" the red head persisted. "Both friends in THUG are Black."
>
> The only other person of color in the room was, like me, a Black person who was often presumed to be "other." He spoke, "Black people can have Hispanic surnames, but even still, I don't remember the character's last name being Rivera. Let's let the kids choose, anyway. If we have enough copies of both and both authors are Black."
>
> I wanted to chime in, but did not. He was correct and looked at me as he spoke. I wanted to let them know that February wasn't the only time you could center Black voices. But my role there was to observe and plan future professional development based on my observations. I knew they needed more voices of color. (Journals, 2018)

I left that day and because I had not read Dear Martin, I googled the list of main characters. The character's name was Emmanuel Rivers and he was Black. I reflected on how deeply the teacher had read the text and I wondered how she storied herself in the text. Still I wondered more about how she storied her children. There was a concept lost on her that I had encountered twice in the field while working on the WITS project – the single story of what it means to be Hispanic. I heard teachers, academics, students, and even other researchers astounded by the concepts of being a Hispanic person who did not speak Spanish, and by being a Black person who was also Hispanic.

On the campus of McKay High School, a Black male teacher once derailed a data conversation with a discussion of how he perceived it a waste of time to have students check a box for Black or white "and then turn around and mark Hispanic or not" (Field notes 2018). While we were normally observers with limited participation in the collaborative meetings, the field research assistant who was with me interrupted a digression that lasted far too long to be productive. Afterward, the WITS writer, Mary, said, "As a white woman, I don't think I can speak fully to that or the need for people to mark boxes at all, but I am fairly certain that they are two different categories." Our team researcher, a blonde haired male, with light colored eyes, spoke.

"She's right," he said. "I'm Mexican. My family is from Mexico and my mother still lives there, but Chestin, didn't you say your grandfather was from there, too?"

I was not accustomed to discussing the factors which comprise my Blackness – there are several. I did this time. "Yes. He was. His parents were from Spain. So technically, when he and I walked in, you saw indicators of our race. Phenotypically, you saw his whiteness and my Blackness, but ethnicity is different."

These experiences centered my belief in the responsibility of teachers to seek more stories and underscored the importance of teacher preservice and in-service developers to require it. They did not understand their ignorance in this matter of race and ethnicity and could therefore not fully understand the implications of these blind spots in working with students from this background. These students could not possibly be fully "seen" if this aspect of their identity was not recognized as a truth of existence. This was something that Jasminne and I spoke of previously, and as she stated early in her interview, she identifies as Afro-Dominican and has a complex relationship with the terms Latina/Latinx. This is related to her experiences as an adult in Texas. Here in the South, she frequently met with individuals who lacked a deep understanding of Blackness in the same manner as the two teachers referenced above.

Jasminne had unpacked her encounters with this societal blind spot in poems and essays that unearth her responses and wonderings regarding the encounter. She said that on some days, "The sun isn't even out yet. I don't have the energy to explain my language, identity, ethnicity, race, culture or life to this man before noon." There were so many. This insight that she has acquired though uncomfortable conversations reminded me of the need for students and teachers to *create texts*. Our texts speak even when we are too exhausted to. They teach. Thus, in a continuation of the movement to challenge what is read, there is a second, softer movement directed toward the centering of student voices in expression of what is written. I believe this movement to be a key factor in the necessary acculturation of the literacy classroom.

Unpacking a Vision for Practice
I taught toward choice in text *and* expression which I heard echoed in Jasminne's interview and from the Black male teacher's contribution to the conversation between his female (white) colleagues at Suburban East High. The white teachers seemed active in taking a step toward increasing representation through the selection of a text by Black authors, and they were prepared for a collective unit. Yet that unit was deficient in the voices of Black teachers and students until the male teacher interjected with the idea of choice. Without him present, they were in rudimentary and monological "seeing." They also selected those texts with a member of the team, most vocal, lacking a deep understanding of what it meant to be Black. This meant that in lecture, there was a great chance of the teachers becoming an imposition on the truths of the very students that they sought to acknowledge (Greene, 2000). I pondered the possibilities for failure and opportunities for growth for this group.

Let us consider, in contrast, the student voice and narrative collection that resonates among the three Black literacy educators (Jasminne, the male teacher, and me). We employed extensive opportunities for choice in text selection, but we often talked about the purpose for reading. Through various interviews with Jasminne, the male teacher, and Dr Ladson-billings, I heard the echoes of "I want them to read something about (insert topic) because I want them to tell me about how they see (insert topic)" from the male teacher. Interviews with the white teachers countered this approach through much discussion on preparing students to be ready for a particular title. Even their selection of supplementary texts was framed as efforts to help engage students in the themes of the title in focus. For the participants of color, the purpose of reading was often framed as an attempt to inspire their students to write. In these transcripts, teachers of color were vocal and direct about seeking student responses to issues over texts. We utilized elements of workshop-based, process-oriented instructional approaches to writing, and as long as the tools of focus were apparent, I did not restrict performance from being a mode under which to assess. In my interview with Dr Ladson-Billings, I asked her to weigh in on this approach to teaching especially amid the four pandemics that she mentioned:

> The workshop & performance based writing approach relies less on writing conventions and more on the substance of writing. Many times, students are reluctant to write because they struggle with grammar, syntax, and spelling and as a result they will not attempt to write. I have found that working with students through a familiar genre allows them to see the variety of ways their voices can be included in their writing.
>
> For example, when I work with students who are writing statements for college admission, I use a classic piece of hip-hop, "I Go to Work" by Kool Moe Dee. I show students the video, which is a take on the James Bond spy theme. Next, I have students read through the lyrics and identify the similes, metaphors, analogies, and other literary devices that writers use. Then, I ask each student to write "8 bars" (i.e., eight lines) of rhyme about themselves. Finally, I ask them to turn those lines into prose.

Dr Ladson-Billings' example resonates with the strategies that Jasminne and I had executed in our teaching. It was reminiscent of what Chris Emdin deemed "an approach to teaching and learning that not only considers what is right for students, but what makes the teacher most effective and fulfilled" (Emdin, 2017, p. 42). It was part of the work. Beyond the job, teachers who are willing to do the work by affording students an accessible platform to use language to explore the world in which they live will find students "engaged in a process of redefining the sociocultural meaning of [their] identity" (Hall, 2007, p. 226) and the world around them.

Burrowed Truths

> There is something vitally important to education in the idea that the consciousness of growing, becoming different, can be tied to some memory of feelings of wonder, of recognition, that can counteract the feelings of futility. (Greene, 2000, p. 272)

Truth 1: For Me, and for Many Teachers of Color, Teaching Counteracts Feelings of Futility in the Plight Toward Equity in Education
As a young teacher, I would have loved to have other teachers of color with whom to partner. Much of the work that I was doing was behind closed doors, because my colleagues found it to be a rogue approach to teaching. They would often say that what they were doing "had always worked," but with increasing populations of students from diverse racial, ethnic, and linguistic backgrounds, there was no

evidence that their strategies *still* worked. In knowing this I felt blessed and burdened as a teacher of color on that campus. I thought of the lack of teachers of color I had when in school and remembered that the first time I considered being one was when I saw my fourth grade math teacher. She was young, beautiful, energetic, and Black. As Jasminne spoke of her encounter with the texts of Angelou and Hughes, I saw myself there. The possibility was born for me because Black teachers existed. In becoming one, I knew that the same could happen for my students.

Part of what made my fourth grade math teacher accessible was that she allowed us to bring in music and she would play "music to math by" as we entered independent practice. This translated in my work as an English teacher when I played music during vocabulary study. I'd first select a Latin root that applied to the sociological objective of our unit. Then I would select five words derived from that root for focus during that week. I planned journal activities that were scaffolded in complexity and required them to interact with the words and the root in a different way each day, and I would ask them to find uses for the words outside my classroom. Each Monday, we would chant them to an instrumental version of Kurtis Blow's "These are the Breaks" and use gestures that they developed as mnemonics for meaning. They were our dance moves and our memory cues, ritually followed by a loud and collective, "*These are the words! – Now break 'em down, break 'em down, break 'em dowwwwwn.*" Only after this progression would I begin an introduction to the root with, "Remember, you can master one word a day."

I unpacked this memory by restorying how Jasminne employed the culture of call and response in her writing courses with WITS and reminded her students that they could become writers "one word at a time." These are appeals to students. They are in many ways a rebuke to the normalcy of schools preoccupied with standardized testing and measurement, but they call upon students to engage, just as choice in assessment form calls upon them to create.

Truth 2: For a Continuity in the Disruption of Inequitable Practice, Normal Is Not an Option

Dr Ladson-Billings noted this in her interview. In response to question regarding the opportunity to reach students in the Gen Z/Gen Alpha age range, particularly those from historically marginalized demographic groups, she discussed the integration of arts in the literacy and said that "given the impact of Inauguration poet, Amanda Gorman, students may be more willing to participate in writing that speaks to their specific situations" (Interview, 2021). And when asked about the dangers of not assessing to move forward in our approach to literacy education and amplifying the voices of students of color, she said:

> The risks are obvious. We are likely to fall right back into the high rates of school failure among marginalized groups as well as a continued lack of engagement. The operative question for me is always, "What are we trying to produce?"
>
> If we have a vision of what we would like to see at the end, perhaps it will give us some insight into how to go about achieving it.

In hearing the voices of two Black women, I heard my own. Research is travel, and in journeying through their stories, I revisited my own. Drawing upon connections in our experiences in literacy education, our shared vision becomes translucent. What we are trying to produce is a system in which more educators value the voices of children who look like us. There is nothing but light that comes through a learning portal that would "force a recognition that students and teachers both need help in reading the surrounding culture, in naming what is lacking, in identifying what might be done in efforts to transform" (Greene, 2000, p. 270). I will continue to unpack toward this justice and hope that "normal" fades as we enter the educational renaissance, or revolution that little girls of color, like my daughters – and like the little girl I used to be – needed it to be.

CONSIDERATIONS AND COMPLEXITY

In consideration of what I needed education to be, I reflect on the power of storying experience, especially autobiographical narratives, as an act of love, an act of self-discovery, and an act of resistance. As a teacher, I wanted that for my students. As a student, I needed it, as Jasminne said, "to survive." So much of my education seemed to ignore multiplicities of self or truth. The lessons given us rested largely on our being receivers of information, not givers. We were offered a singular truth, which I interpreted to be "The American way is best." We were chained to the "truth" that somehow, Americanized life was best. Yet in this, many who are the descendants of historically oppressed and currently bearers of the impact of such generational traumas felt excluded from discourse and therefore less than American. In order for literacy educators to unchain the next generation of learners and free them to travel, there must be a continuation of movements reversing the storied truths of the marginalized.

Some truths have been so deeply silenced by cognitive dissonance that narratives often serve as most effective bridges by which to cross the waters of denial and slowly bring the dominant culture toward acceptance. I still believe that we can all develop a stronger understanding of others through their stories, through which we can travel across the borders that by which we would otherwise be confined (Clandinin & Rosiek, 2006; Lugones, 1987). I wonder if we can expand the approach to literacy education as an act of liberation over the protections of historic continuities of cultural hegemony and associate pedagogies, and I wonder why many teachers see narrative as the "easy" thing to teach. My field notes reflect many who feel that

> ...We spend so much time on narrative that I don't know if we will have time to prepare them for the expository and analytical writing they will have to do on the test. (Field notes, 2018)

Still, others like me believe that narrative is the preparation necessary for all other approaches to writing. Tressie McMillan Cottom addresses this most pointedly in Thick (2019) as she sheds light on Black women's use of personal essays to enter the space of white feminist politics and be represented. Cottom unapologetically embraces narrative construction and analysis as an appeal to the authoritative voices of the dominant culture and to protect our invitation to be heard and seen more fully:

We had learned, or have always known that we cannot change the minds of those on whom we rely to grant us the audience that confers moral authority to speak in public. We could not fix the world, but we could fix our own feet. And so, Black women writers have fixed their feet. We have shoehorned political analysis and economic policy and social movements theory and queer ideologies into public discourse by bleeding our personal lives into the genre afforded us.

For now, at least, it seems that this bleeding of self has found its place in classroom environments, professional development collaboratives, and envisioning a more just system of education. It has become an integral part of the work behind the job for BIPOC literacy educators. We have much to unpack, as we dream of an America that is stronger and greater for the beautiful polyphony of truths.

NOTES

1. Note on the contributions of the interviewees: I extend a note of thanks to Jasminne Mendez for her contributions toward exploring truth claims in this chapter and to Dr Gloria Ladson-Billings for sharing her time and wisdom on instructional methods and cultural implications.

REFERENCES

Auzenne-Curl, C., & Carr, D. (2021). The implications of social media scholarship on forming a knowledge community in black cyberculture: A co-constructed narrative. In C. Auzenne-Curl, C.J. & Craig (Eds.), Developing knowledge communities through partnerships for literacy. Emerald.

Clandinin, D. J., & Rosiek, J. (2006). Mapping a landscape of narrative inquiry: Borderland spaces and tensions. In D. J. Clandinin (Ed.), *Handbook of narrative inquiry: Mapping a methodology* (pp. 35–75). Thousand Oaks, CA: Sage.

Connelly, F. M., & Clandinin, D. J. (1990). Stories of experience and narrative inquiry. *Educational Researcher, 19*(5), 2–14.

Cottom, T. M. (2019). *Thick: And other essays.* New York, NY: The New Press.

Craig, C., Ross, V., Conle, C., & Richardson, V. (2008). Cultivating the image of teachers as curriculum makers. In F. M. Connelly (Ed.), *Handbook of curriculum and instruction* (pp. 282–305). Los Angeles, CA: Sage Publications.

Ebarvia, T., German, L., Parker, K., & Torres, J. (2020). #Disrupttexts: An introduction. *English Journal, 110*(1), 100–102.

Emdin, C. (2017). *For white folks who teach in the hood…and the rest of y'all too: Reality pedagogy and urban education.* Boston, MA: Beacon Press.

Greene, M. (2000). Imagining futures: The public school and possibility. *Journal of Curriculum Studies, 32*(2), 267–280.

Hall, H. R. (2007). Poetic expressions: Students of color express resiliency through metaphors and similes. *Journal of Advanced Academics, 18*(2), 216–244.

Ladson-Billings, G., Brown, K., Camangian, P. R., Dillard, C., Kirkland, D. E., San Pedro, T., … Wilcox, S. E. (2021, February 18). Call us by our names: A kitchen-table dialogue on doin' it for the culture. *Equity & Excellence in Education Virtual Round Table Discussion.* Retrieved from https://tinyurl.com/EEERoundtable

Lorde, A. (1985/2015). Poetry is not a luxury. In S. M. Shaw & J. Lee (Eds.), *Women's voices, feminist visions: Classic and contemporary readings* (pp. 371–373). New York, NY: McGraw-Hill Education.

Lugones, M. (1987). Playfulness, "world"- traveling, and loving perception. *Hypatia A Journal of Feminist Philosophy, 2*(2), 3–19.

Schaefer, L., Downey, C., & Clandinin, D. (2014). Shifting from stories to live by to stories to leave by: Early career teacher attrition. *Teacher Education Quarterly, 41*(1), 9–27.

Stoultzfus, K. (2019, February). The text disruptors. *ASCD Education Update, 61*(2). Retrieved from http://www.ascd.org/publications/newsletters/education-update/feb19/vol61/num02/The-Text-Disrupters.aspx

THE IMPLICATIONS OF SOCIAL MEDIA SCHOLARSHIP ON FORMING A KNOWLEDGE COMMUNITY IN BLACK CYBERCULTURE: A COCONSTRUCTED NARRATIVE

Chestin T. Auzenne-Curl and Daphne Carr

ABSTRACT

Following the mass closing of US schools during the COVID-19 pandemic of 2020, the authors noted an increase in discourse among literacy teachers and literacy coaches on social media platforms. Over a period of 9 months, the authors followed the interactions and work of social media scholars on the Twitter platform. In reflecting on Craig's (1995; Craig, Curtis, Kelly, Martindell, & Perez, 2020) illustrative pillars of knowledge communities and Brock's work on black cyberculture, we use narrative inquiry (Clandinin & Connelly, 2000; Connelly & Clandinin, 1990) to: (1) explore the elements of social media scholarship and (2) reflect on how active engagement in social media scholarship aids in the development of online knowledge communities that amplify and sustain the work of black womxn scholars.

Keywords: Social media scholarship; knowledge communities; black cyberculture; literacy coaching; professional learning; black teachers

NARRATIVE BEGINNINGS

We first met in a face-to-face professional development session. We were both Instructional Coaches for secondary literacy on high school campuses in the same district, and our meeting was past due. We had worked in the same school systems before, but never at the same time. Still, having been labeled as enigmatic-kindred successes by our common supervisors and colleagues, we had heard of one another's work long before we connected in person. Though it is difficult to recall what the specific curricular focus was on that day, we remember that in a sea of white bodies, clad in Vera Bradley, and jeweled lanyards, our darker silhouettes expedited the scan of the room.

Chestin's Notes

My professional and sisterly relationship with Dr. Carr is a factor in my story to live by (Clandinin & Connelly, 1998) as an educator. As a black woman, there are aspects of scholarship, leadership, perception, and negotiations of space that she understands in a way that few others do. When I share these things in the lens of blackness with nonblack scholars, I am often left exhausted by expressions of pity, white-splaining (Blake, 2019), or a call for extensive, didactic restorying (Clandinin & Connelly, 2000). Somehow, Daphne and I know when a release is for ponderance, or a strategic realignment of our wits. It happens through a sense of intuitive interface of cultural cues as language. We speak BLAcademiCK[1] fluently.

Our professional relationship has involved curriculum writing, professional development design and delivery, facilitation of instructional coaching cycles, academic assessment construction, and lesson design for secondary reading and writing. While we have not previously coauthored scholarly publications, we frequently engage in scholarly discourse. After our two-year stint of in-district collaboration, we communicated most frequently in electronic communication, and as we entered the COVID-19 revolutionary period, we extended our discussion and learning via Twitter. Our reflections on this particular platform are captured in this chapter.

Daphne's Notes

"Iron sharpening iron" best illustrates my professional and sisterly relationship with Dr. Auzenne-Curl. We met over six years ago when we were doing similar work at separate locations in the same school district. People who knew both of us assumed we would be good friends because we were both anomalies – "articulate" African-American women coaching curriculum and instruction at high school campuses with predominantly white English department members in a suburban school district. Initially, I chafed at their expectation that having the same job, gender, and skin color as someone I had never met would make us instant friends. But, I could not deny the joy in my spirit when I noticed Dr. AC's side-eyes and deep sighs during a professional development session about closing the literacy gap among children of color. I chuckled to myself and thought, *At last, I have found a kindred spirit....*

Since that initial meeting, we have supported each other through doctoral studies, career moves, a divorce, and deaths in our families. When an administrator's recalcitrance made it difficult for me to arrange an internship for my doctoral program, she rescued me from sitting out a semester by agreeing to serve as my internship supervisor. The internship gave us an opportunity to work together designing professional development experiences and curricular resources for teachers. Her creativity and innovation sparked ideas I enjoyed researching and analyzing. Even though I accepted a promotion in a neighboring district the following year, we continued communicating by phone calls, text messages, and posts on social media. We kept each other abreast of advancements and issues in literacy studies, reminding each other of our identity as scholars by taking each other's ideas seriously. The frequency of this scholarly discourse intensified as we sheltered in place during the early months of the COVID-19 pandemic. We took to social media to see how black scholars and literacy leaders were addressing issues related to equity and lesson design in virtual environments. To our delight, we found what we consider to be a culturally relevant knowledge community of sister-scholars in black cyberculture.

Contextualizing Our Approach

As we continued to ponder the Twitter community of sister-scholars in action, we came to note an intersection of both portfolio-based knowledge communities (Craig, 2007) and Brock's (2020) Critical Technocultural Discourse Analysis (CTDA). In constructing the following analysis of literature on Impostor Phenomenon (IP), CTDA and Knowledge Communities, we became aware of the nature of Twitter as a combatant to the hegemony of higher education and a window to vulnerability and attack.

PRELIMINARY ANALYSES

Imposter Syndrome Among Black Women Scholars

Black women undergraduates, graduate students, and faculty members have reported experiencing the IP in various academic disciplines (Haskins et al., 2019). The phenomenon has been described as a feeling of inadequacy experienced by high-achieving women who doubt their intelligence and competency despite earned degrees, awards, or professional recognition (Auzenne-Curl, 2020; Clance & Imes, 1978). While others view them as accomplished professionals and experts, women who experience IP believe they fraudulently accomplished their achievements through luck, coincidence, or some temporary factor other than skill (Clance & Imes, 1978). Initially, Clarence and Imes attributed the phenomenon to familial influence and the negative stereotypes of independent women who project confidence in their abilities. They surmised that successful women most likely thought of themselves as intellectual frauds to downplay their accomplishments and evade rejection in society for defying traditional gender roles (Clance & Imes, 1978).

Although we can identify with the feelings of anxiety and stress described by Clarence and Imes, their generalizations about the origins of IP do not align with our lived experiences as black women in America. In fact, we find it important to note that Clarence and Imes drew their conclusions based on observations of "primarily white middle-to upper-class women between the ages of 20 and 45" (1978, p. 2). Their generalizations presume whiteness as a default without considering the intersectionality of race, socioeconomic status, and gender (Kendall, 2020). Subsequent studies of the imposter phenomenon have attempted to address the challenges of racial stereotypes and systemic oppression for women of color in addition to familial expectations and social stereotypes (Clance, Dingman, Reverie, & Stober, 1995), but only a few these studies have examined IP in African-American populations (Bernard, Hoggard, & Neblett, 2017). This deficiency in the literature calls us to wonder why. For black womxn, writing about IP can exacerbate the effects. Still, it seems that the topic would be best addressed in a firsthand narrative approach.

> In certain spaces, I was strong and a facilitator of active discourse. I was a consultant in the world of the practical. I worked hands and minds to guide the work. In other [Higher Education] spaces, I was insecure and lacked the language of theoretical discourse. I was often the only person who looked like me in the room and ... microaggressions presented a significant challenge in finding a voice that is representative of the [Black] culture, and simultaneously avoids the exclusion pending...Not to appease the offender, but to protect the seat at the table where changes are born. (Auzenne-Curl, 2020, p. 104)

It can be hard to continue to story the exhaustion of "thrice-better/thrice-charged" in our community. Every moment we spend doing so seems to put us at risk of inheriting more calls to do so, and the tendency of us falling into a narrow scope of what others see as the race-obsessed or angry black woman trope.

Daphne's Notes

> I will never forget the anxiety I felt when my building principal refused to collaborate with me in setting up an internship schedule for a required course I needed to complete as a doctoral student. When I requested a meeting to discuss his reluctance to sign off on the agreement we made last semester, he accused me of being selfish and disrespectful, of placing my personal needs before the needs of students and teachers in my department (even though the schedule I proposed took away my lunch time and added hours to my workday after school). He insisted that I needed to attend the after-school tutorials for struggling students instead of using the time outside of the workday to complete my internship. I had identified the students, organized the curriculum, met with the teachers, and set up a schedule for the tutorial sessions, but I was not "going the extra mile" as a leader. When I reached out to the non-BIPOC (black, Indigenous, and people of color) director of my program for assistance or solutions, she icily responded that it was my responsibility to figure it out. If I could not complete the internship, I would have to take the course with the next cohort and graduate a year later. Though she did not say it, her tone communicated it. Somehow, some way, this was my fault because I was not good enough – or at least, that is the way I felt. And it was not because of my intelligence or my work ethic. It was because I had no community or credibility among the professors in charge of my program. I had no way of proving how "respectable" I was so the professor would understand how unfair my supervisor was being. My professor's unwillingness to intervene would have forced me to placate a superior I knew to be unscrupulous. If Dr. AC had not stepped in by using her newly acquired position as a program coordinator to advocate with the professor on my behalf, I do not know what I would have done. In that moment, I needed more than brains, good self-esteem, and hard work. I needed the grace and muscle of a sister-scholar.

For us, race is not an added challenge to being a woman; it is inextricably linked to our identity as women. From childhood, people within our community have fed us sayings, sermons, and speeches about being "strong black women," women who must be stronger and tougher than white women by necessity, both physically and emotionally. So, we endure the IP and the anxiety to protect the space for one another. It worked for us during the moments above.

We grew up assuming it was our task and our birthright to work more, endure more, and receive less than white women. Though these assumptions were problematic, we did not perceive strength and independence to be only masculine characteristics. Even now, we do not question our interpersonal roles within our families or social circles as much as we struggle to establish a niche for ourselves as scholar practitioners in a white-dominated space. We question whether our scholarly interests sound "academic enough" to be worthy of publication and recognition because what matters to us rarely matters to those who hold positions of power (Bernal & Villalpando, 2002).

More consistent with our experiences are the findings of recent studies that explore the connections between racial discrimination and IP among African-American college students. These studies suggest that instances of racial discrimination can lead to heightened feelings of isolation, anxiety, and depression that result in IP (Bernard et al., 2017). Black American women also appear to experience the phenomenon more often than white females (Haskins et al., 2019). Identifying with women who share similar identities and working with them to achieve social justice can play a crucial role in dismantling IP narratives for women of color (Haskins et al., 2019). We see emergent knowledge communities in social media platforms like Twitter as digital examples of "womanish supports" that can offer places of healing, inspiration, and affirmation for African-American women in the academy (Haskin et al., 2019). By serving as online sanctuaries and support groups, these communities provide a culturally responsive means of combating the debilitating effects of IP on the mental health of black women scholars.

Knowledge Communities and Portfolio-based Knowledge Share

In her 2007 article, "Illuminating Qualities of Knowledge Communities in a Portfolio-Making Context," Cheryl Craig begins by recounting an expression of conflicting views on teacher knowledge transfer by Joseph Schwab and an unnamed contemporary. At its core, the conflict was that the unnamed person's stance on teachers learning from one another represented a "pooling of ignorance" (p.617) while Schwab asserted that it was not ignorance, but "diversities of experience and insight" that resulted from teachers forming such communities.

Craig expands on how her wonderings from this interaction lead to a trend in her research trajectory to study the interactions and patterns of teachers learning in community. Throughout the article, and across her body of research, Craig looks to the function portfolio development in sustaining a story-to-live by, mentoring, and ongoing personal and professional growth (Craig, 1995, 2004, 2007).

As we reflected further, we came to see the same effects of exchanging social media scholarship on Twitter. We felt a part of an online portfolio group. As we reviewed and categorized tweets using hashtags like file folders, Twitter feeds became living records of our learning. It was inviting to us. A fresh space in which to engage with few restrictions or limitations to voice. The authentic engagements among sister-scholars provided critical, collaborative, and emancipatory knowledge (re)construction. Twitter called us into an online portfolio group (Craig, Curtis, Kelly, Martindell, & Perez, 2020) that shares the qualities of a knowledge community:

- Knowledge communities begin with originating events;
- Knowledge communities enable teachers' intra-/interschool dialog;
- Knowledge communities allow teachers' experiences to resonate with one another;
- Knowledge communities evolve and change;
- Knowledge communities cohere around teachers' storying/restorying of experience;
- Knowledge communities fuel ongoing reflection in community;
- Knowledge communities develop shared ways of knowing;
- Knowledge communities feature reciprocity of members' responses; and
- Knowledge communities bring moral horizons into view.

(Craig, 2007, p. 621)

Being online made our communications both safe and dangerous. While we found the online interactions a source of collective mitigation of the impact of IP, the elements that sustained us were not protected from attack and racist trolls. This negativity could easily shift individuals from active participation to weaving a story to leave by. As we entered in this narrative construction, one of our most referenced sister-scholars was attacked by a white female peer and a national journalism title. The span was about two weeks, and the tweet shared questions about diversity in the literary canon. It was something that we had dealt with in public and higher education. Being online meant that the audience was broader, and the vulgarity of the response would drive several sister-scholars to protect their Tweets for a period of time. The backlash and screenshots shared in direct message inboxes prompted a storm of vernacular and didactic responses in solidarity. With black women in particular, we assert that the hegemony of higher education often requires a degree of code-switching since the jargon of academia can isolate practitioners outside of the academy from our message, especially practitioners of color. By employing the linguistic freedom of the Twitter platform, the same message can be shared with a larger audience who may not have access otherwise. Sometimes, the access is restricted due to the rights and permissions of peer-reviewed publications; other times, the lack of authentic cultural voice is the limiting factor.

Reflections on Brock's Work with CTDA and Black Twitter

Our focus on the Twitter platform as a portfolio-based medium for literacy scholarship led us to Brock's (2012, 2016) work with critical cultural discourse analysis (CTDA) as a technique for examining each scholar's interactions on

Twitter. CTDA incorporates technology studies, communication studies, and critical race theory in its examination of online conversations in social media platforms to illuminate how people express culture through technological discourse (Brock, 2012). Brock's technique is unique in its focus on the semiotics of information and communication in social media. By exploring how and why people do digital practice, as opposed to merely quantifying how often people engage in it, CTDA redirects the focus of digital media research studies from questions of use and limited access among underrepresented groups to examinations of cultural context (2016). Its fundamental premise is that digital platforms are not value neutral spaces. Social media platforms like Twitter reflect and extend the cultural practices and ideologies of the societies that produced them, making their interfaces, exchanges, and the contexts in which users engage in them, texts for analysis (Brock, 2012). We adopted this premise for our close reading of various Twitter exchanges while also using Brock's observations of black discursive style on Twitter to examine their online personas. Brock (2012) describes the complexity of this identity as a reflection of the "double consciousness" articulated by W. E. B. Duois (1903) and the practice of signifying, as discussed in works by Gates (1983), Saussure (1959/2011), and Smitherman (1977). The scholar discussed in our reflection negotiates the tension of expressing communal solidarity with other educators of color while advising and challenging white educators about racist literacy instructional practices – all within the same digital platform. Twitter's public broadcast model makes it possible for anyone to comment on these exchanges, whether they are friends, allies, followers, or critics (Brock, 2020). Exchanges between those in the same "in-group" are open to unsolicited scrutiny and antagonism, and so are the responses of scholars and participants to those critiques. Knowing how and when to use black discursive elements through hashtags, network participation in the form retweets and replies, and cultural referents becomes essential to the work of establishing and maintaining culturally relevant learning communities online (Brock, 2012). For us, CTDA provided a model for unearthing and deciphering these rhetorical moves that often take place digitally in plain sight, allowing us to understand more deeply as sister-scholars the intellectual, rhetorical, and tactical demands of social media scholarship on Twitter.

Probing the Concept of Social Media Scholarship in Black Twitter

In an effort to burrow into the phenomenon of sister-scholarship amid the pandemic, we decided to start with our favorite hashtag and turned to Social Media Scholar, Dr. Kim Parker. Dr. Parker is one of four women of color who created #Disrupt Texts in May 2018 to "advocate for a more inclusive and restorative curriculum and pedagogical approach in English language arts" (Ebarvia, German, Parker, & Torres, 2020, p. 100). We began following Dr. Parker on Twitter through her affiliation with #Disrupt Texts and as we sheltered in place during the spring months of 2020, we interpreted #DisruptTexts as a "call" awaiting our response – to follow, to read, to retweet in solidarity with the movement, and to respond with action (Brock, 2016). We had recently experienced a textbook adoption in Texas. Working with districts and campuses that had become increasingly diverse in race, ethnicity, and linguistic background, the conversation surrounding which textbooks, and which ancillary texts were most appropriate. This became an even more complex process as we were forced to complete it virtually. We sought support online.

By June, our focus had become even more narrowed. Dr. Parker captured our interest specifically because of her identification as an African-American woman. Her lived experiences as a native Southerner, along with her academic interests in the "literacy lives of black and Latinx folx" and her personal interests in "mothering a black son," made her privy to the same concerns and conversations we were hearing within the black community as schools responded to the pandemic including inequity in access to technology, lack of engaging literature for students of color, and by July, an increased in requests for literature dealing with racial injustice and police brutality (K. Parker, personal communication, January 8, 2021). As we followed the hashtags and conversation threads of Dr. Parker's posts, we noticed her adept use of Twitter as a platform for advocacy, activism, and professional networking.

Many of Dr. Parker's tweets from June to September 2020 brought attention to the educational needs of black and Latinx families during the pandemic. As schools prepared for distance learning in August, Parker spotlighted the concerns of parents by asking "Is your school/district having parent workshops so they can teach their children this fall? If so, what are some of the topics? If not, why not?" (Parker, 2020). In framing her concern as a series of questions, Parker created space for responses that ranged from anecdotes of neglect or censure by schools to suggestions with hyperlinks connecting followers to websites and resources for parents. The separation of theory and practice, and the community of educators and parents seemed to shrink. All stakeholders were asking questions and whether through direct response, or through referrals and resource recommendations, people were coming together to respond. Kim regularly acknowledged those who joined in to respond, and she frequently retweeted the work of others with gratitude for the share. When a follower posted about sitting through an online workshop that did not allow mostly black and Latinx mothers in attendance to unmute their microphones, Parker encouraged the women to use their collective power to organize and advocate for their needs. To followers who provided answers and resources, she responded with follow-up questions or words of affirmation until the entire thread became a digital portfolio of insightful questions, web tools and ideas for parent outreach programs. The thread was a course, and she was the facilitator.

We also noted Parker's advocacy for black women scholars in her Twitter posts. A post from June 11, 2020, reminded followers that if they were using "mirrors, windows, and sliding glass doors" to explain the benefits of providing children with diverse books to read, they should cite Dr. Rudine Sims Bishop (Parker, 2020). Parker considers her advocacy for citing black women scholars to be "a way of just giving Black women our due for being so good, for so long, on the everyday" (K. Parker, personal communication, January 8, 0). As one of Parker's followers noted, Dr. Bishop's idea has been credited to other scholars by mistake far too often. Ironically, within the same Twitter thread devoted to citing

Dr. Bishop, we noticed a non-BIPOC retweeting Parker's post and restating Dr. Bishop's signature phrase without proper attribution. While some might dismiss this as a harmless or careless omission, we interpreted the retweet as another small yet blatant act of erasure. Anthropologist and social activist Christen A. Smith had such omissions in mind when she established Cite Black Women in 2017 to heighten awareness of black women's contributions to academia since they are "often overlooked, sidelined, and undervalued" despite being "intellectually prolific" (Cite Black Women, n.d.; Smith, Williams, Wadud, & Pirtle, 2021). Parker frequently incorporates the hashtags #CiteBlackWomen and #Citeasista to align her public support of black women scholars with the Cite Black Women movement (Brock, 2016). This practice, according to scholar Meredith Clark, places Parker within a "culturally connected network of communicators" using Twitter to spotlight issues important to black communities (Reid, 2018).

In her support of black scholars and her own intellectual work, Parker sometimes uses direct confrontation or subtle redirection to combat the efforts of non-BIPOC followers to center her agenda around whiteness. This gift of generous scholarship was evident as the movement against racially motivated violence became a global pandemic of its own (Ladson-Billings, personal communication, 2020). As the nation erupted in protests against police brutality after the deaths of George Floyd and Breonna Taylor, Parker gained new white followers on Twitter who were curious about the work and message of #Disrupt Texts (K. Parker, personal communication, January 8, 2021). As Bollen, Gonçalves, Ruan, and Mao colleagues have noted (2011), people with similar interests and dispositions typically gravitate to each other in online social networks. In the wake of significant historical, political, or social events, public mood can spread and escalate quickly across social network ties on Twitter (Bollen, Mao, & Pepe, 2011). People may choose to follow a trending topic or a specific person out of genuine curiosity, marginal interest, or even virulent antipathy.

In June 2020, sister-scholar Parker defended Boston's only black-owned bookstore against hostile emails sent by white customers who were upset because the store could not fulfill immediately over 10,000 orders for the same 10 books about antiracism (Parker, 2020). Previously, Parker had recommended the bookstore to followers in an effort to increase the store's sales. But the events of the summer catalyzed an insatiable desire for books about antiracism and social justice that surpassed the inventory of the local bookstore. Incensed by the harassment the store owner had endured, Parker took to social media to denounce the behavior of her "newly awakened" white followers: "Wanting something when YOU want it is the hilt of white supremacy. This 'sense of urgency' is not okay. DO BETTER. And if you're one of the ppl emailing them to 'demand' your books, then def unfollow me RN. Miss me with your racism" (Parker, 2020). Parker's reply included a link to Showing Up for Racial Justice, a website devoted to providing resources for educating and mobilizing white people who desire to stand up for racial justice. Unlike her straightforward criticism of the bookstore patrons, Parker's handling of followers who seek to take advantage of her professional expertise without providing compensation is more subtle. When a teacher asked for Parker's help in constructing a response to those in her district who might challenge her desire to remove classics from the curriculum, Parker referred the teacher to the #DisruptTexts archives for articles and rationales to support her cause. In other words, Parker asked the teacher to do the work for herself. This is a lesson in protection that black womxn scholars need to see mirrored. In attempting to break from IP, individuals are known to overextend and succumb to workloads that are not equal to the pay. Another sister-scholar had initiated an exchange in which Chestin engaged:

> I saw the post the [Eva] made about citing and paying black women. The call was simple and direct and included "Don't ask us to work for exposure." I couldn't help but add the old Oregon Trail meme with the image of the wagon. The text reads "Died from exposure." She was so right. I retweeted it with a quote and she thanked me. It's difficult when you think that you are alone in the struggle. You ask yourself if you are making too much out of things – especially as a Black woman. There are few of us in ELAR. Fewer in the academy. So, before we were engaging in social media exchanges, we had to wait for conferences and scan a room. Now we see sister-scholars and are drawn in by shared experiences. It really is empowering. In this case, it helped me speak the words, "You have to do this part of the work. Come to me when you have" to a white colleague that seemed unaware of how exhausting her apologetic line of inquisition was. We are happy to have genuine and active allies, but we can't run full courses on racism for every individual who sees us as their one smart Black friend.

Sister-scholars appreciate the way Parker refers her followers to their work, whether it is research in educational technology, history, sociology, or literacy. Her tweets increase their visibility and honor their intellectual production in ways that traditional scholarly practices in face-to-face settings have not. Many times, we saw "thanks, sis" or a simple heart emoji of gratitude for the gift of noticing that Parker provides to many black women and men who labor in silos and shadows because their interests rarely mirror the academic concerns of faculty members at predominately white institutions.

CLOSING REMARKS AND WONDERINGS

We close this chapter with the understanding that Twitter offered us an opportunity to come into community with our sister-scholars. We also understand that this emergent knowledge community is still a novel approach to the sharing of scholarly and practical knowledge. This may mean that it is an invitation to which many may not respond. Our hope is that by our continued engagement, and by extending the lens on the complex nature of interactions here, others will join us. In reflecting on the advocacy, activism, and networking from this study, we address each of the qualities (Craig, 2007) in context COVID-19 evolution:

- The shutting down of schools was an originating event that increased our online knowledge-seeking and our reach for sharing;
- Social media scholars and field practitioners carried on intra-/interschool dialog;

- Our experiences resonated with one another, and the retweets, quoted tweets, and "likes" were measurable, visual affirmations;
- This discourse in the community evolved and changed, and thanks to the online sharing, even "tweeted and deleted" commentary was captured;
- The resultant Call and Response Scholarship (CRS) shifted the conversation from in person and online learning platforms, to a deeper discussion of cultural competency, antibias teaching, and collective restorying;
- As was evident in the aftermath of the attacks on #DisruptTexts founders and allies, the platform fuels ongoing reflection in community and sparks action;
- Through linguistic and sociocultural cues, CTDA helps us understand more about the shared ways of knowing being developed online;
- The reciprocity of social media scholars' responses is key and led to the ability for us to enter in community with Dr. Parker and several other scholars during this period of time; and
- Through this platform, several new dynamic affinity groups and Twitter chats with periodic consistency bring moral horizons into view.

We appreciate and will continue to use our voices in movements such as #DisruptTexts and #CiteBlackWomen in solidarity as the nature of scholarship sharing evolves. Our wonderings are leading us to follow-up studies that explore the vulnerability of those participating in online sharing, and in tracing the membership in the aforementioned affinity groups and a deeper inquiry into the views of social media scholars on the contrasting nature of knowledge shared in higher education and on the Internet. Through continuing this conversation, we hope to learn more about ourselves and to shed light on phenomena for other sister-scholars who may not be aware of the depth of community that is available at a swipe and click of a mouse.

NOTE

1. A term used by the authors to denote the verbal and nonverbal cultural cues read by black womxn scholars in academic and other professional settings.

REFERENCES

Auzenne-Curl, C. (2020). Fear, fellowship, and finding a voice: An autobiographical narrative of being and becoming in an established research community. In C. J. Craig, L. Turchi, & D. M. McDonald (Eds.), *Cross-disciplinary, cross-institutional collaboration in teacher education. Palgrave studies on leadership and learning in teacher education.* Cham: Palgrave Macmillan. doi:10.1007/978-3-030-56674-6_6

Bernal, D., & Villalpando, O. (2002). An apartheid of knowledge in academia: The struggle over the "legitimate" knowledge of faculty of color. *Equity & Excellence in Education, 35*(2), 169–180.

Bernard, D. L., Hoggard, L. S., & Neblett, E. W., Jr. (2017). Racial discrimination, racial identity, and impostor phenomenon: A profile approach. *Cultural Diversity and Ethnic Minority Psychology, 24*(1), 51–61. doi:10.1037/cdp0000161

Blake, J. (2019, February 17). Stop 'whitesplaining' racism to me. *CNN.* Retrieved from https://www.cnn.com/2019/02/17/us/whitesplaining-racism-blake-analysis/index.html

Bollen, J., Gonçalves, B., Ruan, G., & Mao, H. (2011). Happiness is assortative in online social networks. *Artificial Life*, *17*(3), 237–251. doi:10.1162/artl_a_00034

Bollen, J., Mao, H., & Pepe, A. (2011). Modeling public mood and emotion: Twitter sentiment and socio-economic phenomena. *Proceedings of the International AAAI Conference on Web and Social Media*, *5*(1). Retrieved from https://ojs.aaai.org/index.php/ICWSM/article/view/14171

Brock, A. (2012). Blackhand side: Twitter as a cultural conversation. *Journal of Broadcasting & Electronic Media*, *56*(4), 529–549. doi:10.1080/08838151.2012.732147

Brock, A. (2016). Critical technocultural discourse analysis. *New Media & Society*, *20*(3), 1012–1030. doi:10.1177/1461444816677532

Brock, A. (2020). *Distributed blackness: African American cybercultures*. New York, NY: New York University Press. Retrieved from http://opensquare.nyupress.org/books/9781479820375/read/

Cite Black Women. (n.d.). Retrieved from https://www.citeblackwomencollective.org/

Clance, P. R., Dingman, D., Reverie, S. L., & Stober, D. R. (1995). Impostor phenomenon in an interpersonal/social context: Origins and treatment. *Women & Therapy*, *16*(4), 79–96.

Clance, P. R., & Imes, S. (1978). The imposter phenomenon in high achieving women: Dynamics and therapeutic intervention. *Psychotherapy: Theory, Research and Practice*, *15*(3), 241–247. doi:10.1037/h0086006

Clandinin, D. J., & Connelly, F. M. (1998). Stories to live by: Narrative understandings of school reform. *Curriculum Inquiry*, *28*(2), 149–164.

Clandinin, D. J., & Connelly, F. M. (2000). *Narrative inquiry: Experience and story in qualitative research* (p. 211). San Francisco, CA: Jossey-Bass.

Connelly, F. M., & Clandinin, D. J. (1990). Stories of experience and narrative inquiry. *Educational Researcher*, *19*(5), 2–14.

Craig, C. J. (1995). Knowledge communities: A way of making sense of how beginning teachers come to know. *Curriculum Inquiry*, *25*(2), 151–175.

Craig, C. J. (2004). Shifting boundaries on the professional knowledge landscape: When teacher communications become less safe. *Curriculum Inquiry*, *34*(4), 395–423.

Craig, C. J. (2007). Illuminating qualities of knowledge communities in a portfolio-making context. *Teachers and Teaching*, *13*(6), 617–636. doi:10.1080/13540600701683564

Craig, C. J., Curtis, G. A., Kelley, M., Martindell, P. T., & Pérez, M. M. (2020). *Knowledge communities in teacher education: Sustaining collaborative work*. Cham: Palgrave Macmillan.

#Disrupt Texts. (2021, January 02). What is #disrupt texts? Retrieved from https://disrupttexts.org/lets-get-to-work. Accessed on January 24, 2021.

DuBois, W. E. B. (1903). *The souls of black folk*. Project Gutenberg. Retrieved from https://www.gutenberg.org/files/408/408-h/408-h.htm

Ebarvia, T., German, L., Parker, K., & Torres, J. (2020). #DisruptTexts. *English Journal*, *110*(1), 100–102. Retrieved from https://library.ncte.org/journals/ej/issues/v110-1/30854

Gates, H. L. (1983). The "blackness of blackness": A critique of the sign and the signifying monkey. *Critical Inquiry*, *9*(4), 685–723. doi:10.1086/448224

Haskins, N., Hughes, K., Crumb, L., Smith, A., Brown, S., & Pignato, L. (2019). Postmodern womanism: Dismantling the imposter phenomenon for Black American college students. *The Negro Educational Review*, *70*(1–4), 1–25.

Kendall, M. (2020). *Hood feminism: Notes from the women that a movement forgot*. New York, NY: Viking.

Parker, K. [@TchKimPossible]. (2020, August 20). Is your school/district having parent workshops so they can teach their children this fall? If so, what are some [Tweet]. *Twitter*. Retrieved from https://twitter.com/tchkimpossible/status/1296565905489616899

Parker, K. [@TchKimPossible]. (2020, June 11). Dr. Rudine Sims Bishop reminds us white children need to read diverse books so they don't get an exaggerated sense [Tweet]. *Twitter*. Retrieved from https://twitter.com/tchkimpossible/status/1271081414533013504?lang=en

Parker, K. [@TchKimPossible]. (2020, June 24). Is this you? @FrugalBookstore is doing all it can to fulfill orders. Hate email b/c you can't get white fragility is shameful [Tweet]. *Twitter*. Retrieved from https://twitter.com/TchKimPossible

Reid, W. (2018, November 28). Black Twitter 101: What is it? Where did it originate? Where is it headed? Retrieved from https://news.virginia.edu/content/black-twitter-101-what-it where-did-it-originate-where-it-headed

Saussure, F. (2011). *Course in general linguistics*. In P. Meisel & H. Saussey (Eds.); W. Baskin (Trans.): New York, NY: Columbia University Press (Original work published 1959).

Smith, C. A., Williams, E. L., Wadud, I. A., & Pirtle, W. N. L. (2021). Cite black women: A Critical Praxis (A statement). *Feminist Anthropology*, *2*, 10–17. doi:10.1002/fea2.12040

Smitherman, G. (1977). *Talkin and testifyin: The language of black America*. Detroit, MI: Wayne State University Press.

"RESEARCH ACROSS FOUR PANDEMICS: THE END IS A BEGINNING"

Chestin T. Auzenne-Curl and Cheryl J. Craig

ABSTRACT

This concluding chapter discusses how the unfurling of the Writers in the Schools (WITS) Collaborative took place against a backdrop of four pandemics: COVID-19, the movement against racial injustice, climate change, and the inevitable economic despair that spills over into the field of education. The work looks backwards on the chapters in this book and their findings. It also looks forward to the lessons that the WITS Collaborative has taught – and will teach – as it moves toward a future unknown, yet much anticipated.

Keywords: WITS Collaborative; pandemic; COVID-19; racial injustice; climate change; economic despair

INTRODUCTION

From the floodwaters of Harvey to the waves of COVID-19, our research team's exploration of literacy partnerships has brought us to many convergent views of most promising pedagogical practices and many divergent threads of experience in our knowledge construction and reconstruction. During the fall of 2020, Cheryl and Chestin attended two lectures centered on a contextualized view of this period in history as a fourfold pandemic. Both sessions were facilitated by Texas A&M's Visiting Hagler Fellow, Dr. Gloria Ladson-Billings, who is a Professor Emerita at the University of Wisconsin–Madison. In her discussion of the four pandemics, Ladson-Billings outlined the implications of: (1) COVID-19, (2) the movement against racial injustice, (3) climate change, and (4) the impending economic despair on our work as educators.

We felt the heavyweight – the full impact – of all four pandemics. There were days when we struggled to write. All of the pandemics that Ladson-Billings named interrupted our personal and professional lives and impeded our writing progress. Yet, they bore richer fruit when all was said and done. This volume's chapters, above all, demonstrate the inseparability of art and life in the authentic expressions of knowing, doing, and being of *Homo narrans* (storytelling humans).

RESTORYING TRUTHS

In Part I, we mostly were introduced to the story before the story; more specifically, the story before the full-blown "Writers in the Schools (WITS) story." In the opening chapter, we charted the external (Craig) and internal (Auzenne-Curl) conditions shaping our (and possibly others') coming to the WITS Collaborative. Reform efforts have been plentiful in Greater Houston since the 1980s, particularly because Houston is one of the largest and most diverse cities in the United States, one with no majority population reflecting the demographics of America's future. Then, Parts II and III presented "the WITS Collaborative story" kaleidoscopically. After that, toward the end of Part III, we find the imagining of "the story after the story" – the what comes next – morphing into a new "something to pursue" as Greene (2000) declared earlier in this book. Together, these sections set the stage for our restorying of the truths that the chapter authors asserted.

Returning to the questions that sat behind our collection of featured stories, we find that the chapters in this book offer a rich tapestry of WITS lessons and lead to follow. We recognize that we have learned much about knowledge communities as supportive spaces for teacher growth and development. We also know a great deal more about the influence of relationships on the trajectory of teachers' professional development and on their concomitant growth in community. We furthermore have awakened to narratives of experience and their influence on identity construction in the making, particularly against the backdrop of a fluctuating urban milieu in the throes of four pandemics. We now lean into these three assertions by pulling forward for introspection of some key ideas – three narrative truths – appearing in our chapter lineup.

Truth 1: Knowledge Communities Are Supportive Places for Teacher Growth and Development

Chapter-after-chapter, page-after-page, and line-after-line, knowledge communities served as powerful associations and tools for teacher growth and development in relationship with one another and to the WITS Collaborative writers in Greater Houston. In Chapter 2, we learned how Tina and Maryann, who themselves are a knowledge community, focused on strong individuals and teams as they designed the WITS Collaborative. They intuitively knew of the importance of communities of knowing within and across schools and within and across teachers and faculties. Overlaying this – but not hierarchically – the WITS Collaborative was conceived within the WITS organization. The importance of having shared goals in community also rose to the fore in the Curl and Craig chapter. Michael Curl, pulling on his personal practical knowledge as a principal, offered the WITS Collaborative as a suggestion to his campus's literacy faculty, while leaving the final decision in their hands. The pondering of the Collaborative proposal further added to the growth of a community of knowing among the Suburban East Middle School teachers. By no means the last example, but the final one we will share here is the collaborative knowledge community at McKay High School. When Mokhtari and the English team at the underserved campus encountered "tough turf," they found refuge in each other's company. The knowledge community they formed encompassed each other – to be certain – but it also included Mary, their WITS Collaborative writer who like Sarah Jerasa, her fellow WITS Collaborative writer, assessed the unique needs of her partnering campus to ensure that the teachers had a safe space in which to navigate their swiftly changing roles and responsibilities. In each of these examples (among many others), the truthiness of knowledge communities as supportive places for teacher growth and development shines through.

Truth 2: Relationships Influence the Trajectory of Teachers' Professional Development and Growth in Community

Knowledge communities are not the only major theme threaded throughout the chapters of this book. There is also the influence of relationships on the trajectory of professional development and how teacher growth unfurls in community. This entire volume – and the entire WITS Collaborative – is fully dependent on relationships. There is Tina and Maryann, Tina and Tim, Michael Curl and the faculty of Suburban East Middle School, Terri Osborne and the teachers at Suburban East High School, Sarah Jerasa and the teachers with whom she worked, and so on and so forth. One of the distinguishing features of these relationships is that the power differential among them is near equal. While titles indicate people's positions, the way that individuals choose to position themselves in their school contexts and in the WITS Collaborative can best be described as "evenly yoked" or "horizontal" when pursuing tasks at hand. All the writers in the WITS Collaborative sit at the same table. Tim, the CFG® facilitator, sits there too. Maryann and Tina work in the midst of the writers; they are not peering at their pages nor counting their lines over their shoulders. We as researchers join in the mix. We sit as equals and participate as equally engaged colleagues in the broader profession of teaching. The primacy of relationships prevails and positively influences the professional development trajectories of teachers, principals, and writers, in addition to directors, facilitators, and researchers, all who also calibrate their learning along the way. Combined, this makes for strong literacy and English faculties in the Greater Houston school districts and a dynamic WITS organization, an association that each day becomes more ready to share what has been learned nationally and internationally as this book makes abundantly clear. The narrative truth of the importance of horizontal relationships in teachers' growth trajectories is most definitely a second major takeaway point that this volume's chapters offer.

Truth 3: Narratives of Experience Influence Identity Construction on Rapidly Changing Urban Milieus Shaped by Four Pandemics

If teachers' and writers' knowledge communities and growth trajectories are embedded in the WITS Collaborative work, so, too, are their identities. From beginning to end, the development and refinement of identities – both personal and professional – were shaped and reshaped in, and by, the WITS Collaborative. Chestin T. Auzenne-Curl turned a keen eye to identity in the making early on in this book. Readers also see Maryann's and Tina's identities being forged and subtly changed through their ongoing WITS Collaborative work. The identities of writers and poets (Sara, Mary, Jasminne Mendez, Robin Reagler) are also affected; some becoming writers/poets and teachers which especially was true of Mary whose amazing transformation was chronicled. There were also identity shifts on the part of principals (Michael Curl, Terri Osborne), teachers (i.e., Suburban East Middle School, McKay High School, Suburban East High School, among other unnamed campuses), and teacher educators (Daphne Carr, Chestin T. Auzenne-Curl). Tim Martindell, as facilitator, quieted his voice and identity as a teacher and teacher educator while amplifying his voice and identity as a CFG® coach, which ironically meant posing hard questions while mostly staying mum. This point especially was drawn to the fore when he discussed "unknown edges" of facilitation, particularly those having to do with candid discussions around matters of race. Chestin T. Auzenne-Curl and Daphne Carr examine technology, which accelerates social media presence and the development of knowledge communities among black womxn scholars who formed their exemplar. The topics they unpack include racial injustice, police violence, and acts of domestic terrorism faced by black citizens in the United States spearheaded by the George Floyd incident and foreshadowed by quarterback Colin Kaepernick's "taking of a knee" that triggered Nike's controversial "just do it" campaign. Finally, Lobat Asadi explores WITS as it plays out with particular students in a parallel program (Spoken Word), where "poetry is not a luxury" (Lorde, 1993) and student assessments would ideally incorporate multiple literacies perspectives, including environmental literacies.

We cannot end without also mentioning the chapters that brought the Houston area milieu into sharp focus. Chestin T. Auzenne-Curl, Cheryl Craig, and Gayle Curtis characterized in minute detail the Houston devastation left by Hurricane Harvey, while Tenesha Gale reached back in history and explored her concept of gentrimigration, which set the stage for eye-opening discussions of population shifts over time across the region and city. A further example is the Auzenne-Curl and Carr chapter which addressed the virtual growth and development of an online community in fine-grained ways. Then, there is the Robin Reagler chapter elucidating the social narrative history of WITS, alongside its vision and commitment to reach students through creative pursuits, in spite of the dominant neoliberal world that unabashedly privileges statistics while excluding the deeply lived stories emanating from students' and teachers' work and lives. These four, among other chapters, anchor learning, action and community in context, adding both rigor and complexity to the understanding of the WITS Collaborative.

FINAL THOUGHTS FROM THE EDITORS

> What we call the beginning is often the end. And to make an end is to make a beginning. The end is where we start from. (T. S. Eliot)

Over 20 years ago, philosopher Maxine Greene (2000) spoke of the "predictable and the possible" for twenty-first century US education. Amid rising social and political turbulences, she noted that

> ...changes [will be] wrought by technology, by demographic shifts around the world (the movements of refugees, the diasporas), by decolonization, by the new pluralization in tension with media-imposed uniformity, that make it impossible to think in terms of continuities in the histories of schools. (Greene, 2000, p. 267)

It is at this intersection where we return to the beginning (again).

As this volume draws to a close, the world remains in disarray. In particular, the Houston area, which is the primary setting for the topics covered in this book, is recovering from the fourth notable catastrophic event since we partnered with the WITS organization. Our schools are in constant flux. It is difficult to predict the specifics of the changes ahead, even the possible seems distant. We have lost a sense of normalcy in our consideration of how schools function and what teachers do, but this is not necessarily a negative space in which to be. For in it we are called into a collaborative recovery effort, which Greene (2000) foresaw as a time when "differences among diverse groups...will have to be confronted and when possible resolved" (p. 269). In Greene's vision, the collaboration of teachers for the health and functioning of schools would be unquestionably essential.

Predictions

Thinking back to where we first began, we know that reform efforts in schools will always be challenging, particularly since the impetus for change most often comes from outside of campuses not inside of them. We also know that statistics are quick fixes for power brokers desperately seeking solutions to multi-perspectival problems with deep sociocultural, historical, economic roots. However, human experiences reflected by numbers do not have the needed moral purpose or push to move the public's will in the way that people's etched-with-life narratives do. "Information touches the mind, but story sinks into the heart," is how Aesop worded it. From the beginning, Auzenne-Curl and Craig warned of the dangers of unholy unions that Bruner (1986) deduced as perennial barriers.

Possibilities

With foresight and true collaborations for reflective and critical inquiry, we have both the vision and power to move forward from a normal that never served all, and into a space where education not only exudes excellence but deep-seated equity as well. If the pandemics have done one thing – and we include here the snow-demic that we as editors in Texas faced when our book project was due, it is the exposure of inequities: inequities where technological resources are concerned; inequities that leave poor communities mostly of color more affected by COVID-19; inequities that mean that those who are needy are less likely to have the material resources to face hurricanes, snow-demics, and whatever else is thrown our way in this "bring it all on" chapter of national and international history. Yet, within it all lies slivers of possibility "if only we're brave enough to see it" (Gorman, 2021).

Writing this volume became something exceedingly productive to chase that greatly reduced boredom and lessened despair. Communicating what happened with the WITS Collaborative stoked feelings of hope, nurtured communities of knowing, and catalyzed wild possibilities for the future of WITS as a thriving and generative national and international change effort.

The WITS Collaborative has shown both measurable and anecdotal success beyond what was imagined. And yet, as a conscientious educator in this particular moment, I am aware that there is more that can be done. Much more… One of the organizational taglines explains the motivation for WITS' work this way: we do this work "because writing is revolutionary." Framing the WITS future in terms of revolution, I see two mandates. First, WITS Collaborative must make sure that our methodology does not become formulaic. Writing and teaching are both arts. As writers and teachers, we must master formulas and quickly move beyond them, addressing our students' particularities, as well as our own. Second, WITS Collaborative must incorporate more of the lessons we are learning from the prescriptive lens of equity, diversity, access, and inclusion. This is a no quick-fix situation, but one that requires continuous work and refinement that comes from feedback gleaned from students as well as peers. (Robin Reagler, Writers in the Schools, Past Executive Director)

My wish for the WITS Collaborative: that it continues to build on its strengths but takes on new meaning in a current and post-COVID world. How better to process teaching and the art of teaching writing than by processing your own place in this upended world within the supportive community that a Collaborative cohort creates. First and foremost, the WITS Collaborative creates a place for each of us to be a writer, and then to see how being a writer can help our students, too, make sense of what's going on right now in their lives. (Jack McBride, Acting Writers in the Schools, Executive Director)

It is my sincere hope that the Collaborative continues to focus on student growth and impressing upon students the power and legacy of the written word. Further, I hope that the collaborative continues to nourish teachers' spirits through shared knowledge, experiences and community. The bonds that hold a writing collaborative together are strong in that it takes a certain vulnerability to express one's self in writing to colleagues, but the rewards in terms of commiseration, camaraderie, and continuing education make it a fruitful and worthwhile endeavor. (Abdulkader Mokhtari, Partnering Teacher)

One of the strengths of the WITS Collaborative has been its ability to be modified in response to "lessons learned." The basic elements of the model – teachers writing together, planning lessons together and debriefing classroom experiences with the guidance of a professional writer – have allowed each cohort of teachers the ability to create a Collaborative program that is unique to their needs. The WITS

Collaborative in the Age of COVID has offered me an insight into the future possibility of using technology to expand this program on a national level. My one wish for the future of the work of the Collaborative is to offer this job-embedded professional development service to teachers outside of our geographic area. (Tina Angelo, Education Director, Writers in the Schools)

REFERENCES

Bruner, J. (1986). *Actual minds, possible worlds.* Cambridge, MA: Harvard University Press.

Gorman, A. (2021). *This hill we climb. This hill we climb and other poems.* New York, NY: Viking.

Greene, M. (2000). Imagining futures: The public school and possibility. *Journal of Curriculum Studies, 32*(2), 267–280.

Lorde, A. (1993). *Poetry is not a luxury = Lyrik ist kein luxus.* Osnabrück: Druck & Verlagscooperative.

ABOUT THE EDITORS

Chestin T. Auzenne-Curl, PhD, is a Lecturer and Postdoctoral Research Associate in the Department of Teaching, Learning, and Culture, Texas A&M, College Station, TX. A former public school central office administrator and curriculum coordinator, Chestin, has dedicated her work in higher education to investigating the role of teacher educators in the field (TEFs) and worked on several grant-funded projects focused on professional development across teacher life cycles. Chestin has presented and published in a variety of practitioner and scholarly forums including three consecutive years as a recognized Doctoral Scholar in BYU's Invisible College Seminar for the American Educational Research Association's International Pre-Conference. Her most recent publications focus on the role of instructional coaching and mentorship in the retention of secondary English teachers. Chestin served as Cheryl Craig's Postdoctoral Research Fellow and Research Team Lead on the WITS evaluation project.

Cheryl J. Craig, PhD, is a Professor, the Houston Endowment Endowed Chair for Urban Education, and the Program Lead for Technology and Teacher Education at Texas A&M University. She is an American Educational Research Association (AERA) Fellow, a recipient of AERA's Division B (Curriculum) Outstanding Lifetime Achievement Award, and a winner of AERA's Michael Huberman Award for Outstanding Contributions to Understanding the Lives of Teachers. The International Study Association on Teachers and Teaching (ISATT) has awarded her its highest honor: the ST^{2}AR Award for Significant and Exemplary Contributions through Research, Teaching, and Professional Service in the International Field of Teaching and Teacher Education.

ABOUT THE CONTRIBUTORS

Tina Angelo, MEd, is the Education Director for Writers in the Schools, a Houston-based literacy nonprofit. Throughout her 41 years in education, Tina has dedicated herself to two passions – her belief in the power of literacy and her support of classroom teachers. After receiving her BA from The University of Texas, Austin, and her MEd from the University of Houston, Tina spent 24 years as a classroom teacher in high schools in Pearland, Clear Creek, and Houston, and 9 years as a central office administrator. In her role as Manager of Adolescent Literacy for the Houston Independent School District, Tina supported the work of campus-based literacy coaches at 44 middle schools and 36 high schools. She built upon these years of experience to develop the job-embedded professional development model, WITS Collaborative, which has supported classroom teachers K–12 in both public and private schools. In her role as Education Director for Writers in the Schools, Tina focused on providing both job-embedded and customized campus writing workshops for teachers. Her guiding principle is that teachers who see themselves as writers will be more effective as teachers of writing.

Lobat Asadi is a PhD, Curriculum & Instruction, Department of Teaching and Learning at Texas A&M University, College Station is an Associate Instructor at Harvard University Derek Bok Center for Teaching & Learning, Higher Education. Co-editor of Truth and *Knowledge in Curriculum Making,* with her Chair and mentor, Dr Cheryl J. Craig. Lobat is a researcher and storyteller focused on race, gender, cultural, and linguistic relevance and sustainability in education. She is versed in arts-based pedagogies and educational research, with a focus on socially just educational approaches that value multicultural and multilingual learners. She looks to by gender studies, decoloniality, diasporic perspectives, and indigenous methodologies. She lectures in teacher education, multicultural education, intercultural communications, and Teaching English to Speakers of Other Languages, TESOL, courses. She is also a DEI and educational consultant, content and curriculum developer. In her spare time, she is a musician, writer, and non-profit Director at the Asiatic Cheetah Conservation Project, as well as wildlife educator.

Daphne Carr, EdD, is an Instructional Coach for Secondary English Language Arts in Humble Independent School District near Houston, Texas. Daphne has served in Texas public schools for over 20 years as a dual credit and Advanced Placement English instructor, a grade-level team leader, an instructional coach, and a content specialist. Her research interests and professional practice focus on job-embedded professional development for high school English language arts instructors, particularly in writing instruction.

Michael Curl is a proud Campus Principal in southeast Texas. He is a Doctoral Candidate in the Leadership and Innovation Department at St. Thomas University. Michael brings over 18 years of experience in education from classroom teacher to building principal to his writing and consulting work with campuses and districts across the country. He has presented on topics such as increasing equity, building a positive campus culture, and working with underserved youth in public schools. He has been recognized as teacher of the year and principal of the year along with other recognitions for his work in education. Michael's campuses have been recognized by the Texas Education Agency for excellence in closing achievement gaps, academic performance, and postsecondary readiness.

Gayle A. Curtis, EdD, is a Program Manager with the Asian American Studies Center at University of Houston and a Postdoctoral Research Associate at Texas A&M University. After a career as a bilingual teacher and school administrator/principal in urban public schools serving students from richly diverse backgrounds, Dr Curtis turned her efforts to teacher education and research. In 2019, Dr Curtis received the American Education Research Association (AERA) Narrative SIG Outstanding Publication Award for the coauthored article "The Embodied Nature of Narrative Knowledge: A Cross-Study Analysis of Embodied Knowledge in Teaching, Learning, and Life" published in *Teaching and Teacher Education*. She received the 2014 AERA Narrative Research SIG Outstanding Dissertation Award for her dissertation entitled *Harmonic Convergence: Parallel Stories of a Novice Teacher and a Novice Researcher*. Her fields of research include narrative inquiry, self-study, and critical cultural ethnography. Recent publications include an invited chapter in the 2020 *International Handbook on Self-Study Research*.

Tenesha Gale, PhD, is a Middle School Science Educator and Field Researcher. With over 15 years in education, Tenesha's professional roles have included social worker, classroom teacher, teacher coach, and educational researcher. Her research specialization is rooted in sustaining teachers in urban communities, as well as suburban communities in the midst of demographic shifts due to factors such as gentrification. Tenesha is a Gates Millennium Scholar and serves as an advocate for virtual learning platform development.

Maryann Gremillion is a Writer and Educator working with elementary schools, teachers, and nonprofits to build transformative communities. She taught elementary school for 15 years in Houston where she discovered a passion for creative writing and integrating fine arts in content areas. Maryann also worked for 12 years as a writer-in-residence and then program director for Writers in the Schools (WITS) in Houston. Her work has been published in *The Ekphrastic Review*, *Glass Mountain*, *Teachers and Writers* magazine, and several local anthologies. She is excited to complete a book chapter about working with teachers and writers in the WITS Collaborative.

KaLeah Hicks is a Middle School Librarian. She received a BA in English Composition from the University of North Texas and an MS in Educational Technology Leadership from Texas A&M University–Commerce. Prior to becoming a librarian, she taught high school English/Language Arts (ELA), Graphic Design, Journalism and Commercial Photography, and developed curriculum supplements for Socio-Emotional Learning and Secondary ELA. Through her passion for increasing diversity in collection development, KaLeah supports Active Readers Advisory to build more inclusive campus and family libraries.

Sarah Jerasa is a Literacy Scholar, Researcher, and PhD Student at the University of Houston in the Department of Curriculum and Instruction. Her research interests focus on teacher identity as writers, equitable literacy access, and the reading and writing connection in classrooms. Sarah is a former classroom teacher, a National Writing Project fellow, and professional development writing coach for Writers in the Schools. Her most recent research revolves around Research Practice Partnerships to establish mobile library program outreach to increase book access and literacy achievement for students living in book deserts. She is the founder of the Many Truths of Teaching: Teacher Story Project, an online archive of educator interviews to reveal the realities of education through teachers' voices and stories.

About the Contributors

P. Tim Martindell, EdD, is a Middle School English Teacher and Debate Coach at The Village School, as well as an Adjunct Instructor in Literacy Development at the University of Houston–Downtown. In addition to his 25-year teaching career, Tim served as the Houston A+ Challenge program coordinator for literacy and critical friendship, and the past president of both the Texas Council of Teachers of English Language Arts and the West Houston Council of Teachers of English. Tim is a diamond level–writing project trainer with the Abydos writing project and a national-level facilitator of critical friendship practices with the School Reform Initiative. He holds an EdD and MEd in Curriculum and Instruction from the University of Houston and a BS Ed in Communications Education from Miami University.

Abdulkader Mokhtari is a High School English and Dual Credit Government Teacher at Robert E. Lee High School, as well as an Adjunct Instructor at Lee College. Mr Mokhtari has taught for nine years and served as English department head for a time. In addition to teaching English and Government, Mr Mokhtari also served as Assistant Theater Arts Director, helping to produce many award-winning plays. Mr Mokhtari was introduced to the WITS Writing Collaborative in 2017 and has been a vocal proponent of its tenants ever since. Mr Mokhtari holds an MA in Political Science with an emphasis in Political Theory and a BA in Political Science, with a minor in English from The University of Texas at San Antonio.

Terri Osborne is a Dynamic Instructional Leader with experience facilitating learning of Diverse Student Populations. Prior to becoming a campus principal, Terri served as a secondary math teacher, department lead, dean of students, assistant principal, and early college director. Her professional passions include creating advanced academics opportunities for at-risk students and cultivating school environments that embody excellence and collective leadership. Terri holds a bachelor's degree in Architecture from Texas Tech University. Her postgraduate milestones include a Master of Science in Higher Education and a Master of Education in Educational Administration from Texas A&M University–Commerce. Terri is also a Candidate for a Doctorate in Education and Doctoral Scholarship Recipient. She is currently completing dissertation research on the leadership practices that foster academic resilience in students. When Terri is not diligently working or studying, she enjoys reading, biking, and adult intramural sports.

About the Contributors

Robin Reagler, PhD, led Writers in the Schools (WITS) from 1998 to 2020, transforming a small grassroots organization into a national literary movement with 38 member groups. She is a Poet and the Author of *Dear Red Airplane* (Seven Kitchens, 2011, 2018), *Teeth & Teeth* (Headmistress, 2018), *Into The The* (Backlash, forthcoming 2021), and *Night Is This Anyway* (Lily Poetry Press, forthcoming 2022). Her poetry books have won prizes including the Best Book Award, the Charlotte Mew Prize, and the Rebound Award. Her blog, The Other Mother: Letters from the Outposts of Lesbian Parenting, was named best parenting blog by Nickelodcon in 2009. She earned an MFA at the Iowa Writers' Workshop and a PhD at the University of Houston Creative Writing Program.

INDEX

Accountability pressures, 52–53
Activity Logs, 35
Affinity mapping, 31–33
Alternative Certification Program (ACP), 64–65
Annenberg reform movement, 3
Arts-based education, 199, 208

Bildungsroman, 194–196, 206, 208
   culture and, 196–197
   identity and, 209–210
   learner identity, 198
   literacy, 195–196, 202–203
   narrative inquiry, 197
   reading, 196
   relationship, 209
Black cyberculture, 232–233
Black literacy educators, 225–226
Budget concerns, 52–53

Campus demographics, 109
Chalk talk, 31–33
#Citeasista, 239
#CiteBlackWomen, 239
Classroom Collaborative for Professional Development (CCPD), 194–195
Collaborators, in education, 153–154
   Connections activity, 158
   Critical Friends Groups (CFGs®), 155
   gallery walk, 160
   Houston A+ Challenge, 155
   Houston Annenberg Challenge, 155
   interview, 156–157
   paper plate protocol, 159
   protocols, 158–161
   sample school reform initiative protocol, 162
   WITS Collaborative, 156

Commonplaces, 86–87
Community, 22
   classroom, 24–26
   collaborative, 35
   Critical Friends Group® (CFG) protocols, 31
   Goal Setting Protocol, 37–38
   Houston, 39
   site visits, 35
   WITS Collaborative, 22, 30, 34
Comparative reading scores, 9
Comparative writing scores, 10
Consultancy protocol, 31–33
Contextualized commonplaces
   milieu, 120
   students, 119
   subject matter, 119
   teacher, 118–119
COVID-19, 10, 167, 195, 221, 245
   collaborative model and framework, 30
   disruption, 30
   quarantine, 39
Critical Friends Groups (CFGs®)
   protocols, 31, 33, 155
Critical Teacher Talk, 12–13
Critical technocultural discourse analysis (CTDA), 233, 237
Cross-institutional literacy partnerships, 105–108
   campus-wide tools, 110
   enactment, 112–114
   implications, 114–115
   objectives, 108–111
   preparatory considerations, 111–112
   rationale for, 108–111
   workshop approach, 109–110

Cultural literacy, 200, 204–205
Culturally relevant pedagogy, 111

Data Room, 134
Data sources, 47
Destiny High School, 3
Digital literacy, 200
Disruption, 23–24, 29–30, 35–36, 38–39
#Disrupt Texts, 237–238
Diverse learners, 111

Eagle High School, 4
Educational inequities, 34
Emotional literacy, 200, 205
English Language Arts, Reading, and Communication (ELAR), 80
English language learner (ELL), 174–175
Environmental literacy, 200

Funding, 4

Gallery walk, 160
Gentrimigration, 171–172
  administration, 185–186
  climate and culture, 187–188
  co-research participants, 180–184
  Gifted and Talented (GT) program, 181
  Hope demographic composition in 2000, 175
  Hope demographic composition in 2017–2018, 175
  inquiry, 173–176
  literature, 179–180
  methodology, 179
  narrative inquiry, 179–180
  teachers, 185
Gifted and Talented (GT) program, 181
Google Meets, 112

Greater City Independent School District (GCISD), 42–43
Greater Houston, 2, 4, 155–156

Hardy Academy, 3, 153–154
Hope High School, 171–172
Houston A+ Challenge, 153–155
Houston Annenberg Challenge (HAC), 3, 63, 155
Houston A + reform movement, 2–3
Hurricane Harvey, 29–30, 41–43, 119

Impostor phenomenon (IP), 233
Instructional coaching methods, 80, 82–83
Instructional improvement, 91–92
Instructional planning process, 109
International Baccalaureate (IB) school, 143–144

Job-embedded professional development (PD), 23, 85

Knowledge community, 118, 236
  personal practical knowledge and, 7–8
  portfolio-based knowledge share and, 235–237
  social media scholarship, 17
  teacher growth and development, 246–247
  WITS writers, 45
Knowledge sharing, 85

Lesson planning, 31–33
Literacy
  coaching, 83
  cultural, 204–205
  emotional, 205
  multiple, 197–198
  visual, 208
Literacy education, 1, 6, 8, 15, 17
Literary critics, 196

Meaning-making, 221–228
Meetings, 31

Memory Blueprint, 125
Menil Collection, 22
Microlab, 31–33
Microsoft Teams, 112
Multiple literacies, 194–195
   arts-based education, 199
   culture, 196–197
   learner identity, 198–199
   method, 201–202
   multiple ways of knowing, 195
   theoretical, 199–201
Multiple Literacies Theory (MLT), 199–200

Narrative inquiry, 41–42, 46, 80–81, 153–154, 217
   bildungsroman, 197
   description, 69
   gentrimigration, 179–180
   interpretative tools, 69
   meaning-making, 118
   professional development, 43–44
   research backdrop, 69–70
   Writers in the Schools (WITS), 69
Narrative tools, 46, 217
National Council of Teachers of English, 84
National Writing Project (NWP), 131
The No Child Left Behind Act (2002), 70
Numerical literacy, 200

Organization for Economic Cooperation and Development (OECD), 67

Pandemics, 17
Paper plate protocol, 159
Parallel stories, 218
Parent Teacher Association (PTA), 143–144
Personal practical knowledge (PD), 7–8
   principal leadership, 68
Poetry, 194–195
   literature review, 195–199

   method, 201–202
   multiple ways of knowing, 195
   theoretical, 199–201
Political literacy, 200
Portfolio-based knowledge share, 235–237
Principal leadership, 61, 64, 67
   experience, 67–68
   narrative inquiry, 69–70
   personal practical knowledge, 68
   teaching and learning, 67
   Writers in the Schools (WITS), 70–73
Professional development (PD), 41–42, 80, 99, 117–118
   assessment data, 85
   job-embedded, 85
   narrative inquiry, 43–44
   overscheduling, 51
   school collaborative for, 44–45
   solving problems, 85
   student work examination, 85
   teacher, 44
   WITS Collaborative, 119
Professional Learning Community (PLC), 27–28, 71, 120

Racial resegregation, 4–5
Reading scores, 8
Relationship building, 71
Request for proposal (RFP), 111
Rodrigo Elementary teachers, 143–144

Sacramento Area Youth Speaks (SAYS), 10
School-based inconsistencies, 51–52
School budgets, 39
School Reform Initiative protocols, 13
School Writing Project, 100–101
Scientific literacy, 200
Secondary traumatic stress (STS), 43
Self-regulated strategy development (SRSD), 86

Social media scholarship, 17, 231, 233
  Black Twitter, 237–240
  preliminary analyses, 233–240
Socioeconomic resegregation, 4–5
Star High School, 172
State of Texas Assessment of Academic Readiness (STAAR), 82, 138
Storied experience, 217
Suburban East Middle School, 64, 69–70
Supervisory leadership, 87–88

Teacher Educators in the Field (TEFs), 80
  campus and district administrators, 91–92
  campus-level, 89
  content, 84
  district-level, 89–90
  enactment, 88–89
  English Language Arts, Reading, and Communication (ELAR), 80
  interorganizational, 90–91
  non- and for-profit partnerships, 92–93
  pre- and in-service, 93
  process, 84–85
  reflection and evaluation, 85–86
  role identity and expectations, 87–88
  roles targeting, 94
  suggestions, 92
  thinking narratively, 86–87
  Writers in the Schools (WITS), 80–81
  writing-focused, 82
Teacher professional development, 44
Teacher sustenance, urban environments, 121–123
Teacher Talk (TT), 12–13, 29
Teaching quality matters, 67
Texas academic performance report (TAPR), 73

Texas A&M University Research Team, 8, 154
Texas Council of Teachers of Language Arts (TCTLA), 162–163
Texas Education Agency (TEA), 72–73, 136–137, 162–163
Texas Gulf Coast, 41–42
Text rendering, 31–33
Trauma, 50
Twitter, 232

Urban context, 1–6
  methodological foundations, 6–8
  theoretical foundations, 6–8

Visual literacy, 200, 208

Wealthy suburb, 176
Whole Grade Immersion Model, 26
Workshops, 13
Writers in the Schools (WITS), 2–4, 11, 41–42, 246
  Activity Logs, 35
  challenges, 164
  coaching cycle, 157
  collaboration, 70–73
  creative writing instructor, 129–130
  narrative inquiry, 69
  phrases of impact, 56
  practice model, 45
  professional development coach, 45, 101, 129–130
  Professional Learning Community (PLC), 123–124
  protocols, 14
  residency vignettes, 135–146
  site visits, 35
  Suburban East Middle School, 64
  Teacher Educators in the Field (TEFs), 80–81
  teachers' perspectives, 48–49
  workshops for, 13
  writers' perspectives, 53–57

Writers in the Schools (WITS)
    Collaborative, 27, 80–81, 101, 109–110
    campus teachers/administrators, 36–38
    collaborators, in education, 156
    Critical Friends Group® (CFG) protocols, 31–33
    data collection, 133
    monthly meetings, 31
    narrative framework, 25–29
    Parent Teacher Association (PTA), 143–144
    praise and critique of, 54–57
    professional development support, 120
    WITS Houston, 22
Writer's workshop, 162–163
Writer-teacher identity, 129–130, 132
    actualization, 133–134
    coaching residencies, 146–147
    data analysis, 133
    data collection, 133
    Data Room, 134
    limitations, 133
Writing
    collaborative, 34
    free-to-the-public student, 22
    Houston, 22
    personal narrative, 35–36
    reading and, 22
    teaching, 24
    WITS, 26
Writing-focused Teacher Educators in the Field (TEFs), 82
Writing instruction, 119, 126
Writing intervention strategy, 93–94
Writing scores, 8–9
Writing workshops, 111

Zoom, 112